Political Representation

Political representation lies at the core of modern politics. Democracies, with their vast numbers of citizens, could not operate without representative institutions. Yet relations between the democratic ideal and the everyday practice of political representation have never been well defined and remain the subject of vigorous debate among historians, political theorists, lawyers, and citizens. In this volume, an eminent group of scholars moves forward the debates about political representation on a number of fronts. Drawing on insights from political science, history, political theory, economics, and anthropology, the authors provide much-needed clarity to some of the most vexing questions about political representation. They also reveal new and enlightening perspectives on this fundamental political practice. Topics discussed include representation before democracy, political parties, minorities, electoral competition, and ideology. This volume is essential reading for anyone interested in the ideal and the reality of political representation.

IAN SHAPIRO is Sterling Professor of Political Science and Henry R. Luce Director of the MacMillan Center for International and Area Studies at Yale University.

SUSAN C. STOKES is John S. Saden Professor of Political Science and Director of the Yale Program on Democracy at Yale University.

ELISABETH JEAN WOOD is Professor of Political Science at Yale University and Professor at the Santa Fe Institute.

ALEXANDER S. KIRSHNER is a doctoral candidate in the Department of Political Science at Yale University.

D1394524

Political Representation

Edited by

Ian Shapiro, Susan C. Stokes, Elisabeth Jean Wood,
and Alexander S. Kirshner

 CAMBRIDGE
UNIVERSITY PRESS

CAMBRIDGE UNIVERSITY PRESS
Cambridge, New York, Melbourne, Madrid, Cape Town, Singapore,
São Paulo, Delhi

Cambridge University Press
The Edinburgh Building, Cambridge CB2 8RU, UK

Published in the United States of America by Cambridge University Press,
New York

www.cambridge.org
Information on this title: www.cambridge.org/9780521128650

First published 2009

Printed in the United Kingdom at the University Press, Cambridge

A catalogue record for this publication is available from the British Library

Library of Congress Cataloguing in Publication data
Political representation / [edited by] Ian Shapiro . . . [et al.].
    p.   cm.
Includes index.
ISBN 978-0-521-11127-0 (hardback)
1. Representative government and representation.   I. Shapiro, Ian.   II. Title.
JF1051.P583   2009
321.8–dc22   2009035293

ISBN 978-0-521-11127-0 hardback
ISBN 978-0-521-12865-0 paperback

Contents

List of figures   *page* vii
List of tables   viii
List of contributors   ix
Preface   xi

Editors' introduction   1
IAN SHAPIRO, SUSAN C. STOKES,
ELISABETH JEAN WOOD, AND
ALEXANDER S. KIRSHNER

Part I. Representation before representative democracy

1. Hobbes's theory of representation: anti-democratic or
    proto-democratic?   15
    DAVID RUNCIMAN

2. Participation and representation before democracy:
    petitions and addresses in premodern Britain   35
    MARK KNIGHTS

Part II. Theories of political representation

3. Varieties of public representation   61
    PHILIP PETTIT

4. Representative government and popular sovereignty   90
    BRYAN GARSTEN

5. Making interest: on representation and
    democratic legitimacy   111
    CLARISSA RILE HAYWARD

Part III.   Representation and inherited injustice

6.   Critical liberalism   139
COURTNEY JUNG

7.   Settlers and natives in North America   159
MAHMOOD MAMDANI

Part IV.   What role for representative quotas?

8.   Perverse consequences? The impact of quotas for
women on democratization in Africa   211
SHIREEN HASSIM

9.   On quotas and qualifications for office   236
ANDREW REHFELD

**Part V.   Preferences, persuasion, and democratic
representation**

10.   Electoral representation and the aristocratic thesis   271
JOHN FEREJOHN AND FRANCES ROSENBLUTH

11.   Why does the Republican Party win half the votes?   304
JOHN E. ROEMER

12.   The impact of electoral debate on public opinions: an
experimental investigation of the 2005 New York City
mayoral election   324
SENDHIL MULLAINATHAN,
EBONYA WASHINGTON, AND JULIA R. AZARI

13.   Swing voters, core voters, and distributive politics   342
GARY W. COX

Index   358

Figures

1.1 Hobbes's basic theory of representation   *page* 21
1.2 Hobbes's full theory of representation   22
1.3 A Hobbesian theory of democratic representation   27
2.1 Number of petitions and signatures per session
    Source: Taylor (1913)   43
3.1 Representers   63
3.2 Representation   65
11.1 PUNEs and observed policies in two pooled election years   316
11.2 Party-separation "hyperplanes" for the full model and the
    two counterfactual elections   320

Tables

2.1	Petitions to parliament, 1785–1847	*page* 42
2.2	Public petitioning and addressing campaigns, 1640–1840	45
8.1	Women in national parliaments by region, 2005	213
8.2	Women's representation in African countries	217
8.3	Highest ranking countries in terms of women's representation, 2003	218
9.1	Three general aims of qualifications with examples	250
9.2	A typology of justifications	253
9.3	Three forms of political equality	261
11.1	PUNEs and the decomposition of racism's effect ($\delta_0 = 1$)	318
12.1	Summary statistics	329
12.2	Impacts of commitment to vote on voting	331
12.3	Summary statistics for commitment to vote treatment	332
12.4	Post-debate summary statistics	333
12.5	Impact of debate on opinions of candidates	336

Contributors

JULIA R. AZARI is Assistant Professor of Political Science at Marquette University.

GARY W. COX is Distinguished Professor of Political Science at the University of California, San Diego.

JOHN FEREJOHN is the Carolyn S. G. Munro Professor of Political Science and Senior Fellow of the Hoover Institution at Stanford University, and is a Visiting Professor at New York University School of Law.

BRYAN GARSTEN is Associate Professor of Political Science at Yale University.

SHIREEN HASSIM is Professor of Political Science at the University of the Witwatersrand.

CLARISSA RILE HAYWARD is Associate Professor of Political Science at Washington University in Saint Louis.

COURTNEY JUNG is Professor of Political Science at the University of Toronto.

ALEXANDER S. KIRSHNER is a doctoral candidate in Political Science at Yale University.

MARK KNIGHTS is Professor of History at Warwick University.

MAHMOOD MAMDANI is Herbert Lehman Professor of Government and Professor of Anthropology at Columbia University.

SENDHIL MULLAINATHAN is Professor of Economics at Harvard University.

PHILIP PETTIT is the Laurence S. Rockefeller University Professor of Politics and Human Values at Princeton University.

ANDREW REHFELD is Associate Professor of Political Science at University of Washington in St. Louis.

JOHN E. ROEMER is Elizabeth S. and A. Varick Stout Professor of Political Science and Economics at Yale University.

FRANCES ROSENBLUTH is Damon Wells Professor of International Politics at Yale University.

DAVID RUNCIMAN is Senior Lecturer in Political Theory at Cambridge University and Staff Fellow in Politics at Trinity Hall.

IAN SHAPIRO is Sterling Professor of Political Science at Yale University.

SUSAN C. STOKES is John S. Saden Professor of Political Science at Yale University.

EBONYA WASHINGTON is Henry Kohn Assistant Professor of Economics and Assistant Professor of Political Science at Yale University.

ELISABETH JEAN WOOD is Professor of Political Science at Yale University.

Preface

This volume is one of seven books to grow out of the Yale Political Science Department's initiative on Rethinking Political Order. It emerged from a conference on "Representation and Popular Rule" that was held at Yale in October of 2006. The other volumes in the series are *Problems and Methods in the Study of Politics*, edited by Ian Shapiro, Rogers Smith, and Tarek Masoud (Cambridge University Press, 2004); *Rethinking Political Institutions: The Art of the State*, edited by Ian Shapiro, Steven Skowronek, and Daniel Galvin (New York University Press, 2006); *Identities, Affiliations, and Allegiances*, edited by Seyla Benhabib, Ian Shapiro, and Danilo Petranovich (Cambridge University Press, 2007); *Political Contingency: Studying the Unexpected, the Accidental, and the Unforeseen*, edited by Ian Shapiro and Sonu Bedi (New York University Press, 2007); *Divide and Deal: The Politics of Distribution in Democracies*, edited by Ian Shapiro, Peter Swenson, and Daniela Donno (New York University Press, 2008); and *Order, Conflict, and Violence*, edited by Stathis Kalyvas, Ian Shapiro, and Tarek Masoud (Cambridge University Press, 2008).

We are pleased to record our gratitude to Yale University for the financial support that made this initiative possible. Thanks are also due to two anonymous reviewers for their suggestions, and to John Haslam of Cambridge University Press for shepherding the volume into print.

Editors' introduction

Ian Shapiro, Susan C. Stokes, Elisabeth Jean Wood, and Alexander S. Kirshner

> Certainly, gentlemen, it ought to be the happiness and glory of a representative to live in the strictest union, the closest correspondence, and the most unreserved communication with his constituents. Their wishes ought to have great weight with him; their opinion, high respect; their business, unremitted attention. It is his duty to sacrifice his repose, his pleasures, his satisfactions, to theirs; and above all, ever, and in all cases, to prefer their interest to his own. But his unbiassed opinion, his mature judgment, his enlightened conscience, he ought not to sacrifice to you, to any man, or to any set of men living. These he does not derive from your pleasure; no, nor from the law and the constitution. They are a trust from Providence, for the abuse of which he is deeply answerable. Your representative owes you, not his industry only, but his judgment; and he betrays, instead of serving you, if he sacrifices it to your opinion.
>
> Edmund Burke, 3 November 1774 (Burke 1999)

How should we reconcile the ideal that citizens in democracies aspire to control their political representatives with the reality that elected representatives have substantial leeway to act as they themselves see fit? This leeway, which is sometimes described as the monitoring problem, is often portrayed as a defect of the representative process – to be minimized if it cannot be abolished. But, as Burke's speech to the electors of Bristol suggests, this is not the only possible view of the matter. Indeed, even today few would embrace, in its starkest form, the suggestion that representatives should be mere transmission belts for constituent preferences. Burke's formulation might seem like a quaint throwback to an era more elitist than ours. Yet representatives who are excessively responsive to the electorate often confront charges of pandering and flip-flopping.

Our goal in this volume is to explore the relations between representation and democracy, better to understand the tensions between them, and to help work toward an understanding of representation that is both satisfying in its own right and comfortable with democratic understandings of political legitimacy. This agenda leads our contributors to explore predemocratic conceptions of representation, various contemporary theories of representation, the interactions between

1

representation and either replicating or altering inherited injustice (including the effectiveness of, and justification for, representative quotas), and the relations among preferences, persuasion, and democratic representation. We do not claim to supply definitive answers to many of the vexed issues raised in these areas. But our contributors move the discussion forward in ways those looking for distributive answers will have to take into account.

I.   Representation before representative democracy

We usually think of political representation as closely linked to modern conceptions of democracy. This is reasonable, since the ancient Greek view of democracy was based on the idea of ruling and being ruled in turn – scarcely a representative notion. But, as David Runciman demonstrates in our opening chapter, representation has an older pedigree than modern democracy. Indeed, Runciman argues that Thomas Hobbes developed an account of representation that opens up alternative perspectives on the monitoring problem. *Leviathan* might seem to be a surprising point of departure here, because Hobbes vigorously rejected democracy and mechanisms of democratic accountability. Contra Hanna Pitkin's celebrated account of Hobbes's theory of representation, Runciman contends that Hobbes viewed authorization and representation as two distinct and potentially separable activities: individuals authorize the sovereign to act, and in so doing renounce almost all claim to repudiating the sovereign or his actions. Yet the sovereign, on Runciman's interpretation, does not represent the individuals who have authorized him qua individuals; he represents the collective body of them, the Commonwealth.

Representative democracy requires that citizens retain the ability to eject representatives. Yet even democrats, Runciman suggests, may recognize that government officials do not represent individual citizens, but rather a collective entity – such as the people, the district, the state, or some other. From this perspective, the concerns raised by discrepancies between citizens' preferences and the actions of their representatives ought to be assuaged, in that the government does not represent the individuals to whom they are electorally accountable. Rather, the government represents and acts for "the state" or the "the people." Runciman argues for the merits of Hobbes's model in which publics authorize a government to establish a newly created entity – e.g. the United States. The model also fits with the iterative process by which representatives represent the state and citizens respond to the state's actions. Though Hobbes certainly would have resisted a democratic interpretation of his theory,

Runciman suggests that his account of representation may provide a basis for a more persuasive model of democratic representation than theories which treat representation as if it involves only representatives and the represented.

Yet there is no denying that Hobbes offers us a sharply delimited conception of the appropriate political role for citizens. In Chapter 2 Mark Knights demonstrates that Hobbes's sparse characterization of popular engagement lived in some tension with the actual situation in predemocratic Britain. To be sure, only a small proportion of British subjects could vote in premodern parliamentary elections. Moreover, these elections were not intended to give "the People" control over the members of parliament who represented them. Yet, as Knights illustrates, between 1785 and 1847 parliamentary elections were just one of many modes of political representation available to the British public. Local representative bodies, associations, societies, unions, and petitions complicated and checked the ideal of exclusive parliamentary representation. These alternative, and in some cases competing, institutions provided an extra-electoral means of communicating collective political opinion not only to the public, but also to the political elite at Westminster. In an era of comparatively limited suffrage these forums also stood as challenges to parliament's claim to represent the people.

Beginning with a brief overview of extra-parliamentary forms of representation, Knights focuses on petitions and addresses. Because they threatened parliament's legitimacy, the use of the petitions sparked a debate about the relative stature and authority of formal arenas of representation, including parliament, and informal mechanisms, including the petition and the address. Knights demonstrates that even in an era in which formal institutions did not facilitate the responsiveness of representatives, British subjects created informal mechanisms that influenced parliament and more dramatically competed with Westminster's formal representative monopoly. Knights's analysis raises important questions about the mechanisms linking informal and formal representative institutions, as well as about the conditions in which the relationship between them is complementary and the conditions in which it is competitive.

II.   Theories of political representation

Many of us might agree with Runciman that democratic governments represent corporate entities, but few would go all the way in severing the link between representatives and the electorate. If there is a link, what is it? Philip Pettit takes up this question in Chapter 3, distinguishing between the various forms that democratic representation can take. He divides representatives into four groups depending on whether they represent as individuals or within a group, whether they act cooperatively or uncooperatively, and whether, if they act cooperatively, the representation is corporate in nature (e.g. the British parliament). Similarly, on his account, those who are represented may be individuals or groups, and when they are groups, they may or may not be cooperative or corporate. In addition to these distinctions, Pettit outlines three varieties of relationship between representative and *representee* (the term which Pettit, following seventeenth-century usage, deploys) which he describes as simulative, enactive, and interpretative. Roughly speaking, these types of representation correspond to standing for someone, acting for someone, and speaking for someone.

Pettit acknowledges the attractiveness of enactive representation – acting for – because of the hope it holds out of solving the monitoring problem. Enactive representation corresponds with the idea of popular control over political institutions. He insists, however, that in democracies representatives must inevitably make decisions concerning matters about which representees, either as individuals or as collectivities, have no established preferences. Thus the actions of the representative, at least from the perspective of enactive representation, will not track the wishes of the represented. What is required, Pettit maintains, is for the representative to *speak for* the represented; the representative must engage in interpretative representation. If this is not Burkean paternalism, it is surely a step in that direction. This raises the question whether representatives are free to fill in preferences where their constituents' preferences are missing or deemed by the representative to be incoherent or ill-formed, and in what sense this form of representation is democratic. Pettit argues that it can be considered democratic only if decisions are consistent with a set of reasons that all of those represented would recognize as relevant to answering the question at hand.

How are Pettit's distinctions cashed out in actual politics? Pettit presents ideal-typical models of the US and British governments, drawing on his typology to illustrate how these systems can be characterized and their differences demarcated. Washington prioritizes individual representation of the nation (the President), of states (Senators), and of districts (House members). By contrast, the highly disciplined Westminster system prioritizes a corporate form of representation for the entire country (parliamentary government). Citing empirical findings that attribute variation in legislative and political outcomes to these institutional differences, Pettit concludes that the representational priority expressed by a polity's institutional set-up will profoundly shape key political relationships and important substantive outcomes within that polity.

In Chapter 4 Bryan Garsten questions a central premise of Pettit's essay: that democratic representation should be valued because it offers a possible solution to the monitoring problem. Garsten maintains that the "purpose" of representative institutions is to "multiply and challenge government claims to represent the people." Garsten explores the liberal and democratic logic of this conception of representative government by examining the writings of Jean-Jacques Rousseau, Benjamin Constant, and James Madison.

Garsten argues that although Rousseau was a committed defender of popular sovereignty, he nonetheless rejected Pettit's simulative representation. Fearing that representative governments would usurp the people's rightful claim to full political sovereignty, Rousseau favored indirect government. Garsten offers a novel interpretation of the classic debate between Constant and Rousseau, in which Constant did not merely reject Rousseau's conclusions. Indeed, they agree on basic questions about representation. Garsten explains that Constant, like Rousseau, feared the tyrannical outcomes that can arise when democratic governments claim full political sovereignty. For Constant, as for Rousseau, institutions should be established to undermine any single popular representative from claiming to represent the popular will.

Next Garsten explores, in the writings of James Madison and Alexander Hamilton, the sentiment that political institutions should encourage debate about who rightfully speaks for the people. Garsten agrees with them that true demagogues – rulers successfully claiming the support of the people – constitute a grave threat to representative legitimacy. By multiplying the number of government officials who can with some plausibility claim to represent the people, representative institutions encourage disputes and conversation about what the popular will is and who may rightly claim popular authority. Our inherently multivocal forms of government, Garsten argues, are therefore most successful when cacophonous debate about who is the rightful representative of the people drowns out the voice of any particular demagogue. That is how ambition, in Madison's words, is made to counteract ambition.

In Chapter 5 Clarissa Rile Hayward develops a different challenge to the view that democratic representation is fundamentally about solving the monitoring problem. On her account this view fails to account for the many ways in which the actions of representatives actually shape their constituents' interests, rather than simply reflecting preexisting preferences and interests. Hayward uses the example of structural inequalities – inequalities in resources and opportunities built into law – to illustrate the shortcomings of conventional views of the monitoring problem. Because common aggregative and deliberative approaches to democracy theory overlook how political interests are shaped, proponents of these theories fail to recommend institutional reforms that are likely to promote equality or inclusiveness in government. Hayward makes a strong case that merely tinkering with representative forums is unlikely to create incentives for representatives to challenge the structurally entrenched inequities that shape their constituents' lives.

Instead Hayward argues in favor of a contestatory ideal in which political institutions are legitimate if they promote "free and equal struggles over collective norms and principles." Her contestatory approach does not take interests for granted. Rather, institutions should encourage the formation of interests that undermine both inequalities and fixed hierarchies. She advances this case by exploring the example of political jurisdictions in the United States. The growth in suburban municipalities, at the expense of cities, deepened existing inequities (e.g. in public schooling), limiting people's ability to challenge policies that affected them via the democratic process. An approach that understood interests as politically constructed would not only advocate for more effective forms of representation within existing jurisdictions, but it would also militate in support of changes in those jurisdictions. Such an approach, Hayward contends, would put citizens on a more equal footing with one another. It would also make it easier for the disenfranchised to confront institutional barriers to political equality.

III.   Representation and inherited injustice

The historical role of states in creating identities and fixing interests is also at the heart of Courtney Jung's discussion in Chapter 6, entitled "Critical liberalism." Jung argues that existing accounts of group rights, including those that grapple with the appropriate extent and structure of group representation, neglect the ways states create ethnic groups and how states establish unjust institutional arrangements on the basis of group distinctions. Recognizing this, she argues, provides us with greater purchase on what the state owes to whom. Jung's analysis falls into three parts. First she challenges the assumption that groups and identities which constitute society are natural – a perspective the author attributes to theorists such as Will Kymlicka, John Rawls, and Ronald Dworkin. Naturalizing groups and identities creates an impulse to privatize or protect ethnic groups, with the result that culture and democratic politics are insulated from one another. As an alternative, Jung recommends that we investigate where human attachments come from. In doing so, we will not only trace how power has been exercised, but also identify the historical obligations of states.

Like Hayward, Jung is particularly concerned with identifying and reforming institutions that were shaped by, and in turn reproduce, structural injustice. Jung argues that claims for redistribution, special modes of representation, or institutional reconfiguration should be responsive to the specific conditions and policies that shaped the relevant ethnic group. Jung's chapter builds toward a conception of individual rights that is consistent with her theory's focus on politically constructed identities and structural injustice. She argues in favor of membership rights, whereby individual rights accrue to members of structurally disadvantaged groups. Membership rights embody an attractive third way between liberal rights regimes, geared toward preserving inequality on the basis of an ostensible commitment to neutrality, and group rights regimes aimed at shielding unjust group practices from liberal critique. Ultimately, Jung contends that our normative accounts of democracy and representation must address the challenge posed by the following question: "How should democratic institutions process the political claims that arise to protect and contest the exclusions and inclusions set in place by the modern state itself?"

In Chapter 7, Mahmood Mamdani examines a stark instance of how structural injustices become entrenched within and then reproduced by representative institutions. The national system of representation of the United States comprehends two versions of sovereignty. On the one hand, in many cases the decisions of federal organs take precedence over the decisions of lower bodies – such as local and state governments. This hierarchy is consistent with traditional, unitary conceptions of sovereignty. On the other hand, states are thought to retain some element of the sovereign status they compromised when the United States was founded in the eighteenth century. The representative institutions of the United States – including both Houses of Congress and the presidency, whose incumbent is elected by a state-based electoral college – reflect the ingenuity employed to create a single representative political system containing multiple permutations of political sovereignty.

Mamdani notes that, throughout the history of the United States, Native Americans were forced to inhabit a perpetually fluid nether status as wards of the United States – neither guaranteed rights as full citizens, nor recognized as members of free communities within the United States. Not only were Native Americans denied protection under the Constitution, their independence and claims to land were systematically undermined by the state. The singular democratic creativity employed to reconcile federal and state sovereignty was never applied to shape institutions that would recognize Native Americans as members of alternative "sovereign" entities. In devastating contrast to the Founders' remarkable institutional imagination, Mamdani argues that the institutional and legal relationship of the United States to Native Americans mimicked destructive regimes imposed on others by colonial Europe.

IV.   What role for representative quotas?

If representation that reproduces structural injustice is infirm, what should the remedy be? That question is taken up in the next two chapters by authors who explore whether representative quotas and qualifications are a defensible strategy for reforming representative institutions. In Chapter 8, Shireen Hassim analyzes the ways in which quotas for women may paradoxically hinder their effective representation and substantive equality. Her focus is on South Africa, Uganda, and Rwanda, where inherited structural injustice seems to offer compelling reasons to embrace gender-based quotas so as to ensure a substantial presence of women in their respective legislatures.

Yet South Africa, Uganda, and Rwanda are all effectively single-party-dominant systems, even though the dominant political groups within the countries established the gender-based quotas. Hassim identifies two broad mechanisms through which quotas might undercut further democratization and the achievement of substantively egalitarian policies. First, the women elected to these parliaments owe their position to the dominant party. Consequently, they have relatively little political autonomy and therefore often end up supporting the policy of the government against the claims of women's groups in civil society. Despite their lack of political independence, the presence of female representatives in the legislatures provides the dominant parties with a special claim to political legitimacy. Second, quotas might have the effect of increasing the number of women in legislatures without concomitantly establishing a link between those representatives and a political constituency intent on holding those representatives accountable for securing political outcomes that are beneficial to women. Lacking an independent constituency, women representatives are cogs within the larger party machinery. Though Hassim acknowledges that quotas might be a necessary transitional step for achieving more democratic outcomes, she concludes that they are "not a sufficient condition by any means."

Complementing Hassim's study, Andrew Rehfeld takes up the normative basis of electoral qualifications and quotas in Chapter 9. While particular qualifications for elected office might be defended by reference to past injustices or institutional pathologies, he argues, as a general matter they ought to be presumed illegitimate.

Rehfeld defines a qualification as any rule or circumstance that has the effect of creating different probabilities of success for individual candidates. Gender-based quotas fall within this definition of qualifications because they effect the ability of individuals (typically men) to run for office, as well as the ability of all individuals to choose whom they want to govern them. There are, of course, some qualifications for office which are essential to the process of democratic selection – i.e. the qualifications determined by the voters themselves. Accordingly, Rehfeld distinguishes between voter endogenous qualifications, which are not presumptively illegitimate, and voter exogenous qualifications, which are.

Rehfeld then elaborates on the two democratic rights that all exogenous qualifications for office violate: the right to be ruled by someone one chooses and the right to run for office. The existence of a right to choose one's rulers is likely to be intuitive to most democrats, and the relationship between this right and electoral qualifications is straightforward: qualifications impinge on voter choice by assigning a greater probability to a certain kind of candidate. But Rehfeld argues that the equal right to pursue political office is also implied by the democratic principle of equality and by a democratic skepticism of aristocracy. While he does not entirely foreclose the possibility that a polity might be justified in imposing exogenous qualifications for political office, he makes a strong case that such action should have to overcome a strict justificatory test. Ultimately, both Rehfeld's and Hassim's chapters are animated by the shared intuition that the easy embrace of representative quotas and qualifications as mechanisms of political empowerment gives short shrift to the potential political and normative costs of this type of electoral engineering.

V.   Preferences, persuasion, and democratic representation

Are there other grounds for preferring indirect forms of representation, if not Burke's explicit paternalism? This question is taken up by John Ferejohn and Frances Rosenbluth in Chapter 10. They investigate the logical foundations of what they describe as the aristocratic thesis: that indirect decision-making processes or government by an elite might generate better outcomes than direct democratic procedures. Ferejohn and Rosenbluth ask whether representative government produces outcomes that are different from those that direct democracy would generate, and whether those outcomes are better or worse for the people. The authors argue that an agency model – in which the voters are the principals and representatives are the agents – captures central elements of the representative dynamic. Still, they point out that such models fail to account for important aspects of the voter–representative relationship: that voters constitute a plural agent; that they lack important information about their representatives; and that, unlike standard principals, voters are unable to write better contracts for themselves – they can only choose to elect or not elect. Each of these factors makes it harder for constituents to solve the monitoring problem as conventionally conceived. They also imply that representative outcomes will differ significantly from direct democratic outcomes. Ferejohn and Rosenbluth cite empirical findings that the introduction of referendums or initiatives – instruments of direct democracy – into representative democracy tends to push political outcomes toward the preference of the median voter. These observations reinforce the conclusion that representative and direct democratic outcomes differ. Yet do they differ systematically? While Ferejohn and Rosenbluth do not reject this possibility, they conclude that it remains an open question whether representative systems produce *better* outcomes than do direct ones.

John Roemer takes a different approach to the tension between voter preferences and the outcome of representative institutions in Chapter 11. The classic account of the relationship between voter preferences and policy outcomes was given by Anthony Downs. Downsian models do not predict that a political party whose economic policies are in the interests of a small minority of wealthy citizens will be electorally successful. Roemer argues that the Republican Party is such a party, and that a more complicated electoral model than Downs's is needed to account for its long-term electoral viability. After reviewing various explanations for this counterintuitive outcome, Roemer contends that only three are likely to have contributed to the long-term success of the Republican Party: policy bundling (where parties combine less popular policies with more popular ones); voters' conceptions of distributive justice; and imperfect political representation (i.e. democratic institutions are organized in such a way that individuals do not have an equal influence on political outcomes).

Roemer then goes on to describe a four-dimensional model of party policies and voter preferences that allows him to account for the following facts: that the Democratic and Republican parties differ on more than one issue, that there are extreme and moderate factions within both parties, and that voters care about more than one issue (such as taxes, race, and religion). Roemer uses the model to estimate the *policy bundle effect*, which concerns the extent to which voters will support less-preferred economic outcomes (e.g. low taxes) to achieve their preferred outcomes with respect to race, and the *anti-solidarity* effect – how much they simply believe that African-Americans abuse the social welfare state, and vote against redistributive policies on that basis. To estimate the size of these effects, Roemer ran counterfactual elections in which one or both effects were removed from the calculations of the modeled voters. The estimated effect of these race-based factors on the vote totals of the Republican Party in presidential elections was significant. The results suggest that Republicans demonstrated significant political savvy by shifting the political debate away from economic issues. Roemer's finding also adds weight to the increasingly familiar claim that racism has generated the difference in social spending between the United States and advanced European democracies.

Sendhil Mullainathan, Ebonya Washington, and Julia Azari also examine the mechanisms linking the political preferences of American voters with their electoral choices in Chapter 12. In theory, televised political debates provide relevant information that allows voters to make choices reflecting their preferences. To investigate this potential effect, the authors conducted a randomized experiment measuring the impact of a 2005 New York City mayoral debate on likely voters' opinions about the mayoral candidates (Michael Bloomberg and Fernando Ferrer). Previous examinations of the effects of debates typically attempt to gauge the influence of debates by conducting before-and-after viewer interviews. Such studies, however, suffer from familiar problems of potential endogeneity – i.e. debate viewers may be systematically more or less likely to have their views changed by a debate than the voting populace at large. This study was not subject to the same problems, however, since the participants were randomly assigned to watch a debate or a placebo program (*The NewsHour with Jim Lehrer*). Using before-and-after telephone surveys, the authors found that those watching the debate were more likely to report that their opinions of the candidates had changed. Despite the reported difference, those who watched the debate had the same opinions as the control group when asked specific questions about the candidates. This finding suggests both that the debates were uninformative and that voters seemed not to grasp how their own opinions were influenced by the debate. Such a result raises serious questions about the usefulness of political debates, about the mechanisms through which they might actually influence political outcomes, and about how voters incorporate new information.

John Roemer argued that voters are not only persuaded by parties' economic policies but by their stance on other issues, such as those associated with race. In Chapter 13 Gary Cox argues that models that focus only on the attempt of parties to persuade voters miss a number of other partisan activities which may be as important as persuasion in the pursuit of reelection. These activities mobilize reliable voters and coordinate voters, thus serving to prevent, or at least impede, ideologically similar start-up parties from challenging incumbent parties.

Cox's chapter takes particular aim at the argument, made by Susan Stokes, that core voters, who favor a party on partisan or programmatic grounds, cannot credibly threaten to punish their party if it withholds distributive rewards. The implication of Stokes's argument is that parties will focus on swing, not precommitted core voters. In contrast to Stokes, Cox contends that core voters possess two ways of credibly threatening their preferred parties: by abstaining or by voting for a competitor party on the same part of the political spectrum. These two defection strategies in turn map onto two activities that parties must undertake to limit defections: mobilization and coordination. Full models of parties' political activities, Cox argues, should find that as long as mobilizing and coordinating voters are seen as effective strategies for winning elections, parties will shift their focus from swing to core voters.

Cox extends these insights into the legislative arena. Legislative parties do not just convince swing legislators; they also mobilize and coordinate their members. As in the electoral arena, core members or those responsible for mobilizing and coordinating other members (e.g. whips or committee chairmen) should be the chief recipients of pork from the party. If Cox is correct, models which focus only on persuasion are necessarily biased toward finding that parties focus on attracting swing voters, rather than motivating core voters. The analytical payoff here is critical to understanding representation in partisan political systems. If our accounts of party activity mischaracterize what parties do, then they will necessarily mischaracterize whom they represent.

The debates among our contributors do not converge on a single answer to the monitoring problem that was thrown into sharp relief by Burke's speech to the electors of Bristol. Rather they suggest that it is in fact not a single problem. Different voters, indeed even different supporters of a single representative, stand in very different relations to that representative. And representatives often confront multiple, conflicting imperatives vis-à-vis the same voters. Collectively, these authors build a convincing case that we need a better understanding of these complex relations in their multifarious parts before aspiring to develop any general theory of representation.

BIBLIOGRAPHY

Burke, Edmund. 1999. "Speech to the Electors of Bristol," in *Selected Works of Edmund Burke*. Indianapolis, IN: Liberty Fund.

Part I

Representation before representative democracy

1   Hobbes's theory of representation: anti-democratic or proto-democratic?

David Runciman

I.   Hobbes, representation, and democracy

Thomas Hobbes occupies a deeply ambivalent position in the history of modern conceptions of political representation. On the one hand, he is often credited as the thinker who did most to make representation a distinctively modern concept, by emancipating it from its medieval roots and employing it to establish a clear identity for the state as a separate entity in its own right (Skinner 1989, 2002). Hobbes used the idea of representation to ground a secular conception of political authority, and in doing so rescued the idea of political rule from various intractable theological controversies.[1] In this sense, Hobbes's thought is foundational for modern theories of representative government. But for all its apparent modernity, Hobbes's theory of representation suffers from one obvious flaw when judged by the standards of contemporary politics: it appears to be strikingly anti-democratic, and it is very hard to see how an anti-democratic theory can also be viewed as foundational for the political world we now inhabit.

This dual role occupied by Hobbes – both foundational but also oppositional in his perceived relationship to representative democracy – is best captured by his treatment in what remains the most widely cited work on the theory of political representation in English, Hanna Pitkin's *The Concept of Representation* (Pitkin 1967). There, Hobbes is treated first of all as the thinker who did most to clarify the central feature of modern political representation – that it is an "authorization" concept (or what Pitkin goes on to call a "substantive" concept), in which political representation emerges as a form of "acting for" rather than merely "standing for." But Pitkin also makes it clear that Hobbes's theory of representation is not a viable theory, because it stands in direct opposition to the

---

[1] For instance, it is one of the many striking features of Hobbes's theory of representation that his account of theological representation in *Leviathan* – where he discusses at length the manner in which God is "represented" by the Trinity – follows from his account of political representation, and not the other way around (see Hobbes 1996: 339–40).

democratic presupposition that individuals may object to what is being done on their behalf by their political representatives. For Hobbes, a sovereign representative, once authorized, cannot be constrained, and therefore has absolute power to rule as he sees fit.[2] Thus although this may be an "authorization" concept, it is also far too authoritarian by our current standards. So, Pitkin argues, Hobbes is clearly "wrong" about representation, and a different account is needed.

In this chapter, I want to argue that it is possible to close the gap between Hobbes's apparently foundational role in the modern theory of representation and our own democratic expectations of what representation must entail. I believe that Hobbes's thought is not just foundational in the sense that it marks a clean break with the medieval/theological past, but also because it clearly points the way forward to the democratic forms of representation that were to follow. By making sense of what is going on inside Hobbes's theory of representation, it is possible to establish the ways in which a Hobbesian framework for representative government remains the one in which we still have to operate.

In order to make this case, it is important to distinguish the approach I am going to adopt from a number of other ways in which it might be claimed that Hobbes is a more "democratic" thinker than he is usually perceived. One way in which this might be done is to argue that Hobbes's own ideas were designed to be more democratic than commentators have sometimes recognized. A version of this case has recently been made, for example, by Richard Tuck, who has argued for a much fuller overlap than is commonly perceived between Hobbes's political thought and both Aristotle's conception of "extreme democracy" on the one hand and Rousseau's later democratic theory on the other (Tuck 2006). However, though this might help to rescue Hobbes from undue pigeonholing as a straightforward "anti-democrat," it cannot do the same for his theory of representation, because it places the focus on Hobbes's earlier writings in which his theory of representation is not fully articulated, at the expense of *Leviathan*, where it is. Tuck's case rests on treating *De Cive* (1642) as a more significant work than *Leviathan* (1651), where Hobbes's fire is directed against the "democratical gentlemen" whom he blamed for the catastrophe of the English Civil War. But it is no coincidence that *Leviathan* is also where Hobbes firmly identifies representation as the key to his theory of politics, which is something he does not do in his

---

[2] Although Hobbes allows that the sovereign can either be an individual or an assembly (this is one of the ways in which his thought is more democratic than is sometimes supposed), for shorthand here I will treat the sovereign as always a single ruler (and as male, though again Hobbes saw no reason why this should always be the case). This is the shorthand Hobbes himself uses.

earlier works. For this reason, identifying Hobbes in historical terms as a democrat appears to involve rescuing him from his own theory of political representation, so that the gap between democracy and representation remains.[3]

An alternative approach is to argue that Hobbes's theory of representation, while not in itself properly democratic, exercised a strong influence on the ideas of subsequent theorists of representation whom it is possible to think of as democratic theorists in their own right. The strongest version of this argument is one that traces the influence of Hobbes's theory of representation on the political thought of the French Revolution, for example on that of the Abbé Sieyès (Hont 2005). But again, the case is by no means straightforward, not least because Sieyès drew on Hobbes in part because he was seeking to distance his own thought from what he saw as the obvious perils of "crude" democratic theory.[4] It is also striking that some of the theorists who have drawn most heavily on Hobbes's theory of representation are often the ones that many contemporary democrats would be least comfortable identifying with. This is particularly true of Carl Schmitt, whose self-declared "democratic" theory of representation, with its emphasis on plebiscitary leadership and extra-legal forms of political authorization, while echoing Hobbes in a number of respects, hardly rescues Hobbes from the suspicion that he is not a genuine democrat in anything but the most minimal sense of the term (Schmitt 1996). Hobbes's influence on Schmitt recapitulates rather than resolves the problem.

The case I want to make here is not primarily a historical one, and I do not wish to argue that either the earlier variations or the subsequent impact of Hobbes's theory of representation are what make his ideas indispensable for democratic theory. Rather, I want to claim that the formal content of his theory of representation in its best-known and most clearly articulated setting – *Leviathan* – has been too narrowly understood, by being too closely identified with his theory of authorization. In this chapter, I give what I consider to be a fuller account of the formal workings of Hobbes's theory, in order to show how Hobbes's account allows a distinction to be drawn between representation and authorization. With the aid of this distinction, I believe it is possible to establish a much closer connection than is usually allowed between what Hobbes has to say about representation and the functioning of representative

---

[3] This is one of a number of reasons why Tuck's case is not convincing; the others are laid out in Hoekstra (2006).
[4] "For I always maintain that France is not, and cannot be, a *democracy* . . . France is and must be a *single* whole, subject throughout to a common legislation and a common administration" (quoted in Forsyth 1987: 138).

democracy. I am not claiming that Hobbes drew a distinction between authorization and representation in order to make his theory more democratic; if anything, the reverse is true, and Hobbes drew this distinction because of what he saw as the pitfalls of a democratic conception of political authority. What makes the connection between Hobbes's theory of representation and our own understanding of representative democracy is that these pitfalls are still there, and it is only with the aid of a distinction of this kind that it is possible to avoid some of them. Hobbes's wider prejudices against democratic politics served in the end to make his theory of representative government unworkable by our standards. In this respect, he was wrong about democracy. But his understanding of what a theory of representation requires to be workable at all was essentially correct, and applies to democratic politics all the same.

II.   Hobbes on representation and authorization

Pitkin bases her claim that Hobbes is a straightforwardly anti-democratic thinker on his theory of authorization, as laid out in *Leviathan*. Viewed in these terms, the case is a compelling one.[5] For Hobbes, to be the "author" of another person's actions is to "own" whatever actions they perform; in other words, it is to be bound by what they do (Hobbes 1996: 112). Hobbes believed that it was possible to set limits on what one person might do on the authority of another – for example, by authorizing them to act only in certain ways or within certain limits – but that this was only possible within the context of civil society, where contractual arrangements of this kind could be enforced by the sovereign. By definition, the act of authorizing the sovereign itself could not be subject to such limitations, because there was no power in place to enforce them. The ability of the sovereign to hold individuals to their contracts depended on the fact that sovereign authority was unlimited, and therefore binding. So Hobbes states that the individuals who authorize a sovereign to act on their behalf must be the owners of anything and everything the sovereign does in their name. Hobbes accepts that there are some circumstances where this arrangement becomes absurd, as when the sovereign orders the death of an individual subject: given that it is nonsensical for individuals to command their own death, it cannot be plausible that they should treat the command uttered by someone else as though it were their own (ibid.: 151). They may, under such circumstances, resist, which would

---

[5] Though Pitkin does not consider the historical background to this argument (as I also do not here). For a full account of the polemical purposes of Hobbes's theory of representation in *Leviathan*, see Skinner (2005).

be to repudiate the authority of the sovereign. But this caveat is a very slender basis on which to construct any significant limitation of sovereign power, because all other subjects of the sovereign are still bound to obey the command, so that the resistance of the individual freed from their obligations will almost certainly be futile.

The fact that Hobbes allows individuals to disown the actions of their sovereign when faced with death is not enough to make the theory in any sense democratic, since democracy requires not simply that we can disown the actions of our representatives but that we can constrain them in some way. Hobbes's sovereign remains unconstrained, because the disowning of sovereign actions is either futile – when only a few people are threatened – or redundant – as when the population at large is under threat – because a sovereign who threatens the majority of his subjects with death has already returned them to a state of nature, where political authority is void. Pitkin is therefore right to argue that Hobbes's account of political authorization leaves no room for individuals to have a say in what is being done on their behalf by their sovereign. But she is wrong to suppose that this constitutes the whole of Hobbes's account of political representation. For what is striking about the version Hobbes gives in *Leviathan* is that he does not on the whole use the language of representation to describe the relationship between an individual subject and their sovereign. He is careful to limit the description of that relationship to the terminology of authorization and ownership. He talks about representation primarily when he is discussing the relationship between the sovereign and all his subjects, taken as a whole. Individual acts of authorization give the sovereign the right, not merely to act on the authority of each individual, but additionally to "Present the Person of them all (that is, to be their *Representative*)" (ibid.: 121, italics in original). Though this is a somewhat ambiguous sentence – the words "them all" might refer either to a group of individuals qua individuals or to a corporate entity – it is striking that Hobbes does not say that the sovereign represents the "persons" of them all. This makes a corporate reading more plausible. In these terms, representation follows from the authorization of the sovereign but is not strictly equivalent to it, because it is not the individual authors of the sovereign who are represented by his actions as individuals, but the commonwealth itself. When Hobbes talks about the sovereign as "representative" in *Leviathan* (see, for example, ibid.: 128, 184), he emphasizes that what he represents are not the separate persons of his individual subjects, even though these are the people who individually "own" his actions; rather, what he *represents* is the state, which is what their joint ownership of his actions has brought into being. And it is crucial for Hobbes's entire theory of representation that this entity – the person of the state – does not have authority to act on its own behalf, which means it does not have the authority to initiate its own acts of representation.

It is true that Hobbes is not entirely consistent here, and this reading, which emphasizes the corporate character of representation in *Leviathan*, is hard to square with some other passages, where he suggests that representation is indeed the representation of the sovereign's individual subjects. So, for example, in Chapter XVI, Hobbes says of political representation that "it is the *Unity* of the Represener, not the *Unity* of the Represented, that maketh the Person *One*" (ibid.: 114). This suggests that individual subjects, though disunited in their own persons, nevertheless constitute the "represented." Later on, Hobbes warns that

> where there is already erected a Soveraign Power, there can be no other Representative of the same people, but onely to certain particular ends, by the Soveraign limited. For that were to erect two Soveraigns; and every man to have his person represented by two Actors, that by opposing one another, must needs divide that Power, which (if men will live in Peace), is indivisible. (ibid.: 130)

This seems to make it explicit that representation is the representation of every man in "his [own] person," rather than the representation of some group person that transcends the individual. Nevertheless, it is important to note that these two passages, in which Hobbes connects representation with individual persons, are essentially accounts of what political representation is *not*. Hobbes is saying that political representation is *not* the representation of a united multitude; equally, it is *not* to allow individuals to have more than one representative. Both of these ways of thinking about representation are, in Hobbes's eyes, inherently unstable. Indeed, the second passage could be read in an even stronger way, as a warning about what is liable to happen if you do collapse representation into the representation of individuals – they are liable to consider themselves to be represented by someone other than their authorized sovereign. That is why it is so important for Hobbes to emphasize that representation is representation of a single person of the state incapable of thinking in these destabilizing terms.

If one distinguishes between Hobbes's negative statements about political representation – the ways in which it can go wrong – and his positive statements – what needs to be true of it for it to be stable – then a pattern emerges: the authorization of the sovereign by a "multitude" of natural individuals makes the representation of the state possible, but is neither equivalent nor reducible to it. Figure 1.1 makes clear that these can be understood as distinct relationships.

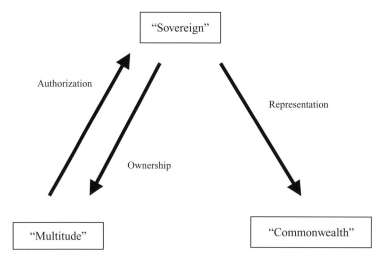

Figure 1.1 Hobbes's basic theory of representation.

The obvious question to ask is why Hobbes might want to separate out representation from authorization, given that the representative nature of the sovereign does not change the basic obligations owed him by his individual subjects. The answer, I think, is that Hobbes was conscious that his bare theory of authorization was insufficient to construct an account of the state, because it did not on its own generate for the state its own collective identity. Even though it was part of the radicalism of Hobbes's theory to found it on individuals (in accordance with his *resoluto-compositive* method), he recognized that representation could not be a purely individualistic relationship. To leave the sovereign as merely the representative of a series of individual "authors" is to reduce politics to a series of personal relationships, each binding, but also each distinct, with the result that the people as a whole remain a fragmented multitude. For the people to assume a collective identity required that they be represented as though they were a single person, not a series of separate individuals. What Hobbes discovered in *Leviathan* was that the language of representation enabled him to do this, notwithstanding the fact that the authority of the sovereign continued to rest on the obligations of his individual subjects. The concept of representation made it possible to separate out the state from the multitude.

While it does not change the basic relationship between the individual subject and the sovereign – and certainly does not democratize it – the idea of the "sovereign representative" does at least raise the possibility that there might be other significant relationships at work in Hobbes's

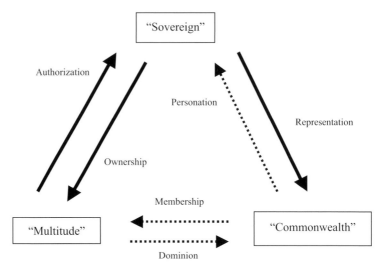

Figure 1.2 Hobbes's full theory of representation.

theory of politics beyond that of authorization: these include the relationship between the sovereign and the commonwealth he represents, and that between the multitude and the commonwealth that their authorization of the sovereign brings into being. These are, as it were, the other two sides of the triangle. Once a second side has been filled in, even if only partially, it is no longer possible to argue that all political relationships are merely replications of the one-sided relationship of authorization and ownership between individual subject and sovereign. Hobbes appears to recognize this. The account he offers in *Leviathan* goes some way to filling in the other sides of the triangle. He does this by extending and enriching some of the terminology that relates to the idea of the "sovereign representative," so that in the end Hobbes's theory of representation includes the notions of "personation," "membership," and "dominion" as well as "authorization" and "ownership." A fuller version of Hobbes's theory of representation is summarized in Figure 1.2, with a brief explanation of the terms as follows:

Personation: Because for Hobbes representation derives from the concept of the "person," he sometimes talks of representation in terms of "personation" – the wearing of a mask, or the inhabiting of a role (ibid.: 112) – so that the representation of the commonwealth makes it possible for Hobbes to describe the sovereign as "bearing the person of the state." But the language of personation does not fit the representation of a multitude of individuals qua individuals, because it is impossible to see how the sovereign could wear a multitude of masks simultaneously. An actor can only wear one mask at a time, and though it is true that an actor could wear a succession of different masks one after the other, it is hard to reconcile this image with Hobbes's understanding of politics; indeed, this is just the sort of fragmentation of the political experience that his theory of representation seems designed to avoid. To see the sovereign as personating the commonwealth at least suggests that the occupant of the "office" of sovereign representative is constrained by the requirement to be a plausible performer of that particular role (Hobbes spells out at some length what these requirements might be in Chapter XXX of *Leviathan*; ibid.: 231–42). Hobbes is adamant that the commonwealth cannot itself constrain the sovereign by its actions, because the commonwealth cannot itself act except through its sovereign representative. But it can, at least potentially, constrain by its implied presence, because even the representatives of things that have no independent existence are limited by the need to keep up appearances. In the case of the sovereign, this means acting in such as a way as to ensure that the subjects he represents appear to be something more than a disunited multitude.

Hobbes also has to consider the question of how the multitude – that is, the individual subjects – might relate to the person of the state. There are in fact two questions here: Do they have any sort of relationship to the state given their role in its creation? And do they have a relationship to the state given the fact that they are ultimately responsible for what is done in its name? One possibility is to answer both questions in the negative, and to insist that the person of the state is simply reducible to the persons of its individual members, so that no independent relationship between them is conceivable. Hobbes might be thought to have good reasons to choose this route, which closes down the possibility of individuals forming a separate relationship with the political community than the one that exists through their sovereign representative. Nevertheless, in both cases, Hobbes offers the basis for an alternative answer, in the following terms.

Dominion: In Chapter XVI of *Leviathan*, Hobbes makes it clear that in the case of "incapable" entities, which are represented but unable to authorize their own representation, authority lies with those who are responsible for the thing in question, or who have brought it into being (ibid.: 113). The state is just such an incapable entity, and those who have brought it into being are the multitude, which at least suggests that they have some kind of latent dominion over it, even if that dominion can never subsequently be exercised because of the hold that the sovereign exercises over them as individuals.

Membership: At the same time, Hobbes deploys the language of membership to describe the relationship between individual subjects and the state to which they belong. For Hobbes, the language of membership forms part of his image of the Leviathan as a kind of body with "members" that enable it to function, as the arms, legs, etc. of the body allow it to function also (ibid.: 168–9). Again, membership in this sense does not imply any kind of independent control, but it does at least mean that what is done in the name of the state depends on the proper functioning of its individual members, joined together as part of a corporate body, rather than simply responding as individuals jointly represented by the same person.

All three of these additional ideas – personation, dominion, membership – follow from the fact that Hobbes makes the sovereign the representative of the commonwealth, not of the multitude. Taken together, they mean that commentators like Pitkin, by focusing exclusively on authorization, offer an account of Hobbes's theory of representation that is much too narrow. But do any of them, either separately or jointly, serve to undercut the force of Pitkin's central claim that Hobbes's account of representation is inadequate because it does not allow anyone to object to what the sovereign does in their name? The answer is no – at least, not as Hobbes uses them. The representation of the person of the commonwealth serves to limit the ways in which the sovereign can act if he is to fulfill his role, but it does not allow anyone to object to what the sovereign does in that role. It simply sets tighter conditions for what will constitute a failure of performance, and ultimately a failure of the state itself. Personation imposes burdens on the sovereign, but does not grant rights to anyone else, just as actors who play a part on the stage are constrained in what they can plausibly do but are not open to objections from the character whose part they are playing. Dominion might offer grounds for objection, but not in the case of the sovereign, who once established exercises control over the forms of dominion enjoyed by his subjects. Membership can be the basis for constraining the actions undertaken by a representative of the group (the members qua members may have certain rights over the determination of group outcomes), but not Hobbesian membership, which is metaphorical, and designed to illustrate that the members are conjoined with the sovereign in whatever he does. These are concepts that open up the possibility of a more democratic conception of representation. But as Hobbes uses them, that possibility is closed down.

Why is Hobbes so adamant that nowhere in the complex of relationships between individuals, sovereign, and the state should there be the basis for anyone to set limits to what the sovereign does, except for the sovereign himself? There are two answers to this question. The first, and most obvious, is that Hobbes was determined not to allow for the kinds of competing claims to political authority that he believed opened the door to civil war. This was the lesson he drew from the events of 1642 onwards: that to allow anyone to claim a "sufficient" basis to challenge the judgment of the sovereign power was to leave the state vulnerable to disintegration (to be "sufficient" in Hobbes's terms meant to have the requisite qualifications). The sovereign existed to close down potentially debilitating differences of opinion among individuals, particularly over what constituted a threat to their existence; allowing anyone to pass judgment over the sovereign's actions would merely open them up again, and ultimately spell the end of the sovereign's ability to act. For Hobbes, this was the strongest argument in favor of his particular conception of political representation. But if it is to be understood as a transhistorical claim, then we can see that Hobbes was clearly wrong. We can now be pretty confident, on the basis of the historical record, that states do not open the door to anarchy if they allow for judgment to be passed on the actions of "sovereign representatives" (or what we would now call governments). Under conditions of relative material prosperity and social stability, we can replace governments that we think have made the wrong decisions without plunging the state into civil war.

But the second answer that Hobbes might give is more persuasive. Hobbes's reluctance to allow anyone the right to object to the way in which they are being represented follows from the formal structure of his theory. In a state in which government authority derives from individuals but is exercised in the name of the people as a whole, it is difficult to see where the right to object should reside. If it belongs with individuals, then political life becomes fragmented, as it appears to allow individuals to exercise a right to opt in or out of collective judgment on their own terms. This was Hobbes's difficulty with resting ultimate political judgment in the multitude. On the other hand, if the group as a whole is allowed to object, then the individualistic basis of the theory is lost, because the group becomes the source of authority of sovereign actions. Hobbes wished to avoid this because he had straightforward intellectual objections to bestowing political rights on shadowy collective entities that had no natural basis. Hobbes was trying to strike a balance between his sense that individuals could not be the final arbiters of political judgment because that would destroy the collective life of the state, and his resistance at the same time to the idea that the collective could act in its own right, because that would trump the judgment of individuals. His theory of representation is a way of trying to circumvent these difficulties. By separating out representation from authorization, Hobbes is attempting to retain a collective identity for the state without granting to the state any distinctive powers of its own.

III.   Hobbesian representation and representative democracy

The problem of trying to strike a balance between the need to give the state a collective identity and the wish to avoid giving the state priority over the judgment of individuals is one that remains for democratic theories of representation. It is hard to see how this balance can be achieved without resort to the kind of formal structure provided by Hobbes. What can be dispensed with from Hobbes's account is the idea that authorization must be a once-for-all event, rather than an ongoing process. But what can be retained is the idea that those whom we authorize to act for us act not in our name as individuals, but in the name of the state, though it is as individuals that we pass judgment on their actions. A democratic theory of representation needs to retain the capacity of individuals to object to what is being done on their behalf by those with political power, while denying to individuals the right to opt in and out of political life as they see fit. If the first is lost, then democracy become authoritarianism (as it does with Hobbes); if the second is allowed, then democracy becomes chaos (as Hobbes feared). The solution, therefore, is to allow individuals to pass judgment on what governments do in the name of the state as a whole.

A version of how Hobbes's theory might be adapted in this way is given in Figure 1.3. It makes use of some of the terms drawn from Hobbes's full theory of representation, but freed from Hobbes's unwillingness to give them a democratic dimension. On this account, individual citizens pass judgment (in elections and through alternative vehicles of public opinion) over government action, and if necessary remove governments they disapprove of, thereby constraining the capacity of governments to act as they see fit. But governments, though authorized by the judgment of individual citizens, do not represent them as individuals (except when government politicians take up the cause of individual citizens, perhaps in representations to a foreign government); rather, they represent them as members of the state as a whole. In this sense, the government personates the state, while individual citizens acting as a multitude retain some dominion over what governments do in the state's name. As members of the state, individual citizens are bound by the actions governments undertake on the state's behalf; likewise, they have rights as members which allow them to pass judgment over those actions. The result is that political representation is an ongoing process that enables

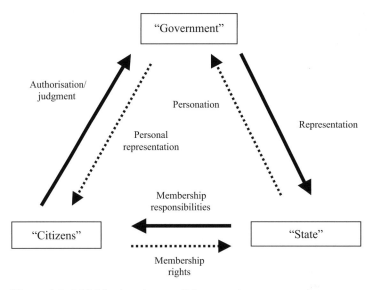

Figure 1.3 A Hobbesian theory of democratic representation.

individuals to judge actions undertaken on behalf of a collective entity to which they belong and for which they are ultimately responsible, without assuming that they are personally represented in every decision taken.

This account of political representation seems to capture an important feature of how many representative democracies do in fact function in practice, though it does not hold for all forms of representative democracy, and nor is it true that any representative democracy functions like this at all times. Different systems place varying amounts of weight on individualistic representation and on tradeoffs between the representatives of different constituencies within the state (something Hobbes wanted to avoid at all costs). The US system in particular places greater emphasis on the representation of individuals and of separate groups within the state than do many other polities (see the discussion of the difference between the "Washington" and "Westminster" models of representation in Pettit's chapter in this volume). But all states, including the US, sometimes need the capacity to undertake actions in the name of the people as a whole. When governments take certain sorts of collective decisions (to go to war, to raise taxes, and so on), it does not make sense to think of each individual member of the state being personally represented in those decisions; otherwise, it would be hard to see how to deal with the fact that many individual members of the state will inevitably object to decisions of this kind.

To put it in semi-Hobbesian terms, there is something implausible about the idea that when government taxes an individual, it is representing that individual in doing so, since the chances are that the person concerned would much prefer not to be taxed. But there is also something unsatisfactory about the idea that when government taxes an individual, it is representing some other group of individuals entirely, as that is likely to make the politics of taxation a highly confrontational business (though of course it often is highly confrontational, particularly in the US; see e.g. Graetz and Shapiro 2005). Governments need to be able to act in the name of the state, or of "the people" understood as a collective entity, not a disparate collection of individuals. What makes this form of political representation democratic is that a disparate collection of individuals can still pass judgment over what governments do in the state's name, either through the ballot box or through other vehicles of public opinion, such as pressure groups and opinion polls. This version of democracy, for all its distance from a Hobbesian conception of politics, shares three key features with Hobbes's theory of representation. First, it separates out authorization from representation: the individuals who give governments the power to act are distinct from the collective entity in whose name governments act. Second, it treats the state as an incapable entity (or in Hobbes's terms, a kind of "fiction") that needs to be represented in order to act at all.[6] The only actors on this account are either individual citizens or governments. The state cannot impose its own will on what governments do or on how individuals judge the actions of their governments. But the state has a necessary presence in democratic political life, because its representation is the means of giving a collective identity to what would otherwise be just a multitude of individuals. Third, despite separating out the state from its individual members, it makes one dependent on the other – on this account, there is no state without individuals to pass judgment on the actions of the state's representatives, and to bear the consequences of what the sovereign does in the state's name.[7]

It is important to emphasize that this is not the only way of reconciling a democratic presumption in favor of individual judgment with the collective identity of groups. Different kinds of groups can square the circle in a variety of different ways. This is another respect in which Hobbes clearly got it wrong. He believed that all groups had to be modeled on

---

[6] The details of this argument are given in Runciman (2000a) and Skinner (2002).

[7] For a discussion of the different forms of collective responsibility for which a corporate conception of political representation might allow, see Runciman (2007).

the representative structure of the state.[8] But groups, particularly small, cooperative groups, can acquire a collective identity in a variety of different ways, without having recourse to Hobbesian forms of representation. The authority of the group can be reduced to the authority of its individual members. Groups can establish their own identity through the joint decisions of their members, either acting unanimously or by their joint agreement to various judgment-aggregation procedures, none of which need require the imposition of a representative to take decisions on their behalf (Pettit 2003). Over time, these decisions may demonstrate the consistency that we expect of any rational agent, so that it becomes possible to speak of the group having its own personality. Moreover, this personality can still be reconciled with a presumption in favor of individual judgment by allowing individual members to exit the group if they are unhappy with its collective decisions, or to remain members but to absent themselves from personal responsibility for what the group does in their name. Hobbes does not allow for any of this, because he does not wish groups other than the state to develop a life of their own.

But the fact that Hobbes is much too restrictive in how he understands group life in general does not mean that he is wrong about the particular character of the state. States are different from other groups, because they do not allow individuals to exit if they are unhappy, nor to absent themselves from responsibility for collective decisions (as Hobbes would be the first to insist, states can only function if individuals who are unhappy about tax-raising decisions taken in their name still have to pay their taxes). Equally, the individual members of states, being a diverse multitude, do not always display the kind of consistency in their judgments over time that would enable them to be described as a collective person in their own right. Public opinion is often fickle. This means that states can only plausibly acquire their own personality through the attempts of their representatives to give them a collective identity over time in a way that is tolerated by public opinion, but is not predetermined by it. In that respect, Hobbes was right to think that the personality of states depends on their being represented as though they had such a personality, rather than their actually having one.

Another way to put this is to say that Hobbes was doubtful about the ability of the individual members of states to agree not merely *that* they need a collective identity, but also *what* that identity should be. The

---

[8] This was achieved either by copying the representative structure of the state with a single sovereign, as in the case of families (Hobbes 1996: 162–3) or by acting on the authority of the sovereign representative of the state, as in the case of business corporations, universities, etc. (ibid.: 159–60).

difference can be captured by looking at what happens if you go the other way around the triangle in Figure 1.3. This is perfectly possible – it could be argued that what happens in political representation is that individuals authorize a collective version of themselves to pass judgments on the actions of representatives appointed by the group but representing them as individuals. This would be a variant on a Lockean conception of political representation: individuals would form themselves into something called a "society" or a "people," who hire and fire governments according to how well the government represents them as a diverse group of individuals. Hobbes's skepticism about such an arrangement derived from his reluctance to rely on individuals agreeing about more than the bare minimum that they needed to. For Hobbes, the bare minimum was an agreement that government was necessary. But on this alternative arrangement, before there can be government there has to be an agreement about the collective identity of the state that is to be governed, and above all about how it is to voice its objections to the way that it is being governed.

It is true that states are often founded on an agreement of this kind, laid out in the form of a constitutional settlement, something that Hobbes explicitly rejects. Again, Hobbes was clearly wrong to imagine that constitutional limitations on sovereign power would invariably serve as recipes for disaster. But against that, it is also true that the process of drawing up and ratifying constitutions accords more closely to a Hobbesian model of political representation than to the alternative version. A constitutional assembly that acts in the name of a people that cannot act for itself (by definition, if it is thought that a people needs to be constituted in order to act in the first place), and then has its actions ratified by a vote of the population at large, fits reasonably well with the picture described in Figure 1.3. Thus the non-Hobbesian version of popular representation could be said to depend on a Hobbesian version to get it off ground. The other thing to be said in favor of Hobbes's account is that it allows for the ways in which the state is represented, and for the ways in which individuals can object to the representation of the state, to shape each other over time. Because Hobbes believes it is not possible to determine in advance any particular constraints on government action, his conceptual scheme of representation is more open-ended than one that requires some agreement on the forms of collective action before popular representation can take place. The collective identity of the state is fashioned out of representation rather than being a precondition of it.

Thus Hobbes's skepticism goes with a more creative conception of representation than might be expected. Because Hobbes is so suspicious of the idea that groups can have an identity before they are represented, he has to allow that they can possess whatever identity their representatives are able to give them. If Hobbes's account is amended to include the input of the state's citizens in this process, then it is consistent with the wide variety of ways in which the governments of democratic states can have their actions conditioned by the judgment of their citizens, without being predetermined by them. This is one of the clear merits of adapting Hobbes's idea of representation for democratic theory: it enables governments and citizens to shape the ongoing life of the state, rather than expecting them to be subordinate to it. Hobbes's skepticism about the possibility of large groups of disparate individuals fashioning a collective identity for themselves out of some kind of common will or group mind has stood the test of time reasonably well, and is widely shared (see Schumpeter 1994). It seems reasonable to accept Hobbes's doubts about the wisdom of giving group persons on the scale of nation-states priority over the individuals by whom they are constituted. But Hobbes's reluctance to give up on the idea of states having their own personality at all also has a lot to recommend it, since it is hard to know what states are if they are nothing but the individuals who happen to inhabit them at a given moment in time. Hobbes's theory of representation is what enables him to combine his well-founded doubts about transcendent claims to group personality with his belief that politics must be something more than a battleground of individual wills. In this respect, it is not as skeptical as it might be, certainly compared to later theories of democracy that insist democracy can be nothing more than the combined choices of individual citizens (Buchanan and Tullock, 1965).[9] For all its anti-democratic polemical force, Hobbes's theory of representation is a measured one, and that is why it remains an important resource for bridging some of the gaps that still exist in the theory of democratic popular rule.

IV.   Conclusion

The account of political representation Hobbes gives in *Leviathan* is an unlikely vehicle for democratic politics. Hobbes himself was not a democrat when he wrote *Leviathan*, and he believed that an idle faith in democracy had helped to cause the English Civil War. But an idle faith in democracy is never a good idea, and Hobbes was right to attempt to

---

[9] Buchanan, in his "Marginal Notes on Reading Political Philosophy," lists as authors congenial to his and Tulloch's approach the following: Plato, Hobbes, and Spinoza. But he goes on: "Of these, and others within this tradition, only Spinoza's work seems to have much in common with our own" (Buchanan and Tullock 1965: 312). Hobbes's theory of representation is one reason for supporting this view of the essential lack of congeniality between their work and Hobbes's view of politics.

ground popular politics on something more solid, even if he was wrong in many of the details. Moreover, his theory of representation was not simply anti-democratic. In its fullest version, it also offers a means to think about the complex relationships between individuals, governments, and states without falling into some of the traps that come from trying to oversimplify those relationships. Many theories of representation do not avoid those traps, with the result that it is all too easy to conclude that there is no satisfactory way of making sense of representation within the terms of democratic theory (Przeworski 1999; Shapiro 2003). The problem is that it is very hard to see how to reconcile the claims of political representatives to take decisions on behalf of individuals with the rights of individuals to judge how well they are being represented. Hobbes offers a way around this difficulty by insisting that it is not simply individuals who are being represented; instead, it is the state that is being represented, and individuals who are involved in the process of making the representation of the state work. This rescues political representation from a constant and ultimately fruitless struggle to reconcile the apparent independence of political representatives to act as they see fit with their supposed dependence as representatives on the views of those whom they represent (Pitkin 1967). On Hobbes's account, political representatives are independent by definition, because they do not purport to represent the views of particular individuals, and the entity that they do represent – the state – has no views of its own.

What Hobbes does not do is offer an explanation of how the views of individuals might bear on the representation of the state. If this is added to Hobbes's account, as I have attempted here, it serves to limit the independence of political representatives without requiring them simply to represent the views of individuals. They act as representatives of the state; individuals judge them on that. In some ways, this is still a pretty minimal account of democracy, and as I have indicated, it describes the workings of some polities better than others. It leaves out all the ways that individuals might want their views taken account of, listened to, and played out before important political decisions are made. It also leaves out all the ways in which political representatives might take up the cause of individual constituents, and seek to represent them. It does not take account of all the groups other than the state in which individuals might find a voice and by which they might be represented. But, though minimal, this account of political representation still has to be compared with the alternatives. The difficulty that conventional theories of representation have in squaring the circle of the simultaneous dependence and independence of political representatives has led to some fairly stark choices. Either democracy abandons the language of representation and employs other terms to describe the relationship between governments and electorates (for example, that of consumer sovereignty: see Shapiro 2003), or representation abandons the idea of national collective identity and looks for other outlets for the representation of individuals (for example, the idea of "representation as responsiveness" in the international arena; see Kuper 2004). Hobbes was trying to avoid the need for choices of this kind. He believed that the idea of popular sovereignty could be reconciled with a conception of representation without placing undue weight on the collective identity of a multitude of separate individuals. His thought remains foundational because (for now, anyway) states founded on the idea of popular sovereignty do not seem to have been able to dispense with the language of representation and replace it with something else. The problem has always been knowing how to combine this dependence on the concept of representation with the democratic conviction that individuals ought to be able to tell their representatives what to do if it is going to make sense to talk about representation at all. Hobbes's triangle offers a way round having to square that circle.

BIBLIOGRAPHY

Buchanan, James and Gordon Tullock. 1965. *The Calculus of Consent. Logical Foundations of Constitutional Democracy.* Ann Arbor: University of Michigan Press.

Forsyth, Murray. 1987. *Reason and Revolution. The Political Thought of the Abbé Sieyès.* Leicester: Leicester University Press.

Graetz, Michael and Ian Shapiro. 2005. *Death by a Thousand Cuts. The Fight over Taxing Inherited Wealth.* Princeton, NJ: Princeton University Press.

Hobbes, Thomas. 1996 [1651]. *Leviathan*, ed. Richard Tuck. Cambridge: Cambridge University Press.
　1998 [1642]. *On the Citizen*, ed. Richard Tuck and Michael Silverthorne. Cambridge: Cambridge University Press.

Hoekstra, Kinch. 2006. "A Lion in the House: Hobbes and Democracy," in *Rethinking the Foundations of Modern Political Thought*, ed. Annabel Brett and James Tully. Cambridge: Cambridge University Press, 191–219.

Hont, Istvan. 2005. *Jealousy of Trade. International Competition and the Nation State in Historical Perspective.* Cambridge, MA: Belknap.

Kuper, Andrew. 2004. *Democracy Beyond Borders. Justice and Representation in Global Institutions.* Oxford: Oxford University Press.

Locke, John. 1988 [1679]. *Two Treatises of Government*, ed. Peter Laslett. Cambridge: Cambridge University Press.

Manin, Bernard. 1997. *The Principles of Representative Government.* Cambridge: Cambridge University Press.

Pettit, Philip. 2003. "Groups with Minds of their Own," in *Socializing Metaphysics*, ed. F. Schmitt. New York: Rowman and Littlefield, 167–93.

Pitkin, Hanna. 1967. *The Concept of Representation.* Berkeley: University of California Press.

Przeworski, Adam, 1999. "Minimalist Conceptions of Democracy," in *Democracy's Value*, ed. Ian Shapiro and Casiano Hacker-Cordon. Cambridge: Cambridge University Press, 23–50.

Przeworski, Adam, Susan Stokes, and Bernard Manin (eds.). 1999. *Democracy, Accountability and Representation.* Cambridge: Cambridge University Press.

Runciman, David. 2000a. "What Kind of Person Is Hobbes's State? A Reply to Skinner." *Journal of Political Philosophy* 8: 268–78.

2000b. "Is the State a Corporation?" *Government and Opposition* 35: 90–104.

2007. "The Paradox of Political Representation." *Journal of Political Philosophy* 15: 93–117.

Schmitt, Carl. 1996 [1938]. *The Leviathan in the State Theory of Thomas Hobbes. Meaning and Failure of a Symbol*, ed. George Schwab. Westport, CT: Greenwood.

Schumpeter, Joseph. 1994 [1942]. *Capitalism, Socialism and Democracy*, ed. Richard Swedberg. London: Routledge.

Shapiro, Ian. 2003. *The State of Democratic Theory.* Princeton, NJ: Princeton University Press.

Skinner, Quentin. 1989. "The State," in *Political Innovation and Conceptual Change*, ed. T. Ball *et al.* Cambridge: Cambridge University Press, 90–131.

2002. "Hobbes and the Purely Artificial Person of the State," in *Visions of Politics*, vol. III. Cambridge: Cambridge University Press, 177–208.

2005. "Hobbes on Representation." *European Journal of Philosophy* 13: 155–84.

Tuck, Richard. 2006. "Hobbes and Democracy," in *Rethinking the Foundations of Modern Political Thought*, ed. Annabel Brett and James Tully. Cambridge: Cambridge University Press, 171–90.

2 Participation and representation before democracy: petitions and addresses in premodern Britain

Mark Knights

Participation and representation are often taken to be alternative forms of popular rule. This chapter nevertheless suggests that, in predemocractic Britain, they were not mutually exclusive, and investigates the informal and participatory ways in which representation occurred outside the formal process of election. In particular it will focus on the mass of petitions and addresses that were presented to both parliament and crown from the seventeenth through to the nineteenth centuries. These not only claimed to represent the people's views but also procured their active participation by obtaining their signatures and by stimulating public debate. Indeed, analysis of the petitions and addresses, and of the debates that they provoked, shows that there was often an ongoing, creative, and dynamic interaction between the represented and their elected representatives.[1] Representation did not end at the moment of parliamentary electoral authorization; and public opinion operated before the advent of democracy. This historical evidence should affect our understanding of the nature of representation and popular rule, both at a theoretical and at a practical level.

One view of representation argues that the represented transfer power to a representative and thus have little political role thereafter, being deemed to consent to what is done in their name. This was essentially the view of Thomas Hobbes in the seventeenth century, who argued that the people transferred all their power to the representative person or assembly, "the great Leviathan," who was the authorized and exclusive but also the "absolute" representative. The "people" became subsumed within and by their representative sovereign (Hobbes 1651: especially Part 1, Chapters 16, 22).[2] Bernard Manin has argued that the system

---

I am grateful to the conference participants and to Mark Philp for helpful comments on earlier drafts of this chapter.
[1] Urbinati (2006) does not discuss petitioning but sees "participation and representation not as alternative forms of democracy but as related forms" (p. 3) and stresses the active and "informal expression of 'popular will'" (p. 10).
[2] Hobbes's views are outlined in detail in David Runciman's chapter.

of electoral representation, which he suggests was devised in the seven-teenth and eighteenth centuries (and which he sees as enduring), did very much the same thing. He sees a representative Leviathan emerging as a result of "the triumph of elections." He argues that through the adoption of elections the people consented to power rather than exercise it them-selves and that elections were inherently aristocratic rather than popular. Indeed, he argues, elections were chosen precisely because they were not democratic, and that "representative government gives no institutional role to the assembled people" (Manin 1997: 8).

To be sure, there is some evidence to support these positions. In Britain in the mid-eighteenth century, elections were seen as securing the consent of the people and they were very often aristocratic and exclusive in nature. Claims were also made that parliament alone was the representative of the people. Yet exclusive parliamentary representation was, especially in the mid/late seventeenth to the early eighteenth century and again in the late eighteenth to the early nineteenth century, more of an ideal than a reality. As Hobbes himself recognized, the urban corporations (who returned four-fifths of elected representatives) were places where the people remained actively involved in governance and were thus, in his eyes, "many lesser commonwealths in the bowels of a greater, like wormes in the entrayles of a naturall man" (Hobbes 1651: chapter 29).[3] The corporations were (chiefly) towns that had obtained royal charters, of which there were only 38 in 1500, but 130 by 1600, 181 by 1640, and 246 by 1833 (Withington 2005: 18; Sweet 1999: 33; Clark 2000: Table 2). The charter created a legally constructed fictional body. "In this guise, the freemen, burgesses and citizens who voluntarily participated in this person could act collectively as a single body, so transcending their individual lives and interests to form an entity that could sue at law and be represented in parliament" (Withington 2005: 8).[4] Through the charter the freemen acquired rights of participation in trade and also in governance. In essence the charter created a self-governing community, albeit one subject ultimately to royal command and one which drew its authority from the monarch. England was a commonwealth within a monarchy.[5]

---

[3] In 1683 Northampton's loyal "address and petition" asserted that "corporations in gen-eral have been the nurseries of sedition and schism . . . for want of necessary inspection from above, they have degenerated by degrees from their allegiance to an imperial power into the corruptions of a commonwealth" (*London Gazette* #1857).

[4] See also Halliday (1998).

[5] Anon. (1701b: 16) depicted the people not as something separate from authority but as the practical constituents of it. In England, the author argued, "Tis hard to find a man who has not sometime been call'd to bear office in his parish or borough."

This insight has recently been developed by historians of the early modern state who argue that in predemocratic Britain it was not the case that the people simply consented to power rather than exercise it themselves. Rather, in the absence of a paid police force or indeed a paid bureaucracy, there was a system of negotiated power and an "unacknowledged republic" of voluntary office-holders. Moreover, it is suggested, the system of representation through parliamentary election was rather remote from the "parish state" that most Britons encountered, in which participation was prized. In this view, then, the British system was something of a hybrid. It had tiers of representatives chosen by elections; but parliamentary elections were only one part. There was a myriad of local posts that were locally elected, and, moreover, a culture of citizenship that saw office-holding and participation as civic duties, and active consent as a civic right. Whilst there is some debate about how long this structure lasted, one recent survey of governance points to it enduring well into the nineteenth century (Collinson 1986–7; Braddick 2000; Braddick and Walter 2001; Wrightson 1996; Goldie 2001; Hindle, 1999; Eastwood 1997 and 2002).[6]

The implication of this research is that elections did not simply "triumph," that the people continued to hold office and self-govern, and that this participation was compatible (even if it was also at times in tension) with electoral representation. To be sure, we should be careful not to exaggerate how much participation occurred or how socially inclusive the higher ranks of local office were, and we should note that there was a good deal of hostility toward both popular rule and democracy. But these caveats do not negate the fact that participation and representation coexisted, and that both as an ideal and as practice the people claimed a representative voice outside elections. The people did not simply authorize their representatives to act for them. Representation, as it developed in seventeenth- and eighteenth-century Britain, was thus a participatory process involving, on occasion, a good deal of direct political activity. An electoral system "differing radically from democracy" was thus not "invented" in the seventeenth and eighteenth centuries (Manin 1997: 4). Citizens were not merely the source of political legitimacy through the consent they gave at elections, but possessed strong notions of self-governance and more than one representative voice in a system of overlapping but legitimate authorities. If that is true, the study of the past may have implications for more modern forms of democratic

---

[6] For a very different analysis see Clark (1985: 374–5), which minimizes the capacity for popular politics in the period: "the common man was still presented with relatively simple options of obedience and revolt."

representation outside election times. For there are representative institutions, such as the petition, that allow citizens an individual and corporate voice even while they have elected representatives. Such institutions reflect a desire to escape the logic of binding authorization and may be one way to strengthen accountability.

I.   Petitioning as a form of representation

The informal means of representation – by which I mean forms of representation that were not electoral, such as the press, petitions, clubs, and associations – developed as a raft of linked practices that supplemented, overlaid, and in some cases claimed to replace, formal representation. They could be associated with elections and they were also used instrumentally in the campaign for a wider franchise; but they were also representative practices in their own right, claiming to speak for the people.

We might identify two important shifts in the context in which such informal means of representation operated over the seventeenth and eighteenth centuries. The first was the recognition of the public as a collective force, of the public as an ideal representation of the people. I have argued elsewhere that this occurred in the late seventeenth and early eighteenth centuries as a result of a combination of frequent general elections, a free press, an ideology of popular sovereignty, and the emergence of a fiscal-military state and party politics (Knights 2005). A second shift is identified by Charles Tilly as a transformation of popular politics, dated as occurring in the mid-eighteenth century and culminating in 1832, "from a significant reliance on patronage to autonomous claim-making in national arenas," a process that he calls "the development of mass national politics." This was accompanied by a "deep transformation" of "the means by which ordinary people made collective claims on other people, including power-holders and the state" (Tilly 1995: 13–14, 53).

Associations, clubs, societies, and unions were participatory, representative institutions that could rival the claims of the national parliament to speak for the people. As T. M. Parssinen has noted, "The association became, in the opinion of its extreme proponents, an anti-parliament. They claimed that it represented the true wishes of the sovereign people more fully than did the corrupt parliament at Westminster, and therefore deserved the people's allegiance in an ultimate conflict between the two bodies" (Parssinen 1973: 504). Equally alarming for the government was the advent of political clubs with mass membership. For example, in Sheffield in 1792 2,500 of the "lowest mechanics" were enrolled in a political society formed after the founders had read Thomas Paine's

Rights of Man (Stevenson 1989: 14). Over a hundred such radical societies were formed by the mid-1790s. Similarly the political unions of the early 1830s grew out of the mass club that agitated for reform, such as the Society for Constitutional Information and the Corresponding Society, as well as the extra-parliamentary popular agitation of Wilkes and the American Revolution. By 1832 there were more than a hundred political unions, aimed at universal manhood suffrage, annual parliaments, and the ballot. Self-consciously trying to unite the interests of "the lower and middle classes of the people," and a mixture of electors and unenfranchised in roughly equal numbers, they could boast 15–18,000 paying members and their rallies attracted over 200,000. Claiming to represent the people, they "played a vital role in seeing the Reform Bill [of 1832] through parliament" (LoPatin 1999: 1, 11–12, 14).

But I want to focus on one very important informal representative institution: the petition and its associate, the address. Petitions and addresses were ubiquitous in the processes of formal government (for example, starting lawsuits or bringing grievances to the attention of local representatives), as well as initiating or lobbying for and against pieces of legislation;[7] but they were also, from the sixteenth century, a key platform through which to represent popular views on national issues of politics and religion (Hoyle 2002). Petitions were often intended and timed to influence representatives at Westminster; but they were also representative in a second and more important sense, since the act of signing involved individuals in a collective action that claimed representative status. Petitioners routinely claimed to speak for the people, to represent the "will" or "feel the pulse" of the people, to show the "bent of the nation." They were the "voice of the country." Of course, unlike an elected representative, who had ongoing authority between elections, petitions had only temporary representativeness; but they often provoked an iterative process of petition and counter-petition so that an ongoing representative contest ensued.

Petitions often created a dialogue with counter-petitioners, thereby stimulating rival representative claims. Thus nineteen counties that petitioned for "root and branch" reform of the church in 1640–1 provoked twenty-nine counter-petitions loyal to the established form of worship,

---

[7] This could be done collectively, as in 1718/19 against calicoes and 1763–6 against the cider tax (Dickinson, 1994: 67–72). There has been no attempt to quantify this petitioning over time, but for an indication of its growing size see Hoppit (1997: 18–21). For studies of petitioning as a means of influencing legislation see Gauci (2001); Sweet (2003); Handley (1990); Brewer (1988). My analysis of public petitions excludes those presented to parliament about trade, though of course these were very significant in number.

claiming over 85,000 names. Petitions promoted between December 1641 and August 1642 came from thirty-eight of the forty counties (Fletcher 1981: 91–3, 192; Maltby 1998: Appendix 1; Maltby 1999: 103–67). Such mass petitioning was new and it helped both to push the country into civil war and to achieve something like a national culture. Third, Zaret suggests, it was the advent of printed petitions, after the government lost control of the press in November 1641, that transformed the power of petitioning as a weapon. He estimates that between 1640 and the restoration of the monarchy in 1660 about 500 petitions were produced and that this created (unintentionally) a sense of public opinion. Indeed he even suggests that print and petitioning in this period created the origins of democratic culture (Zaret 1996 and 2000).

Since there was no franchise determining who could participate, subscriptional activity was also open to sectors of the population who were not participants in the process of formal representation. Thus apprentices and women could and did petition, the former being particularly prominent in seventeenth-century London petitioning and addressing, and the latter particularly important in later anti-slavery petitions.[8] Similarly, unenfranchised towns could, and increasingly did, find in petitions a voice denied them by the formal representative system.[9] Moreover, despite the rhetorical humility customary in the form of a petition, many mass petitions were also implicitly or explicitly threatening in their use of numbers. And they mobilized and invoked the power of the people, as those from the Levelers in the 1640s or from the parliamentary reformers of the nineteenth century show. However, such representations were not limited to radical groups. Addresses were used in very large numbers to demonstrate public loyalty to any particular regime, monarch, or policy; and in doing so loyalists often made conflicting and mutually exclusive representative claims from the radicals. Such campaigns were frequently national in scope (and colonies also joined the early eighteenth-century ones). Indeed this and the widespread publication of them helped engender a sense of the nation and of a national "public opinion."

Despite their importance, there is no study of public petitions and addresses over the premodern period as a whole. Indeed, it is not easy

---

[8] For example, in 1683 the young men and apprentices of Bristol, Westminster and London, and Hull addressed the crown (*London Gazette* #1863, 1866, 1874). For the role of London apprentices see Harris (1987: 42–4, 174–7). For female petitioning in the Civil War period see Higgins (1973). And for later eighteenth-century participation see Colley (1996: 291–4).

[9] This occurred in the later Stuart period. See, for example, Manchester, Leeds, and Halifax presenting addresses in 1683 and 1701 (*London Gazette* #1859, 3761, 3762). See also Phillips (1980: 615–16).

even to compile statistics about how many were presented, either to parliament or to the crown, in order to quantify that importance. While they are often discussed for particular historical moments, there have been few attempts to look at them collectively over time or to relate them to debates about participation and representation. Moreover, their survival in state records is haphazard and many were burnt in the fire that consumed the Houses of Parliament in 1834. This, together with the fact that numbers were often inflated by promoters and disputed by opponents, means that it is often difficult to verify precisely how many signatures they attracted. Table 2.2 (later in the chapter) listing public petitions and addresses 1640–1840 is therefore only a best guess, given the current state of research, about the pattern and size of national petitioning and addressing campaigns. But it does at least allow us to demonstrate its truly vast scale, to chart its fluctuations, and to compare campaigns over time.

From Table 2.2 it is clear that mass petitioning was most prolific in the period 1640–1720 and again 1780–1850. Indeed, the quantity of petitions and addresses in the earlier period is very impressive. Yet four factors at the end of the eighteenth century and in the early nineteenth served to expand petitioning campaigns into mass movements that aimed to represent extra-parliamentary views and achieved a force that was difficult for any government to resist (Fraser 1961: 195–6). The first was anti-slavery. Petitions were used to exert considerable pressure on MPs whenever legislation was being considered to abolish slavery. In 1788 there were 100 petitions with about 60–75,000 signatures; but in 1792 this rose to 500 petitions with 350–400,000 signatures, and in 1814 anti-slavery provoked 800 petitions with 750,000 signatures (Drescher, 1986: 93–4). A second factor was reform. In 1780 the Yorkshire Association, led by Christopher Wyvill, did indeed petition for reform, and included a demand for a "more equal representation of the people" (Black 1963: 49). Twenty-four counties and eleven cities and towns petitioned. But Wyvill was not interested in mass subscriptions on the issue of reform. They did come, however, in 1830–2, so much so that as a result parliament decided that no discussion whatever should accompany the presentation of any petition; otherwise, it was claimed, no public business would get done. Even with this restriction the Chartists continued to use petitioning to agitate for universal representation, though more as a means to maintain political momentum rather than through any belief that MPs would take any immediate notice. The 1842 Chartist 'Grand Petition' had 3,317,702 signatures, was more than six miles in length and was accompanied by a crowd of 50,000 people when it was carted to Westminster. The Chartists gained 1.2 million signatures in 1839; 1.4 million

Table 2.1 *Petitions to parliament, 1785–1847*

Five-year period	Average number of petitions per year
1785–90	176
1801–5	205
1811–15	899
1828–32	4,656
1833–7	7,436
1838–42	14,014
1843–7	16,397

in 1841; and 2 million in 1848, more than twice the size of the electorate. The third factor was the French Revolution and the polarizations that it produced in England. Thus in 1795 over 130,000 signatures were gathered to petitions against the government's repressive sedition bills, which restricted the right to assemble and to speak freely (British Library, Add. MS 27,808 f. 52, estimate by Francis Place). Fourth, these movements tended to combine with other grievances – over Catholic emancipation, the repeal of the Test and Corporation Acts, and so on. Petitioning was thus "an integral part of the system of political representation" (Pickering 2001: 368, 373–4, 381–4).

The impact that these factors had on the amount of public petitioning can be charted from official statistics (see Table 2.1) (*Parliamentary Papers* 1852–3, vol. LXXXIII, p. 166, see http://gateway.proquest.com/openurl?url_ver=Z39.88–2004&res_dat=xri:hcpp&rft_dat=xri:hcpp:fulltext:1852–029528:2) (accessed September 12, 2008).

As Figure 2.1 illustrates, it was not until the twentieth century, once mass democracy had been established, that petitioning faded as a means of representation.

II.   Misrepresentation

Petitioning always raised the issue of the relationship between informal and formal means of representation, between passive consent to elected representatives and active participation by the people in other more direct forms of representation. The elected representatives in parliament usually resented or were hostile to such direct representation. Throughout the premodern period the representativeness of public petitions and addresses was highly controversial and often denied. This could be at

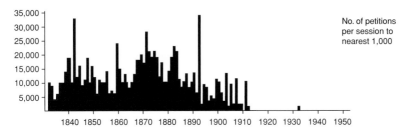

No. of petitions
per session to
nearest 1,000

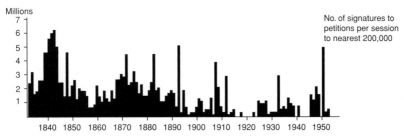

No. of signatures to
petitions per session
to nearest 200,000

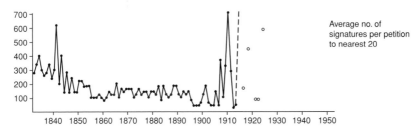

Average no. of
signatures per petition
to nearest 20

Figure 2.1 Number of petitions and signatures per session
Source: Taylor (1913).

the simple level of disputing the accuracy of the numbers claimed. It was suggested that signatures had been invented and that those who signed either did not understand what they were signing or had been misled into doing so. Thus one tactic was to claim that the petition or address was the product not of genuine popular opinion but of individuals or small factions who sought to use the public to give color to their pretense of representativeness. As historians we might share such worries, wondering how far petitions and addresses were representative of non-voters or simply propaganda manufactured by government, the press, or those who already ruled. Were they, as the earl of Lauderdale suggested to Charles II, meaningless pieces of paper "fit for nothing but to wipe his Royal A_" (Anon. 1702a: 20)? In fact we can demonstrate the degree of participatory representation that petitions and addresses afforded to those outside the electorate. John Phillips found that over 50 percent of those who signed petitions in the Middlesex election affair and over economical reform were not voters in parliamentary elections. James Bradley has found the percentage was as high as 81 percent at Poole and 80 percent at Southampton (Phillips 1980: 611; Bradley 1990: 144–5). Clearly such signatories did not see themselves as being represented by those entitled to vote.

However, rather than focus on the mass campaigns of the later eighteenth and early nineteenth century that provided the evidence for Phillips and Bradley, I want to explore the intense contests over representation that petitions and addresses provoked in the first age of party politics, and hence to show how intrinsic such debates were to the formation of Britain's representative system. I propose to examine debates in 1701–2, when a national debate took place about the relationship between formal and informal representation. This occurred (within a context of numerous petitioning and addressing campaigns charted in Table 2.2) because in 1701 an unsigned petition, known as the "Legion Memorial," because it claimed to represent the grievances of two hundred thousand "good People of England," sought to put pressure on parliament to recommence war with France (Defoe 1701).[10] It came hard on the heels of a petition from a Kent grand jury, arguing along similar lines, which was condemned by the House of Commons as "scandalous, insolent and seditious, tending to destroy the constitution of parliament, and to subvert the established government of this realm." The presenters of the Kent petition had been imprisoned by the House of Commons. Legion nevertheless asserted that the people were parliament's "masters" and "superiors" and warned MPs "you are not above the people's resentments." Legion claimed, moreover, that "it is the undoubted right of the people of England, in case their representatives in parliament do not proceed according to their duty, and the people's interest, to inform them of their dislike, disown their actions and to direct them to such things as they think fit, either by petition, address, proposal, memorial or any other peaceable way." Thus if parliament betrayed "the trust imposed in them" it was "the undoubted right of the people of England to call them to account for the same, and by convention, assembly or force may proceed against them as traitors and betrayers of the country." The tract

---

[10] Its representative claim was denied by one author, since it bore "so little proportion to the sentiments of the people and has so small an argument with either honesty or truth, that not one of the good people of England, tho he boasts many thousands, can be concern'd in it" (Anon. 1701a: 27).

Table 2.2 *Public petitioning and addressing campaigns, 1640–1840*[a]

Date	Occasion	Number	Numbers of signatories (max individual; estimate of total where known)
Dec. 1640 – July 1641	Root and Branch	19	4,488 max (Lancs.)
	In favor of Prayer Book	29	14,350 max (Somerset)
Dec. 1641 – Aug. 1642	Grievances (response to Grand Remonstrance)	46	30,000 max (Essex)
1646–9	Levelers	8	"many thousands" (1647)
1658	Addresses for Richard Cromwell's Proclamation as Protector	94	
Dec. 1659 – June 1660	Petitions and addresses for a free parliament and restoration	29	23,500 max (London)
Dec. 1679 – Jan. 1680	Petitions for parliament to sit	7	16,000 max (London)
Spring 1680	Addresses of abhorrence of the petitions calling for parliament	8	
Summer 1681	Addresses of thanks for the king's Declaration	210	6,000 max (Northants), over 40,000 total
Jan. – Sept. 1682	Addresses against Shaftesbury's Association	199	"over 2,000" max (Derbys.)
Aug. – Nov. 1683	Addresses of abhorrence of the Rye House Plot	323	10,000 max (tin miners)
Feb. – June 1685	Addresses of congratulation on accession of James	361	
1687	Addresses of thanks for the declaration of indulgence	197	800 max (Quakers)
1688	Further addresses after second declaration of indulgence	48	
Dec. 1694 – Apr. 1695	Addresses of condolence on death of Queen Mary	201	
Nov. 1697 – Feb. 1698	Addresses of congratulation on peace	260	
Oct. 1701 – Jan. 1702	Addresses against France's recognition of the pretender	344	"near 5,000" max (Northants)
Mar. – May 1702	Addresses of congratulation on accession of Queen Anne	400	

(*cont.*)

Table 2.2 (*cont.*)

Date	Occasion	Number	Numbers of signatories (max individual; estimate of total where known)
Feb. – Aug. 1704	Addresses of clerical thanks for Queen's bounty to church	25	
Aug. – Dec. 1704	Addresses of congratulation on military victories	265	
May. – Oct. 1706	Addresses of congratulation on military victories	303	
Mar. – Oct. 1707	Addresses of congratulation on Union with Scotland	213	
Mar. – July. 1708	Addresses against the Jacobite invasion attempt	338	
July – Oct. 1708	Addresses of congratulation on military victories	98	"several thousand" (Westminster)
Dec. 1708	Addresses of condolence on death of Prince Consort	10	
Sept. – Dec. 1709	Addresses of congratulation on military victories	40	
1710	Tory addresses about dangers to state and pressing for election	92	"many thousand" (Westminster)
1710	Whig counter-addresses	15	533 max (Norwich)
June – Nov. 1712	Addresses of congratulation on imminent peace	291	"many thousand" (Westminster)
Apr. – Sept. 1713	Addresses of congratulation on conclusion of peace	231	"many thousand" (Westminster)
Sept. 1714 – May 1715	Addresses of congratulation on accession of King George	443	
July 1715 – Aug. 1716	Addresses against rebellion and thanks for its suppression	320	
Mar. – Nov. 1717	Addresses of congratulations on victory	50	
1745	Thanks for defeat of Jacobite rebellion	Over 200	
1765	Anti-Stamp Act	20	
May 1769 – Jan. 1770	Middlesex election affair (pro Wilkes)	27	55–60,000 total
	Addresses against Wilkes	76	
1775–6	Anti-aggressive policy toward colonies address supporting government stance	78	6,500 max (Lancs)

Table 2.2 (*cont.*)

Date	Occasion	Number	Numbers of signatories (max individual; estimate of total where known)
1756	Addresses/instructions on loss of Minorca	36	
1779–80	Reform	37	60,000 total
1780	Anti-Catholic relief		50,000 max
1782–3	Economical reform (Wyvill)	35	20,000 total
1784	Addresses in support of royal prerogative (Fox–North)	Over 200	53,500 total
1785	Economical reform (Wyvill)	14	
1788	Petitions for abolition of slave trade	Over 100	11,000 max (Manchester), 60–75,000 total
1789	Addresses on king's recovery	Over 550	
1792	Petitions against slave trade	500	350–400,000 total
1792–3	Addresses in favor of proclamation against seditious writings and activities	386	11,000 max (Liverpool)
1793	Parliamentary reform	36	
1795	Protests against sedition laws	95	131,000 total
Jan. 1795	Petitions against war	17	
Nov. – Dec. 1795	Anti-war petitions and addresses	91	131,000 total
1795–6	Addresses re attempts to assassinate the king	1,800	
1797	Anti-war petitions	>15	
1800	Addresses re further attempt on king's life		
1801	Addresses against war		30,000 max (Yorks)
1803	Addresses on renewal of war		
1803	Addresses on discovery of Despard Conspiracy		
1807	Addresses supporting king's opposition to Catholic relief		
1807–8	Addresses for peace		150,000 from Yorks and Lancs
1812–13	Addresses for peace		Over 50,000 total
1809	Addresses on king's 50th birthday		
1814	Addresses on centenary of Hanoverian succession		

(*cont.*)

Table 2.2 (*cont.*)

Date	Occasion	Number	Numbers of signatories (max individual; estimate of total where known)
1814	Petitions against slavery	800	750,000 total
1816–17	Parliamentary reform (Hampden clubs)	700	30,000 max (Manchester), 1m total
1820	Pro Queen Caroline	*c.* 800	(with over 70,000 female sigs)
1825	Anti-Catholic petitions	over 400	
1828	Anti-repeal of Test and Corporation Acts	28	
1829	Anti-Catholic petitions	Over 2,000	81,000 max (Kent)
	Pro-Catholic petitions	220	
Oct. 1830–Apr. 1831	Parliamentary reform	3,000	21,000 max (Birmingham)
May 1832	Parliamentary reform bill	290	
1833	Petitions against slavery	5,000	1.5 million total
1839–43	Anti-Corn Law petitions	Average of 3,270	(1.15m sigs) per parliamentary session

[a] The figures have been compiled from a large number of primary and secondary sources too numerous to list here, and exclude those presented to parliament relating to economic legislation.

concluded with the warning that "Englishmen are no more to be slaves to parliament than to a king."

The Kent petition and the Legion Memorial sparked an important pamphlet debate about the nature of popular representation, since it pitted a formal representative institution (parliament) against an informal representative one (a petition). *England's Enemies Exposed* attacked the Legion Memorial's claims on the grounds that as soon as electors made their choice "the power and right of the elector devolves intirely upon their representatives; and tho at convenient seasons and in decent words, they may have leave to express their sentiments of things, yet they have no power to compel their members to vote or act, but in conformity to their own private judgments, tho the whole country, city or burrough they represent were of a contrary opinion to that of their representatives" (Anon. 1701d: 30). But against such views Legion also found some ideological support. *Jura Populi Anglicani*, thought to have been written by Whig leader John Somers, repeated the warning of a tyrannical House of Commons and affirmed that "the House of Commons are not the whole People of England's Representatives." The representative body was, it was argued, not the Commons per se but the incorporated people: "The Commons may be said to represent those Freeholders, Citizens and Freemen who chose them; but what are they to the Body of the People, who are represented in the Political State, and are entituled to all the Benefits and Advantages of it?" The tract argued that the people did not delegate power to their representatives "for them to do whatever they please." Rather, deploying Lockean arguments and defending a natural right to petition, it argued that MPs were sent with a trust "which if they should manifestly betray, the People, in whom the Power is more perfectly and fully than in their Delegates, must have a Right to help and preserve themselves" (Somers 1701: preface v, 51).

Jura Populi... Answer'd (1701) nevertheless refuted the idea that the people were above parliament. MPs were "above being directed" and sought to invalidate the voice of any one county as the voice of the nation; rather MPs were only entrusted at a local level: "Each Particular Member of the Honourable House of Commons has a Trust repos'd in him, for the Preservation of the Rights which belong to each distinct County, City or Borrough, and if the Inhabitants of the said Places think themselves aggriev'd, they ought to Address themselves only to those Knights, Citizens or Burgesses they have had the immediate Choice of" and not petition parliament as a whole (Anon. 1701f: 70, 79.).[11] More-over, *Jura Populi*'s claim to popular sovereignty and the limited nature of parliamentary representation infuriated a Tory-dominated Commons which, on February 26, 1702, passed a resolution 'that to assert that the House of Commons is not the only representatives of the commons of England tends to the subversion of the rights and privileges of the House of Commons."

The dispute, which had been hard to disentangle from the Tory impeachments of Somers and other Whig leaders, seems also to have provided an essential context for Jonathan Swift's first political tract, *A Discourse of the Contests and Dissensions between the Nobles and the Commons in Athens and Rome* (1701). Swift took a slightly different tack and argued that in recent years the nation had made "mighty leaps from prerogative heights into the depths of popularity" and the cause of corruption was ultimately political parties. Parties – which of course were themselves in some part representative – made representatives into sheep who followed the herd. As a result, Swift believed, the House of Commons had "lost

---

[11] See also Anon. (1702a: 13).

the universal favour of the numbers they represent." Yet Swift never confronted the ambiguities of the "people" as represented both in an institutional form and as a social or political category with informal representation. Thus on the one hand he argued that "Vox populi vox dei ought to be understood of the universal bent and current of a people, not of the bare majority of a few representatives; which is often procured by little arts and great industry"; but on the other he talked in terms of "an usurping populace" leading to tyranny (Swift 1701: 44–5, 47, 52, 54). This ambiguity was seized on by Charles Leslie, who asked "how shall this universal bent and current of the people be known," if not from the people's representatives? The only alternatives, he suggested, were mob rule or polling "the whole nation," both of which Leslie believed to be absurd (Leslie 1703: supplement, 10). Daniel Defoe did suggest an alternative to Leslie's mob. Whilst supporting Swift's assertion about the dangers of partisanship, and upholding popular sovereignty, he made it clear that when he was "speaking of the rights of the people" he was to be understood as talking about "the freeholders" on the grounds that "Property is the foundation of power" (Defoe 1702: 19).

Swift was answered in *The History of the Last Parliament* (1702). This viewed the attempt to prioritize the collective rights of the people as a partisan attempt by the embattled Whigs "to batter the Power of the House of Commons, under pretence that they were not intrusted with the whole Power of the Commons of England." The manipulative new Whigs, it was alleged, merely wanted "to deceive us in the Sense of the People and . . . palm upon us Mercenary Noise and Clamour for the general Voice and Consent of the People." A "few Men, back'd by a Faction" wanted to "exasperate the People against their Representatives, and by Surprise, and false Representations to make 'em Accessary to the Destruction of their own Rights and Authority" (Drake 1702a: 128, 131, 138).[12] The author of this, James Drake, followed it with *Some Necessary Considerations Relating to Future Elections* (1702), in which he further argued that "the People ought to consider, that when they have made the choice of their Representatives, they have parted with their Power and lodg'd it in them for so long a time as they continue to be such," an argument that Rousseau was to make half a century later (Drake 1702b: 6).

The Kent petition and the Legion Memorial had not been the only form of petition to raise the question of the nature of popular rule. Seventeen instructions presented to MPs after parliamentary elections were printed collectively in *The Electors' Right Asserted*

---

[12] Written mostly by James Drake, but with some assistance from Anthony Hammond.

(Anon. 1701c).[13] The tract countered claims that MPs were "left to the absolute freedom of their own wills, to act without controul," for any MP carried the trust reposed in him by electors which he "ought carefully and faithfully to discharge; or else how can he be properly called their Representative?" Hence it was the "antient custom, continual usage and undoubted right of the freeholders" and electors to deliver instructions to their "delegates." The point was made in the instructions themselves. Gloucestershire thus took it "to be our undoubted Right, to consult with and communicate our Advice and directions to you, now chosen our representatives in Parliament, and from time to time by petition according to law, to express our sentiments to the whole House of Commons." The Bristol electors agreed that "it is no doubt to us that we have a right to direct our Representatives" (Anon. 1701c: 1–4, 11, 13).[14] The role of instructions to MPs, and hence of the representative nature of MPs, was to reverberate for a very long time (Kelly 1984). Instructions were used in 1681, 1701, 1715, 1733, 1753, 1769, 1774, 1783–4, and 1832. The debate that Burke raised over precisely this issue in 1774 was thus part of a much wider and longer one (Dickinson 1976).

III.   Competing representative claims

The 1701–2 debates serve to highlight and introduce a number of points. First, the boundaries between formal and informal representation were contested very early in the emergence of representative government and *remained* contested. Petitions and addresses were seen by many as a legitimate and representative voice of the people, but disputed by others who asserted parliamentary sovereignty. Thus, on the one hand, parliament was championed as the genuine national voice. As one tract put it, attacking the provincial petitions of 1701, "The interest of England is a compound concern, and as solid judgments cannot be made of it, without a due regard to every part of the island; which cannot be expected from a better place than the house of commons, where are representatives from every corner" (Anon. 1702b: 7).[15] On the other, in predemocratic Britain, legitimate representative authority was also vested in a number

---

[13] See also Anon. (1701f).   [14] Not all instructions made such explicit claims.

[15] Anon. (1701e: 15, 47) argued that "their praying the House to have regard to the voice of the people is nonsense; for every little faction lays claim to that appellation and have wore it so threadbare that tis scandalous to make use of it, as appropriating it to a party; for none can be truly called the people of England in a divided capacity; and they are only whole and entire in their representatives in Parliament"; "the Kentish petition was not the petition of the English nation but of a few giddy self-conceited people in a corner of the kingdom."

of formal institutions besides parliament. Grand juries, for example, and corporations had legal power to petition. As we have seen, local governance empowered mayors, aldermen, common councilors and freemen with representative power. Problems occurred when these "local" representatives disagreed with each other, as in 1681 when the Derbyshire grand jurors formulated a Tory address at a time when the county had elected two Whig MPs yet claimed themselves to be "the representatives of the body of your majesties county" (*London Gazette* #1718). Or in 1710 when Gloucestershire's MPs reacted against an address from a grand jury by promoting a rival text. As the Whig John Oldmixon showed in a history of addresses in 1712 which lamented the clamor of the Tories, the disparity between the voice of the people over time, or between the voice of the addresses and the voice of the electorate, could lead to cynicism about the apparent contradictoriness and giddiness of the people. "We are sorry to see them changing like the wind, and fluctuating like Tides," he remarked (Oldmixon, 1709–10: 215). But such frustration was itself a recognition of multiple representative voices. Informal representation complicated the story of formal representation; and this was inherent in the premodern British system.

Second, rival or contested petitions raised anxieties about misrepresentation. In 1710, for example, several tracts sought to expose the fraudulent practices of loyalist addresses. *The Principles and Designs of the High-Church Party Discover'd* (1710) revealed that in one county, Buckinghamshire, very few signatures had been obtained, even though it claimed to show "the general bent of this county." Moreover, it was alleged, the high churchmen had deliberately used a populist slogan – the church in danger – to gull the people to sign (Anon. 1710b: 7–8, 12). Similarly *The High-Church Mask pull'd off or Modern Addresses Anatomized. Designed chiefly for the Information of the Common People* (1710) noted the range of misrepresentative practices: "menaces and promises used, false stories invented, persons and actions misrepresented . . . violent sermons preached to incense the vulgar. In populous places, through persuasion, persons signed to rolls abstracted from the addresses, to which they were afterwards affixed" (Anon. 1710a: 3). Informal representation, it was alleged, was thus every bit as vulnerable to corruption as the electoral system. Such malpractice was exposed by the press; yet the press was also increasingly seen as part of the problem. *England's Enemies Exposed* (1701) thus attacked the Kent petition, Legion Memorial, and several other Whig pamphlets as the product of a partisan propaganda machine. The tract thus sought "to disabuse the nation, and recover the people from the false notions and prejudicate prepossessions, imposed on them by a turbulent malcontented and seditious party, who would lead them blindfold into dangerous errors, set them at variance with their representatives and put them out of love with parliaments" (Anon. 1701d: dedication). Informal (and formal) representation relied on information that was itself a possible partisan misrepresentation.

Third, informal representation helped to strengthen a key principle of representative government, for competing representative claims led to statements in many addresses that they represented the majority rather than the whole. In other words the majority principle came to be embedded not just through or in formal incorporations and elections but also through petitions and addresses. Sandwich's 1681 loyal address thus came from "most of the jurats, most of the common council . . . and others," against the "faction" formed by the "chief magistrate and other his adherents, who formerly have and still do use all possible arts and endeavours to frustrate and stifle all discoveries of duty and loyalty" (*London Gazette* #1735). The majority had thus to struggle against a misrepresentative minority. Lancashire's loyal address of 1713 insisted that it was "the general, the almost unanimous voice of your people, in great contempt of a clamorous but inconsiderable faction" (*London Gazette* #5145). On occasion, however, it was recognized that the corrupting influence of a faction had indeed prevailed so far that a minority had to be legitimized by reference to their loyalty rather than their numbers.[16]

IV.   Conclusion

This chapter has attempted to show the type of predemocratic participatory representative society that existed in the seventeenth and early eighteenth century, and again at the end of the eighteenth into the nineteenth century. The potentially highly participatory state offered many representative moments and contained many overlapping institutions that could each claim legitimately to represent the public. Non-electoral representative institutions thus thrived in premodern Britain. One of the most powerful and most widely deployed of these was the petition and its close associate, the address. Through them both the franchised and unenfranchised could find a voice, particularly after the advent of a free press. Participation in campaigns reflected a popular frustration with the notion of MPs as fully authorized representatives to whom they were bound either by their own direct electoral consent or by their alleged

---

[16] See, for example, Nottingham's 1713 loyal address (*London Gazette* #5128).

tacit consent to parliament's national representative status. These conclusions suggest that Manin's model of representation is overly schematic, for the "triumph of elections" was never complete and often contested; that electoral representation overlapped with a participatory structure of local authority; that participation and representation could thus (albeit sometimes uncomfortably) coexist; and that in Britain there were well-established mechanisms for ensuring that it did. Debate about popular rule over representatives was widespread in the predemocractic era whenever petitions and addresses were presented in any great number. Even so, informal means of representation, particularly in an era of partisan politics and a free press, carried with them their own set of anxieties about misrepresentation and corruption; it was not just the electoral system that was accused of distorting the voice of the people. Yet such accusations themselves stimulated an important debate about the nature of representation.

Finally, it is worth considering how these issues relate to more modern concerns. There are some signs that the very old tradition of petitioning might be being revived, perhaps as a modern parallel of the premodern citizens who felt that their authorized representatives needed to be made responsive to their concerns. There are now many electronic petition sites, including one at Downing Street that in 2006 attracted 1.7 million signatories to a single petition. A paper petition about threats to close post offices recently collected over 4 million signatures, making it the largest in British history.[17] Whatever the issue, and in whatever form, petitioning might be seen as an important institutional balance to the idea that a representative has consensual authorization through elections to declare the will of the people. As Hanna Pitkin put it in her seminal study of representation, "in a representative government the governed must be capable of action and judgment, capable of initiating government activity, so that the government may be conceived as responding to them . . . a representative government requires that there be machinery for the expression of the wishes of the represented, and that government respond to these wishes unless there are good reasons to the contrary" (Pitkin 1967: 232–3). Elections may be the best form of such machinery; but the premodern state had others that acted as important cogs in it.

---

[17] See http://petitions.pm.gov.uk/ (accessed January 10, 2007). The attention that the e-petition received, perhaps because of its novelty, outstripped that given to the 4 million strong petition in October 2006: one thousand sub-postmasters were on hand to present a petition so large it covered the bottom level of a London double-decker bus. See www.telegraph.co.uk/news/main.jhtml?xml=/news/2006/10/19/npost119.xml (accessed September 12, 2008).

BIBLIOGRAPHY

Anon. 1701a. *The Ballad or some scurrilous reflections in verse... answered.* London.
  1701b. *The Claims of the People, Essayed.* London.
  1701c. *The Electors' Right Asserted.* London.
  1701d. *England's Enemies Exposed.* London.
  1701e. *The History of the Kentish Petition, Answer'd Paragraph by Paragraph.* London.
  1701f. *Jura Populi... Answer'd.* London.
  1701g. *A Letter from Some Electors to one of their Representatives in Parliament shewing the Electors Sentiments.* London.
  1702a. *The Legionites Plot.* London.
  1702b. *A Letter to a New Member of the Ensuing Parliament.* London.
  1710a. *The High-Church Mask pull'd off or Modern Addresses Anatomized. Designed chiefly for the Information of the Common People.* London.
  1710b. *The Principles and Designs of the High-Church Party Discover'd.* London.
Black, Eugene Charlton. *The Association. British Extra-Parliamentary Political Organisation, 1769–1793.* Cambridge, MA: Harvard University Press.
Braddick, Michael J. 2000. *State Formation in Early Modern England 1550–1700.* Cambridge: Cambridge University Press.
Braddick, Michael J. and John, Walter. 2001. *Negotiating Power in Early Modern Society: Order, Hierarchy and Subordination in Britain and Ireland.* Cambridge: Cambridge University Press.
Bradley, James. 1990. *Religion, Revolution, and English Radicalism: Nonconformity in Eighteenth-Century Politics and Society.* Cambridge: Cambridge University Press.
Brewer, John. 1988. *The Sinews of Power: War, Money and the English State, 1688–1783.* Cambridge, MA: Harvard University Press.
Clark, J. C. D. 1985. *English Society 1660–1832.* Cambridge: Cambridge University Press.
Clark, Peter (ed.). 2000. *Cambridge Urban History of Britain 1540–1840.* Cambridge: Cambridge University Press.
Colley, Linda. 1996. *Britons: Forging the Nation 1707–1837.* London: Vintage.
Collinson, Patrick. 1986–7. "The Monarchical Republic of Queen Elizabeth I." *Bulletin of the John Rylands Library* 69: 394–424.
Defoe, Daniel. 1701. *Mr S_r, The Enclosed Memorial you are charg'd with.* London.
  1702. *The Original Power of the Collective Body of the People of England Examined and Asserted.* London.
Dickinson, Harry T. 1976. "The Eighteenth Century Debate on the Sovereignty of Parliament." *Transactions of the Royal Historical Society*, 5th ser., 26: 189–210.
  1994. *The Politics of the People in Eighteenth-Century Britain.* Basingstoke: Macmillan.
Drake, James. 1702a. *The History of the Last Parliament.* London.
  1702b. *Some Necessary Considerations Relating to Future Elections.* London.
Drescher, Seymour. 1986. *Capitalism and Anti-Slavery.* Basingstoke: Macmillan.

Eastwood, David. 1997. *Government and Community in the English Provinces, 1700–1870*. Basingstoke: Palgrave Macmillan.

——— 2002. "Local Government and Local Society," in *A Companion to Eighteenth Century Britain*, ed. H. T. Dickinson. Oxford: Blackwell, 40–54.

Fletcher, Anthony. 1981. *The Outbreak of the English Civil War*. London: Edward Arnold.

Fraser, Peter. 1961. "Public Petitioning and Parliament before 1832." *History* 46: 195–211.

Gauci, Perri. 2001. *The Politics of Trade. The Overseas Merchant in State and Society 1660–1720*. Oxford: Oxford University Press.

Goldie, Mark. 2001. "The Unacknowledged Republic," in *The Politics of the Excluded c. 1500–1850*, ed. T. Harris. Basingstoke: Macmillan, 153–94.

Halliday, Paul. 1998. *Dismembering the Body Politics: Partisan Politics in England's Towns, 1650–1730*. Cambridge: Cambridge University Press.

Handley, Stuart. 1990. "Local Legislative Initiatives for Economic and Social Development in Lancashire 1689–1731." *Parliamentary History* 9: 231–84.

Harris, Tim. 1987. *London Crowds in the Reign of Charles II. Propaganda and Politics from the Restoration until the Exclusion Crisis*. Cambridge: Cambridge University Press.

Higgins, Patricia. 1973. "The Reactions of Women, with Special Reference to Women Petitioners," in *Politics, Religion and the English Civil War*, ed. Brian Manning. London: Edward Arnold, 179–224.

Hindle, Steve. 1999. "Hierarchy and Community in the Elizabethan Parish: The Swallowfield Articles of 1596." *Historical Journal* 42 (3): 835–51.

Hobbes, Thomas. 1651. *Leviathan*, ed. Richard Tuck, 1996 edn. Cambridge: Cambridge University Press.

Hoppit, Julian (ed.). 1997. *Failed Legislation 1660–1800*. London: Hambledon.

Hoyle, Richard. 2002. "Petitioning as Popular Politics in Sixteenth-Century England." *Historical Research* 75: 365–89.

Kelly, Paul. 1984. "Constituents' Instructions to Members of Parliament in the C18th," in *Party and Management in Parliament 1660–1784*, ed. Clyve Jones. Leicester: Leicester University Press, 103–67.

Knights, Mark. 2005. *Representation and Misrepresentation in Later Stuart Britain: Partisanship and Political Culture*. Oxford: Oxford University Press.

Leslie, Charles. 1703. *The New Association. Part II*. London.

London Gazette. Various issues. London.

LoPatin, Nancy. 1999. *Political Unions, Popular Politics and the Great Reform Act of 1832*. Basingstoke: Macmillan.

Maltby, Judith. 1998. *Prayer Book and People in Elizabethan and Early Stuart England*. Cambridge: Cambridge University Press.

——— 1999. "Petitions for Episcopacy and the Book of Common Prayer on the Eve of the Civil War, 1641–1642," in *From Cranmer to Davidson: A Church of England Miscellany*, ed. Stephen Taylor (Church of England Record Society, 7). Woodbridge: Boydell and Brewer, 103–67.

Manin, Bernard. 1997. *The Principles of Representative Government*. Cambridge: Cambridge University Press.

Oldmixon, John. 1709–10. *The History of Addresses* (2 parts). London.

Parliamentary Papers 1852–3, vol. LXXXIII. London: House of Commons Parliamentary Papers Online. Proquest database.

Parssinen, T. M. 1973. "Association, Convention and Anti-Parliament in British Radical Politics 1771–1848." *English Historical Review* 88: 504–33.

Phillips, John. 1980. "Popular Politics in Unreformed England." *Journal of Modern History* 52: 599–625.

Pickering, Paul. 2001. "And your Petitioners &c: Chartist Petitioning in Popular Politics 1838–48." *English Historical Review* 116 (2): 368–88.

Pitkin, Hanna. 1967. *The Concept of Representation.* Berkeley: University of California Press.

Somers, Lord John. 1701. *Jura Populi Anglicani.* London.

Stevenson, John. 1989. "'Paineites to a Man'?: The English Popular Radical Societies in the 1790s." *Bulletin of the Society for the Study of Labour History* 54 (3): 14–25.

Sweet, Rosemary. 1999. *The English Town 1680–1840: Government, Society and Culture.* London: Longman.

2003. "Local Identities and a National Parliament, c. 1688–1835," in *Parliaments, Nations and Identities in Britain and Ireland, 1660–1850,* ed. Julian Hoppit. Manchester: Manchester University Press, 48–63.

Swift, Jonathan. 1701. *A Discourse of the Contests and Dissensions between the Nobles and the Commons in Athens and Rome.* London.

Taylor, A. A. 1913. *Statistics Relating to Sittings of the House,* &c. Typescript returns of the House of Commons.

Tilly, Charles. 1995. *Popular Contention in Great Britain 1758–1834.* Cambridge, MA: Harvard University Press.

Urbinati, Nadia. 2006. *Representative Democracy. Principles and Genealogies.* Chicago: University of Chicago Press.

Withington, Phil. 2005. *The Politics of Commonwealth. Citizens and Freemen in Early Modern England.* Cambridge: Cambridge University Press.

Wrightson, Keith. 1996. "The Politics of the Parish in Early Modern England," in *The Experience of Authority in Early Modern England,* ed. Paul Griffiths, Adam Fox and Steve Hindle. Basingstoke: Macmillan, 10–46.

Zaret, David. 1996. "Petitions and the 'Invention' of Public Opinion in the English Revolution." *American Journal of Sociology* 101: 1497–1555.

2000. *Origins of Democratic Culture: Printing, Petitions and the Public Sphere in Early Modern England.* Princeton, NJ: Princeton University Press.

Part II

Theories of political representation

3   Varieties of public representation

Philip Pettit

I.   Background and basics

Systems of representative government, I shall assume, are designed to give control over government to the people. Far from being an alternative to democracy, as some have taken them (Manin 1997), they embody an institutional framework – or rather a family of frameworks – for realizing the democratic ideal of giving *kratos* to the *demos*, power to the people. The distinction between a participatory and a representative system is not one between democracy proper and some faint approximation but a distinction between rival proposals for the implementation of democracy.

My focus in this chapter is on representation in this democratic, popularly enabling sense. Thus the target of the chapter is narrower than it might have been. As Hobbes in particular argues, the idea of representation may be used, not just of representatives who are subject to the continuing or periodic control of the people, but also of a hereditary, absolute monarch. The defenders of parliament in the 1640s tried to give its members a monopoly right on the use of the word (Skinner 2005), but Hobbes argued against them that it was absurd that a monarch who "had the sovereignty" over his subjects "from a descent of 600 years" should not be "considered as their representative" (Hobbes 1994: 19.3). His own view, to the contrary, was that "the King himself did . . . ever represent the person of the people of England" (Hobbes 1990: 120).

But though my focus is narrower than Hobbes's, it is broader than the target to which many contemporary theorists give their attention. As will appear, I use the notion of representation in such a way that any public authorities, and any citizens who assume a legitimate role in public

I benefited enormously from discussion at the Yale conference where a first version of the chapter was presented in November 2006; from discussion and commentary (by Ian McMullin) at a seminar in Washington University, St. Louis, in April 2008; from exchanges with Eric Beerbohm, Nate Kemp, Frank Lovett, Evan Oxman, and Andrew Rehfield; and from the comments of two anonymous referees. I am grateful to Bryan Garsten for directing me to expressions of the indicative ideal among anti-federalist writers.

discourse, may make a legitimate claim to represent the people (Richardson 2002). Others apply the notion, however, only to elected representatives – elected members of the legislature and, where relevant, of the executive and the judiciary. The concept of electoral representation is more tightly circumscribed than my looser concept of democratic representation, but I think that it does not offer the same generality of perspective.[1] I hope that this chapter may help to vindicate that claim.

There are three factors in any relationship or system of representation, whether in my sense of representation or in any other. First there are the representatives or, using a seventeenth-century word, the representers; I prefer this term since the other has an exclusively electoral connotation. Second, there are the represented or, as I shall say, the representees. And, third, there is the relationship that exists between those two parties: the representation that is exercised by representers on behalf of representees.[2]

Representers

Representers may be individual agents or groups of individual agents. And in the case where a group serves in this role, the members may each act for their own ends, according to their own judgments, or they may act on a shared intention to further this or that end. In this latter case the individuals will each intend that together they promote the agreed end and they will each do their bit for the promotion of the end, expecting that others will play their parts too (Bratman 1999); they will be a cooperative grouping, not a mere collection of individual agents.

The cooperative grouping that combines around a joint intention comes itself in two forms. The members may act for shared goals, now on this occasion, now on that, without ever forming a joint intention governing their continuation over time. Or they may form the special, shared intention that over time they together should constitute a corporate agent or agency: a body that simulates the performance of a single agent with a single mind. The intention shared in this case will be that they together cooperate in the organized pursuit of agreed ends according to agreed judgments. The ends will usually be an evolving set of ends selected under agreed procedures, and the judgments an evolving body of judgments selected under agreed procedures (Pettit and Schweikard 2006). The distinctions are mapped in Figure 3.1.

[1] For a very congenial and insightful account of representation in a broader sense than that of electoral representation, see Rehfeld (2006).
[2] On the emergence and development of the concept of representation in the late seventeenth and early eighteenth century, see Knights (2005).

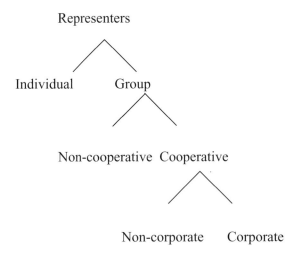

Figure 3.1 Representers.

These distinctions are readily illustrated. The member of the legislature who represents a certain constituency or the President who represents the people as a whole exemplifies the individual representer. And the legislature or the executive as a whole exemplifies the group representer. The members of such a group may behave as a collection of independent agents, each with their own brief, or as a cooperative grouping. And if they behave as a cooperative grouping, then they may or may not incorporate in the manner of a body with a coherent, evolving set of goals and judgments.

The US Congress might be seen as an unincorporated, cooperative grouping that does battle, now on this issue, now on that, looking in each case to see if a more or less ad hoc majority can be assembled to support a certain line. There is some concern with securing coherence between the lines supported over time, of course, as well as coherence with the Constitution. But this concern can take second place to the other concerns of members – say, their concern to display their colors back home. This will especially be so if in any case a presidential veto is likely, or if the Supreme Court is expected to reject or reinterpret the legislation.

The Westminster parliament might be seen, by contrast, as an incorporated, cooperative agency whose members assume a higher degree of responsibility for legislating on coherent lines, at least within the time-frame of a given parliament. The members acquiesce in a procedure whereby a fixed majority will be established and that majority – say, a single, incorporated party – will bring forward a coherent program of legislation to be enacted after parliamentary discussion in the name of the parliament as a whole.

Representees

So much for the possibility of variation on the side of the representers in a democratic system. There is a corresponding degree of variation on the side of the representees. The representee may be a single individual, as when the member of a legislature takes up some cause on behalf of a constituent. Or the representee may be a group. The group represented may be cast as a mere collection, such as perhaps the electors in a given district, or they may have a more cooperative aspect. And the cooperative representee may be incorporated or unincorporated. In other words the distinctions on the side of the represented may correspond to those that we map on the side of the representing.

The loose pressure group or the ethnic minority that succeeds in finding a spokesperson in the legislature or elsewhere will often be an unincorporated entity whose members are united around just a single issue. But equally an entity with a corporate or quasi-corporate form of organization may figure as representee. The states that are represented by the Senate of the US or Australia are surely entities of this kind.

The ultimate representee in any democratic system will be the people as a whole: a body that might be taken as a mere collection but is usually depicted as an incorporated entity. It is of the essence of a democratic system that it is supposed to create a state that represents the people as a whole, acting in their name on the international stage and in dealings with individual citizens and groups of citizens (McLean 2004). Thus John Rawls (1999) says that the government in a well-ordered society – ideally, a liberal democratic society – will be "the representative and effective agent of a people" (ibid.: 38) – "the political organization of the people" (ibid.: 26). The disordered society where a small group usurps power, like the unordered society where political organization fails utterly, will be marked by the absence of precisely this system-wide level of representation.

Representation

Not only are there variations of these kinds in who are represented and who do the representing: that is, in the relata at either end of the representative relationship. There are also variations in the nature of the relationship. I argue that there are two fundamentally contrasting

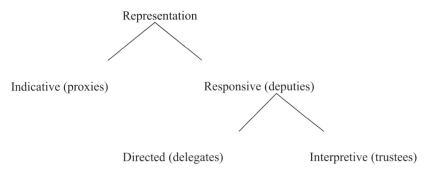

Figure 3.2 Representation.

varieties of representation, indicative and responsive. Indicative representers *stand for* the representees in the sense of typifying or epitomizing
them; how they act is indicative of how the representees would act.[3]
Responsive representers *act for* or *speak for* the representees, playing the
part of an agent in relation to a principal; how they act is responsive to
how the representees would want them to act. Both sorts of representation, so I shall assume, have to be authorized by the representees.

Authorized indicative representers I describe as proxies, authorized
responsive representers as deputies. Deputies divide, in a traditional distinction, into delegates who are more or less explicitly directed by representees and trustees who have interpretive discretion in determining how
to construe their representees. The distinctions appear in Figure 3.2.

Three metaphors have dominated the tradition of thinking about the
meaning of representation (Skinner 2005). One of these metaphors is
drawn from representation in the pictorial arts, and it maps onto indicative representation. As the painting is indicative of how the subject of
the painting looks, so on this image should representers be indicative
of representees: they should be proxies. The other two metaphors are
drawn respectively from the courts and from the theater: from the way
in which an attorney represents a client, and an actor represents a character. These reflect the two different modes of responsive or deputy-
style representation: one directed, the other interpretive. As the attorney acts under the explicit or implicit direction of a client, so should

---

[3] Pitkin (1972) casts the indicative relationship as descriptive representation: as involving
nothing more than the sort of relationship that holds between statistical sample and a
population. But she misses the fact that a representee population may appoint a descriptive representer with a view to having things done as it would do them, or want them
done; the possibility is nicely illustrated by the British Columbia citizens' assembly that
I discuss later. It is only such controlled representation that I describe as indicative.

representers act under the explicit or implicit direction of their representees: they should be delegates. As the actor constructively interprets the mind of a character, so should representers interpret the mind of representees: they should be trustees.

The following two sections review these two conceptions of representation, looking at how they might apply with different sorts of representers and representees but focusing in particular on the representation of a people. The fourth section then asks how these forms of representation might be organized in a democracy, focusing on a particular problem that is raised by responsive representation of the interpretive kind. In order to illustrate the usefulness of the distinctions, the paper concludes with an appendix that considers issues of representation in the presidential and parliamentary systems that are exemplified respectively by Washington and Westminster.

II.   Indicative representation

The standard case

In the standard form of this first conception, the assumption is that there are a number of representers, that the representees are the people as a whole, and the indicative requirement is that the representers should be a reliable or representative sample of the representees. They should faithfully reproduce significant differences among the population, and reproduce them in proportion to their realization within the community. We are familiar nowadays with the idea of indicative representation in the context of statistics. The random sample that is polled in the statistical exercise is a representative sample in the sense of being a good indicator of the population as a whole.

This conception of representation goes naturally with the pictorial or figurative metaphor. As Quentin Skinner (2005: 163) argues, it appears in those parliamentarian writers in England of the mid-seventeenth century who look for a "speaking likeness" of the people in those who rule them, "describing Parliament as a 'representation' – a picture or portrait – of the body of the people."

The relationship that is envisaged between the body of representatives and the body of the people is certainly figurative, as in the likeness between a portrait and the subject of the portrait. But it might best be conceptualized as the relationship whereby a painting or sculpture, particularly one of an abstract kind, can exemplify a feature of the subject: the mass of a body, the elegance of a movement, and so on. As a tailor's swatch contains pieces of cloth that exemplify the purportedly significant features of various fabrics, so figurative works exemplify purportedly significant aspects of an object or substance or situation or whatever (Goodman 1969). And as figurative representations can play this part to an aesthetic purpose, so politically representative bodies ought to serve in a parallel, democratic role. They ought each to exemplify and indicate the presumptively significant aspects of the people they represent, reproducing salient variations amongst its members and in a proportion that corresponds to their distribution in the population.

The idea of indicative representation figures early in democratic theory, since it is the sort of representation that is achieved or is likely to be achieved under the lottery system that was favored by the Athenians and that also played an important part in later regimes such as those of the Italian city-republics (Waley 1988; Hansen 1991). This lottery system might be taken as a version of the technique of random sampling, but random sampling put to use in the service of advancing goals espoused by the people as a whole. While it may have been motivated by a desire to have a regular turnover in the representer body, the important thing from our viewpoint is that it would have ensured a degree of proportional and indicative representation.

The indicative idea also appears in the jury system, as that was developed in medieval Europe (Abramson 1994). To be subjected to the judgment of one's peers, whether in determining that there is a legal case to answer, or that one is legally liable, is to be exposed, not to a random arbiter – a chance enemy, perhaps – but to a body that stands in for the community as a whole. The idea is that the jurors should represent a cross-section of the community, or at least of the fully enfranchised members: in medieval Europe, the mainstream, propertied males.[4]

The ideal of indicative representation was entrenched in the thinking of many of those associated with the American War of Independence and the French Revolution. Melanchton Smith could write in 1788, in opposing the American Constitution: "The idea that naturally suggests itself to our minds, when we speak of representatives is, that they resemble those they represent; they should be a true picture of the people" (Ketcham 2003: 342). Again, it was powerfully endorsed in a speech given by Mirabeau to the French Constituent Assembly in January 1789, though he used the image of a map rather than a picture to get it across. According to this version of the model:

---

[4] It is significant that a supporter of the anti-federalist cause in 1787 could complain that in the enlarged United States there would not be a representative body in legislature or jury "which possesses the same interests, feelings, opinions, and views the people themselves would were they all assembled" (Ketcham 2003: 265).

a representative body is to the nation what a chart is for the physical configuration of its soil: in all its parts, and as a whole, the representative body should at all times present a reduced picture of the people – their opinions, aspirations, and wishes, and that presentation should bear the relative proportion to the original precisely as a map brings before us mountains and dales, rivers and lakes, forests and plains, cities and towns. (Pitkin 1969, 77)

With the growth of electoral machinery, the indicative idea was naturally applied to elections for the legislature, providing support for making the electoral system more and more proportional (Mill 1964). Is it also behind the practice of organizing the legislature around geographically dispersed districts? It is hard to believe that it did not play some role in justifying that practice but the evidence, according to Rehfeld (2005), is against this hypothesis. Still, districting does induce a similarity in one dimension – nowadays a fairly unimportant one – between the population as a whole and the legislature that represents it.

The indicative idea survives in the continuing enthusiasm for proportional representation and has been given new life in campaigns for supplementing electoral representation with novel, statistically representative bodies. It is there in the general policy of organizing citizens' juries that would review various policy issues (Stewart, Kendall, and Coote 1994). It is present in the notion of the deliberative opinion poll that is chosen as a random sample and then canvassed for its view on one or another issue at two separate times: first, before members of the sample make contact, and, second, after they come together to receive background information, to hear different points of view, and to debate the right line to take on the issue under consideration (Fishkin 1997). A particularly striking example appears in the citizens' assembly that was recently established in the Canadian province of British Columbia (Fung and Fagotto 2006; Ferejohn 2007). A more or less representative sample of 160 citizens was assembled and given the task, over much of 2004, of reviewing the existing electoral system in the light of various hearings and discussions, and making a recommendation on whether or not it should be amended. The group recommended a change that then went to referendum and won more than 50 percent support – just short of the quota required to trigger a change.[5]

The similarity between representer and representee does not mean, in itself, that the representee has any degree of control over the representer.

---

[5] Since everything is a perfect indicator of itself, a limit case of indicative representation is the participatory democracy where the whole population is present to vote, not just a sample. Far from being cast as the contrast point for indicative representation, the compulsory, participatory arrangement can be seen as a special case. The case is so special, however, and so infeasible, that I ignore it in this discussion.

The connection between them is not one under which the representer has to track the dispositions of the representee, and respond by acting in conformity to those dispositions. Rather it is a connection under which the representer is a good indicator or model of how the representee might have been disposed to act or speak, if in the position of the representer. Thus the people of British Columbia did not control the citizens' assembly but, given that the assembly was a microcosm of the people, it might be thought to model the decision that the people as a whole would have made had it been given the same information.

But while the indicator relationship does not necessarily give control over representers to representees, it is possible for representees to exercise control by selecting suitable indicators as their representers, by subjecting them to constraints designed to ensure that they remain indicators, and by deselecting them if they fail to act appropriately. Such authorized, indicative representers, as indicated earlier, I describe as proxies of the representees; they stand in for those who determine their selection.

Suppose that I see someone who thinks like me, as we say, and is a good indicator in a certain domain of how I tend to respond on various issues. While I do not directly control what he or she does, I do assume a position of indirect control when I decide to authorize that person to act in my stead, say on a committee. By appointing that person rather than someone else, I make it more likely that the committee will act in a congenial manner: act, as they would have been led to act, had I myself been a member. And this indirect control can be further strengthened by additional measures. I may put other constraints or incentives in place that make it more likely that the person will simulate what I would have done on the committee: for example, I might take steps to insulate the person against special, warping motives. And I may retain the power of de-selecting the person, should he or she, for whatever reason, not serve my interests well. The person is my proxy, someone who takes my place, with my authority.

The extended case

These observations about the control that is possible with indicative representers should prompt us to recognize that while indicative representation has traditionally been associated with the proportional representation of groups, the model can also apply in very different contexts.

Consider the professional or quasi-professional public figures who are appointed by government, often under strict regulations and often with a (limited or unlimited) tenure that is independent of those who do the appointing. Obvious examples will be judges and prosecutors, public auditors and ombudsmen, agency heads and the members of public commissions. These figures will serve as proxies for the public, being appointed under public authorization because of the likelihood that they will serve the public well.

This likelihood may not be based on a similarity of nature between representers and representees, but it will be based on a similarity in the tendency of their wishes. There will be a convergence between the goals the representers are professionally constrained and motivated to implement – at least ideally – and the goals that the public would want to promote in the domain of their operation. The representers are recruited to public service, plausibly, on the grounds that their interests, if things go well, are likely to be indicative of the interests of the public. And they can be subjected to constraints that make it even more likely that this will be so. Such figures can be cast as proxy representers of the people on the same grounds that certain proportional bodies can be cast as proxies.

Think of those who serve on a central bank like the Federal Reserve in the US. Or think of those who are members of an election commission of the kind that is given responsibility in many countries, at arm's length from parliament, to draw the boundaries of electoral districts. Absent dependency on the elected officials who appoint them – absent reliance on those officials for continuing tenure, for example – such individuals may be moved by motives of professional reputation to act reliably in a manner that answers to the interest of the people as a whole. And this will be especially likely if their performance is subject to public check and commentary. It is surely more likely that an independent electoral commission would act in this way, for example, than that elected members of a parliament or congress would do so, since elected representatives would have special party interests in the shape of district boundaries (Pettit 2004).

The idea of appointing professional figures was not unknown to traditional democratic theory. A good example is provided by the official known as a "podesta," who played a very important role in the life of twelfth- and thirteenth-century Italian city-republics (Waley 1988). The podesta, who might serve at different times in different cities, was an outsider appointed for six months to a year in order to run a city's affairs. He was given a range of issues to control, was often forced to act without having contact with special interest groups within the citizenry, and was subjected to intense scrutiny at the end of his tenure. Since he might hope to be appointed as podesta by different cities at different times, he would also have been susceptible to reputational motives for doing his job to the satisfaction of the citizenry. Such a figure would have been a good example, in our terms, of an indicative representer: a proxy agent who takes the place of those he represents.

But it is not just public appointees who can count as indicative representers in the extended sense we are examining. For another sort of example, think of the whistle-blowers who can expose abuses in public life, or the "private attorneys general," as they have been called (Rabkin 1998), who serve the public well by challenging certain laws before the courts. The fact that the public or people give whistle-blowers protection, and the fact that they give private attorneys general a license to use the courts as they do, means that these figures are authorized to act in their characteristic manner. In the aggregate they serve the public well, by most accounts, acting as they do on convergent if not always identical interests. Their authorization by the public means that like formally appointed officials, they can be seen as representers who are employed in their characteristic roles, precisely because of the indicative relationship between their dispositions and the presumptive dispositions of the people as a whole.

III.   Responsive representation

Directed responsiveness

Where the indicative idea is that a microcosm or model of the people should rule because it is likely to be a good indicator of how the people as a whole would decide the issues that come before it, the responsive idea takes the complementary line. In this conception the representer tracks what the representee wants and responds with appropriate action, playing a very different role from that of being a passive indicator of the representee's disposition.[6] The judicial metaphor in which the lawyer or attorney acts for the client offers an illustration of the idea in which the representee explicitly or implicitly directs the representer. As the lawyer tracks the client's wishes, so the responsive representer is to track the wishes of the representee.

---

[6] I take indicative and responsive representers to be indicative and responsive only in a positive mode. If an indicative agent pursues something, that indicates that it is something that the principal would favor; but if the agent does not pursue something, that does not indicate that it is something the principal would not favor. If a principal has an interest in something, the responsive agent will not have an interest in it but if the principal does not have an interest in something that does not mean that the responsive agent will not have an interest in it. This assumption means that a responsive agent may not be indicative, as an indicative agent may not be responsive.

Under the responsive conception of representation, the wishes of representees exercise a degree of control over how representers act, and they do this with the authorization of the representees themselves; the representative process materializes, if not at their initiative, at least with their knowledge and acquiescence. Indicative representers are recruited or licensed to act because they are or can be made to be indicative. Responsive representers are recruited or licensed to act because they are or can be made to be responsive. Where I describe representers who are authorized to serve in an indicative role as proxies, I describe representers who are authorized to serve in a responsive role as deputies. We shall see that apart from directed deputies who answer to the metaphor of the attorney, there are also interpretive deputies who answer better to the metaphor of the actor.

Responsiveness among representers may materialize spontaneously, as a result of a natural love or reverence or fear of the representees, or it may be manufactured by contextual incentives or constraints that elicit suitable attentiveness. Let the representees form an intention that something be done by the representers and, at least in the directed version of responsive representation, the representers will become disposed to do it. The representers may respond to instructions issued by the representees – that is, to the manifestations of their wishes – or they may not need any such instruction, being disposed to respond to the wishes that the representees manifestly hold. Such explicitly or implicitly directed deputies I describe, in a received term, as delegates of those they represent: they are agents who serve as voiceboxes for the represented (Pitkin 1972; but see Urbinati 2000).

The category of delegates is often taken to be illustrated – rightly or wrongly, as we shall see – by those who serve in the legislature, or perhaps the executive, in sensitivity to the wishes of the electorate.[7] The control that the people exercise over such public representers may take an active, hands-on form, as when the representees impose suitable constraints on representers or give them explicit instructions. But it may often be just virtual in character, constituting a sort of hands-off, arm's-length control (Pettit 2001); while this may also be possible with indicative representers, it is particularly salient with responsive ones. Hands-off control will materialize when the representers behave in a congenial fashion and the representees stand by, ready to reveal relevant attitudes, or impose relevant constraints, only in the event that the representers stop

---

[7] For a state-of-the-art assessment of political, responsive representation, see Mansbridge (2003). Mansbridge (forthcoming) defends congenial views on indicative representation, as I learned when this paper was in press.

performing to their taste. In this case the representees ride herd on the representers, to use an image from cowboy life. They intervene in the affairs of the representers, eliciting suitable motivation or information, only on a need-for-action basis.[8]

Might the control of responsive representers be increased by ensuring that they are indicative as well as responsive? The hope that it can be increased in this way motivates the drive for ensuring proportionality among elected deputies. The case for proportional, electoral representation is made in John Stuart Mill's classic work on representation (1964 [1861]), as indicated earlier, and it is reinforced by contemporary theorists such as Anne Phillips (1995) and Thomas Christiano (1996). There are many reasons to think that salient divisions among a represented population should be reflected in an elected house of representatives. But it is not so clear that ensuring such proportionality will ensure the indicative reliability that we might expect, for example, in the British Columbia citizens' assembly.

The reason is that no matter how much proportionality is imposed on a parliament or congress, the fact that members are chosen by election from among those who are ready to stand at the polls introduces a framework of motivation that is going to undermine the prospect of parliament operating as a reliable model or microcosm of the people. Those who stand for election are not going to be typical of the society, and even if they are typical, their performance in the legislature is bound to be affected by a special motive: the interest in being elected and reelected. In order to constitute a model of the people, legislators would need to go about their business without a thought for anything but what by their lights it is best to do. And no elected officials can be expected to do that; they are bound to be subject to what from the point of view of the indicative model is a deeply warping influence.

As suggested, there is a serious question as to whether public, responsive representers really can serve as delegates who are explicitly or implicitly directed by their constituents. Directed, responsive representation supposes that the mind of representees is made up and manifested to representers. There are explicit or implicit directives available to express

---

[8] The notion of control employed across the distinctions we have made is quite univocal. We can say that one party, A, exercises control over another party, B, to the extent that A raises the probability – robustly raises the probability (Lovett 2007: 712–13) – that B will behave in a congenial manner above the level that that behavior might have had in A's absence (Dahl 1957; Pettit 2007). A will have such an effect if A actively elicits the deputy or proxy performance sought. But A will also have this effect in the case where A stands ready to intervene on a need-for-action basis. A will guard against the possibility that B has a change of mind and by raising the probability that B will behave congenially even in that case, A will raise the absolute probability of such behavior.

the mind of representers and the responsive representational job is to track those directives. The problem that we should now note, however, is that representees in the public worlds rarely provide representers with a fully formed, directive mind. Thus responsive representation often has to become interpretive or constructive in a manner that evokes the metaphor of the actor rather than that of the attorney.

Interpretive responsiveness

Where attorneys have to be guided by the explicit or implicit directives of clients, actors bear a much less constrained relationship to the scripted characters that they are required to play. The actor interprets the character, taking the spare lines of the dramatist and giving them life in a pattern of emphasis and presence that makes interpersonal sense; the interpretation lets the character portrayed be understood as a person amongst persons. Representation in this interpretive sense is described by Hobbes (1994: 16) as personation: an act in which the representer speaks with authority for another, in particular for another individual or group of individuals.

Like any form of responsive representation, the interpretive sort that answers to this metaphor has to be authorized by the representees, at least if it has democratic credentials. Representees have to authorize the representers to speak for them, even though they do not provide the representers with the words to use. Where responsive representers on the attorney model are voiceboxes of the people, as we might say, responsive representers on the actor model are spokespersons. Where I describe attorney-like deputies as delegates, I follow tradition in describing actor-like deputies as trustees (Pitkin 1972).

The authorization that representees give interpretive deputies means that those who speak for them do not report the mind of their constituents, as a journalist or opinion survey might report that mind. Subject perhaps to certain provisos, the representees are deemed to think what their authorized spokesperson – or body of spokespersons – says that they think. The authorization is not just a prediction to the effect that the representers will be a pretty good guide to what they think. It is a guarantee that, at least within certain limits and under certain conditions, they can be taken to be minded as the representing words portray them as minded. They can be held to those words.

Responsive representation has to be interpretive with an individual representee if that person is a minor – here authorization may be supplied by a court – or if the person does not express his or her mind on some particular issue where the representer needs to act. But the context in which responsive representation is most clearly required to be interpretive is one of political representation, where there are a number of individuals in the position of representees, and the representer is forced, at whatever level of grain, to ascribe a coherent, enactable set of attitudes to them – a single mind.

Suppose that one or more representers are acting for an unincorporated collection or multitude. Whatever control is exercised by the representees in the multitude it had better allow the representers to act for a consistent set of goals, according to a consistent set of judgments; otherwise the representative actions are liable to undercut one another. Or if that requirement is thought too strict, on the grounds that many agents fall short of consistency, then the control certainly ought to allow the representers to be responsive to charges of inconsistency. They should not be required to have to admit that what they hold or seek on behalf of their representees is an inconsistent package; else they and their constituents would be a laughing stock.

Might the representees impose an arrangement under which they control what the representers do in a goal-by-goal or judgment-by-judgment way, and still hope to satisfy such a coherence constraint? It turns out that they could not. And that suggests that the responsive representation of a multitude is bound at a certain point to become interpretive. Those who serve in such responsively representative roles will have to be spokespersons, not voiceboxes: they will have to be deputies in the trustee mould, not in the mould of the delegate.

The most obvious way in which a multitude might hope to control the actions of its representers would be by forcing those agents always to follow the majority vote of its members. But the "discursive dilemma" shows why this will not work in general (Pettit 2001: ch. 5). The votes of entirely consistent individuals on logically connected issues can generate a set of inconsistent positions on those issues. Suppose that A, B, and C want to establish a majority collective view on three issues: whether p; whether q; and whether p&q. They might be judges in a court who have to decide on whether a plaintiff in tort did harm (p), had a duty of care (q) and so was liable for damages (p&q) (Kornhauser and Sager 1993). It is perfectly possible for A, B, and C each to have a consistent set of views on these issues and yet for the group to be forced by majority voting into endorsing an inconsistent set.

That will happen, for example, if the votes that the individuals submit are as follows. A and B vote that p, C votes against; B and C vote that q, A votes against; and so only B votes that p&q. A and C vote that not-p&q, thereby giving a majority verdict that p, that q, and that not-p&q. The following matrix should make the pattern vivid.

	P?	Q?	P & Q?
A	Yes	No	No
B	Yes	Yes	Yes
C	No	Yes	No
Majority vote	Yes	Yes	No

This paradox is of general significance, since it turns out that no voting system is guaranteed to produce a consistent output from consistent inputs if it is to work with all patterns of input and if, roughly, it is to treat both individuals and issues even-handedly (List and Pettit 2002). The lesson is that if the representers of a multitude are required to enact a coherent mind, furthering a consistent set of goals according to a consistent set of judgments, then they cannot be controlled by representees on an issue-by-issue basis. Such control is liable to provide representers with an inconsistent set of attitudes to enact: a set of attitudes like the judgments that p, that q, and that not-p&q.

The lesson, put more positively, is that in a case like this responsive representation has to be interpretive or constructive. It has to involve, not the faithful reflection of a pre-given mind, but a constructive interpretation in virtue of which the multitude is imputed a coherent mind or mentality. When that occurs, the multitude will assume the status of a corporate agent.

The idea that the interpretive representation of a multitude can transform it into a corporate agent is present in Western thought from at least the fourteenth century. In 1354, Albericus de Rosciate could say that a collegial agent, although it is constituted out of many members, is one by virtue of representation: *collegium, licet constituatur ex pluribus, est tamen unum per representationem* (Eschmann 1946: 33, fn 145). The theme dominates the work of legal theorists of the time, such as Bartolus of Sassoferrato and his pupil, Baldus de Ubaldis, who make much of the way represented groups, in particular the represented people of a city, could figure as corporate agents or persons (Woolf 1913; Canning 1983). Arguing that the *populus liber*, the free people of a city-republic, is a corporate person, Baldus explains that this is because the council represents the mind of that people: *concilium representat mentem populi* (Canning 1987: 198).

The theme reappears in the writings of Thomas Hobbes in the seventeenth century. He makes representation, a term that he uses as an alternative to personation, central to the possibility of a group's creating and enacting a single mind. "A multitude of men are made one person, when they are by one man, or one person, represented." Where does the unity come from? From the fact that the representing individual – or body – will speak with one voice, thereby testifying to one mind in the group: "it is the unity of the representer, not the unity of the represented, that maketh the person one" (Hobbes 1994: 16.13).

IV.   Representation and democracy

Varieties of democratic representation

Democracy, on the Lincolnian formula, is government of the people, by the people and for the people. Representation has to have a place in any democratic constitution insofar as it is only by courtesy of representers that government can hope to be by the people; popular participation is inevitably restricted to the occasional referendum.

There is obviously room in a democratic constitution for indicative representation, of both the standard and the extended kind. The British Columbia citizens' assembly exemplifies a standard variety of indicative representation that any democracy could usefully institute. And the extended variety of indicative representation is bound to have a place insofar as every plausible democracy requires some statutory officers and bodies, such as judges, ombudsmen, and electoral commissioners, as well as a possibility of contestation by public attorneys general and by other informal invigilators of government.

Equally clearly, there has to be room in a democratic constitution for responsive as well as indicative representation. In order for many reliably indicative representers to be appointed to office, as statutory officers will have to be appointed, there must already be elected and presumptively responsive representers in place. But in any case there are quite independent reasons why no plausibly democratic regime could operate on the basis of indicative representation alone. Such representation requires that people have a standing interest in decisions being made after a more or less determinate pattern, as in requiring judges to adjudicate cases according to established law. And in many cases there would be no such interest available to guide indicative authorities. Thus popular representation is bound to require a role for responsive as well as indicative representation.

Democracy has to make room, then, both for proxies and for deputies. This is not the place to investigate the best way of networking such different kinds of representers in a satisfactory democratic dispensation, nor the best way of frameworking their activities by suitable constitutional and other constraints. Some of the relevant issues will be highlighted by the discussion in the appendix, which constitutes the final section of the chapter, on the operation of the Washington and Westminster systems. But in the remainder of this section I discuss one serious problem that may be raised about the democratic control of those responsive representers, those deputies, that operate in an interpretive rather than a directed mode. This is a telling issue since the argument at the end of the last section suggests that all public deputies will have to be interpretive trustees rather than directed delegates.

A problem

The medievals who spoke of the representation of a people – as I take it, their interpretive representation – generally appear to have had an intuitively democratic form of representation in mind, at least relative to a citizenry of mainstream, propertied males. They looked to a form of representation in which the individual people not only consented to being represented but exercised an influence over what representers said and did as a corporate spokesperson. They took it for granted that the council of a city-republic would be appointed, at least in good part, by voting and rotation – under the *regimen ad populum* – so that the city or people could be described, in Bartolus's words, as a *sibi princeps*, a prince unto itself (Woolf 1913: 155–60, 180).

Hobbes went beyond this in arguing that the interpretive representation whereby a people assumes the unity of a person might be practiced by a monarch with absolute powers or by a committee of aristocrats: and this with the authorization of members of the people. He did not think that there could be democracy with representation by others, arguing that democracy would require the people to self-represent, ruling themselves in a committee-of-the-whole; this theme was later taken up by Rousseau (1973). Mistakenly, in view of the discursive dilemma, he thought that this self-representation could be achieved under a regime of majority voting (Hobbes 1994: 16.15–17), as indeed did Locke (1960: Bk 2, ch. 8.96) and Rousseau (1973: Bk 4, ch. 2).

The issue as to whether interpretive representation can be democratized is important, given that interpretation is going to be unavoidable when a multitude is responsively represented. We took responsive representation, being a relationship of tracking the representees, to require the control of those representees. The question here is whether such control is available with interpretive representation as well as with responsive. How might interpreters – authorized interpreters, as we can assume – be subjected to the control of representees?

Participation in the committee-of-the whole, as envisaged in Hobbes's vision, is not a feasible way of imposing democratic control. Contemporary societies are just too big to allow for a participatory regime, in particular the sort that would require members to adjust in face of majority support for inconsistent positions. And neither is an electoral regime going to provide an effective democratic discipline. Elected representatives cannot be responsively controlled by the majority attitudes of the population, since those attitudes may be incoherent. And if the only restriction on those members springs from the desire to be reelected, or from the fact of having to live under the laws proposed, still it will leave them free to construct the mind of the people in a relatively unconstrained fashion. So is there any alternative or supplementary discipline that might be imposed on interpretive representers?

A solution?

At the time of the civil rights disputes in the United States, as at many other junctures in American history, the protagonists made rival claims as to what was the way of thinking about racial relations that represented the mind of the American people. Was it the much-vaunted heritage of a state like Mississippi in which strict segregation had been enforced on public transport, in public schools, and in other public amenities? Or was it the message of equality and respect that had long been enshrined in the Constitution and its amendments? The division on this issue created a fault line that ran through the legislatures, the courts, the media, and out onto the streets. Ultimately the constitutionally supported message won out and became a theme around which citizens generally rallied. But did this victory constitute a democratic breakthrough: a win for the right interpretation of the people's mind over the wrong interpretation? Or was it a victory of what was morally right over what was morally wrong? Or was it just a victory for the stronger over the weaker, the more numerous over the less numerous?

I think that there is only one base on which the line taken in a case like this can be justified as the right rather than the wrong interpretation of the people's mind. This is the base provided by considerations in the family of what Rawls (1993, 1999) describes as public reasons. My own view is that the victory in the civil rights disputes can be cast as a democratic victory, so far as the line that emerged triumphant is the only line that had the support of such public reasons.

Central to the idea of a democratic polity is the assumption that citizens can debate with one another about what government and the state should do from positions of relative equality: positions in which they can see public action as action that they together license and support (Larmore 2003). So at any rate I assume. Given this assumption, it follows that any proposal as to what government is to do should be supported by the sorts of considerations that all can equally recognize as relevant, even if they weight them differently. If one group can argue for a certain policy only on the ground that it is good for its own members, or in line with their particular view of the world, then that cannot be expected to pass muster under the discipline of public debate – not, at least, unless the policy can also be shown to benefit other groups or not to do them any harm (Elster 1986a).

The existence of a political society in which members address one another in arguing for this or that public policy ought, under the assumption of equality, to generate a currency of public reasons. These will be reasons that get established in the course of debate and argument as considerations that are appropriately invoked in assessing public measures and initiatives. If the members of the society cannot find a fund of considerations on which to draw in argument about public policy – a fund of considerations that all will take to be relevant, even while they weight them differently – then the exchanges between them will degenerate into power struggles and they will live in the precincts of civil war.

The assumption of equal positioning in public debate makes it inevitable that certain core considerations are endorsed in any democratic society: in particular, the claim of each member to equal respect and concern. But there are many considerations that may receive endorsement in one society and not in another. One society might endorse considerations that support a system of more or less exclusively private ownership, for example, another considerations that support a system that allows for considerable public property. One society might foster considerations that promote the development of certain cultural norms, another promulgate considerations that provide support for quite different conventions. And so on.

The considerations acknowledged and valorized in any society will typically leave issues of detailed policy underdetermined, of course; what they rule out will be the policies that are unthinkable, certainly indefensible, in the discourse of the public sphere. But even when there are many candidate policies for dealing with a given issue, all of which pass muster in public debate, the public reasons acknowledged in that debate may support one or another procedure for resolving the tie. The supported procedure might involve a parliamentary vote, or reference to an expert committee, or resort to referendum, or even the use of a citizens' assembly.

As a democracy grows, then, we may expect that the trial and error process whereby participants float considerations and find that they are accepted or rejected will generate a currency of considerations that all valorize, and valorize as a matter of common access. Those considerations will provide the blocks out of which any case for changing or conserving the way things are done will have to be built; they will indicate the sorts of presumptions or premises on the basis of which arguments in public policy are to be made. This observation is at the heart of Rawls's conception of public reasons, although he spells it out only occasionally. In one version, he says, "the political culture of a democratic society that has worked reasonably well over a considerable period of time normally contains, at least implicitly, certain fundamental ideas from which it is possible to work up a political conception of justice suitable for a constitutional regime" (Rawls 2001: 34–5).

Returning to our original question, then, how can one argue that the interpretations of the people's mind that are selected and given authority in public life really are the correct interpretations: the interpretations that are controlled in an appropriate sense by the representees? The only available base for arguing this in a large-scale democracy has to be that they are the interpretations that emerge in a process where public reasons are the primary selectional force. The interpretations may be uniquely consistent with considerations that are given the status of public reasons. But more likely they will be that particular set of interpretations, among the sets that are compatible with public reason, that are selected under procedures endorsed in public reason.

Go back, then, to the civil rights case. The argument of public figures in Mississippi and other southern states may have been in line with some local traditions. But it seems clear that in the opinion of the courts, the media, and the vast majority of US citizens those traditions conflicted with the requirements of the idea of equality as that figured and still figures in American law and culture. It is doubtful if the civil rights movement would have won the day had there not been a widespread acceptance that practices of segregation were not supported in the currency of public reasons that were accepted in the country. The inconsistency with public reasons may not have been enough on its own to bring about the changes that occurred in the 1950s and 1960s but, arguably, it was an essential prerequisite for the success of the civil rights movement.

It is time to sum up the overall argument of the chapter. We have seen that representers and representees may be individuals or groups and, if groups, that they may be mere collections, mere cooperatives, or full-scale corporate entities. We have also seen that the relations of representation come in two broad types, with representers figuring as indicative proxies under the first variety, responsive deputies in the other. And, focusing on issues of politics, we have argued that both sorts of representation are bound to have a place in a democratic regime; that responsive representation is likely to require interpretive trustees, not directed delegates; and that interpretive, responsive representation, however constructive, can be democratically controlled under a discipline of public reason.

But are these ideas and distinctions of any use in considering empirical systems? In order to vindicate their claim to significance I conclude with observations on two ideal types of system, one associated with Washington, the other with Westminster. The distinctions we have made enable us to mark a nice difference in representational priority between these two models: inevitably, these two rather toytown models. And that difference clearly matters.

V.   Appendix: The Washington and Westminster systems[9]

Philip Pettit and Rory Pettit

The Washington model

The Washington system employs individual elected representers at a number of sites. Broadly speaking, members of the House represent districts, members of the Senate represent states, and the President represents the people as a whole. The representation at this level is responsive in character, with members of the House being apparently committed to the service of their districts, members of the Senate to the service of their state, and the President to the service of the nation or union.

Representation is practiced in this system, however, not just at the level of individuals, but also at the level where members of Congress cooperate with one another and with the President and other members of the administration. It is this group, Congress-cum-administration, that ultimately gets various measures into law, performing a representative function that parallels the representative work of the individuals in that group. Where individuals may serve their different constituencies in a responsive way, this group will be expected to serve the people as a whole in a responsive manner. What it promulgates as law and policy is meant to count, under suitable controls, as the law and policy supported by the people.

---

[9] This builds in some part on R. Pettit (2007).

Given the complexity of views in any district or state, the individual representation of constituency is bound to be fundamentally interpretive. The member of the House or the Senator will have to construct the mind of the constituency he or she serves, operating as a trustee rather than a delegate. Since the views of the people as a whole are even more complex, the representation of the people by the Congress-cum-administration is also bound to be interpretive. But how can the Congress-cum-administration serve as an interpretive representer of the people – a reliable trustee – if it is composed of individuals who often have conflicting briefs? They have to serve as trustees both for their constituency and for the nation or people as a whole.

Congress-cum-administration does not constitute a corporate entity with a coherent set of goals and judgments. If it did, then that entity might be a reliable system-wide trustee, imposing constraints on its members to support suitable policies. Congress-cum-administration operates, rather, as a loose aggregation that provides a majority, now for this compromise and coalition, now for that. It has to get enough members on side in order to create the requisite support for any bill that passes into law. But the majority it musters in support of one bill may be different from the majority it musters in support of another. And in each case it will have to manufacture the majority by buying off various members with favors that will play well with their electors back home. In operating on this pattern, the Congress-cum-administration will be subject to various constitutional constraints, but it is not clear that these provide anything but the lightest level of regulative control.

In this system there is an inherent tension between two sorts of forces. There are pressures on individual members of Congress to represent their different constituencies responsively, on pain on not being reelected. And at the same time there is pressure at the group or system level to generate and maintain a body of law that has the coherence required, and the fit with system-wide public reasons, to pass as the voice of the people (Dworkin 1986).

These forces are quite likely to interact so as to produce laws that fail to fit with one another, and perhaps even with the Constitution. The laws themselves will often involve subclauses designed to pick up the support of swing voters, and such complexity can make the demands of coherence hard to identify. But even when those demands are obvious, the desire to strike a popular, electorally helpful posture is liable to generate support among members of Congress for laws that fail to fit with one another. In that case the buck passes to the President, who may veto the law. And, failing a presidential veto, the buck will pass to those members of the public who may combine to challenge the law and to the courts that will adjudicate that challenge. If there is a coherent body of law emerging at the end of the process, that will be a product of this interplay of different factors, not the work of any single corporate body.

This result can be summed up by saying that the Washington system prioritizes the individual-level representation of constituencies at a possible cost to the group-level or system-level representation of the people as a whole. It allows members of Congress to serve as trustees for their constituencies, thereby raising a problem for how the administration-cum-Congress can serve as a trustee for the people as a whole. It is directed at ensuring not so much a representative government as a government of representatives – something that resembles what Edmund Burke (1999) described as a congress of ambassadors.

The Westminster model

The reason why the Washington system of representation prioritizes individual-level representation goes back to the fact that the executive or administration is elected directly, not by members of the Congress. This separation means that the fate of the administration does not depend on how the members vote. And so those members are free to vote as they wish, with party constraints serving only as a relatively light discipline, at least under normal conditions. This marks the crucial difference between the Washington and the Westminster regimes.

In the Westminster system the administration stands or falls with the support of the individual members of parliament, in particular the lower House. And that means that those parliamentary representatives who have succeeded in electing an executive – the members of the winning party or coalition – will have to stick together in order to maintain that executive in power. In effect, the party or coalition will have to be organized so that its members are forced to cleave to an agreed party line, on pain of losing party membership and the chance of being reelected. The party or coalition will become a self-policing corporate entity.

Given this pressure, the behavior of parliamentary representatives cannot be dictated by a desire to please those back in the constituency, and to promote the prospects of reelection; they cannot serve as trustee representatives for the constituency. If their party gets enough members into parliament to be able to select the executive, then members will be bound by the party whip to stick on most important matters to the party line. And if their party fails to do this, then they will be bound by the party whip to present a solid face of opposition to the party in power, playing by the same hard-ball rules. This necessity is manifest to voters, of course, so that legislators will be elected in great part on the grounds of which executive they promise to support in office – usually, an executive composed of members of their own party – not on the grounds of how well they are likely to serve the local constituency.

In the Westminster system, then, the individual-level representation of constituency gets put in a decidedly second place, since individual members will tend to vote as their party votes and will be expected even by those who elect them to vote that way. But if that is the weakness of the system, the strength is that the parliament will operate very efficiently to generate a body of legislation that can be expected to be internally coherent, to cohere with established law and principle, and to be generally responsive to the public reasons that carry weight among the people as a whole. The legislative program for any parliament will have to be planned by a corporate body: the party in power. This party will have had to ensure the coherence of its legislative program. It will have had to advertise the program as that which it would implement in office. And once in office it will have to stick to the program, at least in general outline. Short of being a minority or coalition government, it will have no excuse for departing from it and any departure will be subject to a powerful challenge from the opposition, the media, and the public.

We saw that the Washington system prioritizes the individual-level representation of constituency at a cost to the system-level representation of the people. These comments on the Westminster system show that things there are almost exactly the other way around. The system prioritizes the group-level representation of the people, giving parliament the cast of a corporate body, albeit a body controlled by members of the party that holds office. And it does this to the detriment of the individual-level representation of constituency. In contrast to the Washington model, it is directed at ensuring a representative government rather than a government of representatives.

Significance

The difference of representational priority has enormous implications for other aspects of the two systems, including implications that bear on the claims of each to be a satisfactory democratic regime.[10] The significance of the difference in representational priority comes out in differences of sensitivity to a variety of pressures. We can illustrate the point, somewhat speculatively, with reference to local pressures, expressive pressures, lobby pressures and the pressure of public opinion.

---

[10] Other assessments of the two systems tend not to focus on this issue of representational priority: see Shugart and Carey (1992); Linz and Valenzuela (1994).

Local pressures   Under the Washington system members of Congress are bound to be influenced, for good or ill, by a concern for how their votes will play back home. This localism may occasionally bring real benefits to their district, as when members can secure legislative favors. The members of a Westminster parliament will have little occasion to think locally in this manner, since their votes will be controlled by the party; local efforts will be restricted to providing some local advisory services and to playing the part of a celebrity in local events.

Expressive pressures   To act in a purely instrumental way is to act out of a concern for the outcome of what one does; to act purely expressively is to act out of a concern for the posture associated with acting in that manner (Brennan and Lomasky 1992). The members of Congress will often be in a situation where they cannot affect the outcome, even as part of an effective majority, and where relevant they will be motivated to take positions on an expressive basis. They will be tempted to grandstand on issues like prostitution and drugs and crime, for example, focusing on the symbolic rather than the substantive utility of doing so (Nozick 1994). The members of a Westminster parliament will be less exposed to this pressure. The party in power will always be able to affect outcomes, with the result that concern for outcome should balance if not eliminate the concern for posture and thereby reduce expressive motives. Something similar may be true of the party out of power, for it will always have to think about what to do if it wins office.

Lobby pressures   The members of a Washington Congress, being more or less free to vote as they will, are going to be subject to intense lobby pressure for their vote, especially when the lobbies involved can provide campaign finance for those who vote congenially. The members of a Westminster legislature, not being free to vote against their party, will not be subject to the same lobbying pressure, at least not outside the ministry. Lobbies will have to buy over whole parties in order to have a legislative impact, not just the swing voters on any issue.[11]

Public opinion   The members of Congress will not necessarily be responsive to a high level of public opinion in favor of a particular measure. Whether a response is forthcoming will depend, first, on how far

---

[11] The very fact that the party in power puts up a unified legislative program for the duration of a parliament may facilitate the influence of an opinion-forming elite in the process whereby that program is formed. And that particular danger may be relatively absent under the Washington system.

that opinion generates local pressure on the representer to do something; second, on how expressively beneficial or costly will be the posture of support; third, on how far lobby pressures are silent or supportive on the issue; and, fourth, on how far the transaction costs of getting a majority together in support of the measure are manageable. But if public opinion strongly supports a given measure, then the party in office under the Westminster system can usually be expected to back the measure. It will not be subject to the same local, expressive and lobbying concerns; there will be low transaction costs involved, since it will already be organized as a corporate entity; and, as an effective agent in power, it will be expected to respond to public opinion and will run an electoral risk if it fails to do so. The difference between the two models may help to explain why the public support for gun control that generally emerges in the wake of gun outrages routinely elicits a response in Westminster systems and routinely fails to do so under the Washington model.

If these thoughts are on the right lines, then the representational priority adopted in a system of government is going to have an enormous influence on how the system and the society as a whole works. Let the system go toward Washington and it will activate local, expressive, and lobby pressures and reduce the impact of aggregate public opinion. Let it go toward Westminster and it will reduce local, expressive, and lobby pressures and intensify the impact of public opinion.

These predictions should be qualified for variation in other factors, of course, and need to be tested against empirical observations. But assuming they are broadly on the right lines – and there is some evidence that they are (Foweraker and Landman 2002) – they emphasize the importance of the issue of representational priority. There are various normative standpoints possible on that issue, of course, so that some thinkers may favor the Washington model, some the Westminster. But no one is likely to think that the issue is insignificant. It demonstrates, if demonstration is needed, that the theory of representation matters.

BIBLIOGRAPHY

Abramson, J. 1994. *We, the Jury: The Jury System and the Ideal of Democracy*. New York: Basic Books.
Bratman, M. 1999. *Faces of Intention: Selected Essays on Intention and Agency*. Cambridge: Cambridge University Press.
Brennan, G. and L. Lomasky. 1992. *Democracy and Decision*. Cambridge: Cambridge University Press.
Burke, E. 1999. "Speech to the Electors of Bristol," in *Selected Works of Edmund Burke*. Indianapolis, IN: Liberty Fund.

Canning, J. P. 1983. "Ideas of the State in Thirteenth and Fourteenth Century Commentators on the Roman Law." *Transactions of the Royal Historical Society* 33: 1–27.

1987. *The Political Thought of Baldus de Ubaldis*. Cambridge: Cambridge University Press.

Christiano, T. 1996. *The Rule of the Many: Fundamental Issues in Democratic Theory*. Boulder, CO: Westview Press.

Dahl, R. 1957. "The Concept of Power." *Behavioral Science* 2: 201–15.

Dworkin, R. 1986. *Law's Empire*. Cambridge, MA: Harvard University Press.

Elster, J. 1986a. "The Market and the Forum: Three Varieties of Political Theory," in *Foundations of Social Choice Theory*, ed. J. Elster and A. Hilland. Cambridge: Cambridge University Press, 103–30.

Eschmann, T. 1946. "Studies on the Notion of Society in St Thomas Aquinas: St Thomas and the Decretal of Innocent IV Romana Ecclesia, Ceterum." *Medieval Studies* 8: 1–42.

Ferejohn, J. 2007. "The Citizens' Assembly Model," in *Designing Deliberative Democracy: The British Columbia Citizens' Assembly*, ed. H. Perse and M. Warren. Cambridge: Cambridge University Press, 192–213.

Fishkin, J. S. 1997. *The Voice of the People: Public Opinion and Democracy*. New Haven, CT: Yale University Press.

Foweraker, J. and T. Landman. 2002. "Constitutional Design and Democratic Performance." *Democratization* 9: 43–66.

Fung, A. and E. Fagotto. 2006. "The British Columbia Citizens' Assembly." Kennedy School of Government, Harvard University. Cambridge, MA.

Goodman, N. 1969. *Languages of Art*. London: Oxford University Press.

Hansen, M. H. 1991. *The Athenian Democracy in the Age of Demosthenes*. Oxford: Blackwell.

Hobbes, T. 1990. *Behemoth or The Long Parliament*, ed. F. Toennies. Chicago: University of Chicago Press.

1994. *Leviathan*, ed. E. Curley. Indianapolis, IN: Hackett.

Ketcham, R. (ed.). 2003. *The Anti-Federalist Papers*. New York: Signet Classic.

Knights, M. 2005. *Representation and Misrepresentation in Later Stuart Britain: Partisanship and Political Culture*. Oxford: Oxford University Press.

Kornhauser, L. A. and L. G. Sager. 1993. "The One and the Many: Adjudication in Collegial Courts." *California Law Review* 81: 1–59.

Larmore, C. 2003. "Public Reason," in *The Cambridge Companion to Rawls*, ed. S. Freeman. Cambridge: Cambridge University Press, 368–93.

Linz, J. J. and A. Valenzuela (eds.). 1994. *The Failure of Presidential Democracy*. Baltimore, MD: Johns Hopkins University Press.

List, C. and P. Pettit. 2002. "Aggregating Sets of Judgments: An Impossibility Result." *Economics and Philosophy* 18: 89–110.

Locke, J. 1960. *Two Treatises of Government*. Cambridge: Cambridge University Press.

Lovett, F. 2007. "Power," in *A Companion to Contemporary Political Philosophy*, ed. R. E. Goodin, P. Pettit, and T. Pogge. Oxford: Blackwell.

McLean, J. 2004. "Government to State: Globalization, Regulation, and Governments as Legal Persons." *Indiana Journal of Global Legal Studies* 10: 173–97.

Manin, B. 1997. *The Principles of Representative Government*. Cambridge: Cambridge University Press.

Mansbridge, J. 2003. "Rethinking Representation." *American Political Science Review* 97: 515–28.

forthcoming, "A 'Selection Model' of Political Representation," *Journal of Political Philosophy*.

Mill, J. S. 1964. *Considerations on Representative Government*. London: Everyman Books.

Nozick, R. 1994. *The Nature of Rationality*. Princeton, NJ: Princeton University Press.

Pettit, P. 2001. *A Theory of Freedom: From the Psychology to the Politics of Agency*. Cambridge: Polity Press; New York: Oxford University Press.

2004. "Depoliticizing Democracy." *Ratio Juris* 17: 52–65.

2007. "Republican Liberty: Three Axioms, Four Theorems," in *Republicanism and Political Theory*, ed. C. Laborde and J. Manor. Oxford: Blackwell, 102–30.

Pettit, P. and D. Schweikard. 2006. "Joint Action and Group Agency." *Philosophy of the Social Sciences* 36: 18–39.

Pettit, R. 2007. "Reconceptualising Democratic Representation," BA honors thesis, Department of Philosophy, University of Sydney.

Phillips, A. 1995. *The Politics of Presence*. Oxford: Oxford University Press.

Pitkin, H. F. (ed.). 1969. *Representation*. New York: Atherton Press.

1972. *The Concept of Representation*. Berkeley: University of California Press.

Rabkin, J. A. 1998. "The Secret Life of the Private Attorney General." *Law and Contemporary Problems* 61: 179–203.

Rawls, J. 1993. *Political Liberalism*. New York: Columbia University Press.

1999. *The Law of Peoples*. Cambridge, MA: Harvard University Press.

2001. *Justice as Fairness: A Restatement*. Cambridge, MA: Harvard University Press.

Rehfeld, A. 2005. *The Concept of Constituency: Political Representation, Democratic Legitimacy, and Institutional Design*. Cambridge: Cambridge University Press.

2006. "Towards a General Theory of Political Representation." *Journal of Politics* 68: 1–21.

Richardson, H. 2002. *Democratic Autonomy*. New York: Oxford University Press.

Rousseau, J.-J. 1973. *The Social Contract and Discourses*. London: Dent.

Shugart, M. S. and J. M. Carey. 1992. *Presidents and Assemblies: Constitutional Design and Electoral Dynamics*. Cambridge: Cambridge University Press.

Skinner, Q. 2005. "Hobbes on Representation." *European Journal of Philosophy* 13: 155–84.

Stewart, J., E. Kendall, and A. Coote. 1994. *Citizens' Juries*. London: Institute of Public Policy Research.

Urbinati, N. 2000. "Representation as Advocacy: A Study of Democratic Deliberation." *Political Theory* 28: 758–86.

Waley, D. 1988. *The Italian City-Republics*, 3rd edn. London: Longman.

Woolf, C. N. S. 1913. *Bartolus of Sassoferrato*. Cambridge: Cambridge University Press.

4   Representative government and popular sovereignty

Bryan Garsten

Are representative governments working well? The answer to that question depends on what we think the purpose of representative government is. Most research in political science presumes that the purpose of representative government is to represent the will of the people by translating popular sentiment or public interest into governmental policy. It therefore presumes that a good measure of the performance of representative democracy, at least in its representative capacity, involves comparing policy results with public opinion as it is or as it should be. The classic study of constituency influence in the House of Representatives by Miller and Stokes, for example, focused on "the extent of policy agreement between legislator and district" (Miller and Stokes 1963). More recent work continues to investigate similar relations: Page and Shapiro look for "congruence between changes in policy and changes in opinion" and assume that "normative concepts of democracy" would mandate something close to "direct democracy" (Page and Shapiro 1983). Stimson, Mackuen, and Erikson ask "whether the national system is efficient in turning popular sentiment into policy" (Stimson *et al.* 1995). These studies, and many more like them, presume a principle close to the one that Bartels articulates clearly: "The appeal of representative democracy hinges on the responsiveness of elected politicians to the preferences and interests of their constituents" (Bartels 1991). Occasionally the notion of responsiveness is examined in more depth (Manin 1997; Manin *et al.* 1999), but most of the political science literature simply presumes that the purpose of representative government is to be an instrument of the popular will.

The author would like to thank the following people for their comments and suggestions on previous versions of this chapter: Costin Alamariu, Onur Bakiner, John Ferejohn, Hélène Landemore, Karuna Mantena, David Mayhew, Paulina Ochoa Espejo, Pasquale Pasquino, Melissa Schwartzberg, Annie Stilz, Susan Stokes, Elisabeth Wood, the members of the Brown University Political Philosophy Colloquium, and the participants at the conference on "Representation and Popular Rule" at Yale University, fall 2006.

In this chapter I do not deny the importance of responsive government; Robert Dahl is surely right to suggest that the notion of responsiveness is central to any understanding of modern democracy (Dahl 1971). But the relationship between representative government and popular sovereignty is more complicated than an emphasis on responsiveness alone would suggest. In this chapter I want to indicate the nature of the problem and put forward a view of the purpose of representative government that is quite different from one that prioritizes responsiveness, a view drawn largely from two of the early theorists of representative government in France and the United States, Benjamin Constant and James Madison. At the end of the chapter I will briefly suggest the sorts of empirical research questions that might be investigated in light of this broader view of representative government.

The broader view that emerges from considering these thinkers is, in summary, this: a chief purpose of representative government is *to multiply and challenge governmental claims to represent the people*. This goal is quite different from asking the government as a whole to represent the popular will as it can be found through any particular vote or poll. It is also different from the goal of asking it to represent the popular will as it could be imagined to emerge from a process of deliberation or from an independent analysis of the public interest. In asking instead for a government to multiply and challenge representative claims, representative government aims (on this view) to provoke debate about precisely what the popular will is and thereby to prevent any one interpretation of the popular will from claiming final authority. It aims to foster and institutionalize popular impatience with our rulers, to both fuel and channel popular grievances against those in power. For conceptual reasons to be mentioned later, it is always possible to claim that a government is not fully or adequately representative. Representative government attempts to capitalize on this fact. By trying to insure that there are always competing claims to represent the people present in government at the same time, it makes any particular claim to fully represent the people implausible, and it helps to combat the use of such claims to justify the concentration of power. Counterintuitive as it sounds, a fundamental purpose of representative government, as Constant and Madison saw it, is to *oppose* popular sovereignty in the sense that it is usually understood – to undermine the idea that government can adequately represent the people.

To avoid misunderstanding, let me make one point clear at the outset: the suspicion of government efforts to turn popular sovereignty into policy that lies at the heart of this conception of representative government does not rest on a belief that the public is incompetent, unintelligent, or lacking in virtue. It does not even rest on the idea that public opinion must be, in Madison's words, "refined and enlarged"; it does not begin from a sense that public sentiment must be filtered through the minds of representatives or through a deliberative process before being allowed access to political power. There may be some validity to these ideas. Perhaps representatives sometimes are, by virtue of their competence or their deliberations or the influence of their office, better decision-makers than the people themselves. But this aristocratic point is not at all the consideration that lies behind the argument for representative government that I want to examine here. Too often, it is thought that such doubts about the capacities of ordinary citizens are the only reasons that one might have (aside from the practical impediments to gathering large groups) for preferring representative government to direct democracy. The aim of this chapter is to suggest that there are other reasons, more fundamentally democratic reasons, for creating a form of government that always remains at some distance from public opinion, and whose claim to represent that opinion can never be made fully convincing.

The aristocratic argument against popular sovereignty and direct democracy is often traced to Edmund Burke, whose suspicion of popular politics can be seen in his famous skepticism about the French Revolution and whose statement to his own constituents has become the emblematic articulation of the view that representatives should use their own judgment rather than merely echoing the opinions of their constituents (Burke 2000, 2003). The view to which I want to draw attention is not drawn from Burke. It is instead drawn from Burke's enemies and critics – from Rousseau, whose writings helped to inspire the French Revolution, and from Benjamin Constant, who defended that Revolution against Burke's attack. Constant is often portrayed as a critic of Rousseau's, since he opposed the notion of popular sovereignty associated with Rousseau. And since Constant was one of the first writers in any language to use the word "liberal" in politics, and one of the first to outline a full account of liberal, representative government, his relation to Rousseau is viewed as emblematic of liberalism's relation to democracy: liberalism, because of its support for representative rather than direct democracy, is often viewed as fundamentally undemocratic. The argument that I want to suggest here draws the democratic Rousseau and the liberal Constant much closer to one another, and so suggests that the phrase we use to describe our own form of government, "liberal democracy," is not in fact an oxymoron. It is true that liberals such as Constant are suspicious of efforts to institutionalize popular sovereignty directly. But it turns out that on this point Constant was merely following Rousseau. If we can understand Rousseau's reason for harboring this suspicion, we will come closer to seeing the democratic argument for this liberal position.

I.   Rousseau on popular sovereignty

None of the canonical political theorists defended the sovereignty of the people more insistently than Rousseau did. With the concept of the general will he sought to capture the intuition that all citizens had to be regarded as equal, that no one could impose his or her views on the rest, and that the only legitimate source of authority in politics was the vote of the people as a whole, where every individual had an equally weighted vote. He thought that people's authority could not be transferred or alienated, even if the people wished it; nor could it be represented. Institutions that claimed to hold the people's sovereignty for them were, he wrote, an inheritance from the feudal past and signs of political corruption. In a healthy polity citizens would fly to the assemblies themselves rather than allowing representatives to do the work of sovereignty for them (Rousseau 1997). On the basis of such statements, political theorists have regarded Rousseau as an inspiration for participatory democracy, and populist politicians since Robespierre have quoted from Rousseau's *Social Contract* to advance their cause.

But the truth is that Rousseau, in spite of his radically democratic understanding of sovereignty, did not advocate any form of direct democratic government in the *Social Contract*. In fact he warned against democracy: "If there were a people of Gods, it would govern itself democratically. Such a perfect government is not suited to men," he wrote. And further:

In the strict sense of the term, a genuine Democracy never has existed, and never will exist. It is against the natural order that the greater number govern and the smaller number be governed. It is unimaginable that the people remain constantly assembled to attend to public affairs, and it is readily evident that it could not establish commissions to do so without the form of administration changing. (ibid.: 3.4)

This passage might make it sound as if Rousseau's primary reason for warning against direct democratic government was practical. Later in the book, however, he explicitly argued against the view that in large modern states it is impossible for the people to gather together and vote on important questions. He pointed out that Rome, no small polity, routinely asked citizens to vote directly on matters of importance, and he insisted that such regular meetings of the citizenry could be held in modern times as well (ibid.: 3.12). Whether he was right does not matter.

The point is that his reason for opposing direct democratic government was not simply that it was impracticable to gather all the citizens in a large state together.

Rousseau's deeper reason rested on a theoretical distinction that he regarded as crucial, a distinction to which he worried his readers would not pay enough attention. This was the distinction between *legislation* and *execution*. The legislative power was analogous to the faculty of the will in an individual person; it was the power to decide what to do, and it was the power that the *sovereign* had the authority to wield. The executive power, on the other hand, was analogous to the physical power of the individual; it carried out the decisions of the sovereign will and applied them to particular situations. This was the power that *government* wielded. The key point about these two powers, according to Rousseau, was that they had to be kept distinct from one another in a polity. The reason was that the sovereign will had to remain *general* in order to retain its unique legitimacy. Only legislative acts that were general in scope could be viewed as equally touching all citizens. And only the fact that the general will touched all citizens equally made it compatible with the freedom of all citizens. For if submitting to the general will meant submitting to the rule of *particular* other people, it would seem to require giving up one's freedom. Democratic sovereignty gained its special claim to legitimacy from the fact that it did not require this, the fact that, as Rousseau put it, "each, by giving himself to all, gives himself to no one" (ibid.: 1.6). If submitting to the sovereign general will was different from submitting to a ruler, as Rousseau insisted it was – if it was more democratic and more compatible with freedom – that was only because the sovereign could not mandate anything that was not general enough to affect all citizens equally. But acts of government were *necessarily* particular. They affected different people in different ways, and they reflected particular officials' judgments about particular issues. Therefore, as soon as a sovereign power engaged in executive acts of government, it would lose its claim to be "no one" and would become someone in particular, a ruler with distinct goals and interests. This meant that the sovereign could not govern. Only by remaining separate from most acts of government could the sovereign popular will maintain its general character and thus preserve its unique democratic legitimacy. *Usurpation* was Rousseau's name for the confusion of sovereignty and government; it occurred whenever the government claimed the authority that rightfully belonged to the sovereign. According to Rousseau, usurpation could be minimized and delayed, but it was difficult, if not impossible, to avoid; with time, it would eventually bring the downfall of all governments, leading to tyranny or despotism (ibid.: 3.10).

The problem with direct *democratic* government was that it asked the same people to act as both sovereign and government. In theory one person could play both roles without mixing them, but in practice it would be difficult to keep the two roles separate in one's mind. The people, while they were acting as a government, would tend to claim sovereign authority for their actions. And we might think, why not? The people themselves were, after all, the sovereign; if the people in their capacity as governors were usurping the authority of the sovereign, they were only usurping that authority from themselves. But Rousseau would insist that we consider this case more carefully: the party doing the usurping is "the people" acting in pursuit of particular interests or considerations. The party whose authority is being usurped is "the people" acting according to the general will. Rousseau's argument for the absolute sovereignty of the democratic people applies only to the latter version of "the people." If this sovereign authority is replaced by a people acting instead according to particular interests – either private interests or the interests of government as a particular body in society – then its legitimacy disappears. Thus, to say that a direct democracy has usurped the sovereign authority of the people is another way of saying that the people have become corrupted by private concerns, that they are no longer exercising their will in a way that is general enough to be democratically legitimate. In the chapter on democracy Rousseau therefore articulated his reason for being suspicious of direct democratic government in this way:

It is not good that he who makes the laws execute them, nor that the body of the people turn its attention away from general considerations, to devote it to particular objects. Nothing is more dangerous than the influence of private interests on public affairs, and abuse of the laws by Government is a lesser evil than the corruption of the Lawgiver [the sovereign], which is the inevitable consequence of particular considerations. (ibid.: 3.4)

Of course we might disagree with Rousseau's view that a popular will is only legitimately sovereign if it has a general or "uncorrupted" character. Then we would face the formidable task of explaining why a mere tally of votes should have any particular moral legitimacy; why accepting a majority vote as legitimate is not simply an example of might making right. Perhaps there are non-Rousseauian ways to make the case for democratic sovereignty, but this is beyond the scope of this chapter. Here, I assume that Rousseau's argument for popular sovereignty is powerful, and I ask why that line of reasoning does not also make the case for direct democratic government. Rousseau's reason was that usurpation was particularly likely in democratic governments, and that usurpation destroyed the conditions under which a people's will could rightfully be called sovereign. Therefore, even though Rousseau claimed that "the legislative power belongs to the people and can belong only to it," he just as firmly insisted that the executive power "cannot belong to the generality [of the people] in its Legislative or Sovereign capacity" (ibid.: 3.1). His theory of sovereignty was democratic but his theory of government was not.

Direct democracies were not the only governments that Rousseau thought were likely to fall into usurpation, but they were especially ill-equipped to resist the impulse because they include no institutional separation of the legislative and executive roles. In other forms of government, the people acting as sovereign could check or slow the process of usurpation by expressing its judgment about the actions of the government. The most important practical recommendation of Book 3 of the *Social Contract* was that every form of government should be subject to periodic referenda in which all citizens could vote on two questions: whether the present form of government should continue, and whether the present office-holders should continue in office (ibid.: 3.12–14, 18). It is clear enough how this would work in an elective aristocracy: the people as a whole would vote on whether the few of them who had governmental offices should retain power. But in a direct democracy the people as a whole (as sovereign) would have to render judgment on themselves, the same people as a whole (as government). The problem is not that this is conceptually impossible; Rousseau mentioned that the British House of Commons sometimes transformed itself into a committee of the whole to discuss a matter and then transformed back into itself to hear the recommendations of the committee, so the same group of individuals performed two distinct roles (ibid.: 3.17). But Rousseau did not think such an arrangement was to be recommended if one wanted to prevent, or at least slow, the corruption of the people and the usurpation of its sovereign authority. The periodic referenda that he recommended to preserve the sovereignty of the people would work best if the people voting in them were not evaluating their own performance. Direct democratic government required every citizen to be judge in his own case, dividing himself into sovereign citizen and governing citizen. Rousseau suggested that usurpation was more easily avoided or delayed if this division were institutionalized in a distinction between the people and its government. Strikingly, he suggested that the sovereign people's *distance* from the particular work of governing was precisely what enabled it to protect its own sovereignty.

Rousseau's famous opposition to "representation" must be understood in light of what has just been discussed. The relationship between sovereign and government was not one of "representation," as he most often used the term. Government did *not* represent the people in the sense of bearing their sovereign authority. Government officials held their power by "nothing but a commission, an office in which they, as mere officers of the Sovereign, exercise in its name the power it has vested in them, and which it can limit, modify, and resume" (ibid.: 3.1). Sovereign authority always remained with the people and could not be transferred to government; any effort by the governors to claim sovereign authority for themselves, by saying that they represented the people, was nothing other than a form of usurpation.[1] The key point – and the counterintuitive one – was that the distinction between sovereign and government, and the distance that it recommended between the people and the government, was wholly consistent with (and was in fact a consequence of) the impossibility of "representation" in Rousseau's understanding of the word. In his terms, efforts to "represent" the sovereign people were efforts to usurp their authority.

Popular sovereignty in Rousseau thus functioned not only in a positive sense, as a way of thinking about what basic law the people might actively authorize and legislate, but also – more fundamentally – in a negative sense (Pasquino 2007). The negative function of popular sovereignty is to remind us that governing institutions and officers are *not* sovereign. Popular sovereignty understood in this way offers an argument to use against would-be usurpers. The statement that "the people" and *only* "the people" is sovereign is, precisely because of its abstract generality, a rebuttal of any claim that a particular official or assembly might make to fully represent or embody the popular will. This negative function of popular sovereignty is itself institutionalized in the regular referenda through which the people can reject the government and government officials. While Rousseau opposed "representation," the recommendations that he made about government were not so different than those at the heart of our practice of representative democracy: he suggested that governmental functions should be delegated and that periodic popular elections should be held to judge the performance of the delegates.

---

[1] Rousseau did say that acts of the government should be presumed to be consonant with the sovereign general will so long as there was an opportunity for the sovereign to voice opposition and it did not do so (ibid.: 2.1). But if the people did make its sovereign will known, no governmental authority had any standing at all to contest that will: "The instant the People is legitimately assembled as a Sovereign body, all jurisdiction of the Government ceases, the executive power is suspended, and the person of the last Citizen is as sacred and inviolable as that of the first Magistrate; because where the Represented is, there is no longer a Representative" (ibid.: 3.14). In this passage Rousseau slipped into using the language of representation to describe the relation of government to sovereign, but the general point is clear: sovereign authority always remains with the people and is never taken over by their governors.

The most significant differences between what Rousseau suggested and the basic structure of our liberal democracies are (a) that our regular elections ask only the second of the two questions that Rousseau thought should be put to the sovereign people – we ask whether office-holders should be changed, but not whether the offices themselves, the constitutional framework of government, should be changed; (b) that Rousseau did not envision the role of political parties; and (c) that Rousseau did not recommend the elaborate institutional checks and balances that we have, such as separation of powers and federalism. These differences are important, and so I do not claim that Rousseau had a modern theory of representative government. But he did prefer an indirect system of government to a more direct form of democracy, and he did so for democratic reasons. His suspicion of governmental claims to represent the popular will arose from his desire to protect the sovereignty of the people against potential usurpers. Many of the institutional arrangements promoted by theorists after the democratic revolutions in France and America can plausibly be viewed, I think, as aiming to do the same thing.

II.   Liberal democracy

Benjamin Constant, after having watched the course of the French Revolution from its hopeful beginnings through the Terror and eventually to Napoleon's *coup d'état*, argued that the remedies for usurpation found in Book 3 of the *Social Contract* had been wholly ineffective. In fact, Constant thought, Rousseau's writings had been used as a justification for new and more pernicious forms of despotism by politicians who claimed to act in the name of the people. Rousseau had meant to give sovereignty to the people, but politicians had quickly found that they could arrogate that sovereignty to themselves precisely by claiming to represent it, just as Rousseau had feared they would.

Constant thus began his major work on liberal politics, *Principles of Politics Applicable to All Representative Governments*, with a chapter on popular sovereignty in which he repudiated part – but only part – of Rousseau's thought. He insisted, against Rousseau, that there was no such thing as *absolute* sovereignty, not even if it was placed in the hands of the people themselves. "When you establish that the sovereignty of the people is unlimited, you create and toss at random into human society a degree of power which is too large in itself, and which is bound to constitute an evil, in whatever hands it is placed ... There are weights too heavy for the hand of man," he wrote (Constant 1988). To limit sovereignty he asserted that there was "a part of human existence which by necessity remains individual and independent, and which is, by right, outside any social competence" (ibid.). These parts of human existence were protected by rights, and no government that interfered with them was legitimate, no matter on what grounds it did so. Thus Constant moved directly from his criticism of Rousseau to the fundamental commitments of liberalism and to the notion of limited government.

Beneath this disagreement with Rousseau about whether popular sovereignty was absolute, however, lay a more fundamental agreement with him. Constant did not dispute the idea that popular sovereignty was the only rightful source of political authority. In fact, he made the argument even more succinctly than Rousseau had, insisting that the only alternative to popular sovereignty was force, which was clearly illegitimate. What Constant feared was not the idea of giving sovereignty to the people, but the practical implication that particular individuals or assemblies would claim the right to exercise that sovereignty on behalf of the people. He acknowledged that Rousseau had feared precisely the same thing:

Rousseau himself was appalled by [the] consequences [of his theory]. Horror-struck at the immense social power which he had thus created, he did not know into whose hands to commit such monstrous force, and he could find no other protection against the danger inseparable from such sovereignty, than an expedient which made its exercise impossible. He declared that sovereignty could not be alienated, delegated or represented. This was equivalent to declaring, in other words, that it could not be exercised. It meant in practice destroying the principle which he had just proclaimed. (ibid.)

Constant's difference with Rousseau was therefore more one of strategy than one of ultimate intention. He thought that Rousseau's distinction between sovereignty and government, and the related claim that sovereignty could not be represented, were arguments that were too abstract to be successful in preventing governors from trying to usurp sovereign authority. Once someone introduced a justification of absolute sovereignty into the political universe, no set of arguments, no matter how sophisticated, would succeed in preventing political actors from trying to use that justification to support their own power. Sovereignty and government could not be kept distinct (Constant 2003). The abstract idea of a sovereign people tended to become concrete in the form of demagogues claiming to rule in the name of the people. Popular leaders became aspiring tyrants. In the first version of *Principles* he described this process in a striking passage. Whenever the government wants to grab power, he wrote, it quotes the imprescribable prerogative of the whole society ... The government can do nothing, it says, but the nation can do everything. And soon the nation speaks. By this I mean that a few men, either low types or madmen, or hirelings, or men consumed with remorse, or terror-struck, set themselves up as its instruments at the same time as they silence it, and proclaim its omnipotence at the same time as they menace it. In this way, by an easy and swift maneuver, the government seizes the real and terrible power previously regarded as the abstract right of the whole society. (ibid.)

Constant and Rousseau were thus united in their worry about government misuse of the language of popular sovereignty. Constant, of course, had the advantage of hindsight, having seen not only Robespierre use this language but also, later, Napoleon, whose particular form of despotism legitimated itself through elections and democratic justifications. Constant devoted another work exclusively to describing Napoleon's democratically tinged despotism, and the second term in the title he chose for that work, "Conquest and Usurpation," echoed Rousseau's language of "usurpation" (Constant 1988).

The real difference between Rousseau and Constant lay in their views of how best to combat the danger that usurpation posed. The philosophical part of Constant's solution, as we have seen, was simply to deny that sovereignty could ever be absolute, to insist that the individual should be afforded rights with which no authority could rightfully interfere. This part of his solution is difficult to say much about, because Constant was not clear about the grounding of these rights. But there is also another part of his solution, the part that he wrote much more about, which focused on institutional design. Constant's specific proposals, which varied over time, demonstrate an inability to settle on one best means of carrying out his ideas. Early in his career he seems to have been more republican, while later he embraced the idea of a constitutional monarchy. But what lay beneath all of his different institutional proposals was a fundamental and unchanging desire to find ways of institutionalizing resistance to centralizing and usurping authority. This is true even of his later arguments on behalf of a constitutional monarchy. He justified a monarch by arguing that it could be made into a "neutral" power that could check and keep in place the various "active" powers of government. When he defended the monarch's power to dissolve representative assemblies, he claimed that it was a means of checking the assembly. Why did the assembly need checking? It is important not to misinterpret his point here (Holmes 1984). His worry about the assembly was not that the people itself would act tyrannically through it. Unlike later liberals such as Alexis de Tocqueville and John Stuart Mill, he was not preoccupied with the danger that the people themselves would become a tyrannical majority. Instead he suggested that it was the *representatives* who often became dangerous once they were separated from the people: "An assembly, the power of which is unlimited, is more dangerous than the people" (Constant 1988). When he supported a monarch's right to dissolve an assembly, he viewed this monarchical right as a way of defending the people against their own representatives: "The dissolution of assemblies is by no means, as some have argued, an insult to the rights of the people" (ibid.). On his plan, the monarch could not replace the representatives' policy with his own will, but could only send the matter back for consideration by the next group of representatives to be elected. In exercising this power, the monarch was contesting the claim of the current representatives to be adequately representing the popular will. A very similar argument had been used to justify the monarch's "suspensive" veto during the Revolution. Even Constant's support for constitutional monarchy, then, has a democratic justification: it was part of an institutional plan to insure that no governmental power could advance a claim to act in the name of the people without being subject to challenge from another governmental power capable of making the same claim. If usurpation could not be avoided, the best that could be done was to multiply the sites of usurpation and set them against one another.

That Constant was not worried about the people so much as about their representatives can also be seen in the fact that he opposed the Abbé Sieyès's system of indirect election for representatives. Sieyès had set up an elaborate set of electoral colleges to filter public opinion in the course of selecting delegates. Constant opposed the system and favored replacing the electoral colleges with direct elections (ibid.). And in the earlier, more theoretical version of *Principles*, he included an entire chapter devoted to arguing against the view that representatives, or those in government, were better suited to rule than the people themselves. The people who say that "light has to come from elevated places" may be right when speaking of uncivilized societies, he wrote, but their argument is wholly out of place in modern civilized societies with an educated class of any significant size. It was a mistake, he thought, to "attribute to governments the superiority of enlightenment": "We can reply to those who want to subject the intelligence of the many to that of the few what a famous Roman said to his son when the latter proposed to take a town, with the sacrifice of three hundred soldiers. Would you care to be one of this three hundred?" (Constant 2003).

Thus it is a serious misunderstanding of Constant's liberalism to regard his suspicion of government efforts to directly enact popular sovereignty as a suspicion of the people itself. Far from favoring the rule of elites, he was suspicious of those who claimed to represent the people, those who used the language of popular sovereignty to justify their own rule. His targets were not the people as a whole but the individuals such as Robespierre and Bonaparte who had usurped the people's authority.

If we turn to Constant's counterparts in the United States – those theorists who had framed the Constitution in the aftermath of the American Revolution – we find that many of them had had concerns similar to the ones that Constant voiced. James Madison, for example, harbored a similar wariness about the danger of popular demagogues, especially in light of activity in the state legislatures trying to respond to the post-revolutionary debt crisis. And, like Constant, Madison thought the solution to this problem was not to allow any one part of government to become the sole institutional locus of popular sovereignty. Too often, Madison's defense of representative government is reduced to his famous remark in *Federalist* 10 (Hamilton *et al.* 2003) about the need to "refine and enlarge" public opinion. But this consideration does not explain his stance on many of the provisions in the Constitution. The truth is that he opposed giving sovereign authority even to the most "refined" version of public opinion. He did not, for instance, think that the Senate should have conclusive authority over the House of Representatives, even though he thought that the quality of deliberations would be higher there. Instead, he favored having two separate institutional efforts to represent the popular will present in government at once. He also favored staggering elections in the Senate, so that the assembly would contain members who were elected at different times, and who thus reflected different snapshots of the popular will taken at different times. Each group of elected officials – each chamber of Congress, the winners from each election cycle – has a plausible case to make that they represent the popular will, and yet they may often disagree. What this means is that no group of representatives can plausibly insist that they are the only representation of the popular will; none can claim popular sovereignty without their claim being contested by others with at least as plausible a claim (Ackerman 1991). Madison's position cannot be captured by saying that he feared the legislature or the people would become too powerful, because in the 1790s his worries were centered on the executive and he turned to popular electoral politics as a remedy (Ferejohn 2003). The common thread in his various political positions over the years was not an opposition to popular politics or the legislature's representation of the people, but a determination to resist allowing any one part of government, legislature or executive, to claim sovereignty for itself.

Nor was Madison the only one of the American founders to take a position similar to the one we have seen in Constant. Alexander Hamilton's defense of the Supreme Court's power of judicial review in *Federalist* 78 uses an argument much like the one that Constant would use to support a constitutional monarch's right to dissolve the legislative assembly. Just as Constant said that the monarch should be able to appeal over the heads of the representatives to the people themselves, Hamilton suggested that the Supreme Court's ability to strike down legislation was designed to prevent "legislative encroachments" and to insure that "the intention of the people" was preferred to "the intention of their agents" (Hamilton *et al.* 2003). And even on the other side of the political spectrum we find Thomas Jefferson sometimes making similar arguments. Jefferson, the American founder closest to Rousseau in spirit, argued in his *Notes on the State of Virginia* that a concentration of power was despotic even if it was found in the most representative branch, the legislature. In a passage strikingly similar to what can be found in Constant's writings, Jefferson argued that despotism arose not from the fact that power was given to one person rather than many, but from the fact that it was concentrated in one institution, unchecked by others:

It will be no alleviation [to despotism], that these powers will be exercised by a plurality of hands, and not by a single one. One hundred and seventy-three despots would surely be as oppressive as one. Let those who doubt it, turn their eyes on the republic of Venice. As little will it avail us, that they are chosen by ourselves. An *elective despotism* was not the government we fought for. (Jefferson 1984)

Jefferson went on to advocate as a solution to this problem the separation of powers and a system of checks and balances, which is why Madison cited this passage at length in *Federalist* 48 when defending the proposed Constitution. Across the political spectrum at the American founding, then, the theorists of representative government shared the suspicion of representatives that Constant would make central to his writings.

Of course the authors of the Constitution did not respond to this fear by looking for an alternative to representation. They also did not take Rousseau's advice to institute regular referenda on the form of government as a whole. Jefferson did propose something in this spirit in the form of new constitutional conventions every generation, but Madison and the framers rejected it for reasons set out in *Federalist* 49. Instead they sought to deal with the problem of usurpation by *multiplying* the points of representation within government and creating a contest between them. It has been remarked that what distinguishes the system of representative government instantiated in the Constitution from the "mixed regime" described in classical sources such as Polybius is that in our system every branch is ultimately responsible to the people. In the classical mixed regime, the people were represented by one of the powers, but the other powers were supposed to represent the nobles or the rich or other orders of society. In insisting that all three branches, and also all levels of government, local, state and federal, are in some sense representations of "the people," the American system aims to multiply the plausible claims to represent the popular will. In Rousseau's language, it multiplies the sites of usurpation. This multiplication in turn challenges any particular branch's claim that its representation is determinative. Perhaps, if all three branches and all levels of government come to reflect a similar sentiment over a sustained period of time, then the government as a whole can be said to represent the popular will in a particularly authoritative way (Ackerman 1991). But at least in the ordinary course of politics such agreement is not to be expected or even hoped for. In fact, the system seems designed in part to resist registering any unified representation of the popular will. By striving to have multiple representations of the popular will present in government at the same time, the system aims to encourage contestation about what precisely it is that the people want. There is plenty of anecdotal evidence, at least, that the system achieves this goal; no piece of rhetoric is more omnipresent in American politics than the politician's claim to represent what the American people want or need – a claim made on every side of every issue by every sort of politician.

From this perspective the various debates among political theorists and philosophers about what exactly political representation is, and the debates among political scientists about what sorts of institutions best reflect the will of the people, can be seen in a different light. These debates are precisely the kind that the system of representative government is designed to encourage and accommodate. Those who claim with Madison that public opinion must be refined and enlarged, such as contemporary proponents of deliberative democracy, will find within representative government a place for their views; but so will those who argue primarily for the representation of special interests or of unrefined, populist manifestations of public opinion. What no party will find sympathy for in the theory of representative government that I am drawing out here is the idea that its particular interpretation of public opinion should be the final or authoritative interpretation. By locating the source of sovereignty in an abstract entity, "the people," whose voice can be heard only through the various interpretations of its many spokespeople, representative government instigates constant debate about what the popular will actually is. It calls for "interpretive representation" of the kind that Philip Pettit describes in his contribution to this volume, but it does not allow Rawlsian public reason or any other theory to dictate one definitive interpretation. The constant contestation over how the popular will should be interpreted gives political life in liberal democracies much of its vitality and energy. It drives politicians to explore different interpretations and to try to make their interpretations persuasive; representative government understood in this way aims to foster a politics of persuasion (Garsten 2006). It also fuels the media, which helps to multiply and amplify different iterations of the popular will, and which investigates any claim to represent that will and exposes its problems. It is no accident that the proponents of this vision of representative democracy, Constant and Madison, were also great spokesmen for the importance of a free press (Constant 1988; Madison 1888).

The view of representative government that I am describing takes advantage of a peculiar feature of the concept of representation itself. As Hanna Pitkin and others have noticed, the concept of representation seems to be structured in a way that makes its complete realization impossible. A representation that is identical to the represented object in every way is nothing other than the object itself, which is therefore not re-presented but simply *present*. Representation implies the absence of what is being represented (Pitkin 1967). Thus, political representation of the sovereign people implies that the people are not actually present themselves in government. The impossibility of fully and completely representing the people's will – the impossibility that Rousseau highlighted – is therefore integral to the concept of representation itself. Representation properly understood requires a distinction between representatives and the people. This is the distinction that demagogues aim to obscure whenever they claim to fully represent the people; it is the distinction that representative government, with its indirectness, aims to preserve; and it is the distinction that Rousseau, with his warnings about mixing sovereignty and government, wanted to protect. In this sense we can say that both Rousseau and the theorists of liberal representative government were responding to a feature inherent in the concept of representation itself. Liberal democratic governments – representative governments – are those that recognize the conceptual impossibility of adequately representing the popular will.

Of course this is not the only interpretation of representative government that could be drawn from the history of political thought. There is a competing story that can be traced from Chapter 16 of Hobbes's *Leviathan*, through Sieyès, the architect of the first National Assembly during the Revolution in France, and straight through to a commonly invoked understanding of the state today. In this alternate story, the sovereign power of the people is inert unless it is given coherence and agency by being represented in one unified authority – a single ruler, a single assembly, or a government as a whole understood as having the mission of responding to one representative will. Hobbes is the crucial starting point for this story: he argued that a multitude could only be considered as a *people*, in the sense of being one entity capable of action, if it was represented in a single sovereign: "For it is the *Unity* of the Representer, not the *Unity* of the Represented, that maketh the Person One" (Hobbes 1996). And Sieyès, in spite of his many blueprints for institutions that would divide the government in various ways, insisted with Hobbes that a people or "nation" could not be a coherent entity except through a single representation. He opposed any effort to appeal past the representatives to the people themselves, viewing the suspensive royal veto, for example, as a compromise on the principle of representation; he insisted that the National Assembly was "the sole authorized interpreter of the general will" (Sieyès 1996). From the perspective outlined earlier, we might say that when the representatives of the Third Estate, inspired by Sieyès, gave themselves the name of "National Assembly" and then proceeded to govern, they thereby joined the people (the Nation) with the government (the State) in just the manner that Rousseau had warned against. Robespierre would, once in government, find himself unable to resist a similar act of usurpation. Insofar as we continue to think of ourselves as living in "nation-states" and ask only that the state reflect our will as accurately as possible, we treat our government as a more complex version of the National Assembly.[2] If we accept this view of our governments, we implicitly accept the usurpation reflected in the joining of nation and state. We may insist that the representative nation-state nevertheless respects popular sovereignty, but we can do so only by adopting a view of popular sovereignty closer to the account put forth by Hobbes and Sieyès than to the democratic account we saw in Rousseau.

Thus there are at least two conceptions of representative government that might guide our thinking. One views representative government as a "liberal democracy" in the sense that I have tried to invoke by joining the democratic Rousseau with the liberal Constant; the other views this form of government as a "nation-state" in the way just described. It is true that liberal democracies are nation-states, and therefore that some degree of usurpation is all but inevitable (as Rousseau himself acknowledged). Still, the emphasis in the two views is quite different. The first view of representative government accents the negative function of popular sovereignty and tries to multiply usurpations so as to weaken them,

---

[2] If the term "nation" is understood precisely as Sieyès understood it, i.e. as a state, then the phrase "nation-state" becomes a tautology, as Istvan Hont argues (Hont 2005).

while the second view pursues a governmental representation of popular sovereignty and does not regard usurpation as a threat.

Today there are a host of ideas about where the authoritative version of the popular will might lie. Some suggest that it can be found in a mandate issued by a particular election or poll; others argue that it resides in the Constitution as interpreted by the Supreme Court. Some argue that it can be found whenever a particular consensus emerges about certain issues and makes its way through various governmental institutions and procedures over a sustained period of time (Ackerman 1991). Still others look for the authoritative popular will in the views that a people might express after being allowed to deliberate with adequate information and fair procedures (Fishkin 1991). These are all plausible arguments about where the popular will might be expressed in our system of representative government. But insofar as they imply that one expression of the popular will should be sovereign, they all implicitly adopt the second view of representative government described above; they all view the government as a nation-state trying to enact a singularly authoritative interpretation of the popular will, rather than as a liberal democracy trying to encourage the multiplication and contestation of claims to represent the people.

III.   Research questions

In addition to asking which vision of representative government seems most attractive, scholars should also ask which vision best reflects what is actually going on in our system. What sort of empirical research questions could be formulated, in light of the issues raised here? We already have research designed to test how responsive government as a whole, or particular parts of it, is to public sentiment, and this line of investigation should surely continue. But we could also try to test the extent to which our system of representative government does what I have suggested early liberal theorists wanted it to do: multiply and challenge governmental efforts to represent the popular will. The institutional features of the US system that I mentioned in this regard – staggered elections with overlapping terms of office, the different chambers of Congress and branches of government, and so on – are familiar features of the constitutional system of "checks and balances" often mentioned in textbook accounts of government. These textbook structural features of constitutional government deserve serious consideration by political scientists (Manin et al. 1999). Work finding that the Senate and House do not differ much on measures of responsiveness (Stimson et al. 1995) begins to approach such questions, but does not fully address them. The question is not just how responsive these institutions are to public opinion on a uniform scale of responsiveness, but whether they are responding *differently* to the same public opinion. For example, the House and Senate seemed to respond differently to the proposed impeachment of President Clinton. At the time this chapter was written those same chambers were responding differently to President Bush's proposed strategy for the war in Iraq. Yet both houses claim to represent the popular will. Political scientists should investigate what considerations explain these different representations of the popular will. What is it about the different institutions that influences the kinds of claims they make, and the extent to which those claims are accepted by others? To what extent is there in fact a practice of conflict between these institutions? David Mayhew's work on congressional opposition to the president in the United States offers an example of the kind of work that could be done in this vein (Mayhew 2001).

To see whether claims to represent the people are successfully being multiplied and challenged, we would also have to investigate whether one kind of claim, or one institutional source of claims, is consistently winning out, and whether any one institution is effectively being granted final or sovereign authority on many issues and over a long period of time. I do not know what we would find. Some political commentators worry that the growth of the executive threatens this multiplicity, while others would point to the Court's use of judicial review as the real threat. Empirical and historical research could yield insights into such questions. We could also look to see whether there is more diversity among governmental interpretations of the popular will at particular times, and why. How does the multiplication and contestation of claims change in response to stimuli such as wars, economic disturbances, technological innovations, and demographic trends?

Having a research agenda based on this broader understanding of the purpose of representative government would not only provide useful descriptive information, it would also be normatively desirable. As things stand now, if any of the studies of responsiveness mentioned at the beginning of this chapter were to find that a particular institution in government did accurately and reliably "translate" popular sentiment into policy, there would be a strong tendency, I think, to conclude that that institution should have final authority, that it was the legitimate bearer of our sovereignty. If responsiveness is the purpose of representative government and the criterion of its legitimacy, there would be no reason to deny this conclusion. I hope in this chapter to have indicated why it is plausible to think that this conclusion might be wrong, and to think so for democratic reasons. Popular sovereignty can be understood in a negative sense, as Rousseau himself often seems to have understood it.

A government institutionalizes the negative sort of popular sovereignty when it helps us to resist the ever-present temptation to grant final and exclusive authority to the government, no matter how much we approve of its interpretation of popular sentiment at any particular moment. What popular sovereignty as a normative ideal does, on this theory, is ask us to be on the lookout for usurpation and the demagogic appeals that accompany it. To evaluate the health of representative democracy, we should look not only at whether institutions are responding to our opinions, but also at whether the structure of government succeeds in multiplying and challenging claims to represent our opinions. Representative government is working well when no claim to represent the people goes uncontested.

BIBLIOGRAPHY

Ackerman, Bruce A. 1991. *We the People: Foundations*. Cambridge, MA: Belknap Press.
Bartels, Larry M. 1991. "Constituency Opinion and Congressional Policy Making: The Reagan Defense Buildup." *American Political Science Review* 85 (2): 457–74.
Burke, Edmund. 2000. "Speech to the Electors of Bristol," in *On Empire, Liberty and Reform*, ed. D. Bromwich. New Haven, CT: Yale University Press, 50–7.
2003. *Reflections on the Revolution in France*, ed. F. M. Turner and D. M. McMahon. New Haven, CT: Yale University Press.
Constant, Benjamin. 1988. *Political Writings*, ed. B. Fontana. Cambridge: Cambridge University Press.
2003. *Principles of Politics Applicable to All Governments*, trans. D. O'Keeffe, ed. E. Hofmann. Indianapolis, IN: Liberty Fund.
Dahl, Robert Alan. 1971. *Polyarchy: Participation and Opposition*. New Haven, CT: Yale University Press.
Ferejohn, John. 2003. "Madisonian Separation of Powers," in *James Madison: The Theory and Practice of Republican Government*. Stanford, CA: Stanford University Press, 126–55.
Fishkin, James S. 1991. *Democracy and Deliberation: New Directions for Democratic Reform*. New Haven, CT: Yale University Press.
Garsten, Bryan. 2006. *Saving Persuasion: A Defense of Rhetoric and Judgment*. Cambridge, MA: Harvard University Press.
Hamilton, Alexander, James Madison, and John Jay. 2003. *The Federalist Papers*, ed. C. L. Rossiter and C. R. Kesler. New York: Signet Classic.
Hobbes, Thomas. 1996. *Leviathan*, ed. R. Tuck, rev. student edn. Cambridge: Cambridge University Press.
Holmes, Stephen. 1984. *Benjamin Constant and the Making of Modern Liberalism*. New Haven, CT: Yale University Press.
Hont, Istvan. 2005. *Jealousy of Trade: International Competition and the Nation-State in Historical Perspective*. Cambridge, MA: Harvard University Press.
Jefferson, Thomas. 1984. *Notes on the State of Virginia*, ed. M. D. Peterson. New York: Library of America.

Madison, James. 1888. "Virginia Resolutions," in *The Debates in the Several State Conventions on the Adoption of the Federal Constitution as Recommended by the General Convention at Philadelphia in 1787*, ed. J. Elliot. New York: Burt Franklin.

Manin, Bernard. 1997. *The Principles of Representative Government*. New York: Cambridge University Press.

Manin, Bernard, Adam Przeworski, and Susan C. Stokes. 1999. "Introduction," in *Democracy, Accountability, and Representation*, ed. A. Przeworski, S. C. Stokes, and B. Manin. Cambridge: Cambridge University Press.

Mayhew, David. 2001. "Congressional Opposition to the American Presidency: An Inaugural Lecture Delivered before the University of Oxford on 27 November 2000." Oxford: Oxford University Press.

Miller, Warren E., and Donald E. Stokes. 1963. "Constituency Influence in Congress." *American Political Science Review* 57: 45–56.

Page, Benjamin I., and Robert Y. Shapiro. 1983. "The Effects of Public Opinion on Policy." *American Political Science Review* 77 (1): 175–90.

Pasquino, Pasquale. 2007. "Constitution et pouvoir constituant: Le double corps du peuple," in *Sieyès*. Paris: Presses Universitaires de la Sorbonne, 13–24.

Pitkin, Hanna Fenichel. 1967. *The Concept of Representation*. Berkeley: University of California Press.

Rousseau, Jean-Jacques. 1997. *The Social Contract and Other Later Political Writings*, ed. V. Gourevitch. Cambridge: Cambridge University Press.

Sieyès, Emmanuel Joseph. 1996. "Dire de l'abbé Sieyès sur la question du veto royal," in *La Monarchie républicaine: la constitution de 1791*, ed. F. Furet. Paris: Fayard, 406–17.

Stimson, James A., Michael B. Mackuen, and Robert S. Erikson. 1995. "Dynamic Representation." *American Political Science Review* 89 (3): 543–65.

5 Making interest: on representation and democratic legitimacy

Clarissa Rile Hayward

Political representation has no necessary link to democratic legitimacy. As Hanna Pitkin (among others) has argued, there are ways of "making present" in a political sense people who are not literally present that stand at odds with basic democratic principles, such as political equality and inclusiveness in collective norm-making (Pitkin 1967: ch. 2).[1] Representation is often considered a means to promoting legitimacy, however, when those who are subject to the norms representatives make first authorize those who represent them, and then hold them accountable for their choices and their actions. Such specifically democratic forms of representation often are understood to promote legitimacy in government under conditions in which all cannot participate directly in norm-making, if and to the extent that they enable and motivate representatives to track the interests of the represented (Przeworski, Stokes, and Manin 1999: 2).

Call this understanding of the democratic value of representation "the conventional view." Although the conventional view does not provide the only way to understand the link between representation and democratic legitimacy, it provides one important way. In this chapter, I make trouble for the conventional view. In so doing, I join other theorists who have begun the project of rethinking this orthodox understanding of the nature and the value of political representation. David Plotke, for instance, has argued it is not the case that representation is a second-best alternative to direct, participatory democracy: an unfortunate necessity that follows from the complexities of modern political life (Plotke 1997).[2] Bernard

This chapter was first presented at the fall 2006 meeting of the American Political Science Association, the fall 2006 Yale Conference on Representation and Popular Rule, and the spring 2007 Center for Interdisciplinary Law and Policy Studies workshop at Ohio State University's Mortiz College of Law. Thanks to all participants in these sessions, especially Khalilah Brown-Dean and Jenny Mansbridge.

[1] Hobbesian representation, which is characterized by a total lack of responsibility or obligation on the part of the representative, is one example Pitkin (1967) discusses at length.

[2] Participation in representative government is, Plotke claims, itself an important and democratically valuable form of political participation (Plotke 1997).

Manin has challenged the conventional view's implicit assumption that the key institutions of modern political representation – elections – are egalitarian and democratic (Manin 1997). Andrew Rehfeld has challenged the conventional view's tendency to conflate the empirical fact of representation with legitimacy, or with *democratic* representation (Rehfeld 2006).

In what follows, my own contribution to this project will center on the role that interests play in representation. Drawing on constructivist approaches to the study of democratic politics, which stress the endogeneity of political interests to political processes, I will argue that, because the role of government with respect to interests is never simply to track them, but always also to help shape and reshape them, legitimacy requires more than simply "making present" the interests of all. It requires shaping political interests in democracy-promoting ways.

To advance this argument, I begin by considering one of the principal concerns about the conventional view that democratic theorists have articulated in recent years: difficulties posed for it by the problem of structural inequality. After analyzing arguments in favor of what some term "descriptive representation" as a solution to such difficulties (Section I), I turn to the question of the relation between structural inequalities and political interests. Illustrating with the example of racial inequalities in the contemporary United States, I make the case that political decisions and political actions that produce structural inequalities produce corresponding political interests (Section II). Under such conditions, political institutions – electoral constituencies, political jurisdictions, and other institutions of representative democracy – promote equality and inclusiveness in government, not by tracking all interests equally, but by encouraging the formation of new political interests (Section III).

I.   Descriptive representation and political legitimacy

The conventional view, then, provides one way of thinking about the value political representation holds for democratic politics. It provides an account that runs into difficulties, however, in the face of deep and enduring social hierarchies: hierarchies produced by what, in the following discussion, I will refer to as structural inequalities. By "structural inequalities" I mean asymmetries in access to resources and opportunities and in the social capacity to act, which are built into structures such as laws and other institutions.[3] Structural inequalities are political in origin. They are not simply the product of natural differences between individuals or groups, although they are often justified by appeals to allegedly natural differences. And structural inequalities are institution-alized. They are not simply the product of ongoing acts of aggression or discrimination, although they are often accompanied by and rein-forced by such acts. Racial inequalities in the contemporary United States are one example, and the principal example on which I draw in this chapter.

Why do structural inequalities pose a problem for the conventional normative view of representation? The principal reason is that those whom they disadvantage often cannot, by virtue of their positions in the hierarchies structural inequalities define, authorize representatives and/or hold them to account. In some cases, structural inequalities formally or informally exclude those whom they disadvantage from participation in elections. In other cases, although the disadvantaged are not formally or informally excluded, they form numerical minorities in every electoral constituency, or in most. But even when neither condition obtains – when those whom they disadvantage are permitted to vote *and* form a numerical majority in some districts or in the population as a whole – structural inequalities often translate into a lack of access to the organizational and financial resources needed to back candidates, mount successful electoral campaigns, and effectively hold representatives to account.

The result may be a male-dominated legislature in a patriarchal society. It may be a legislature in a racialized society that is comprised mostly, or even entirely, of members of dominant racial groups. It may be mostly, or only, wealthy representatives in a legislature that governs a class-divided society. If the disadvantaged cannot constrain such representatives to "act for" them, or if such representatives do not understand the needs, experiences, and/or perspectives of the disadvantaged (the worry is) rep-resentative institutions will fail the test of democratic legitimacy.[4] Politi-cal representation will ensure only that government tracks the interests of those who occupy privileged positions in extant hierarchies, rather than the interests of all who are governed by the norms representatives make.

---

[3] This definition is similar to that offered by Iris Young (2000: 98), according to whom, "[s]tructural *inequality* consists in the relative constraints some people encounter in their freedom and material well-being as the cumulative effect of the possibilities of their social positions, as compared with others who in their social positions have more options or easier access to benefits."

[4] I borrow the phrase "act for" from Pitkin, for whom it means, roughly, "act in the interests of" (Pitkin 1967: ch. 6).

One intuitively appealing response to this problem, and one which several recent theorists have defended, centers on what Pitkin called "descriptive representation" and what others have termed "the politics of presence" or "self-representation" for the disadvantaged (Pitkin 1967: 81; Dovi 2002; Mansbridge 1999; Phillips 1995; Williams 1998; Young 1990: ch. 6).[5] Stated at its most basic, the argument for descriptive representation is that, in a political society that is both internally divided and hierarchical, people who are disadvantaged by structural inequalities should be represented by people who share their positions of disadvantage. Those who defend descriptive representation make the case for devising institutional means (quotas, for instance, majority–minority electoral districts, and/or various forms of proportional representation) to ensure, or at least to make it highly likely, that people disadvantaged by structural inequalities will be represented by people who share their positions in extant hierarchies: in other words (and to paraphrase Jane Mansbridge), to ensure that "blacks . . . represent blacks, and women . . . represent women" (Mansbridge 1999).

Descriptive representation and advocacy

There are at least two analytically distinct reasons why a democrat might endorse descriptive representation as a remedy for problems posed by structural inequalities. The first centers on the motivations of representatives. If one assumes that people – not excluding people who hold political office – are motivated principally to pursue their interests, then one might regard electoral accountability alone as an insufficient guarantee that those who represent disadvantaged groups will act in ways that advance their constituents' interests. Self-interested representatives, after all, regardless of whom they represent, may stand to gain more by acting against their constituents' interests while in office than they stand to lose by failing to secure their votes at the end of term. For this reason, one might make the case that, in addition to accountability, a further check on representatives' inclinations to pursue their self-interest at the expense of the interests of their constituents is necessary. The interests of representatives, one might argue, should be made to correspond as closely as possible to the interests of the people they represent.

This line of reasoning is at least as old as James Mill's *Encyclopedia Britannica* article, "On Government" (Mill 1825). Here Mill makes the

[5] Pitkin is critical of descriptive representation, which she suggests is most appropriate "in contexts where the purpose of representation is to supply information about something not actually present" (Pitkin 1967: ch. 4, here 81).

case that political elites will be motivated to make laws that serve the interests of those who elect them – as opposed to laws that serve their own interests as individuals, or the corporate interests of the governing elite – if and only if they know that they, too, will be governed by the laws they make (ibid.: 18). It is for this reason that Mill argues for frequent elections and for relatively short terms of office. To be sure, he does not advance an argument for descriptive representation: for the representation *of* the interests of a particular class or subgroup of a political society *by* members of that class or group. Indeed, he does not even think it necessary that members of every class or subgroup be permitted to vote.[6] Still, if one extracts from Mill's essay its elemental logic, it supplies one set of premises from which a democrat might make the case for descriptive representation. If people are motivated to advance their own interests (this logic suggests), and if interests vary systematically with position in social hierarchies, then in a hierarchical society the interests of the disadvantaged are best represented by political elites who share their positionality.

To adopt a view such as this one, it is worth underscoring, is not necessarily to assume a complete homogeneity of interests among members of the relevant structurally disadvantaged political group. Clearly, every group defined by position in hierarchical relations of power (African-Americans, for example, Latinos, women, poor people) is characterized by an internal differentiation of interests, just so long as its members are positioned in multiple power relations. The interests of middle-class and professional African-Americans, to cite one well-known example, depart in non-trivial ways from those of poor and working-class African-Americans, or at least they do with respect to some political issues and some proposed policies.

Still, to the extent that structural inequalities follow group lines (to the extent that residential racial segregation persists at all income levels, for example), and to the extent that important aspects of people's lives – their material well-being, their opportunities to develop their capacities and to

---

[6] Mill does make the case for a relatively broad franchise, on the grounds that representatives will be motivated to serve all interests in the larger society if and only if those interests are shared by the members of "the choosing body" (the electorate). But he is notoriously lax in his application of this claim. No harm is done to the principle of representation, he argues, if women are excluded from voting. No harm is done if people who do not hold property are denied the franchise, or if everyone under the age of forty is denied the vote. In such cases, the interests of those who are excluded from voting, Mill asserts, are "included in the interests of other individuals" who are permitted to vote: their husbands and their fathers, in the case of women and young people, and in the case of the propertyless, their fellow citizens who own property, but only in small amounts (Mill 1825: 21).

achieve their aims and their ends – are shaped by their membership in dis-advantaged groups, their political interests will vary systematically with group membership. African-Americans, regardless of social class, are subjected to racial discrimination in employment, in housing, in interactions with the police, and in other contexts. What is more, due to their historical and contemporary experiences of racial subjugation, they tend to perceive their fates as linked to the fate of their racial group (Dawson 1994). African-Americans therefore tend to use racial group interest as a proxy for individual interest when they are forming and acting upon political preferences (ibid.).

Whenever patterns such as these obtain, a democrat might endorse descriptive representation on the grounds that representatives whose interests overlap substantially with those of their constituents make the best advocates. Melissa Williams (1998: ch. 5) illustrates using the example of civil rights legislation in the United States. If African-Americans are represented mostly or only by whites in debates about, and in collective decision-making processes centered on, civil rights laws, then they are represented by people whose interests are not affected by the proposed legislation in the same ways their interests are. African-American representatives, by contrast, who share their black constituents' positions in power relations constructed around race, make (to borrow Williams's language) more "trustworthy" advocates.

Descriptive representation and deliberation

Alternatively, democrats might endorse descriptive representation on the grounds that representatives whose experiences and perspectives overlap substantially with those of their disadvantaged constituents make the best participants in deliberative processes that are aimed at discovering shared or common interests (Williams 1998: chs. 4–5).[7] Again, the idea that representative institutions can be ordered in ways that promote common interests is hardly new. Political philosophers from Burke to Madison to (J. S.) Mill have conceived interests on a spectrum from the particular to the public, and they have searched for institutional mechanisms to promote the representation of the latter (Burke 1854–6; Madison 1969; Mill 1975). In many instances, these thinkers' motivations have been conservative, in the sense that among their principal aims has been the preservation of status quo hierarchies. For Madison, for instance, "the first object of government" is the protection of the allegedly natural

---

[7] The two reasons are analytically distinct, but not mutually exclusive (Williams 1998: chs. 4 and 5).

bases of those social hierarchies that are constructed around property ownership and wealth. Promoting the public interest – a function which Madison argues representative institutions are uniquely suited to fill – involves controlling the effects of majority factions that have a particular interest in overturning class-based hierarchies (Madison 1969).[8]

Nevertheless, a democrat might take this notion of the representation of public interests, and she might employ it in a more egalitarian fashion. She might argue, for instance, that at least in some cases, people have shared interests in helping to alleviate the adverse effects structural inequalities have on the disadvantaged. If such effects are harmful to the political society as a whole – if they threaten national security or stability, for example, or if they undermine ethical norms or moral principles that are widely endorsed by members of the political society – then a democrat might regard descriptive representation as offering important epistemic advantages. All political actors view collective problems from perspectives that are only partial. In a hierarchical society, the perspectives of the dominant differ systematically from those of the disadvantaged. The latter are best positioned to understand how, and to persuade others that, structural inequalities undermine common interests. Hence, if only those who are privileged by structural inequalities are present in legislatures, and even if some – even if all – representatives are motivated to promote the public good, they may not understand how best to do so (Williams 1998; Mansbridge 1999, 2003; Young 1990, 2000).

Authorization, what is more, is an insufficient guarantee of the effective representation of the disadvantaged in deliberative processes, since much of what representatives do when they deliberate is not, and cannot be, directed by constituents at the moment of electoral choice. Jane Mansbridge offers the example of Carol Mosely-Braun's opposition in 1993 to an amendment to a bill introduced by Jesse Helms that would have extended the United Daughters of the Confederacy's design patent for their insignia, which featured the Confederate flag. Prior to Mosely-Braun's intervention, by Mansbridge's telling, the design patent had not been debated in state or national politics. It had not been discussed in any electoral campaign. It was an issue that Mosely-Braun first brought to the attention of her fellow senators and the public. According to Mansbridge, "[t]he most important reason for her action seems to have been the particular sensibility, created by experience, that led her to notice the Confederate flag and be offended by it" (Mansbridge 1999: 647).

The example illustrates a more general phenomenon, which was discussed by Pitkin and which has been emphasized by others since: the

---

[8] Factions of propertyless people and debtors are two examples Madison cites.

unavoidable autonomy of political representatives. A non-trivial part of what representatives do while in office involves responding to changes that occur in the political environment between elections. Representatives identify collective problems that did not exist and/or that were not on the table at the time of their campaigns. They respond to new conflicts, new crises, new opportunities and possibilities. They develop, evaluate, and debate about new proposals. Political representatives, when they engage in deliberation with one another, engage in debates that cannot be charted or plotted in advance. Hence descriptive representation (one might argue), because it brings to deliberative fora people who share at least some of the relevant experiences and perspectives of the disadvantaged, is crucial for democratic politics under conditions of structural inequality.

II.   The political construction of interests

As should be clear from the above, these two sets of reasons correspond roughly to two approaches to theorizing democratic politics: approaches typically identified as, respectively, "aggregative" and "deliberative" democracy. Because the benefits and the shortcomings of each have been discussed at length elsewhere, I will not rehearse them here (see, e.g., the essays collected in Macedo [1999] and Elster [1998]). Nor will I engage in the kind of careful textual exegesis that would be necessary to explore important distinctions within the bodies of democratic theory that are typically labeled "aggregative" and "deliberative." Instead, my account will be deliberately stylized. Its aim is to point up broad differences in how political theorists might understand the role that interests play, and the role that they should play in democratic politics.

Interests in aggregative and deliberative democratic theory

By the aggregative view, the interests that inform and motivate the choices people make are relatively stable across political interactions. The processes through which interests are formed, interpreted, and articulated are more or less exogenous to this model. The aggregative model assumes, in addition, that the interests that matter the most for politics are typically people's particular interests: what it is that serves their good as individuals and as members of subgroups of their political society, and/or what individuals and group members believe to serve their good (their preferences). Political actors are assumed to pursue their interests even if – and by some accounts especially if – those are at odds with the interests of other individuals and subgroups. Democratic politics is a matter of fairly aggregating conflicting particular interests, in order to arrive at a collective choice that is legitimate, because it is responsive – and equally so – to all whom it affects (see Dahl 1989: chs. 6–9).

For example (and to continue with the case of race in the contemporary United States), because African-Americans are disproportionately concentrated in urban school districts with overcrowded, underfunded, and underperforming public schools, while people constructed as "white" are disproportionately suburban and wealthy, and have disproportionate access to resource-rich, high-performing schools, a theorist of aggregative democracy likely would expect most blacks to act in ways that promote their interests in the improvement of urban education and/or the redistribution of educational resources and opportunities. She would expect most whites, by contrast, to act in ways that promote their interests in keeping resources in their local public schools. The principal advantage of descriptive representation, by this view, is that it would ensure that blacks' particular interests were represented whenever choices about education (or other collective choices that affect them) were made.

As the example makes clear, however, on the aggregative model there are real limits to descriptive representation as a solution to the problem of the chronic underrepresentation of the interests of African-Americans, or for that matter of any subset of a collectivity that forms a numerical minority. If the purpose of descriptive representation is to ensure governmental responsiveness to the interests of all, including those who are disadvantaged by structural inequalities, and if political actors are motivated principally to promote their particular interests, then descriptive representation cannot ensure governmental responsiveness to disadvantaged minorities whose interests vary systematically from those of dominant majority groups. African-Americans are a numerical minority in the US, and in every state of the US. Thus even if they are represented in proportion to their numbers in state and federal legislatures, and even if their representatives advocate effectively for their interests, those representatives themselves will remain in the minority.

Hence the appeal to some theorists of descriptive representation of a more deliberative model of democracy, which assumes that the interests that shape and motivate the political choices people make are relatively fluid over the course of political interactions. The deliberative model assumes, in particular, that people's perceptions of what it is that serves their good can – and that in some non-trivial subset of cases they do – change in response to the reasoned exchange of opinions and arguments. The deliberative model assumes, further, that although people often are motivated to pursue their particular interests, they also can be motivated to pursue common or collective interests, even when such action is at odds with their particular interests as they understand them at the outset of deliberation. Democratic politics, by this view, is not principally a matter of aggregating particular interests. It is also – and from a normative perspective it is most importantly – a matter of encouraging open, inclusive, and egalitarian forms of rational argumentation, with a view to discovering shared or common interests. Representation promotes legitimacy in government, not by tracking *any* interests, but by tracking people's post-deliberative interests, or their interests as they (would) understand them after subjecting them to free, equal, and public rational argumentation (Benhabib 1996; Habermas 1990, 1996; Manin 1987).

In the case of racial disparities in access to educational resources, a deliberative democrat might emphasize the importance of enabling urban blacks to persuade suburban whites that their shared interests in having an educated citizenry, and/or their common interests in promoting the principle of equal opportunity, outweigh whites' particular interests in keeping local schools relatively resource-rich. The principal advantage of descriptive representation, by this view, is that it gives voice to the perspectives and the claims of those who are disadvantaged by extant hierarchies. It thus enables them to persuade their more privileged interlocutors to reconceptualize their political interests and/or to sacrifice their particular interests for the common good.

Again, the example makes clear the limits to descriptive representation as a solution to the problem of the underrepresentation of those who are disadvantaged by structural inequalities. Even if black representatives understand the perspectives of their black constituents, even if they share (some of) their relevant political problems and experiences (if they know what it means to struggle with a failing school system, for example), they will not necessarily be able to persuade the representatives of whites to act in ways that promote educational redistribution. To be sure, the privileged sometimes sacrifice their particular good to advance what they understand to be the shared or the common good. More often than not, however, those who are privileged by extant power relations pursue their particular interests in maintaining their privilege: in paying relatively low taxes for a top-notch public education, to continue with the present example, or in reducing the competition their children will face, down the road, for positions in elite universities. Even if black representatives advance compelling claims about the advantages of educational redistribution for American society as a whole, even if they advance philosophically sophisticated arguments based on widely endorsed moral or ethical principles, it seems pollyannaish to hope or to expect that the representatives of suburban whites will heed their claims.

Making interests

These shortcomings notwithstanding, both the aggregative and the deliberative approaches offer important insights about the role that interests play in democratic politics. Theorists of aggregative democracy rightly underscore that among the most reliable predictors of how political agents act are their particular interests. Even many deliberative democrats grant this point. Many grant that, even if there are instances in legislatures and in other political settings when actors with conflicting particular interests discover new common interests, much of politics remains a matter of deciding what to do in the face of conflicting interests, and many collective decisions are coercive in the sense that they further the interests of some of the individuals and groups they affect, but not others (Mansbridge 1996).

Interests are important motivators of political action, and theorists of aggregative democracy are right to emphasize this is the case. At the same time, deliberative democrats are right to underscore that interests are not fixed or static: that much of what happens in democratic politics is not simply a matter of *responding to* people's interests and preferences (by advancing them, or by failing to) but also of *shaping* what it is that people want and/or what it is that serves their good.

Typically, deliberative democrats emphasize only one way in which political action shapes interests: they stress that reasoned argumentation changes how people understand or interpret their interests and/or how they weigh them against competing claims. But if an actor's political interests are her interests only relative to some particular set(s) of collective norms (if I have an interest in maximizing my income and my wealth, for example, only relative to the norms of a capitalist economy), then any political action that shapes relevant institutions (the legal construction of property rights, for instance) also, unavoidably, shapes political interests.[9] Political action that produces structural inequalities – collective choices that result in institutional norms that define unequal access to resources and opportunities and to the social capacity to act – tends to produce corresponding sets of political interests. For those whom structural inequalities privilege, it tends to produce interests in exploiting

---

[9] "Shapes" is important, since institutions do not *determine* interests. Faced with the norms of a capitalist economy, I might nonetheless reject the aims of income- and wealth-maximization. I might, for instance, adopt religious ascetic ends and define my interests in terms of my own spiritual development. If so, however, either these interests are not *political* interests (perhaps I pursue self-denial solipsistically, wholly indifferent to how my society structures its economy) or capitalist norms *do* shape my interests, by helping define the worldly practices and the desires I reject and resist.

and perpetuating their privilege. For those whom structural inequalities disadvantage, it tends to produce interests in escaping, if possible, and if not in minimizing or managing the effects of disadvantage. If democrats devise ways to represent interests such as these – to "make present" political interests which themselves are the products of structural inequalities – the likely result is the perpetuation of hierarchy.

Consider again the interests that many black Americans share in the redistribution of educational and other opportunities and resources. By producing both race-based residential segregation and also a highly differentiated and decentralized system of schooling, political actions taken by local municipal officials and by state and federal legislatures (among other actors) helped to construct and maintain these interests. At the same time, they constructed a set of "white" interests that center not only on reaping the benefits of an inegalitarian educational system, but more generally on maintaining relatively high levels of local public service provision with minimal tax expenditure.

"White" interests in perpetuating racial privilege, it is worth underscoring, are neither natural nor necessary. Indeed, had the collective norms that helped to produce the interests of today's suburban whites been subjected at the point of decision to the forms of rational argumentation that deliberative democrats recommend, many of them likely would not have withstood that test. The decisions that helped produce racial segregation, for example (such as collective decisions in the early part of the twentieth century to engage in racial zoning, or decisions through mid-century to permit and to enforce racially restrictive covenants), were informed by claims about racial differences that were, at best, unsubstantiated. These included, perhaps most notably, the claim that African-Americans, by virtue of their race, pose a threat to property values.[10]

Although people constructed as white, if they believed the racist claims in circulation at that time, may have believed that racial segregation served their interests, no doubt for many of them it did not. Processes of racial segregation constrained not only the housing choices of African-Americans, but also the housing choices of many so-called

---

[10] This claim was advanced especially forcefully by prominent members of the real estate industry. Frederick Babcock, for example, in his influential *Valuation of Real Estate* asserted, "Among the traits and characteristics of people which influence land values, racial heritage and tendencies seem to be of paramount importance. The aspirations, energies, and abilities of various groups in the composition of the population will largely determine the extent to which they develop the potential value of land" (Babcock 1932: 86). Rose Helper (1969), who systematically surveyed mid-century real estate textbooks, appraising manuals, and National Association of Real Estate Boards (NAREB) publications, found that almost all endorsed some version of this claim about the relation between race and property values.

"ethnic whites." In many instances, the fear of racialized others that racist claims incited prompted working-class people to abandon neighborhoods in which they had invested substantial resources and had established important networks (Sugrue 1996).

Once these claims had informed collective decisions that in turn helped produce structural inequalities, however, the result was a new "white" interest in racial exclusivity. A case in point involves decisions made by New Deal housing agencies such as the Home Owners Loan Corporation (HOLC) and the Federal Housing Administration (FHA), which are widely credited with nationalizing the practice of redlining (Jackson 1985). The latter agency defined racial segregation in the neighborhood surrounding a property as a necessary condition for that property to receive a favorable rating for a federal loan guarantee. It specifically recommended the use of racially restrictive covenants to promote segregation.[11] In the postwar years it channeled the vast majority of state-backed mortgages to racially exclusive white suburbs.[12]

The FHA mortgage program affected people's interests profoundly. It favorably affected the interests of many working- and middle-class white Americans by dramatically lowering their down-payments and interest rates and by extending their amortization periods, thus making it possible for them to purchase and to own private homes. It adversely affected the interests of many African-Americans to whom it denied this important opportunity to accumulate wealth. But, because it extended loan guarantees to white home buyers *on the condition that their homes be sited in racially exclusive enclaves*, the FHA not only differentially affected interests, but also helped to create a new constellation of race-based political interests.

A parallel argument could be developed about processes of disinvestment from urban public schools and from other institutions in the ghettoized sections of America's cities. By channeling resources away from black ghettos and to newer cities and suburbs, as well as to the central business districts and the gentrifying residential sections of older cities, state and federal legislatures, local redevelopment authorities, and

---

[11] In its 1938 *Underwriting Manual*, the FHA advised that neighborhood ratings should reflect the presence of "Adverse Influences," which it defined to include "incompatible racial and social groups." "Recorded restrictive covenants," the manual asserted, "should strengthen and supplement zoning ordinances [and] . . . should include . . . prohibition of the occupancy of properties except by the race for which they are intended" (FHA 1938: par. 937).

[12] From the start of the FHA program though the early 1960s, a period during which this agency insured mortgages on close to a third of new housing in the United States, African-Americans received less than 2 percent of these state-insured mortgages. Even these went disproportionately to racially segregated neighborhoods in the South (Squires 1994).

powerful private actors such as builders and developers, made collective decisions that did not obviously serve the interests of all middle-class people, or of all people constructed as white (Baxandall and Ewen 2000; Frieden and Sagalyn 1990; Gelfand 1975; Hirsch 1998). Urban disinvestment exacerbated non-trivial collective problems, among them joblessness, crime, victimization, and a host of social problems associated with concentrated poverty (Massey and Denton 1993; Wilson 1987).

Again, such actions differentially affected interests. Urban blacks, for instance, were made to bear disproportionately the financial, social, and psychological costs of "slum clearance" (Fullilove 2004; Teaford 1990, 2000). But they also created new political interests: interests that corresponded to the structural inequalities they defined. For many poor and working-class African-Americans, they created interests in managing or minimizing the effects of the collective problems they localized in so-called "slums." For the many whites whom they privileged, by contrast, they created interests in keeping the effects of collective problems at bay, by zoning them out of their (urban and suburban) enclaves.

III.   Reconstructing interests

The example points to what I want to suggest is a larger problem with the conventional view of representation's democratic value: it is insufficiently constructivist about political interests. Representative institutions do not promote political equality and inclusiveness in government by enabling and motivating representatives to track the interests of those they represent, if and when political interests themselves reflect structural inequalities. If representative institutions are to be democracy-promoting under conditions of deep and enduring hierarchy, they need to do more than simply "make present" the interests of all. They need to encourage the formation of new political interests. In particular, they need to encourage among those who are disadvantaged by extant hierarchies new oppositional interests, and among those who are privileged by extant hierarchies, new interests in addressing – rather than simply in avoiding the effects of – collective problems.

Interests in contestatory democratic theory

If the arguments for descriptive representation sketched above (Section II) correspond, respectively, to aggregative and deliberative understandings of what democracy is and what it requires, this more constructivist approach is informed by an account of democratic politics typically labeled "contestatory" (Connolly 1991; Mouffe 2000; Tully 1999, 2000,

2002; Wolin 1996). Legitimacy in government, by the contestatory view, is not a matter of the fair aggregation of particular interests. Nor is it a matter of the realization, or the approximation, of rational consensus about shared interests. Instead, legitimacy is the product of inclusive and egalitarian political contests, which center on ethical and moral principles, as well as on collective decisions. In contradistinction to the deliberative approach, by this view the orientation of participants in political contest is not mutual agreement, but success. When people engage in political struggles, that is to say, their aim is to win. In contradistinction to the aggregative model, by the contestatory view, political struggle has a status that is not merely empirical, but also normative. Politics not only *in fact does*, but also *should* involve contests over both principles and norms.

What lends success-oriented contestation this normative status? Contestatory democrats have offered multiple answers to that question. Some have suggested that contestation is of value for democracy because it is instrumental in promoting other democratic goods, such as a willingness to engage respectfully and non-violently with political opponents.[13] Others have suggested that the political changes that result from contestation – the destabilization of institutions and the repeated revision of collective norms – themselves hold democratic value.[14]

The most compelling reasons, however, are Arendtian in their logic (Arendt 1958: 176–7; Pitkin 1981; Honig 1995). If human agency and human plurality place what is sometimes called "collective autonomy" out of reach – if, that is to say, democratic political actors never attain sovereignty over the effects of their actions, much less over the social constraints that delimit their fields of possible action – then democratic freedom cannot be equivalent to the independence of action, or to non-interference with action, or to what Patchen Markell has called "masterful agency" with respect to one's action (Markell 2003; Hayward 2000). Instead, democratic freedom is best understood as a capability that is both social and relative: a politically produced capacity to participate in

---

[13] See, for example, Connolly (1991). This particular line of reasoning makes contestatory democracy *less* distinctive from deliberative democracy than do others, however. Deliberative democrats often argue for some forms of contestation on the Millian grounds that they are instrumental to promoting other democratic goods: namely, the discovery of rational and reasonable interests. This line of reasoning is also largely unsubstantiated. There is little reason to believe that contestation over norms and principles encourages mutual respect across lines of difference. For a persuasive critique along these lines, see Deveaux (1999).

[14] See, for example, Wolin (1996). Again, this line of reasoning is less than persuasive. It is unclear why the destabilization of institutions and the revision of collective norms are, in and of themselves, democratic goods. For a persuasive critique of this line of reasoning, see Markell (2006).

those struggles through which the norms that govern action are made and remade. Legitimate government, by this view, is realized just to the extent that people who stand to one another in relations of interdependence and mutual vulnerability are enabled – and constrained – to participate in free and equal contests over the terms of those relations.[15]

This chapter is not the place for a comprehensive or a systematic discussion of the differences that separate contestatory from aggregative, and from deliberative theories of democracy.[16] But one difference that, for present purposes, is worth highlighting is the value for democratic politics that this approach accords to political interests. By the aggregative view, the principal reason interests should influence political outcomes is that the agents those outcomes affect "have" them – or more precisely: the agents those outcomes affect believe they have them and, other things equal, are likely the best judges of whether they do.[17] That it is in my interest to do x or to have y, by this view, is an objective fact about me as a political agent (or, at least, very likely a fact about me, given my belief that it is). Hence, if I am deserving of inclusion in some democratic process because the outcomes of that process affect me, then the process should be structured such that my interests relative to its outcomes are tracked.

By the deliberative view, by contrast, interests should influence outcomes, not simply because the agents whom those outcomes affect believe they have them, but because – and *only if* – their beliefs about their interests have withstood, or in principle could withstand, the test of intersubjective reason. It might be the case that I believe it is in my interest

---

[15] By including the phrase "and constrained," I do not mean to suggest that people should never be able to opt out of participating in democratic struggles or contests, but rather that they should not be able to opt out of engaging their political opponents *while continuing to act in ways that affect them*. This point is developed below.

[16] As in the previous section, my aim here is not textual exegesis. Instead, it is an explication of a particular alternative understanding of what makes democratic politics legitimate, and how representative institutions might contribute to that end. Hence my argument is not necessarily one that all theorists who self-identify as contestatory democrats would endorse. Nor is it necessarily one that all who self-identify as aggregative or deliberative democrats would reject. I draw in this section on the work of James Tully, for example, who presents his understanding of contestatory democracy as a version of deliberative democracy. More generally, I would include in this category readings of Habermas that emphasize the importance of the revisability of both the outcomes of and the rules that structure discourse, and that de-emphasize consensus as a political ideal.

[17] Thus, for Dahl, the "principle of the equal consideration of interests" (which states that "the good or interests of each person must be given equal consideration"), combined with the "presumption of personal autonomy" (the claim that, absent "a compelling showing to the contrary everyone should be assumed to be the best judge of his or her own good or interests"), justify the use of democratic procedures for determining collective norms (Dahl 1989: 85, 100).

to do *x*, but that I would believe it is in my interest to do *not-x* if I had perfect information, complete autonomy, and an unconstrained set of alternatives from which to choose. If so, my belief about my interest is irrational (Elster 1997). By the same token, it may be the case that it is in my interest as a private individual to do *x*, but that I also have a public interest in doing *not-x*, which I share with other actors whose interests are affected by the relevant norm. If so, my interest in doing *x* is unreasonable.[18] Democratic processes, the deliberative claim is, should be structured such that they track only those interests that are rational and reasonable.

On this question of the democratic value of political interests, the contestatory view is at once more demanding than the aggregative, and less demanding than the deliberative democratic position. If interests are contingent in the sense that they are always the product of some particular configuration of institutional norms, then it cannot be the case that interests should influence outcomes just because those affected "have" them. The privileged might have an interest in maintaining their privilege by naturalizing or otherwise depoliticizing its foundation. But if so, that does not mean that that interest *should* influence political outcomes.

Still, interests can be of democratic value without being fully rational and fully reasonable in the strong (Rawlsian) sense of that term.[19] The disadvantaged might have interests that conflict with those of the privileged, for example, and irreducibly so – there may be a case of a zero-sum conflict of interests among those affected by a norm or a proposed norm – and yet it might be the case that their interests should influence outcomes. The relevant question is neither which interests people happen to have, nor whether the interests people have are fully rational and reasonable. Instead, it is whether political interests promote – or whether they inhibit – free and equal struggles over collective norms and principles. When power relations are hierarchical, therefore, and when hierarchies are relatively enduring because they are the product of inequalities that are structural in form, then the interests that should affect outcomes include interests in destabilizing inequalities and in subverting entrenched hierarchies. Political institutions, including institutions of political representation, should encourage the formation of interests such as these.

---

[18] Or, more precisely, it would be unreasonable for me to pursue my interest in doing *x*, if and to the extent that the choice whether to *x* is a political choice which affects not only me, but also others. Were I to pursue my interest in doing *x*, I would, in Elster's terms, employ behavior appropriate to the market in the political forum (Elster 1997).

[19] "Reasonable" in the Rawlsian sense means, roughly, concerned to live with others on terms they might accept (Rawls 1993: 48–54).

Contestatory democracy and representative institutions

Thus the standard complaint against contestatory democratic theories – that, in political contests, those advantaged by extant hierarchies always win – is misplaced. The privileged often win *not* by engaging in free and equal political contests with their opponents, but rather by avoiding such contests altogether. Still, a different complaint carries weight. Theorists of contestatory democracy – unlike theorists of deliberative and aggregative democracy – have had relatively little to say about the legitimacy, or about the comparative democratic value, of different political institutions.[20] This is the case in no small part due to the emphasis many place on the democratic value of transgressing institutional forms. If democracy is (to borrow Sheldon Wolin's language) "fugitive" – if it appears only during those "rebellious" episodes when ordinary people use collective power to undo some entrenched political system or some established political order – then *whatever* new order they create – whatever institutions, whatever laws, whatever rules and procedural norms – will be, by definition, not democratic, but the end or the edge of democracy (Wolin 1996). Thus, for Wolin, "Institutionalization marks the attenuation of democracy: leaders begin to appear, hierarchies develop, experts of one kind or another cluster around the centers of decision; order, procedure, and precedent displace a more spontaneous politics" (ibid.: 39). Democracy, by this view, is a "moment" or an "ethos" more than a political form or a set of institutional arrangements (Wolin 1996; Connolly 1991).

If one conceives the normative justification for democratic contestation in more Arendtian terms, however – if one sees the value of political contest, not in transgression or rebelliousness per se, so much as in the capacity it creates for the agentive and egalitarian making and remaking of relations of power – then one can articulate guidelines for developing and for evaluating political institutions, including institutions of political representation. One important such guideline is that institutions should constrain those agents who (would) act in ways that affect collective norms to engage politically the other agents those norms (would) affect. Such engagement need not be direct. It can be mediated by parties, by elections, and by other institutions of representative democracy. But, at the limit, no single participant in a relation of power, and no subset of participants in such a relation, should be enabled to act unilaterally to affect its terms.

This guideline points up what, from a contestatory democratic perspective, is the principal problem with despotical rule. The problem is

---

[20] One exception is James Tully. See especially Tully (1995).

not that the despot decides and acts in ways with which her subjects do not (or would not) agree, much less that her opinions and theirs are not properly aggregated. Instead, the problem is that the despot works on her subjects like an artisan on material. Rather than acting in a way that interacts with, that is responsive to, the actions of the others her action affects, the despot extends into politics the logic of what Arendt calls fabrication (Arendt 1958: Part IV). Even if the decisions that she makes are decisions with which her subjects (might) agree, even if the decisions that she makes do not prevent her subjects from behaving as they wish to behave, the rule of the despot undermines democratic freedom (Pettit 1997).

Such unfreedom, of course, can obtain absent despotical rule. Such unfreedom can obtain even absent rule by *any* identifiable agent who "works" on the fields of action of other actors. Deeply entrenched norms and institutions can subject people to forms of impersonal power that are as far removed from their influence as the dictates of a tyrant. A second guideline, then, is that institutions should render the terms of power relations in principle open to political challenge and revision. To say so is not to imply that constant change is necessary or desirable. But change must be possible. To the extent that the terms of power relations are removed from the reach of some or all participants (to the extent, for example, that they are naturalized or sacralized), democratic freedom is abridged.

Consider again the example of power relations structured around "race" in American cities and suburbs. One important set of institutional norms that helps set the terms for the management of these power relations consists in norms defining electoral constituencies and political jurisdictions: institutions (such as local school districts and other special-purpose governments, as well as general-purpose governments such as urban and suburban municipalities) that determine whom representatives represent, and in the making of which collective norms.

Local constituencies and political jurisdictions in the United States are exceedingly fragmented: a trait that, in the context of racial and socioeconomic residential segregation, enables the privileged to act in ways that profoundly affect the disadvantaged, but without engaging them politically. In 2002 (the year of the most recent census of American governments), there were nearly 88,000 local governments in the United States. Of these, nearly 39,000 were general-purpose governments.[21]

---

[21] The exact figures are 87,849 and 38,971, respectively (US Bureau of the Census 2002). In the Pittsburgh metropolitan area (the most politically fragmented of America's major metropolitan areas), 412 general-purpose governments averaged less than 6,000 residents each (Dreier, Mollenkopf, and Swanstrom 2004: 45).

This level of political fragmentation is a relatively recent development in the US. Through much of the nineteenth century, most American cities expanded by annexing their surrounding territories. Beginning in the early decades of the last century, however – just when the black population surged in the urban north, and when the mass production of automobiles and tract housing opened the suburbs to the middle and the lower-middle classes – state legislatures throughout the nation shifted from a pattern of enabling urban annexation to one of legally restricting annexation, permitting suburban municipalities to incorporate, and granting them significant governance authority (Briffault 1990).

By mid-century, most American suburbs could engage in a fairly wide range of autonomous political decision-making. Most could make land use decisions autonomously. Most could pass exclusionary zoning ordinances, for example, if there was a high enough level of local public support. Most could set admissions policies for, and they could raise taxes to fund, public local schools. More generally, most American suburbs could exclude would-be residents who lacked the resources needed to gain entrance, and they could raise and spend taxes to fund services which they made available to residents only. The privileged thus were enabled to retreat to relatively homogeneous political jurisdictions where they could form constituencies and elect representatives whose decisions would affect the disadvantaged, but where the disadvantaged were excluded from authorizing those representatives and from holding them accountable.

In the US, local constituencies and jurisdictions are not only fragmented; they are also territorially based. The latter trait, as Richard Thompson Ford has argued, serves both to naturalize these institutions and to depoliticize them (Ford 1999). Territoriality, Ford's claim is, encourages people to conceive constituencies and jurisdictions in one (or in both) of two (logically inconsistent) ways: as the natural product of organic communities, which predate the exercise of state power, or as politically neutral tools through which states administer policies and laws which treat all people equally. In the US, Ford argues, territorial jurisdictions work to legitimize race-based social hierarchies of the sort sketched in Section II, above: hierarchies that likely would be widely perceived as illegitimate if not perpetuated through the legal mechanism of the territorial jurisdiction.

It is in large part due to the fragmentation and the territorial grounding of political jurisdictions that many urban blacks have political interests in *managing* educational and other inequalities (for example, by working locally to increase property taxes and/or to shift public expenditures toward schooling) or in *minimizing* them (by working through state courts to press for school finance reform, for example), rather than in *eradicating* these inequalities altogether (by instituting cross-district desegregation plans, for instance, or by eliminating residency requirements for public school attendance). It is not in their political interests to pursue the latter objectives for the simple reason that these courses are next to impossible to chart within the extant structure of representative institutions. By the same token, it is because local constituencies and jurisdictions enable them to do so that many suburban whites have interests in *avoiding the effects of* failing schools (for example, by passing zoning ordinances that effectively prevent poor and working-class people from living in their municipalities, thus keeping student need relatively low and the property tax base relatively high) rather than in *addressing* these and related collective problems.

In a context like this one, changing political interests requires changing the definition of electoral constituencies and political jurisdictions. There are multiple ways to do so. Some theorists have made a case for a substantial centralization of governance functions to the metropolitan and/or the regional level (Young 1990 ch. 8). Others have argued for periodically redrawing municipal and other political jurisdictional boundaries, with a view to promoting political equality and inclusiveness in government (Briffault 1996). Still other theorists have proposed various forms of cross-jurisdictional voting, so that, for instance, city dwellers and residents of older "inner-ring" suburbs would be permitted to vote in the elections of neighboring affluent suburban municipalities whose decisions significantly affected them (Ford 1994). Each approach has its practical strengths and limitations (Hayward 2003), but the basic principle motivating each is the same. Representative institutions should ensure that it is in the interests of all to address problems that are, in a causal sense, collective. They should constrain people who are privileged by extant hierarchies to engage politically those whom their decisions and actions affect, and they should grant those who are disadvantaged by structural inequalities the collective power to change, rather than simply to negotiate, those inequalities.

IV.   Conclusion

In this chapter, I have argued against the conventional view, according to which representative institutions promote democratic legitimacy by enabling and motivating representatives to track the interests of the represented. Under conditions of structural inequality, I have argued, legitimacy requires that representative and other political institutions shape interests in democracy-promoting ways. Specifically, it requires that they encourage among the privileged interests in engaging in political contests over collective problems and collective decisions, and among the disadvantaged oppositional interests in subverting entrenched hierarchies.

What it means to encourage the formation of such political interests, and which specific institutional changes that requires, will vary from case to case. In some cases, descriptive representation may be one important step. But for the reasons sketched above, descriptive representation often will not be enough. The challenge, then, is to restructure representative institutions so that they do not simply *track* the interests of all, but rather *change* political interests in ways that promote democratic inclusiveness and political equality.

In many cases, changing interests will require enabling the formation of new alliances and new solidarities among groups that, individually, form minorities in the relevant population, and that are differently disadvantaged by extant hierarchies. More generally speaking, the aim is not to aggregate the interests of the governed, whatever those interests happen to be. Nor is it to ensure that collective norms promote the interests of all, because they are the product of the rational agreement of all. Instead, the aim is to ensure that those who stand in relations of power to one another engage in free and equal contests over the terms of those relations. To the extent that they engage one another through political representatives (whom they elect and hold accountable), representative institutions should help make and remake political interests in ways that promote such contests.

BIBLIOGRAPHY

Arendt, Hannah. 1958. *The Human Condition.* Chicago: University of Chicago Press.
Babcock, Frederick Morrison. 1932. *The Valuation of Real Estate.* New York: McGraw-Hill.
Baxandall, Rosalyn and Elizabeth Ewen. 2000. *Picture Windows: How the Suburbs Happened.* New York: Basic Books.
Benhabib, Seyla. 1996. "Toward a Deliberative Model of Democratic Legitimacy," in *Democracy and Difference*, ed. Seyla Benhabib. Princeton, NJ: Princeton University Press, 67–94.
Briffault, Richard. 1990. "Our Localism, Part II – Localism and Legal Theory." *Columbia Law Review* 90 (March): 346–454.
  1996. "The Local Government Boundary Problem in Metropolitan Areas." *Stanford Law Review* 48 (May): 1115–71.
Burke, Edmund. 1854–6. "Speech to the Electors of Bristol," in *The Works of the Right Honorable Edmund Burke*, 6 vols., ed. Edmund Burke. London: Henry G. Bohn, vol. IV.

Connolly, William. 1991. *Identity\Difference: Democratic Negotiations of Political Paradox*. Ithaca, NY: Cornell University Press.

Dahl, Robert. 1989. *Democracy and its Critics*. New Haven, CT: Yale University Press.

Dawson, Michael. 1994. *Behind the Mule: Race and Class in African-American Politics*. Princeton, NJ: Princeton University Press.

Deveaux, Monique. 1999. "Agonism and Pluralism." *Philosophy and Social Criticism* 25 (4): 1–22.

Dovi, Suzanne. 2002. "Preferable Descriptive Representatives: Will Just Any Woman, Black, or Latino Do?" *American Political Science Review* 96 (4): 729–43.

Dreier, Peter, John Mollenkopf, and Todd Swanstrom. 2004. *Place Matters: Metropolitics for the Twenty-First Century*. Lawrence, KS: University Press of Kansas.

Elster, Jon. 1997. "The Market and the Forum: Three Varieties of Political Theory," in *Deliberative Democracy: Essays on Reason and Politics*, ed. James Bohman and William Rehg. Cambridge, MA: MIT Press, 3–34.

(ed.). 1998. *Deliberative Democracy*. Cambridge: Cambridge University Press.

Federal Housing Agency (FHA). 1938. *Underwriting Manual, Underwriting and Valuation Procedure under Title II of the National Housing Act*. Washington, DC: US Government Printing Office, para. 937.

Ford, Richard Thompson. 1994. "The Boundaries of Race: Political Geography in Legal Analysis." *Harvard Law Review* 107 (June): 1843–1921.

1999. "Law's Territory (A History of Jurisdiction)." *Michigan Law Review* 97 (4): 843–930.

Frieden, Bernard and Lynne Sagalyn. 1990. *Downtown, Inc.: How America Rebuilds Cities*. Cambridge, MA: MIT Press.

Fullilove, Mindy Thompson. 2004. *Root Shock: How Tearing Up City Neighborhoods Hurts America, and What We Can Do About It*. New York: Ballantine Books.

Gelfand, Mark. 1975. *A Nation of Cities: The Federal Government and Urban America, 1933–1965*. New York: Oxford University Press.

Habermas, Jürgen. 1990. "Discourse Ethics: Notes on a Program of Philosophical Justification," in *Moral Consciousness and Communicative Action*, trans. Christian Lenhardt and Hierry Weber Nicholsen. Cambridge, MA: MIT Press, 116–94.

1996. "Three Normative Models of Democracy," in *Democracy and Difference*, ed. Seyla Benhabib. Princeton, NJ: Princeton University Press, 21–30.

Hayward, Clarissa. 2000. *De-facing Power*. Cambridge: Cambridge University Press.

2003. "The Difference States Make: Democracy, Identity, and the American City." *American Political Science Review* 97 (4): 501–14.

Helper, Rose. 1969. *Racial Policies and Practices of Real Estate Brokers*. Minneapolis: University of Minnesota Press.

Hirsch, Arnold. 1998. *Making the Second Ghetto: Race and Housing in Chicago, 1940–1960*, second edn. Chicago: University of Chicago Press.

Honig, Bonnie. 1995. "Toward an Agonistic Feminism: Hannah Arendt and the Politics of Identity," in *Feminist Interpretations of Hannah Arendt*, ed. Bonnie Honig. University Park: Pennsylvania State University Press, 135–66.

Jackson, Kenneth. 1985. *Crabgrass Frontier: The Suburbanization of America*. New York: Oxford University Press.

Macedo, Stephen (ed.). 1999. *Deliberative Politics: Essays on Democracy and Disagreement*. New York: Oxford University Press.

Madison, James. 1969. "Federalist 10," in *The Federalist Papers*, ed. Clinton Rossiter. New York: New American Library of World Literature, 77–89.

Manin, Bernard. 1987. "On Legitimacy and Political Deliberation." *Political Theory* 15 (3): 338–68.

   1997. *The Principles of Representative Government*. Cambridge: Cambridge University Press.

Mansbridge, Jane. 1996. "Using Power/Fighting Power: The Polity," in *Democracy and Difference*, ed. Seyla Benhabib. Princeton, NJ: Princeton University Press, 46–66.

   1999. "Should Blacks Represent Blacks and Women Represent Women? A Contingent 'Yes.'" *Journal of Politics* 61 (3): 628–57.

   2003. "Rethinking Representation." *American Political Science Review* 97 (4): 515–28.

Markell, Patchen. 2003. *Bound by Recognition*. Princeton, NJ: Princeton University Press.

   2006. "The Rule of the People: Arendt, *Archē*, and Democracy." *American Political Science Review* 100 (1): 1–14.

Massey, Douglas and Nancy Denton. 1993. *American Apartheid: Segregation and the Making of the Underclass*. Cambridge, MA: Harvard University Press.

Mill, John Stuart. 1825. *Essays on Government, Jurisprudence, Liberty of the Press, and Law of Nations*. New York: Kelley.

   1975. *Considerations on Representative Government*, in *John Stuart Mill: Three Essays*. Oxford: Oxford University Press.

Mouffe, Chantal. 2000. *The Democratic Paradox*. London: Verso.

Pettit, Phillip. 1997. *Republicanism: A Theory of Freedom and Government*. Oxford: Oxford University Press.

Phillips, Anne. 1995. *The Politics of Presence*. Oxford: Clarendon Press.

Pitkin, Hanna Fenichel. 1967. *The Concept of Representation*. Berkeley: University of California Press.

   1981. "Justice: On Relating Private and Public." *Political Theory* 9 (3): 340–1.

Plotke, David. 1997. "Representation is Democracy." *Constellations* 4 (1): 19–34.

Przeworski, Adam, Carol Stokes, and Bernard Manin. 1999. *Democracy, Accountability, and Representation*. Cambridge: Cambridge University Press.

Rawls, John. 1993. *Political Liberalism*. New York: Columbia University Press.

Rehfield, Andrew. 2006. "Towards a General Theory of Political Representation." *Journal of Politics*, 68 (1): 1–21.

Squires, Gregory. 1994. "Community Reinvestment: The Privatization of Fair Lending Law Enforcement," in *Residential Apartheid: The American Legacy*, ed. Robert Bullard, J. Eugene Grigsby, III, and Charles Lee. Los Angeles, CA: CAAS, 257–86.

Sugrue, Thomas. 1996. *The Origins of the Urban Crisis: Race and Inequality in Postwar Detroit*. Princeton, NJ: Princeton University Press.

Teaford, Jon. 1990. *The Rough Road to Renaissance: Urban Revitalization in America, 1940–1985*. Baltimore, MD: Johns Hopkins University Press.

2000. "Urban Renewal and Its Aftermath." *Housing Policy Debate* 11 (2): 443–65.

Tully, James. 1995. *Strange Multiplicity: Constitutionalism in an Age of Diversity*. New York: Cambridge University Press.

1999. "The Agonic Freedom of Citizens." *Economy and Society* 28 (2): 161–82.

2000. "Struggles over Recognition and Distribution." *Constellations* 7 (4): 469–82.

2002. "The Unfreedom of the Moderns in Comparison to their Ideals of Constitutional Democracy." *Modern Law Review* 65 (March): 204–28.

US Bureau of the Census. 2002. "Preliminary Report No. 1: The 2002 Census of Governments." Available at: http://ftp2.census.gov/govs/cog/2002COGprelim_report.pdf (accessed June 8, 2009).

Williams, Melissa. 1998. *Voice, Trust, and Memory: Marginalized Groups and the Failings of Liberal Representation*. Princeton, NJ: Princeton University Press.

Wilson, William Julius. 1987. *The Truly Disadvantaged: The Inner City, the Underclass, and Public Policy*. Chicago: University of Chicago Press.

Wolin, Sheldon. 1996. "Fugitive Democracy," in *Democracy and Difference*, ed. Seyla Benhabib. Princeton, NJ: Princeton University Press, 31–455.

Young, Iris Marion. 1990. *Justice and the Politics of Difference*. Princeton, NJ: Princeton University Press.

2000. *Inclusion and Democracy*. Oxford: Oxford University Press.

Part III

Representation and inherited injustice

6   Critical liberalism

Courtney Jung

Representative democracies struggle with the demands of ethnic minorities. In the last decade of the twentieth century, these struggles were exacerbated by the rise of new cultural claims and claimants. Democratization engendered discussions about citizenship and membership, which raised questions of national identity and belonging. The Soviet Union disintegrated as its component units exercised their rights to national self-determination; the European Union attempted to develop new standards for the protection of minorities; and indigenous rights were enshrined in international law. The demands of ethnic minorities punctuate the political landscape in rural and urban areas, in developed and developing countries, in the East and in the West, reshaping the terms of political debate, and raising new points of political contestation.

Liberal democrats worry about this political turn. They worry about the extent to which democracies can accommodate the competing claims of ethnic groups, and they worry about their obligations to do so. They are concerned in particular because they believe that demands for bilingual education, autonomy, and cultural respect represent fundamental demands for the recognition of human identity, and that they therefore engage a deeper level of commitment than other claims. As such they impose greater obligations on the democratic state. They also pose a greater threat, as democratic institutions struggle to process and accommodate the deeply held but incompatible cultural commitments of their citizens.

Critical liberalism responds to these concerns with a theory of obligation that is rooted in the structural origins of groups rather than in the cultural difference of groups. States are obligated to engage and respond to the claims of indigenous peoples, other ethnic minorities, African-Americans, women, immigrants, and so on, not because of who they are, or because they may command human attachment, but as a result of the historical record of exclusion and selective inclusion through which they have been constituted. The obligation of states lies in the fact that states themselves have forged social groups, and the identities they anchor, by using such markers as cultural practices, alleged phenotypical traits, biological sex, property ownership, and wealth to organize access to power and delimit the boundaries of citizenship.

In the first section of the chapter I develop a structural theory of obligation. In the second and third sections, I draw out the normative implications of such a theory. In the second section I argue that a constructivist theory of identity formation demands that the normative standing of particular claims be established through the framework of structural injustice rather than cultural difference. In the third section I introduce the category of membership rights – rights that recognize that social groups are constructed and nevertheless acknowledge that they often play a central role in determining life chances. I draw examples from the politics of indigenous rights to illustrate some of my arguments.

I.   A structural theory of obligation

Normative political theorists of democracy and multicultural citizenship have largely ignored the political and strategic context in which cultural claims are formulated and advanced. Such theorists have been content, for the most part, to begin from the premise that people feel strong attachments to their cultural groups (Rawls 1985, 1993; Dworkin 1978; Kymlicka 1995), that human identity is in fact constituted by cultural group membership (Sandel 1982; Galston 1995), and that human authenticity arises in dialogue with members of one's own cultural group (Taylor 1994). They assume that demands for bilingual education, local-level self-government, territorial autonomy, and public support for the cultural practices of minority groups are the political expression of a universal human need for the affirmation and preservation of the cultural groups to which we belong.[1]

Will Kymlicka best expresses the general consensus that there is no real point in trying to explain the cultural attachments of individuals. As he says, the bond between individuals and their cultural groups is simply "a fact . . . whose origins lie deep in the human condition, tied up with the way humans as cultural creatures need to make sense of their world, and that a full explanation would involve aspects of psychology, sociology, linguistics, the philosophy of mind, and even neurology" (Kymlicka 1995: 90). Such attachments, Kymlicka and others insist, importantly shape human identity. By making an appeal to neurology, Kymlicka suggests they may even be biologically hard-wired. The challenge for democratic

---

[1] Seyla Benhabib's *The Claims of Culture* (2002) is a notable exception to this trend. She focuses attention instead on the ways in which culture is deployed for political purposes.

theorists, he and others believe, is not where they come from, but how to deal with them.

Against this backdrop, claims for recognition take on the air of a reflexive reaction against the homogenizing threats of modernity and the frequency with which supposedly insular and intact cultural units come into contact with one another, with the penetrating reach of the modern state, and with neo-liberal economic policies (Yashar 1998, 2005). Demands for cultural preservation seem to stem from a protective instinct in defense of the familiar, local, and particular against the threat of Nike, Eminem, and English.

This initial assumption is not neutral, and it has played a crucial role in framing the terms of debate over what democratic states owe to ethnic minorities. The contemporary normative discussion over multicultural citizenship is divided between those who insist that democracy requires the privatization of cultural commitments, and those who believe that democracies have an obligation to protect, or preserve, the cultural groups in which their citizens have membership. Both impulses, to privatize or to protect the ethnic group – to insulate democratic politics from culture, or to insulate culture from democratic politics – are rooted in assumptions that make a fetish of culture.

Privatizers worry that religious and cultural commitments anchor what is most fundamental in human identity, and that such convictions are therefore not amenable to the normal give-and-take of negotiation and moderation that representative democracy requires. Claims that rest on belief or tradition threaten to tear apart the public sphere. Because they cannot be moderated, they should instead be excluded from public deliberation, leaving citizens free to express, preserve, and exercise their preexisting religious and cultural commitments in private. Democratic society will only be maintained if it is protected from debate between competing conceptions of the whole truth (Rawls 1971, 1985; Macedo 1995). If the public sphere is to remain neutral, and equally available to everyone, it must be limited to reasoning that everyone could understand and agree to. Typically, privatizers invoke groups that are unsympathetic, such as Christian fundamentalists, Nazis, or skinheads, and invite us to imagine what would happen if their viewpoints were to achieve dominance through the democratic process (Macedo 1995).[2]

Protectionists agree that religion and culture represent fundamental human commitments, but they argue that this is a reason to protect, not to privatize, the collective units in which citizens hold membership. They argue for the recognition of group rights, though they sometimes

---

[2] Stephen Macedo (1995) writes about the Christian right, for example.

disagree over which groups and which rights the state should protect. They maintain that respect for the individual entails respect for his culture, and that cultural and religious minorities should therefore be protected from majoritarian politics that threaten the capacity of a culture to reproduce itself (Taylor 1994). They argue that democracy requires respect for difference (Galston 1995), and that individual freedom depends on access to one's own societal culture (Kymlicka 1995). Protectionists tend to invoke sympathetic groups, such as indigenous people and the Amish, and to suggest that the laissez-faire character of privatizing liberalism threatens to extinguish the traditions and lifestyles of these ancient and vulnerable communities to the detriment of all mankind.

Theorists on both sides make a compelling case by invoking fear of tyranny of the majority. Privatizers raise the possibility that hate-mongering skinheads might take over local governments in some parts of the United States, which is a genuine concern. Protectionists invoke the threat to the survival of indigenous languages and traditions, which is palpable almost everywhere. Each of them is correct in thinking that the procedural character of democracy may threaten minority interests and empower dangerous majorities. Their instinct to preclude such outcomes by limiting democracy has nevertheless left them vulnerable to compelling criticism.

By denying cultural groups the grounds to contest politics, privatization has the effect of naturalizing the cultural status quo, leaving little viable choice to minorities but assimilation. And it is not only that others are forced to assimilate to liberalism, as Macedo claims when he argues the case for liberalism with a spine (Macedo 1995). They are also forced to assimilate to the dominant language, religion, culture, etc., all of which, absent contestation, will be naturalized as part of the backdrop of social exchange. As critics contend, privatizing cultural commitments really does limit the capacity of minority groups to navigate and prolong many of their own cultural practices (Taylor 1994; Kymlicka 1995).

On the other hand, by arguing for the right to collective self-government and cultural autonomy, which is also an exemption from democratic politics, protectionists have come under fire for depriving group members of the political means to contest the norms and boundaries of their own cultural and religious groups. Unless we can assume the complete internal coherence of the cultural group, or that the cultural group is literally an organic unit, collective rights that draw their legitimacy from cultural norms alone run the risk of violating individual rights. Recognition is always partial, privileging those who hold power within the cultural group (Okin 1999), and freezing the cultural boundaries and practices that are salient at the moment of recognition (Appiah 1994). Ironically, this often gives the state more leverage to adjudicate what counts as tradition, insisting, for example, that only pre-contact practices warrant special exemptions, or that only those people who continue to live on their ancestral lands qualify as genuinely indigenous.

The deepest criticisms of each side stem from the paradox that, despite their different commitments, both privatizers and protectionists support the exclusion, or exemption, of cultural groups from democratic politics – either to protect the supposed neutrality of the state, or to protect the supposed integrity of the cultural group (Jung 2001). The common impulse to exclude derives in turn from the fact that, whether they recommend privatization or protection, normative theorists employ the same assumptions regarding the crucial role of culture in constituting individual identity. Culture should be protected or privatized precisely, they believe, because demands for cultural recognition arise from a universal and transhistorical human need for cultural group recognition. Most people feel a strong attachment to their cultural groups and practices, they say, and such attachments have normative standing. From such attachments flow obligations.

Nevertheless, there is a prior level of politics that has been obscured by a fixation on the fact of cultural difference. The debate over minority rights is often conducted in a register that leaves many fundamental questions of power, access, politics, and exclusion largely off the table. It does so mainly because it has neglected questions about where cultural claims come from, and why they are salient in contemporary political discourse. Although many theorists concede that ethnic identities are constructed, they draw no analytical connection between the origins of demands for cultural group recognition, on the one hand, and the just disposition of such demands, on the other (Barry 2001; Carens 2000; Dworkin 1978; Galston 1995; Kymlicka 1995; Macedo 1995; Rawls 1971, 1985, 1993; Taylor 1994). Theorists who have actually confronted this question insist that the fact that social groups are constructed has no bearing on how they are managed, or what they are owed, by liberal democratic institutions (Walzer 1983: 31; Kymlicka 1995).

Such theorists have attempted to bypass the significance of constructivism for normative theory by saying "yes, ethnic groups may be constructed, but regardless of where they come from, or how they change, human beings are fundamentally attached to, and indeed constituted by, the (constructed) cultural groups they are born into." Indeed this is a reasonable response to the "weak-constructivist" claim that a group's culture is shifting and subject to reinvention and that traditions are often transformed by such outside influences as colonial and postcolonial governments. It is certainly true, and has been amply shown, that many of the traditions that are portrayed as ancient are in fact new. But this critique issues a feeble challenge to the existing corpus of literature on multiculturalism and democracy, which takes no position on where culture comes from, focusing instead on the extent to which human well-being depends on access to one's own societal culture, regardless of where such culture comes from or how it may change.

The "strong-constructivist" argument is different, however, and offers grounds for a fundamental reconsideration of the line of thinking that has driven the debate over multiculturalism and democracy. The strong-constructivist argument holds that it is human attachment itself that is constructed. It is not that people do not have fundamental attachments – of course they do. Instead, as Akeel Bilgrami has argued, religious or cultural identities are not fundamental because they are the spontaneous expression of "the subject's irreducible interest in the definition of itself" (Bilgrami 1992: 831). They are fundamental because of the way (or to the extent) they have developed in particular historical and cultural contexts (ibid. 1992: 831, 833).

The likelihood that cultural practices and traditions will rise to the level of "ethnicity," generating boundaries with social significance and the weight to invest a distinction between "us" and "them" with authority and commonsense meaning, is contingent. The extent to which human beings identify themselves as members of ethnic groups depends on the extent to which cultural practices have been vested with public and social significance. Whether individuals perceive their identities to be most fundamentally mediated by ethnicity, or by gender, race, or class, or even by such personal attributes as intelligence, profession, or marital status, reflects structural conditions rather than law-like psychological traits. Like race, class, and gender, culture develops political resonance when it has been used as a marker of selective inclusion and exclusion by states organizing access to power.

One implication of the strong-constructivist argument for liberal democratic theory is that it lodges responsibility for the relative salience of cultural group membership in the state. It draws a direct connection between how groups are formed and what they are owed. Movements form around gender, sexuality, race, and culture because these social categories have regulated political access and the organization of power, not because they express people's deepest sense of themselves. This does not make them any less potentially real or valuable to human experience, but it does mean that the ostensible reality, importance, and value of culture depend not on cultural practices alone but on the social and structural forces that lend them weight in our lives.[3]

Tracing the origins of political salience is relevant not only as an exercise in exposing the way power operates, but also as a way of establishing the historical responsibility of states. The real normative torque of cultural politics is anchored in the structural location that certain groups occupy as a result of historical discrimination and exclusion. Groups that are constituted through exclusion and oppression, that have come to shape political identity because their members have suffered in common, and that occupy a position of structural inferiority, have grounds for redress that lie in their own particular history. The legitimacy and scope of ethnic group claims lie in the structural location of the group, not in differences of tradition and practice, and not in the extent of human attachment to such traditions.

The appropriate question for normative political theory therefore is not "How can democratic governments accommodate the preexisting and deeply held cultural commitments of their citizens?" but instead "How should democratic institutions process the political claims that arise to protect and contest the exclusions and inclusions set in place by the modern state itself?" Taking seriously the historically and politically constituted character of ethnicity leads neither to privatization nor to protection but to a transformative engagement that sustains a more critical conception of liberalism.

II.   Structural injustice

Cultural norms and practices generate ethnic boundaries and sentiment, the capacity to bear attachment, and relevance as political identities through the way that such markers as language, tradition, alleged phenotypical traits, and cultural norms have been used by states to mark the boundaries of citizenship. Human beings identify themselves as members of ethnic groups, and perceive cultural practices as relevant

---

[3] A structural account of identity formation does not erase the possibility of agency. Human beings rework, challenge, and revalue their categories of membership, shaping the meaning and contours of their own identities. Nevertheless, the categories of membership they revalue are those that have been publicly marked, and the project of cultural retrieval does not take place in isolation – culture is deployed, reworked, and invoked in engagement with politics. The fact that human beings are also at work in the construction of their own identities does not diminish the relevance of focusing on the structural dimension of identity to establish the normative and political standing of oppressed groups.

markers of identity, to the extent that culture has been used to organize society. Ethnicity is the deeply contextualized result of a particular historical experience, not a universal category of human political organization.

The most direct implication of constructivist theories of identity formation for normative frameworks of multiculturalism and democracy is that universal solutions are mismatched to the task of adjudicating the claims of cultures and the responsibilities of democratic states. This follows directly from the insight that ethnicity arises as a result of structural configurations that are particular to different societies and historical experiences. What ethnic groups are owed by liberal democratic governments depends on the historical conditions that have given rise to particular ethnic groups.

As a result, claims should be judged on the basis of the existence of historic and ongoing injustice, and not on the degree to which a group is culturally distinct. Jeff Spinner-Halev has called this type of injustice, which has roots in the past but persists to the present, enduring injustice. Enduring injustice, he says, has both historical and contemporary components (2007: 3, 7). Spinner-Halev argues that injustices endure because they are beyond the scope of liberal conceptions of justice – they cannot be remedied through individual rights or a fair system of distributive justice (ibid.: 7).

The structural injustice framework focuses attention instead on the causes of historical and ongoing injustice. Structural injustices are those with systemic roots that persistently, over the course of generations, structure access and power to the disadvantage of people who have some trait, such as biological sex or skin color, in common, with the effect of generating a sense of common identity. They are woven into the fabric of a society's political institutions and laws, through its norms and mores, and into the very texture of everyday life. Structural injustices persist across generations because they have structural systemic roots in the history of liberal democracy.

The cause of such injustice is therefore the same as its normative force. Injustices that flow from laws and policies put in place by the state – structural injustices – offer particular normative standing to those who have suffered from them, and whose "groups" have been shaped by them. On this account, persistent injustice is caused by the failure of actually existing liberal democratic history, rather than the failure of liberal democratic theory, as Spinner-Halev contends. A critical conception of liberalism, which foregrounds this history, can offer a remedy.

The fact that constructivism forces normative theory to turn for answers to the particular condition of structural injustice (or privilege) that is the condition of the group's existence has a number of corollary implications. There are four reasons that the claims of ethnic groups are more appropriately legitimated through the structural injustice framework than through the cultural difference framework.

First, by resting group claims in particular historical experiences, critical liberalism is able to cut through orthodox group distinctions, offering a theory of multiculturalism and democracy that has something to say about race, gender, and class. It allows normative theorists to use the same standard – the particular set of structural relations that has constituted the group – to contemplate the moral and political standing of all groups. Ethnic groups need not be treated in a category apart from race or class groups.

This is useful because it sidesteps the classificatory reification that confuses our thinking on these questions. There is a poor fit between actual groups, such as indigenous peoples and African-Americans, and the categories that are used to determine how they should be treated by liberal democratic institutions, such as race, class, and ethnicity. Over the last five hundred years, indigenous people in Mexico have been reclassified by race, class, and ethnicity. Each designation located them in a distinct policy space, with important implications for their experience of political exclusion and incorporation, and for the scope and substance of their political claims. But the fact that a single population has been serially "raced," "classed," and "ethnicized" should alert us to the ways in which these categories are deployed by states, in line with dominant ideologies of human classification, to render their populations legible (Jung 2008). Such categories, which have been used by states to classify their populations, most obviously through censuses, are reified when they are redeployed to establish the proper standing of groups and to evaluate the legitimacy of the claims they make.

Second, following the same logic in the other direction, critical liberalism is also able to distinguish among cultural groups, affording them different standing. Insisting that the legitimacy of ethnic group claims rests on structural conditions and historical obligations – and not on cultural difference or attachment – allows critical liberalism to parse similarities and differences among groups in a way that is more satisfying than the recommendations that multiculturalists have been backed into by their commitment to cultural distinctiveness. Part of the reason that theoretical debates over cultural group rights sometimes seem lodged at too high a level of abstraction is that, by locating rights to self-determination and territorial autonomy in cultural difference, multiculturalists give the same grounds to Kurds and other victims of genocide as they do to Serbs or to Afrikaners. All groups can claim cultural difference, and such claims give all groups the same moral standing.

Yet it somehow does not ring true that all groups that stake a claim to cultural distinctiveness are equally legitimate, or should have the same normative standing. This is a point that some multiculturalists have recognized, but the logic of their own arguments gives them very little room to distinguish among cultural groups. Will Kymlicka, for instance, makes a case for according different rights to First Nations, national minorities, and immigrants, based primarily on the degree to which they maintain intact societal cultures and whether or not they have chosen to live in their current location (Kymlicka 1995).

Yet this argument follows on from his main point, which is that liberal democracies have a responsibility to protect the groups he calls societal cultures because individual freedom, and the capacity to make meaningful choices, relies on access to one's own culture. This is a powerful claim, and it is a universal claim. The subsequent distinction Kymlicka draws among cultural groups is counterintuitive against this backdrop. If freedom – which he says is the primary commitment of a liberal democratic society – depends on maintaining cultural group membership, how can such societies accord greater cultural protection to some groups than others? If basic freedom itself is at stake, liberal democracies cannot be governed by pragmatic decisions that protect the individual freedom of First Nations people but not of immigrant minorities.

I suspect instead that our instinct to try to distinguish among claims, and to accord different status to Afrikaner demands for a *Volkstaat* than we do to Kurdish demands for a homeland, depends not on the degree to which each group maintains an intact societal culture (the Afrikaner language and culture is both distinctive and robust), but on the degree to which the group has been constituted through discrimination and oppression, or privilege. Viewed through the prism of structural injustice, groups in structurally superior positions, which stand in structural relations of power over other groups, have weaker standing, and command less normative legitimacy, than groups in structurally inferior positions, even when both can claim cultural distinctiveness. Although the distinction Kymlicka draws between groups seems surprising from the perspective of cultural distinctiveness, it makes sense through a structural injustice framework.

The third way in which the appeal to structural injustice advances politics beyond an appeal to communal integrity is that it expands the arena of the politics of recognition. Ethnic minorities do not only demand cultural protection and bilingual education. They have also been subjected to a raft of injustices that cut in the other direction, namely inadequate integration, racism, exclusion from full citizenship, insufficient access to healthcare, welfare, and social service benefits, and poor or non-existent educational opportunities. With this litany of structural injustices behind them, they can make claims for representation, redistribution, and restitution, and not only for recognition.

Furthermore, from the perspective of political organization, cultural groups may make a strategic error when they anchor their political claims in cultural difference. By locating culture at the center of political voice, indigenous peoples and others who would mobilize ethnic difference risk being backed into demands for cultural protection and the preservation of tradition, which do not issue a fundamental challenge to many of the structural relations that are the condition of their disadvantaged position. The claims of culture issue a feeble challenge to the neo-liberal economic order for instance, or to the structural location of indigenous populations at the bottom of that order. Some states may even be eager to confer self-government on their indigenous populations, using territorial autonomy to abjure state responsibility for providing development and social services.

Finally, this type of claim centers the issue of the historical recollection of injustice, which is important to people whose identity has been constituted by such injustice. As Waldron says, "it is a well known characteristic of great injustice that those who suffer it go to their deaths with the conviction that these things must not be forgotten" (Waldron 1992: 5). The descendants of those who suffer such injustice are normally just as committed to keeping the memory alive, insisting that the fact that such injustice occurred be publicly acknowledged and made part of the public record.

The political significance of memory should not be underestimated. It is widely acknowledged that the indigenous rights movement in Latin America was precipitated through mobilization against planned celebrations of the five-hundredth anniversary of the "Discovery of the Americas" in 1992. Indigenous people throughout Latin America rose up to insist that their own governments, and the government of Spain, acknowledge the violence and oppression that the so-called discovery had entailed. They defiantly renamed the anniversary "Five Hundred Years of Oppression."

As Waldron goes on to say, "reparations may symbolize a society's undertaking not to forget or deny that a particular injustice took place, and to respect and help sustain a dignified sense of identity-in-memory for the people affected" (ibid.: 6). To forget is considered immoral, a sign of disrespect toward those who suffered and died, and of contempt toward the present community. A society offers respect to the community by acknowledging, mourning, and seeking to redress, the historic injustices that have been perpetrated against it.

Beyond maintaining "identity-in-memory" for those who suffered, the retrieval of injustice establishes the present identity of groups against whom harm was historically perpetrated. In international and domestic forums alike, indigenous peoples establish their standing through a catalogue of the harms they have suffered. As Melissa Williams has argued, "collective memory may surface as a response to discriminatory treatment, creating a solidarity and group self-consciousness that would not otherwise exist" (1998: 186).

Moreover, as Williams shows, the framework of historic and ongoing injustice offers "a schema for identifying groups that have a strong claim to recognition within political institutions" (ibid.: 176). As she says, "the claims of marginalized ascriptive groups to special representation in politics are legitimized by a clear and strong connection between present inequality and the kinds of past discrimination that were sanctioned by dominant social groups and often enforced by the state" (ibid.: 177). There are both objective and subjective criteria by which such claims can be measured. The objective criterion is the historical record: "evidence provided by law, documents, and other generally accepted sources that the discrimination actually occurred." The subjective criterion, however, is provided by memory – "the meaning the past has for members of those groups who were the targets of discrimination and oppression" (ibid.: 177).

Constructivist theories of identity formation generate the deep normative implication that developing a universal theory of multicultural citizenship is a mistaken enterprise. In every case, how democratic institutions should process the claims of culture is a political matter, rooted in a particular logic and history of political incorporation and exclusion. It is a matter that is therefore more appropriately, and fruitfully, addressed through the framework of compensatory justice than through the framework of communal attachment, identity, and cultural group difference. The structural injustice framework seeks to transform the future by offering restitution for a past that has actually constituted the social groups that play a principal role in shaping life chances.[4]

The framework of structural injustice establishes a direct line of responsibility between the actions and the obligations of states. States have obligations toward oppressed populations, not because they have distinctive cultural practices, but because the state has discriminated against them

[4] In his excellent book *Postcolonial Liberalism*, Duncan Ivison also makes an argument for considering indigenous claims through the prism of historic and ongoing injustice. He nevertheless comes to this argument from a completely different route. Melissa Williams also includes the concept of historic injustice as part of her argument for legislative representation for historically disadvantaged groups (Ivison 2002; Williams 1998).

on the basis of those distinct cultural practices. If the state has not done so, it can reasonably claim that the fact that a group has distinct cultural practices generates no responsibility on the part of the state. But since modern states have been built on conceptions of nationhood that often invoke cultural (and racial) markers to legitimate state boundaries, most contemporary states cannot claim that they have not discriminated on the basis of cultural difference, and the structural injustice framework therefore establishes a clear contemporary line of obligation that links "ethnic" politics, including indigenous politics, to the Westphalian (and postcolonial) state system. In so doing, it attempts to sidestep the normative instabilities that are produced by claims to standing that rest on "identity."

III.   Membership rights

Membership rights flow from a constructivist account of identity formation along three streams. First, through membership rights, states offer redress for structural injustices that have harmed individuals because they are members of low-status groups. Second, membership rights stretch "identity" politics beyond culture, to include demands for redistribution and representation as well as recognition. Third, membership rights offer a framework for forging oppositional and independent political challenges that may be able to break out of the narrow political space offered by culture and identity. Membership rights ground a deeper and potentially more challenging engagement between the state and its citizens than either individual or collective rights.

The category of membership rights tries to respond to the question of what kind of rights are compatible with the fact that groups are constructed and, more specifically, with the fact that they have been constructed precisely through the unequal allocation of rights, representation, and citizenship. Neither individual nor collective rights respond appropriately to the fact that states have played an important role in constructing contemporary boundaries of ethnic group membership by using cultural practices, language, and tradition to mark the boundaries of exclusion and selective inclusion. Membership rights are differentiated individual rights that take seriously both the constructed character and the social weight of groups.

The liberal commitment to individual rights is rooted in a universal framework of equal treatment. For many liberals, justice and equality are anchored in a conception of neutrality that requires that every individual be treated equally. As Joseph Carens has pointed out, this is an important ideal, and one which "provides grounds for criticizing policies and practices that exclude or marginalize distinct groups of citizens" (Carens 2000: 178).

But, given the legacy of differentiation and discrimination that structures all contemporary societies in different ways, equal treatment will not be sufficient to provide all individuals with equal opportunities. An undifferentiated conception of citizenship treats everyone as if they are in fact equal, whereas states themselves have created differences of access, recognition, and prestige, as well as wealth, education, and services, with lasting implications. Given the central role they play in determining life chances, the constructed character of groups does not imply that they have no social or political character, or that they carry no normative weight. Individual rights, which treat everyone equally, respond inadequately to injustices that have been suffered as a result of putative group membership.

Nevertheless, against the backdrop of constructed histories, the normative weight of ethnic groups does not extend to collective rights to "self"-government that rely on organic conceptions of the group. It is no coincidence that demands for collective rights – rights that accrue to the group as a whole rather than to individual members of the group – rest on essentialized notions of group history, boundaries, and identity. They must, because there must be an identifiable unit to which (or whom) a right accrues. As Charles Taylor has pointed out, the Herderian notion of a cultural group, as *a Volk* (singular) that should be true to *it*self (singular) underpins the very idea of a collective right (Taylor 1994: 31). If a cultural group is as likely to be internally divided, to have shifting boundaries, and to be of varying levels of importance to different members of the group, then it follows logically that a collective right will be captured by some powerful segment of the group – that is, by individual members of the group (Okin 1999). Such groups are not organic units, and they need therefore to justify their authority through the principles of representation and human rights, in the same way that states are obliged to establish the legitimacy of their rule. Rights that treat a collective as a single unit are logically incoherent in the face of the fluid, constructed, and multiple dimensions of the collective units in which people claim membership.

Membership rights try therefore to steer a path between individual and collective conceptions of rights in a way that is consistent with the constructed character of groups. Differentiated individual rights are sensitive to the structural conditions that constitute individual human beings and that afford them differential access to most of the things that matter in contemporary societies. When the rights of some citizens have been distorted and degraded by discrimination and oppression directed at members of particular groups, such members can legitimately demand membership rights that offer all of the normal entitlements of citizenship along with some distinctive entitlements.[5] Such rights retain the non-negotiable concern of liberalism for the well-being of individuals, while nevertheless acknowledging that individuals are embedded in groups or categories that have (negatively) affected their life chances, but also, importantly, offer opportunities for political agency.

Membership rights nevertheless endorse a conception of differentiated individual rights that is justified on the basis of structural rather than cultural difference. Some structural differences have culture as their organizing principle – people suffer discrimination and exclusion because they have different cultural practices. But others suffer because they are Black, or poor, or gay, or women. The principle behind membership rights is that the liberal democratic state owes differentiated rights that are responsive to the demands of members of each of these groups for the same reason – because the state has played a central role in ordering society in such a way that people who have the same phenotypical traits, biological sex, sexual orientation, or cultural practices might perceive such markers as a binding identity.

In so doing, membership rights attempt to move beyond the controversy over individual versus collective rights that has fixed debates over multiculturalism and democracy and narrowed the scope of such politics. The attempt to reconcile concern for the well-being of individuals with a desire to be responsive to the demands of groups has dominated the normative theoretical agenda. But this controversy has limited our attention to one particular category of rights, namely third-generation cultural rights, obscuring the demands that many groups also make for first- and second-generation rights, and crowding out a broader analysis of how such rights work with third-generation rights.

Membership rights bundle civil and political, social and economic, and cultural rights, refocusing attention on the premise, which is taken for granted in the field of human rights law, that the three generations of rights are interdependent and mutually supportive (Scott and Macklem 1992). A focus on collective/cultural rights, to the exclusion of civil

---

[5] The idea of differentiated individual rights is well entrenched, both in actually existing constitutions and in political theory. Joseph Carens (2000) explains, for example, that the concept of "citizen-plus" status was coined in the 1966 Hawthorn–Tremblay Report that sought to reconcile Canadian citizenship with Indian status. As he says, "Clearly the goal here was to achieve some sort of evenhanded justice, granting distinctive entitlements out of a sense that this was a fair way to respond to the history and circumstances of Indians in Canada" (ibid.: 187). What I argue here is that it is this conception of rights that is conceptually matched to a constructivist account of identity and group formation.

and political and social and economic rights, will actually undermine the possibility of securing a robust cultural framework. In the face of poverty, discrimination, and hopelessness, culture can disintegrate, further marginalizing people who have been constituted by exclusion and by their inability to shape the terms of their inclusion. Such groups should not have to make a choice between demands for recognition, redistribution, and representation (Fraser 2000).

Unlike a cultural difference framework, which legitimates the demands of ethnic groups for such cultural rights as language preservation and cultural autonomy, a structural injustice framework justifies extending the political reach of so-called ethnic groups to demands for redistribution and participation as well as some forms of cultural protection. A structural injustice framework therefore covers more political ground than a cultural difference framework. Using structural injustice, activists can insist on rights to political representation, the protection of civil liberties, individual freedoms, protection from discrimination, and social and economic welfare, that may not be covered by demands for cultural protection and recognition, or even by autonomy and self-government.

Membership rights therefore have a strategic effect on the scope of opposition politics. Such rights expose groups constituted through structural exclusion to alliances among groups, whereas, as many people have argued, some forms of a politics of identity spell the demise of alliances across groups and the twilight of common dreams (Gitlin 1995). Because they do not derive from cultural specificity, membership rights have a universal logic, notwithstanding the fact that they accord special rights to members of some groups and not others. The grounds of structural injustice on which they tender such rights establish the basis for alliances among all sorts of groups (women, indigenous peoples, African-Americans) that have suffered such injustice. Groups that anchor their demands in cultural difference may instead turn inward, lacking grounds to make common cause with potential allies.

Logically, the proposition that membership rights should include first- and second-generation rights, and not only third-generation rights, follows from the account advanced here of the structural foundations of group identity. That is, the blinkered fixation with collective and cultural rights that has focused normative debates on multiculturalism and democracy, as well as many activists who mobilize so-called identity groups, follows from the assumption that what relevantly distinguishes such groups is cultural difference. If instead the legitimating principle of group standing is structural injustice, the political demands of groups may extend beyond culture.

Finally, rights may also play an important role in opening up the political space of oppositional politics. Where such rights are enshrined in constitutions, they recast oppositional politics as a demand that the state fulfill its own promise. As such, rights can structure politics as an immanent critique, harnessing the prevailing de jure ideology against the de facto inequalities it sustains. Rights offer a way into the political realm because they expose the gap between promise and fulfillment, offering a powerful discursive strategy and point of intervention to activists who are seeking to engage the state. Through rights, activists politicize the contradiction between the dominant ideology and their reality (Crenshaw 1995: 111).

Individual rights have nevertheless been criticized as atomizing. Such rights may divert politics into the courtroom, and sacrifice collective political organization to individual legal strategies (Tushnet 1984; Gabel and Kennedy 1984). The focus of attention on the individual may undermine collective solidarity, and encourage the pursuit of private happiness over the pursuit of the common good.

Collective rights may also divert attention from the public political sphere, redrawing the boundaries of the polity around minority groups, and directing attention inward. One of the goals of collective rights is to establish the priority of subgroup boundaries, and to reduce the points of interaction and dependence between group members and the national society and institutions that threaten their culture and have rendered their subordinate status. Collective rights are not designed primarily to foster transformative engagement between group members and state institutions.

Membership rights may engender such engagement. Such rights offer standing to excluded peoples, generating incentives for collective political solidarity. Indigenous activists, for example, played an important role in developing and entrenching the concept of indigenous rights in international law. But indigenous rights – which have the scope of membership rights rather than collective rights – have in turn fostered the formation of an international indigenous rights movement. Whereas individual rights may fail to motivate collective action, membership rights furnish a framework that is distinctly political.

At the same time as they generate incentives for collective solidarity, membership rights should also sustain a framework for creative reappropriations of identity, and for challenges to state-imposed categories of membership. Membership rights should have more room than collective rights for multiple and overlapping memberships, for moving among memberships, and especially for the rejection of membership. Whereas collective rights can serve to reify existing categories, boundaries, and hierarchies, membership rights are designed to adapt to shifts in structure and social meaning.

IV.   Conclusion

The argument for justifying political claims through an appeal to structural injustice follows directly from a structural account of the origins of social groups. The obligations of states lie not in the fact that people have distinct cultural practices but in the fact that states have used such cultural practices to establish the boundaries of inclusion and exclusion. States have also used such markers as race, gender, and class to establish the boundaries of citizenship, which extends the obligations of states beyond "ethnic" groups alone to categories of people who have been "raced," "gendered," and "classed." A structural injustice framework establishes the link not only between the state and the groups it has constituted, but also among groups that have been similarly constituted, notwithstanding the different markers that have been employed to denote irreconcilable difference. A structural theory of obligation links state responsibility to state actions.

Membership rights respond to structural injustices. They arise to the extent that groups have been constructed through the unequal allocation of rights and representation, precisely because group membership therefore plays an important role in determining life chances. Membership rights are differentiated individual rights that are assigned to individuals whose group membership has operated as a source of exclusion, discrimination, or oppression. They are designed to redress such structural injustices, to put individuals on an equal footing in a robust, and not merely formal, sense. To this end, membership rights bundle civil and political, social and economic, and cultural rights.

Critical liberalism proposes a reformulation of the paradigm that has guided both normative theorizing and political activism around the issue of ethnic minority rights, offering a normative framework that transforms the scope of so-called identity politics and provides an alternative theory of state obligation toward ethnic and other dispossessed categories.

In general, however, a critical conception of liberalism has less to say about which solutions will be negotiated in particular instances – whether the appropriate response to social group demands is affirmative action, representative quotas, or self-government – and more to say about the way in which political dialogue is framed. A more critical conception of liberalism is aimed at shaping democratic deliberation in ways that take responsibility for the past, and reorienting the rights framework at the core of liberalism. These framing constraints make some settlements more likely than others, and they will affect the scope of such solutions as self-government. But just which solutions will be negotiated in particular instances is still an explicitly open question, to be determined by the historical context that has shaped the social group, and by politics.

BIBLIOGRAPHY

Appiah, Anthony. 1994. "Identity, Authenticity, Survival: Multicultural Societies and Social Reproduction," in *Multiculturalism*, ed. Amy Gutmann. Princeton, NJ: Princeton University Press, 149–63.

Barry, Brian. 2001. *Culture and Equality: An Egalitarian Critique of Multiculturalism*. Cambridge, MA: Harvard University Press.

Benhabib, Seyla. 2002. *The Claims of Culture: Equality and Diversity in the Global Era*. Princeton, NJ: Princeton University Press.

Bilgrami, Akeel. 1992. "What is a Muslim?: Fundamental Commitment and Cultural Identity." *Critical Inquiry* 18 (4), Summer: 821–42.

Carens, Joseph. 2000. *Culture, Citizenship, and Community: A Contextual Exploration of Justice as Evenhandedness*. Oxford: Oxford University Press.

Crenshaw, Kimberlé. 1995. "Race, Reform, and Retrenchment: Transformation and Legitimation in Antidiscrimination Law," in *Critical Race Theory*, ed. Kimberlé Crenshaw, Neil Gotanda, Gary Peller, and Kendall Thomas. New York: The Free Press.

Dworkin, Ronald. 1978. "Liberalism," in *Public and Private Morality*, ed. Stuart Hampshire. Cambridge: Cambridge University Press.

1985. *A Matter of Principle*. London: Harvard University Press.

Fraser, Nancy. 2000. "Rethinking Recognition." *New Left Review* 3 (May–June): 107–20.

Gabel, Peter, and Duncan Kennedy. 1984. "Roll over Beethoven." *Stanford Law Review*, I (29): 1–55.

Galston, William. 1995. "Two Concepts of Liberalism." *Ethics* 105 (3 April): 516–34.

Gitlin, Todd. 1995. *The Twilight of Common Dreams: Why America Is Wracked by Culture Wars*. New York: Holt.

Ivison, Duncan. 2002. *Postcolonial Liberalism*. Cambridge: Cambridge University Press.

Jung, Courtney. 2001. "The Burden of Culture and the Limits of Liberal Responsibility."*Constellations* 8 (2): 219–35.

2008. *The Moral Force of Indigenous Politics: Critical Liberalism and the Zapatistas*. Cambridge: Cambridge University Press.

Kukathas, Chandran. 1992. "Are There Any Cultural Rights?" *Political Theory* 20 (February): 105–39.

Kymlicka, Will. 1995. *Multicultural Citizenship*. Oxford: Oxford University Press.

Macedo, Stephen. 1995. "Liberal Civic Education and Religious Fundamentalism: The Case of God v. John Rawls?" *Ethics* 105: 468–96.

Macklem, Patrick. 2001. *Indigenous Difference and the Constitution of Canada*. Toronto: University of Toronto Press.

Okin, Susan. 1999. *Is Multiculturalism Bad for Women?* Princeton, NJ: Princeton University Press.

Rawls, John. 1971. *A Theory of Justice.* London: Oxford University Press.

    1985. "Justice as Fairness: Political not Metaphysical." *Philosophy and Public Affairs* 14 (3): 223–51.

    1993. *Political Liberalism.* New York: Columbia University Press.

Sandel, Michael. 1982. *Liberalism and the Limits of Justice.* Cambridge: Cambridge University Press.

Scott, Craig and Patrick Macklem. 1992. "Constitutional Ropes of Sand or Justiciable Guarantees?" *University of Pennsylvania Law Review* 141: 1–148.

Spinner-Halev, Jeff. 2007. "From Historic to Enduring Injustice," *Political Theory* 35 (5): 574–97.

Taylor, Charles. 1994. "The Politics of Recognition," in Amy Gutmann, ed. *Multiculturalism.* Princeton, NJ: Princeton University Press.

Tushnet, Mark. 1984. "An Essay on Rights." *Texas Law Review* 62: 1363–1403.

Waldron, Jeremy. 1992. "Superseding Historic Injustice." *Ethics* 103: 4–28.

Walzer, Michael. 1983. *Spheres of Justice.* New York: Basic Books.

Williams, Melissa. 1998. *Voice, Trust, and Memory: Marginalized Groups and the Failings of Liberal Representation.* Princeton, NJ: Princeton University Press.

Winbush, Raymond, A. (ed.). 2003. *Should America Pay? Slavery and the Raging Debate on Reparations.* New York: HarperCollins.

Yashar, Deborah. 1998. "Contesting Citizenship: Indigenous Movements and Democracy in Latin America." *Comparative Politics* 31 (1): 23–42.

    1999. "Democracy, Indigenous Movements, and the Postliberal Challenge in Latin America." *World Politics* 52 (1): 76–104.

    2005. "Citizenship Regimes, the State, and Ethnic Cleavages," in *Contesting Citizenship in Latin America.* Cambridge: Cambridge University Press, 31–53.

Young, Iris Marion. 1990. *Justice and the Politics of Difference.* Princeton, NJ: Princeton University Press.

7   Settlers and natives in North America

Mahmood Mamdani

I.   A colonized population

The legal position of Native Americans under US law has been the subject of two key debates. The first revolves around state versus federal claims to sovereignty over Native Americans. The second is over the relationship of Indians to the political community that is the United States. The first debate has been resolved in favor of federal sovereignty. The second has revolved around two issues – tribal autonomy and individual citizenship rights – and has yet to reach a satisfactory resolution. Tribal autonomy is subject to federal plenary powers; at the same time, Native Americans are a special class of citizens: both citizens and wards of the United States, they are without any constitutionally guaranteed rights.

State sovereignty was historically the preferred shield for settlers wanting to advance local interests. States vied in the courts for full jurisdiction over Native Americans and African-Americans residing within their boundaries and, in extreme cases, went to war over it. *State v. Forman* (1835) was the first case to confirm state criminal jurisdiction over Indian tribes in direct contradiction to Supreme Court decisions to the contrary (Harring 1994: 42). By the 1880s, most states with significant Indian populations asserted such criminal jurisdiction and simply exercised it. Some, such as California, did so expressly by statute; others, such as Wisconsin and New Mexico, did so with support from judicial opinions under existing state law (ibid.: 49–50). Finally, in 1953, Congress enacted Public Law 280 authorizing states to assume criminal and civil jurisdiction over Indian reservations within their borders, with or without the consent of the tribes involved.[1] None of this, however, should detract from the fact that whatever powers states enjoyed over Indian

---

[1] In 1963, the State of Washington assumed full jurisdiction over consenting Indian tribes but only partial jurisdiction over non-consenting tribes. The assumption of partial jurisdiction depended on three factors: the status of the land on which the regulated conduct occurred, the subject matter of the regulated conduct, and the race of the person involved in the activity, Indian or non-Indian (Newton 1983–4: 281).

communities were a result of federal delegation; whether during the colonial era or after, the Indian question has been an exclusive prerogative of the federal government and not the states.

This much is clear from an examination of how the crown and the US Constitution dealt with key aspects of Indian policy: land, Indian affairs, trade, and treaties and wars. Every colony the crown established in North America had one legal characteristic in common – *the soil* granted to the colonies was subject to the unextinguished right of occupancy of the Indian tribes. The crown, however, retained the title to all lands occupied by those tribes and the exclusive right to extinguish the tribal right of occupancy. The Proclamation of 1763 both limited Indian Territory to west of Mississippi and put it beyond the reach of settlers. The United States built on this tradition after 1776. Native Americans have never been accorded the legal status of full title by the US government; the land they held was put in a different conceptual category, called variously "Indian title" or "right of occupancy" (Castile and Bee 1992: 63). Their land rights have been more qualified, akin to usufruct (use) rights of African peasants that obtained under forms of communal tenure instituted during the British colonial era.

Indian affairs refers to contacts between Indians and settlers. Initially regulated by the individual colonies, the crown began to remove control of Indian affairs from the colonists in 1755 and vested two British superintendents with full responsibility for regulating political relations with the Indians. In matters of *trade*, a plan was proposed in 1764 to remove Indian trade from the control of the colonies and put it into the hands of officers appointed by the crown. Though never formally adopted, it was used by the British superintendents until 1768, when the regulation of trade was returned to the colonies. The provisions on Indian affairs and trade were reproduced in the final copy of the "Articles of Confederation," accepted by the Continental Congress in 1777, which contained the provision that Congress had the sole and exclusive right and power of "regulating the trade and managing all affairs with the Indians not members of any of the states," followed by an ambiguous qualification – "provided that the legislative right of any state within its own limits be not infringed or violated." The Articles also provided that no state could make treaties or alliances or engage in war with the Indians without the consent of Congress, unless actually invaded or in great danger of being invaded (Johnson 1973: 981–2).

The provisions in the Articles of Confederation were carried into the US Constitution, different articles in which gave the federal government the unqualified right to extinguish the tribal right of occupancy and establish control over Indian "trade" and "affairs," including making treaties or war. It is worth underlining the different ways in which the Constitution treated the Native American and the African slave. Unlike the chattel slave who "was subject to the internal laws of the US without his consent or participation," Indians were classified in law as "free persons," but they were excluded from representation, and thus were not citizens. Not only was the Indian "not a member of the new national community," he was seen as "a threat" who "had to be controlled" (ibid.: 985–6). Unlike persons of African origin who were to be mastered, Indians were enemy peoples. In *Federalist* 24, Alexander Hamilton described "the savage tribes on our western frontier" as natural enemies of the US and natural allies of the British and Spanish, and cited the presence of the Indian tribes as reason for keeping a national defense force. In *Federalist* 25 Hamilton raised the specter of the territories of Britain, Spain, and the Indian tribes encircling the Union from Maine to Georgia as a common danger (ibid.: 984). The 1866 Civil Rights Act that guaranteed "the same rights" to citizens explicitly excluded Indians from citizenship (ibid.: 217). Even when Indians did become citizens, starting after the First World War, they were not considered citizens by birth, and their citizenship rights remained qualified by earlier historical limitations. As we shall see, Indians – unlike other citizens of the United States – were defined as *both* citizens and wards. As Johnson says, "though Indian affairs are not strictly 'foreign' affairs, they are in a constitutional sense 'external' affairs." That power over Indian affairs is "to be exercised as an attribute of national sovereignty" means that "authority rests in the federal government even in the absence of an affirmative constitutional grant" (ibid.: 987). The Indian was thus different from the Black person in politics, and therefore in law. The Black person was marked by *individual* servitude, but Indians were colonized as peoples comprising so many *tribes and nations*. The specificity of the Indian question was fully elaborated by Chief Justice John Marshall in a set of Supreme Court rulings over a decade, 1823 to 1832.

Marshall's verdict

Supreme Court opinion subordinating Native Americans to the jurisdiction of the federal government is set out in three seminal opinions, rendered over a decade by Chief Justice John Marshall, in three crucial cases, *Johnson* v. *M'Intosh* (1823), *Cherokee Nation* v. *Georgia* (1831), and *Worcester* v. *Georgia* (1832). Marshall was a member of the founding generation, and developed a legal model of Indian rights that relied upon the same basic language used by the Constitution to define US Indian policy. Both a jurist and a historian, he was loath to confuse legal and historical judgment. While upholding the legal order, his judgments often provide acute and rare insights into the relationship between law, history, and politics. Marshall's single most important contribution was to underline federal recognition of Indian nations as "domestic dependent nations." By so doing, he both incorporated Native American communities within the scheme of constitutional federalism and defined the limits of doing so. Was the Marshallian doctrine of "domestic dependent nations" a victory for those who sought autonomy within the United States, or did it mark – however gracefully and skillfully – the gravestone of Indian autonomy and Indian rights? Two views are on offer. One has been advanced by Charles Wilkinson who sees the Marshall trilogy as having "conceived a model that can be described broadly as calling for largely autonomous tribal governments subject to an overriding federal authority but essentially free of federal control" (Wilkinson 1987: 24; Williams 2005: 228). A lesser degree of conviction is conveyed by the Native American legal theorist Robert Williams Jr. who has argued that Marshall built a "model of inferior and diminished Indian rights" (Williams 2005: 48–9).

It is worth going through each judgment in the Marshallian trilogy, for together they laid the foundation stone of federal Indian policy for the next century and a half. The first of the opinions, *Johnson* v. *M'Intosh* (1823), gets to the heart of the matter distinguishing Native Americans from American settlers and states that Native Americans are a conquered people. The significance of *Johnson* is that it is the opinion in which Chief Justice Marshall unquestioningly incorporated the European colonial era's "doctrine of discovery" as the keystone for defining the legal position of Native Americans under US law. This is how Marshall's argument proceeded.

On the discovery of this immense continent, the great nations of Europe were eager to appropriate to themselves so much of it as they could respectively acquire . . . But, as they were all in pursuit of nearly the same object, it was necessary, in order to avoid conflicting settlements, and consequent war with each other, to establish a principle, which all should acknowledge as the law by which the right of acquisition, which they all asserted, should be regulated as between themselves. This principle was, that discovery gave title to the government by whose subjects, or by whose authority, it was made, against all other European governments, which title might be consummated by possession. (*Johnson* v. *M'Intosh* 1823: 572–3)

True, Indians continued to possess the title of occupancy, but this was inferior to the right of domain that discovery gave to a European power and which was "an exclusive right to extinguish the Indian title of occupancy, either by purchase or by conquest" (ibid.: 587). Marshall was under no illusion that the doctrine of discovery was "opposed to natural right, and to the usages of civilized nations," but he argued that it was "indispensable to that system under which the country has been settled." Thus, he concluded, in as unequivocal a confirmation as one is likely to come across in legal texts, that politics trumps law:

Conquest gives a title which the Courts of the conqueror cannot deny, whatever the private and speculative opinions of individuals may be, respecting the original justice of the claim which has been successfully asserted. The British government, which was then our government, and whose rights have passed to the United States, asserted title to all the lands occupied by Indians, within the chartered limits of the British colonies . . . The title to a vast portion of the lands we now hold, originates in them. It is not for the Courts of this country to question the validity of this title, or to sustain one which is incompatible with it. (ibid.: 588–9)

Loath to paint necessity as virtue, Marshall nonetheless acknowledged the dark side of the history of right: that might creates right. Can one speak of Native Americans possessing "rights" in such an arrangement, no matter how qualified, as "inferior" or "diminished"? Marshall answered this question in *Cherokee Nation v. Georgia* (1831). He began by affirming that the Cherokees were indeed a state, "a distinct political society, separated from others, capable of managing its own affairs and governing itself" (ibid.: 14–15). But he doubted whether these tribes can be "denominated foreign nations" for they are territorially "a part of the United States," "within the jurisdictional limits of the United States," and "under the protection of the United States." He suggested they be more appropriately designated as "domestic dependent nations":

They occupy a territory to which we assert a title independent of their will, which must take effect in point of possession when their right of possession ceases. Meanwhile they are in a state of pupilage. Their relation to the United States resembles that of a ward to his guardian.

And then he proceeded to define the relationship between ward and guardian:

They look to our government for protection; rely upon its kindness and its power; appeal to it for relief to their wants; and address the president as their great father. They and their country are considered by foreign nations, as well as by ourselves, as being so completely under the sovereignty and dominion of the United States, that any attempt to acquire their lands, or to form a political connexion with them, would be considered by all as an invasion of our territory, and an act of hostility. (ibid.: 16)

A ward is like a child in law. A ward holds no property right, only a right of use. A ward cannot bring independent action in courts of the United

States (Williams 2005: 61).[2] Without property rights and the right to maintain an action in court, Indians were not citizens; rather than rights-bearing members of the political community called the United States, they lived on the territory of the United States on sufferance of its citizens and their representative political institutions, particularly Congress. So Marshall concluded his judgment:

> If it be true that the Cherokee nation have rights, this is not the tribunal in which those rights are to be asserted. If it be true that wrongs have been inflicted, and that still greater are to be apprehended, this is not the tribunal which can redress the past or prevent the future. (ibid.: 18)

The conundrum that Native Americans faced can be glimpsed from the key facts surrounding *Worcester* v. *Georgia* (1832). The case originated from an attempt by the state of Georgia to extinguish the tribe as a distinct, self-governing society within its borders. Georgia's solution was to strip the Cherokee of their tribal citizenship and lands, and thereby to integrate them as a free people but under white racial dictatorship in the state. The result would be to place individual Cherokees in the same position as free Blacks – subject to the onerous, racially discriminatory legal regime imposed by Georgia on all "free persons of color" within its sovereign borders. Section 15 of the Act passed by the legislature of Georgia on December 19, 1829 spelt out the consequences in no uncertain terms:

> And be it further enacted, that no Indian or descendant of any Indian, residing within the Creek or Cherokee nation of Indians, shall be deemed a competent witness in any court of this state to which a white person may be a party, except such white person resides within the said nation. (*Worcester* v. *Georgia* 1832: 7)

As legally designated second-class citizens of color, they would be unable to vote, unable to serve in the state militia, and unable to send their children to Georgia's public schools under the racial apartheid laws

---

[2] Marshall then went on speculate as to why the founders did not provide constitutional rights for Native Americans:

> In considering the subject, the habits and usages of the Indians, in their intercourse with their white neighbors, ought not to be entirely disregarded. At the time the constitution was framed, the idea of appealing to an American court of justice for an assertion of right or a redress of wrong, had perhaps never entered the mind of an Indian or of his tribe. Their appeal was to the tomahawk, or to the government. This was well understood by the statesmen who framed the constitution of the United States, and might furnish some reason for omitting to enumerate them among the parties who might sue in the courts of the nation.

This speculation can only be excused as an attempted rationalization.

that would apply to the Cherokees under state jurisdiction. In addition, the "Cherokee codes" would enable the state to take control over the immensely valuable Indian lands within its borders and make them available to Georgia's white citizen farmers and plantation owners. So the choice for the Cherokee was between a colonial subjugation to the federal government and racial subjugation to settlers in the form of a second-class citizenship in the state of Georgia. In mid-nineteenth-century United States, the former was the lot of Indians and the latter of Blacks.

It is also worth noting that the Court failed to arrive at a unanimous verdict as regards the legal status of the Cherokee within the United States; instead, the justices divided three ways, offering three different interpretations. Marshall's position, that the Cherokee nation was not a foreign nation but a domestic dependent nation, was shared by only Justice McLean. Justices Thompson and Story believed that the Cherokee were indeed a foreign nation, even if defeated. The two remaining justices, Baldwin and Johnson, believed that the Cherokees were a conquered people with no status as a nation at all, either foreign or domestic (Harring 1994: 30–1). The interesting fact is that none of the justices were willing to think outside the box, beyond the historical fact of conquest, to contemplate either their coexistence or their integration as a free people within the political community called the United States. I shall return to this point after considering the third case.

In his third and final opinion on the subject, *Worcester* v. *Georgia* (1832), Marshall returned to the question of power and to its claims, first to the "doctrine of discovery," and then to ask whether the right that followed upon discovery was an effect of a superiority of civilization or of brute force. He began by reflecting on the world in 1491: "America, separated from Europe by a wide ocean, was inhabited by a distinct people, divided into separate nations, independent of each other and of the rest of the world, having institutions of their own, and governing themselves by their own laws." He then dismissed the idea that discovery could be the basis of a claim of dominion:

It is difficult to comprehend the proposition, that the inhabitants of either quarter of the globe could have rightful original claims of dominion over the inhabitants of the other, or over the lands they occupied; or that the discovery of either by the other should give the discoverer rights in the country discovered, which annulled the pre-existing rights of its ancient possessors. (*Worcester* v. *Georgia* 1832: 33)

He next posed a rhetorical question, as to whether the right of domain could be the effect of superiority in civilization: "Or has nature, or the great Creator of all things, conferred these rights over hunters and fishermen, on agriculturists and manufacturers?" Finally, he concluded that the claim of dominion lay in the naked fact of conquest:

> But power, war, conquest, give rights, which, after possession, are conceded by the world; and which can never be controverted by those on whom they descend. We proceed, then, to the actual state of things, having glanced at their origin; because holding it in our recollection might shed some light on existing pretensions. (ibid.: 33–4)

Worcester went on to reflect on the nature of that power: first, on who had the right to exercise it and, second, on whether there were any limits to that exercise. On the first question, Marshall was unequivocal, holding that it is the federal government, and not the individual states, that possesses the exclusive right to exercise control over Indian affairs (Williams 2005: 63). But on the second question he equivocated, leaving plenty of room for further interpretation. To begin with, Marshall defined the limits of the "principle of discovery": if it "shut out the right of competition among those who had agreed to it," it could *not* "annul the previous rights of those who had not agreed to it." These were "the rights of those already in possession, either as aboriginal occupants, or as occupants by virtue of a discovery made before the memory of man." What were these rights of the original occupants? According to Marshall, they were the right to sell – but only to the discoverer; they had the right of occupancy, but subject to the superior right of domain that belonged to the discoverer (*Worcester* v. *Georgia* 1832: 34–6).

    Worcester has been regarded by many as a landmark victory for Indian rights. But none of these rights is "inalienable," and none is protected by a constitutional guarantee. While its principle of federal supremacy in Indian affairs theoretically immunizes tribal Indians from different forms of state encroachments on tribal rights and interests (Williams 2005: 69), its focus on the relation between the same Native Americans and the federal government does no more than affirm a colonial relationship between the United States and Native Americans.[3] The notion of tribal sovereignty was not without substance: in placing treaty Indians outside the domain of state law, the Supreme Court gave them effective protection against state jurisdiction. But in doing so, the Supreme Court placed these same Indians squarely within the domain of federal law, at the mercy of Congress, and without any protection. At the heart of this relationship is a lack of constitutional definition and protection of Indian rights, a situation that continues today and that explains the shifts and

---

[3] Williams notes that his response to an 1828 address made by his close friend and colleague on the court, Justice Joseph Story, suggests that Marshall himself was keenly aware of the Indian's essential fate as perpetual colonial subject under US control (2005: 226–7).

turns in the legal position of Indian communities – as summed up in the doctrine of tribal sovereignty – in the United States over the past two centuries and more.

II.   Tribal sovereignty

Indian sovereignty historically rested on two independent pillars: control over land as the principal means of subsistence, and the community's right to organize and administer its own affairs. Two turning points mark the step-by-step erosion of the economic and political ground that supported these pillars: the 1763 Royal Proclamation that for the first time referred to a portion – and not the whole – of North American territory as Indian Country, and the 1871 pronouncement by the US Congress that no more treaties would be entered into between the United States and Native American communities. Both formally acknowledged processes that had been in motion for some time: the loss of land in the first instance, and the loss of political independence in the second.

The term Indian Country[4] was first used in the famous Royal Proclamation of 1763, issued by King George III. Prior to that there was no reference to a place called Indian Country, since all attempts to access land in North America began with the recognition that it belonged to Indians (Wilkinson 1987: 89). Three types of practices predominated in the early days. The first was that of *renting*, as when Maine settlers rented land from Indians. The other two involved the *purchase* of land from Indians, either by individual settlers (as when Dutch and English colonies made grants of Indian land to settlers and then expected them to purchase it individually from Indians – that is, if the land had not been confiscated from Indians in war) or by the colony concerned (as English successors to the Dutch did in the Middle Atlantic colonies, when the colony bought the land wholesale from the Indians, then granted it piecemeal to settlers, thereby obviating the need for individual settlers or groups of settlers to bargain with the Indians). This third type of practice was adopted by the English crown when it took control of Indian affairs from some of the colonies, and then by the USA on the formation of the confederation and then the Union. Eventually, all three – the colonies, the crown and the US – refused to recognize Indian claim to Indian lands beyond simple possession or occupancy. And yet the fact was that all three had in the past paid money to the Indians in exchange for a

---

[4] From this point of view, Indian tribes are viewed as foreign nations and their aggregated reservation areas are technically known as "the Indian Country," with each reservation being "Indian Country."

formal quitting of their claim. Did this not, at least implicitly, acknowledge Indian ownership of land? In time the United States Supreme Court, trying to resolve the inconsistencies of theory and practice, referred to the purchase from Indians as the purchase merely of their "right of occupancy," as distinct from a right of domain or ownership (Macleod 1928: 203–4).

It is the distinction between the right of use and the right of domain over the same land that became the cutting edge of a process which acknowledged Indian right to use land but denied their sovereignty over it. Tribes were free to sell land, but only to the nation said to be their protector. For example, Article 2 of the treaty of the US with the tribes of the territory northwest of the Ohio, of January 9, 1789, *guaranteed them the possession of their lands forever*, provided that "the said nations, or either of them, shall not be at liberty to sell or dispose of the same, or any part thereof to any sovereign power, except the United States; nor to the subjects or citizens of any subject power, nor to the subjects or citizens of the United States" (ibid.: 440). A renewal of the treaty of October 22, 1784 with Iroquois tribes, except the Mohawks, fixed "a boundary line between the Six Nations and the territory of the United States," once again, "forever." Similarly, according to the Hopewell treaty of November 28, 1785, the Cherokees "do acknowledge themselves to be under the protection of the United States of America, and of no other sovereign whatsoever" (ibid.: 440–1).

A second limitation on tribal sovereignty concerned criminal jurisdiction. So the treaty of January 1789, with the Delaware and other tribes northwest of the Ohio, stipulated that the United States should extend its criminal jurisdiction over them, applying the criminal law of the territory or the state which surrounded the tribal domain. Practically that same limitation was contained in the Creek treaty of 1790 (ibid.: 442). A further limitation, as in the 1805 treaty with the Piankeshaw, went with a change in language from "protection" to "care and patronage" to describe the relation of the US with the tribe, a sure sign that the status of the tribe had been degraded from a protectorate to a community of "wards" (ibid.: 443).

During the treaty era, tribal sovereignty referred to *the right of use* granted tribes, usually in perpetuity, by treaties. Even though the treaty era ended in 1871, Section 2079 of the Revised Statutes, March 3, 1871, which declared the end of treaty-making, also guaranteed the sanctity of all previous treaties, as in the following clause – "provided, further, that nothing herein contained shall be construed to invalidate or impair the obligation of any treaty heretofore lawfully made or ratified with any such Indian nation or tribe." But the provision that the statute was not to be retroactive in its application created an anomaly. The 1871 statute created wards of Indians, but the non-retroactive provision recognized the independence of treaty Indians, however qualified. Thus the Commissioner of Indian Affairs complained to the President two years later (1873) of "the anomalous relation of the Indian tribes to the government, which requires that they be treated as sovereign powers and as wards at one and the same time" (ibid.: 537).

The doctrine of "tribal sovereignty" persisted because it was susceptible to multiple uses. To get an idea of the range of uses, we can look at the extremes. When it comes to asserting federal over state jurisdiction, the notion of "tribal sovereignty" had real bite; but when it came to asserting Native American "sovereignty" in their relation with the federal government, its significance was more rhetorical than real. Without a consideration of the multiple uses to which it has been put, it is difficult to understand why the doctrine of "tribal sovereignty" continues to survive in the language of the law to this day.

Thus, federal courts have continued to use the doctrine of tribal sovereignty to check local white interests, as when Justice Hugo Black held in *Williams* v. *Lee* (1959) that the Navajo possessed "the right to govern themselves," a right that the state of Arizona could not infringe by enforcing state civil law on the reservation (Harring 1994: 289). But rather than give real content to "sovereignty," the doctrine did the reverse: it defined in perpetuity the boundaries of a conquered, colonized, community – the "tribe" – in its relations with the federal government. The fact was that Indian tribes were no longer sovereign; the notion of "tribal sovereignty" referred to a continuing practice of internal self-administration, rather than any real independence of administration from external forces. In this context, "tribal sovereignty" defined more a de facto state of affairs – which continued only so long as it was tolerated by those in power – than a statement of constitutionally enforced principles.

At the heart of this de facto state of affairs was a regime of legal dualism that was defined racially (as in a colonial setup) rather than territorially (as it would be in a federal setup).[5] The Intercourse Act of 1834

---

[5] Alaska was the one place where a significant number of Native Americans lived under the same law as whites. For this there were historical reasons. Alaska was bought in bulk from Russia and there were no treaties with Native American communities. Natives constituted a substantial majority and there were few whites. American courts came to Alaska only in 1884 and in the nineteenth century, Alaskan natives lived under the same law as Alaskan whites (Harring 1994: 207). There is also the case of the Pueblos. In *US* v. *Joseph* (1876), the court decided that the Pueblos had a settled (i.e. civilized) domestic existence and were therefore not subject to the same laws passed for the protection and civilization of "wild tribes." As in Alaska, the laws of New Mexico Territory applied to the Pueblo just as they applied to other people in the state. This was overruled in *US* v. *Sandoval* (1913). And finally there were the Indians of Oklahoma, a case we shall look at later in some detail (Harring 1994: 45–6).

provides that the general laws of the US will apply to crimes committed any place in the US, except in "Indian Country" where it will apply only "where a non-Indian is the criminal or victim, not where the affair is between Indians" (Macleod 1928: 535). The relationship was defined by Justice Taney in *United States* v. *Rogers* (1846): tribes in Indian Country may have authority over Indians within their lands, but the United States has authority over whites, as well as the right to determine who belongs to which racial category. Therefore, two criminal jurisdictions coexisted side by side in Indian Country, with the United States exercising the power to determine who fell under which jurisdiction (Harring 1994: 61). With federal district courts having criminal jurisdiction over whites and over Indians who committed crimes against whites, a jurisdictional void was created. On the one hand, Indian courts lacked jurisdiction over non-Indians in Indian Country; on the other, federal courts lacked jurisdiction over crimes committed by Indians against Indians. Non-Indians came to Indian Country for several reasons. Given several hundred years of intermarriage and intertribal migration, there were not only many non-Indians integrated as Indians, but also many persons born of intermarriages known as "mixed bloods." If Indian was defined as a racial status, as it was by US courts, the definition of Indian would be up to US authorities; but for Native Americans who saw Indian as more a political than a racial identity, as membership in a political community, this group were Indians.[6] The last category of non-Indians similarly attracted were criminals who found refuge in Indian Country because there was often no US court within a hundred miles or more (Harring 1994: 63–5, 166).

That federal courts lacked jurisdiction over crimes committed by Indians against Indians – an aspect of a residual "Indian sovereignty" – was highlighted by *Crow Dog* (1881). The details of the case were as follows: on August 5, 1881, Kan-gi-shun-ca (Crow Dog) shot to death Sin-ta-ga-le-Scka (Spotted Tail) on the Great Sioux Reservation in Dakota territory. Because the two men had taken up radically opposed positions in the debate over how to relate to white power, the killing had political significance. In the ongoing debate on the reservation, Spotted Tail had called for a realistic recognition of the overwhelming nature of white power and thus favored a qualified embrace of "civilization" as identified with that power, whereas Crow Dog had stood for the outright

---

[6] Take, for example, the facts in *US* v. *Rogers* (1846) where Rogers, a white man, claimed that he had been adopted into the "Cherokee tribe of Indians, and having married a Cherokee Indian woman" under tribal law, had renounced his US citizenship. His novel legal argument to the court was that, politically speaking, he was an Indian and therefore exempt from the US criminal jurisdiction over non-Indians in Indian Territory (Williams 2005: 73).

repudiation of white power in defense of Indian "tradition." The families met and settled the matter, but police hunted down Crow Dog and state courts convicted him of murder. In December 1883, the US Supreme Court reversed the conviction, holding that the United States had no criminal jurisdiction over Indian tribes in "Indian Country," because the tribes, inherently sovereign, retained the right to administer their own law as an element of that sovereignty (Harring 1994: 1). But even in this landmark case, Indian sovereignty was not defined as the hallmark of Indian independence from external constraint, but as a sign of the specific nature of its subordination to the external power that was the United States, and thus of its alienation from the political community called the United States. This is how Justice Mathews defined the relationship of Indians to the United States:

They were nevertheless to be subject to the laws of the United States, not in the sense of citizens, but as they had always been, as wards, subject to a guardian; not as individuals, constituted members of the political community of the United States, with a voice in the selection of representatives and in the framing of the laws, but as a dependent community who were in a state of pupilage, advancing from the condition of a savage tribe to that of a people who, through the discipline of labor, and by education, it was hoped might become a self-supporting and self-governing society. (*Ex Parte Crow Dog* 1883: 568–9; Williams 2005: 77)

Plenary powers

Congress responded to *Crow Dog* (1883) by defining the status of Indians as wards of the United States. The result was to repudiate, in deed if not in word, any claim to Indian "tribal sovereignty."[7] The congressional response extended federal law to tribal Indians under the Major Crimes Act (1884).[8] Two years later, the Supreme Court recognized in *United*

---

[7] But the tendency among those who write of federal Indian law is to see a divide between cases that affirm Indian sovereignty and those that repudiate it. This is how Wilkinson assesses the historical significance of *Crow Dog*: "A line of cases affirming sovereignty runs through *Worcester*, *Crow Dog*, and *Talton* v. *Mayes* 163 US 376 (1895) while an opposing line of cases denying that sovereignty and giving the United States 'plenary powers' over the Indian tribes begins with *Kagama* and *Lone Wolf* and dominates Indian law in the first half of the twentieth century" (Wilkinson 1987: 24; Harring 1994: 9).

[8] As we shall see, this was followed by the imposition of a repressive system of administrative justice, under the authority of the Bureau of Indian Affairs, for lesser offenses on reservations. The IRA proposal was for the Indian agent to serve as judge in courts without juries, with a right of appeal only to the commissioner of Indian affairs, and with few due process protections (a second-class citizenship at best) (Harring 1994: 134). An Act of Congress of March 3, 1885, arrogated to the US the right to punish the reservation Indians for crimes committed against one another, and reserved to state courts the right to punish the crimes of Indian against Indian off-reservation, and the crimes of non-Indian against non-Indian on-reservation (Macleod 1928: 537–8).

States v. *Kagama* (1886) how very fundamentally Congress had changed the terms on which Indian communities could govern themselves. That sanction is known as the plenary power doctrine. This new doctrine put the tribes completely under the control of Congress and the US political process, and legally justified Congress's assertion of total power over the tribes (Harring 1994: 101). Even if accented by an unmistakable arrogance of power, one is struck by the extent to which the language of *Kagama* marks a continuation of the language used by Justice Mathews in *Crow Dog*:

These Indians are the wards of the nation. They are communities dependent on the United States. Dependent largely for their daily food. Dependent for their political rights . . . From their very weakness and helplessness . . . there arises the duty of protection. And with it the power . . . The power of the General Government over these remnants of a race once powerful, now weak and diminished in numbers, is necessary for their protection, as well as to the safety of those among whom they dwell. (Harring 1994: 142, 147–8)[9]

In spite of congressional plenary powers, the notion of "Indian sovereignty" continues to be an important point of reference in federal Indian law. Wilkinson argues that it is the scholarship of Felix Cohen during the 1940s that played a cardinal role in preserving the doctrine of tribal sovereignty for modern courts. Cohen retrieved and reinforced Marshall. As late as *US* v. *Wheeler* (1978), the Supreme Court distinguished "Indian tribes from both cities and federal territories, which derive their power from the states and the federal government respectively" and "found that Indian tribes possess a third sovereignty in the US" (Wilkinson 1987: 61). And Wilkinson concurs: "Perhaps the most basic principle of all Indian law, supported by a host of decisions hereinafter analyzed, is the principle that those powers which are lawfully invested in an Indian tribe are not, in general, delegated powers granted by express Acts of Congress, but rather inherent powers of a limited sovereignty which has never been extinguished" (ibid.: 57–8). Both the courts and the writers who shared this judgment were right in acknowledging the distinctive historical *origin* of Indian sovereignty, and that it predated the United States, but their argument did not fully recognize the historical *developments* that had eroded this claim. Thus, *history* (and origin) hardly illuminated the *scope* of Indian sovereignty in the present. For the contemporary reality is that there is no limit to how far Congress may breach this historical sovereignty. Even today if tribes have a right to define the tax regime or adjudicate conflicts within reservations, the fact

---

[9] For full quotes from the court's judgment re the extra-constitutional powers of Congress – thus not subject to judicial review – over Indians, see Williams (2005: 81–3).

is that this right is subject to sufferance by Congress, and can be repealed by Congress at will, and without review by the Supreme Court – a fact that Wilkinson himself is compelled to recognize.[10]

More recently, the Supreme Court has been less willing to tolerate ambiguity on this question. Robert Williams has outlined the debate in his recent book on the Rehnquist court. Two points of view can be discerned in recent Supreme Court decisions. On the one hand is Chief Justice Rehnquist's outright dismissal of the notion of "Indian sovereignty" in *Oliphant* (1978) as untenable, either legally or politically:

Indians are within the geographical limits of the United States. The soil and people within these limits are under the control of the Government of the United States, or of the States of the Union. There exists in the broad domain of sovereignty but these two. There may be cities, counties, and other organized bodies with limited legislative functions, but they ... exist in subordination to one or the other of these. (Williams 2005: 110)

Chief Justice Rehnquist further reiterated this point of view in *United States* v. *Lara* (2004) when he held that Congress, under the Constitution's plenary grants of authority over Indian affairs, has the power "to enact legislation that both restricts and, in turn, relaxes those restrictions on tribal sovereign authority" (ibid.: 150). Justice Thomas, in contrast, began by stating his express disagreement with the Lara majority's holding "that the Constitution grants to Congress plenary power to calibrate the metes and bounds of tribal sovereignty." In Justice Thomas's view, "the tribes either are or are not separate sovereigns, and our federal Indian law cases untenably hold both positions simultaneously":

It seems to me that much of the confusion reflected in our precedent arises from two largely incompatible and doubtful assumptions. First, Congress (rather than some other part of the Federal Government) can regulate virtually every aspect of the tribes without rendering tribal sovereignty a nullity. Second, the Indian tribes retain inherent sovereignty to enforce their criminal laws against their own members ... It is quite arguably the essence of sovereignty not to exist merely at the whim of an external government. (cited in Williams 2005: 159)

While conceding that states can have their sovereignty diminished by Congress, Thomas explained that the states of the Union are part of a

---

[10] According to Wilkinson: "Wheeler dealt with the source of tribal powers, not with the difficult question relating to their scope." Even if the Supreme Court ruled in *Menominee Tribe of Indians* v. *United States* (1968) that the federal government may terminate its recognition of a tribe but that does not terminate its existence, until the tribe does so, this was not a recognition of sovereignty but identity: "Indians are properly viewed not as members of a race but as citizens of a government with whom the United States has a special government-to-government relationship" (Wilkinson 1987: 62, 73, 75–6, 86).

"constitutional framework" that recognizes their sovereignty and "specifically grants Congress authority to legislate with respect to them." The tribes, according to Thomas, are not part of the constitutional order and their sovereignty is in no way guaranteed by the Constitution (ibid.: 159). Rather than be treated as a fait accompli, argues Justice Thomas, this most unsatisfactory situation demands a clear resolution.

What, then, is the difference between "Indian sovereignty" and the two forms of sovereignty recognized in the Constitution of the United States: federal and state? The first is historical: that Indian sovereignty in the Americas preceded that of all settler states. The second is contemporary: the very establishment of the United States, and consolidation of settler power, extinguished Indian sovereignty. The fact is Indian communities continue to exist in a *colonial* relationship to the United States, and this is why the notion of Indian sovereignty finds neither recognition, nor definition, nor protection in the US Constitution, whether as originally drafted or as amended thereafter.

This brings us back to that great jurist, Chief Justice Marshall, and his deliberations on the colonial conquest of Native America. In his reflections on the Indian question, Marshall tried to think of a future outside the box, the settler conquest of the native:

The title by conquest is acquired and maintained by force. The conqueror prescribes its limits. Humanity, however, acting on public opinion, has established, as a general rule, that the conquered shall not be wantonly oppressed, and that their condition shall remain as eligible as is compatible with the objects of the conquest. Most usually, they are incorporated with the victorious nation, and become subjects or citizens of the government with which they are connected. The new and old members of the society mingle with each other; the distinction between them is gradually lost, and they make one people. Where this incorporation is practicable, humanity demands, and a wise policy requires, that the rights of the conquered to property should remain unimpaired; that the new subjects should be governed as equitably as the old, and that confidence in their security should gradually banish the painful sense of being separated from their ancient connexions, and united by force to strangers. (*Johnson* v. *M'Intosh* 1823: 589)

The thought is bold: conquest must not only draw the curtain on the independence of a previously existing political community, it must also open the possibility of creating a new political community, where conqueror and conquered, whether joined or separate, shall be as equal members. But this is where Marshall hesitated, uncertain that this principle of "civilized" society could apply to natives in the Americas.

But the tribes of Indians inhabiting this country were fierce savages, whose occupation was war, and whose subsistence was drawn chiefly from the forest. To leave them in possession of their country, was to leave the country a wilderness;

to govern them as a distinct people, was impossible, because they were as brave and as high spirited as they were fierce, and were ready to repel by arms every attempt on their independence. (ibid.: 590)

Thus, argued Marshall, "that law which regulates, and ought to regulate in general, the relations between the conqueror and conquered, was incapable of application to a people under such circumstances" (ibid.: 591). So Marshall concluded by reconciling himself to political reality as it exists, even if it "be opposed to natural right, and to the usages of civilized nations":

However extravagant the pretension of converting the discovery of an inhabited country into conquest may appear; if the principle has been asserted in the first instance, and afterwards sustained; if a country has been acquired and held under it; if the property of the great mass of the community originates in it, it becomes the law of the land, and cannot be questioned . . . However this restriction may be opposed to natural right, and to the usages of civilized nations, yet, if it be indispensable to that system under which the country has been settled, and be adapted to the actual condition of the two people, it may, perhaps, be supported by reason, and certainly cannot be rejected by Courts of justice. (ibid.: 591–2)

There is a limit to the justice courts can dispense; that limit is defined by the political power. Courts do not establish rights, power does! It was to Marshall's credit and testimony to his moral courage that he tried to think through the colonial question. But that he failed to think of a future where the native would be as free as the settler, indeed where native and settler would cease to be opposed political identities, was his failing. If the strength set him apart from contemporaries, he shared the failing with them. The challenge for successive generations, including for us, is to reflect on the question Marshall had the courage to pose, the colonial status of Native Americans, so as to craft a future he failed to contemplate – a world of political equality between erstwhile natives and settlers.

III.   Separate and unequal futures

A common thread that runs through the history of settler power in the United States is the separate and unequal futures for settlers and natives. Within this broad framework there have been a number of shifts. The settler enterprise began with the promise of separate representation for Indians in the US Congress, then moved on to the idea of two states, one white, the other Indian, on each side of the Mississippi, except that the native state would be a protectorate of the settler state. When westward expansion in the nineteenth century destroyed that vision, settlers crafted other, but more cruel, futures for natives, all within an explicitly colonial context. One of these was forced assimilation, the other compulsory segregation.

Creating Indian states

In early treaties with Indian communities – sometimes called nations, other times tribes – both the English crown and the United States offered these communities independent representation in Congress. On the face of it, these seemed offers to coexist in political equality under a common political roof, made to all Indian tribes that believed in peaceful coexistence with whites. Later, the terms of the offer changed to a contradictory mix of equality and protection – and finally, to a form of colonial paternalism. The first treaty of the US, then a confederation, was made with the Delaware, in September 1778. Article 6 invited the Delaware nation "to form a state" by joining with "other tribes, friendly to the interest of the United States," and provided that "the Delaware nation shall be the heads" of the state "and have a representation in Congress."[11] The Hopewell Treaty of November 28, 1785, with the Cherokees contained a provision acknowledging the right of the Cherokee nation "to send a deputy of their choice, whenever they think fit, to Congress."[12]

During the second phase of its relations with Indian communities, the US deliberated on, and sometimes publicly considered, a two-state policy. It began as a promise to those tribes willing to move east of the Mississippi. In his last annual message to Congress in 1825, President Monroe proposed that after their removal west of the Mississippi, the tribes could be confederated into a protectorate of the United States and used to extend the influence and trade of the United States westward to the Pacific (Macleod 1928: 446). In 1834, once again, the United States Congress considered a proposal for a permanent homeland for Indians, with a governor and a council of tribal representatives, that might ultimately become a state of the Union, but then dismissed the idea (Kiernan 1978: 40–1). Indian removal to the west followed a dual approach: semi-captivity for Indians who resisted assimilation and promises of statehood for those who came on board the "civilizing mission."

---

[11] This is how the full provision reads in Article 6: "The parties further agree, that other tribes, friendly to the interest of the United States, may be invited to form a state, whereof the Delaware nation shall be the heads, and have a representation in Congress." See *Worcester* v. *Georgia* (1832), p. 39.

[12] This is how Article XII of the Treaty read: "That the Indians may have full confidence in the justice of the United States, respecting their interests, they shall have a right to send a deputy of their choice, whenever they think fit, to Congress." See, "Treaty of Hopewell with the Cherokees, November 28, 1785," in Prucha (1976: 8).

With the Civil War and the Reconstruction era that followed, the pendulum swung yet again between two contrasting proposals. The single-state solution envisioned Indians as becoming part of the United States as a political community; the two-state solution was premised on the establishment of a separate state for Indians. The former initiative was part of the 1867–9 Southern constitutional conventions that swept the Reconstruction South in the wake of the Civil War. These constitutions established the South's first state-funded systems of compulsory education and the first systems of providing poor relief. All guaranteed civil and political rights for Blacks. It is in the context of what a Texas paper called "the equal rights revolution" that Florida granted Seminole Indians two representatives in the state legislature (Foner 1988: 319–20). The latter was given a fresh lease on life with the new treaty offered to the Five Civilized Tribes which had already moved west of the Mississippi.

Largely abandoned by the Union and courted by the Confederacy, the Five Civilized Tribes had followed the leadership of a slave-owning elite and joined the war effort of the South. After the Civil War, retribution was to follow. Based on guidelines from the Secretary of the Interior, the Commissioner of Indian Affairs offered new treaty arrangements to the Indians. One of six key stipulations he outlined called for the formation of "one consolidated government after the plan proposed by the Senate of the United States, in a bill for organizing the Indian territory" provided "other arrangement be made." The Harlan Bill (named after the Secretary of the Interior) called for the formation of an Indian state on terms different from those enjoyed by all other states. These were the terms of a Protectorate. As spelt out by the Commissioner, this would be "a regular territory of the United States, with a governor appointed by the President having an absolute veto over the legislative council and acting ex officio as superintendent of Indian affairs." At the same time, "tribal citizens would elect a council, and the Territory thus constituted would send a delegate to Congress." When the Indian nations refused to accede to such an arrangement, they were forced to sell large parts of their land to the US "for use by other Indians, thus dividing the Indian Territory roughly in two; the Five Civilized Tribes retained the eastern half, while the remainder was to be used as homes for western tribes who were to be settled on reservations as part of the government's policy of consolidation. Slavery was prohibited, and the freedmen were granted certain rights within the nations" (Prucha 1976: 375–6; Kiernan 1978: 80–1). The boundaries of Indian Territory shrank further: from continental US in 1491, to west of the Mississippi after Indian Removal, to the future state of Oklahoma during the Civil War, to its eastern part thereafter. Each time the promise of autonomy lasted only until the next rise in the settler tide.

Once the treaties of 1866 had been signed, Ely S. Parker, Commissioner of Indian Affairs, urged that action be taken to organize the general council spoken of in the treaties, and suggested: "The next progressive step would be a territorial form of government, followed by their admission into the Union as a state" (Prucha 1976: 377–8). The first annual report of the Board of Indian Commissioners, issued that same year, on April 10, 1869, spelt out a combined policy for "civilized" and "uncivilized" Indians, whereby both could be brought together in the Indian Territory that would become a state of the Union:

> The policy of collecting Indian tribes upon small reservations contiguous to each other, and within the limits of a large reservation, *eventually to become a state of the Union*, and of which the small reservations will probably be the counties, seems to be the best that can be devised. Many tribes may thus be collected in the present Indian territory. (ibid.: 107–8, emphasis mine)

The next time a state solution was proposed for Native Americans was when Congress appointed the Dawes Commission on March 3, 1893. The three commissioners were authorized to negotiate with the Five Civilized Tribes (the Cherokee, the Choctaw, the Chickasaw, the Muskogee [or Creek], and the Seminole) "for the purpose of the extinguishment of the national or tribal title to any lands within that Territory now held by any and all of such nations or tribes," so as "to enable the ultimate creation of a state or states of the Union which shall embrace the lands within said Indian Territory" (Commission to the Five Civilized Tribes (Dawes Commission), March 3, 1893, ibid.: 189). On the face of it, the Commission's mandate was to extinguish and replace "national or tribal titles" with the "creation of a state or states of the Union." But we shall see that the real object of pursuit was the rich agricultural and mineral lands in Indian Territory highly coveted by whites. According to the mandate, as we shall see, the dissolution of national or tribal governments was to go alongside another dissolution – that of national or tribal land – so as to allot titles to individual Indians and thereby to declare the remaining land as surplus and secure it under US custody. The move would shatter the hopes of the Five Civilized Tribes who, more than any other group of Indians, had embraced the promise of "civilization," and tried their best to adapt to the settler way of life. It would also be the last time the US would offer any Indian community the mirage of separate statehood.

IV.   Forced assimilation

The experience with "civilization" proved to be equally disillusioning. There is little to suggest Indian resistance to new ways so long as their freedom was not in question. The contention between "civilization" and "tradition," with one set up as the alternative to the other, arose under conditions where civilization seemed to go along with loss of independence and tradition was a safeguard of independence. As we shall see with the Five Civilized Tribes in Indian Territory in eastern Oklahoma, their experience with the "civilizing mission" was contradictory and disenchanting. Though openness to civilization was initially demanded of them as a condition for autonomy within the United States, the actual results of "civilization" were given as reasons for ruthlessly undercutting that autonomy.

Nothing in the early accounts of Native Americans suggests that they shunned European immigrants. This is why we need to begin by distinguishing voluntary integration from forced assimilation. Macleod writes:

The Indians were always eager to have their children educated by Europeans. Indian parents would trustfully turn children over to some trader, whom they came to admire for his apparent wisdom and wealth, to be taken to the coast and to be trained according to European ways. Within a specified length of time the young apprentice was to be returned to his parents. The white guardian would instead ship the boy or girl to the slave market, and, in time, inform the Indian parents that their child had died. (Macleod 1928: 303)

Until King Philip's War in 1674, white and Indian children sat together in the same classrooms in the schools of the New England colonies. Until the Indian wars of 1675, men such as Peter Fontaine and Colonel Byrd in Virginia openly advocated intermarriage of the races as the best way of building a common future, and so did Lawson of the Carolinas until the disastrous Indian war of 1715 (ibid.: 374–5).

But even later assimilation did not always have to be *forced* on reluctant Native American communities. Several consented, and for good reason. The fate of those who resisted could not be ignored by those bearing witness. In a context where force was increasingly the arbiter between settler and native, those who were convinced of the superiority of the force of the settler were keen to look for ways of becoming reconciled to it. Leading that search were the Cherokee.

The Five Civilized Tribes moved to the west, most in the 1830s and the Seminole in the 1850s, where they constituted themselves as "nations" and proceeded to make changes under federal pressure. The Cherokee and the Choctaw most readily adapted to the creation of new legal and political institutions parallel with those in the United States. The contest between "civilization" and "tradition," the former a synonym for the white man's way and the latter for the Indian way, triggered a protracted debate in their ranks. The Cherokee, for example, built a modern prison, whereas the Creek maintained that a prison was not fitting punishment for an Indian. Of all the nations of the Indian Territory, the Creek and the Seminole most successfully excluded whites and tried to preserve their traditional ways (Harring 1994: 58–9). The debate between "civilization" and "tradition" had the most tragic outcome among the Creek: this nation of perhaps ten thousand people had five civil wars between 1860 and 1908 – roughly one per decade – and on several occasions had parallel governments, one representing those calling for adaptation to "civilization" and the other those championing "tradition" (Harring 1994: 73–4, 76, 78–9, 82–92, 284).

Although the Treaties of Removal had included strong protection of Indian lands and Indian autonomy, they also contained language that would justify strong federal intervention when the times so demanded. Take, for example, the Choctaw Treaty of 1830:

The United States under a grant specially to be made by the President of the US shall cause to be conveyed to the Choctaw nation a tract of country west of the Mississippi River, *in fee simple to them and their descendents, to inure to them while they shall exist as a nation and live on it* . . .

The government and people of the United States are hereby obliged to secure to the said Choctaw Nation of the Red People *the jurisdiction and the government of all the persons and property that may be within their limits west*, so that no Territory or State shall ever have a right to pass laws for the government of the Choctaw nation or the Red People and their descendents; and that no part of the land granted them shall ever be embraced in any Territory or State; but the US shall forever secure said Choctaw Nation from, and against, all laws except such as from time to time be enacted in their own National Councils, *not inconsistent with the Constitution, Treaties, and Laws of the United States*; and except such as may, and which have been enacted by Congress, *to the extent that Congress under the Constitution are required to exercise a legislation over Indian Affairs.* (cited in Prucha 1976: 374–5)

Two kinds of guarantees were given in strong language. The first concerned land, and the second persons and their possessions. Land was to be granted "in fee simple" and not simply as a right of occupancy, and more or less in perpetuity, "while they shall exist as a nation and live on it"; the treaty also secured to the Choctaw nation "the jurisdiction and the government of all the persons and property that may be within their limits"; but these guarantees were subject "to the extent that Congress under the Constitution are required to exercise a legislation over Indian Affairs." Here, then, was the clause that the Supreme Court would later use to justify the right of congressional rule by decree over Indian tribes.

Creek treaties were compromised from the outset (Harring 1994: 65–6, 69–70). To begin with, the federal government reserved the right to decide who was a Creek and who was not. Given the historic alliance between Creeks and Blacks, the federal government demanded the right

to decide whether a Black admitted into the Indian nation – or the off-
spring of a union between a Creek and a Black – was an Indian or not
(ibid.: 68ff, 97ff).

In the period that followed the Civil War, congressional rule by decree
tightened the squeeze so much that both the right of tribal property and
tribal property itself tended to go under as the era of removal gave way to
that of reservations, an institution that combined compulsory segregation
with forced assimilation.

The Dawes Act

At the heart of forced assimilation[13] was a program of forced decol-
lectivization as a way of forcibly appropriating Indian lands. "Common
property and civilization cannot coexist," a Commissioner for Indian
Affairs laid down succinctly in 1838: only separate holdings could breathe
enterprise, morality, and progress into Indians (Kiernan 1978: 38). Not
surprisingly, the debate on Indian rights got particularly hot when it came
to their right to sell off land. Every speculator who hoped to benefit from
the sale of Indian land championed the right of Indians to sell their land
(Williams 2005).

Probably the most ambitious attempt to force assimilation on Indian
tribes took place towards the end of the nineteenth century. Its legislative
instrument was the Dawes Act (the General Allotment Act) of 1887
and, following it, the Curtis Act of 1897. The two Acts applied to the
two halves of what was later to become the state of Oklahoma. The
earlier Dawes Act applied to the western part which was designated
Oklahoma Territory, and where the same reservation status pertained and
the same laws applied as those that governed Indian communities outside
Oklahoma. The eastern part was known as Indian Territory. There, the
legal situation was defined by early treaties and legal precedents that
explicitly pertained only to groups removed as part of the Indian Removal
Act. The Five Civilized Tribes in eastern Oklahoma were consistently
excepted from federal laws, such as the Major Crimes Act and the Dawes
Act, which had been applied to the Plains Indian tribes that were later
settled on reservations in the western part of the state. Also excepted were
the Osages, Miami, Peoria, and Sacs and Foxes in the Indian Territory,

---

[13] On the process of assimilation, read Prucha (1984: 609–757); for primary documents,
Prucha (1973); see also Hoxie (2001) cited in Harring (1994: 13). On Locke: read
Pagden (1998) and Macpherson (1964). On Burke, critic of the Royal Proclamation of
1763, which imposed British authority to the rear of the American settlers as a barrier
to their westward expansion, which he saw as the fulfillment of a divine plan, see Hall
(2005: 74–7).

the Seneca Indians in New York, and the strip of Sioux lands in Nebraska (Prucha 1976: 255).

The exception was not popular among two groups of whites with a direct interest in Indian Territory: on the one hand, reformers who had long called for "the Americanization of all the Indians"; on the other, a rapidly growing population of white farmers from the surrounding states of Arkansas, Texas, and Kansas, who coveted "rich acres only partially used by the Indians" (ibid.: 373). The exception turned out to be short-lived; ten years after the Dawes Act, its provisions were embedded in a new Act, the Curtis Act, and applied to the "civilized" tribes in Indian Territory (ibid.: 96–7). Together, these Acts authorized the President of the US to break up the land of any reservation into separate farms, and confer citizenship alongside. Proceeding on the assumption that "it is doubtful whether any high degree of civilization is possible without individual ownership of land," the stated objective of the Act was "to individualize the Indian problem and thus lead more rapidly to a disintegration of tribal relations."

The Dawes Commission issued its report on November 20, 1894 (cited ibid.: 190–5). The report began by narrating how the United States had contracted different treaties and patents and "conveyed to the several tribes the country originally known as the 'Indian Territory'," but how a part of this same Territory had been ceded to the United States by the same tribes for white settlement (and, we may add, for the establishment of reservations for other Indian tribes being pushed west), and how the remaining part was subject to stipulations contained in the treaties, mainly that "these tribes were to hold this territory for the use and enjoyment of all Indians belonging to their respective tribes," and that "their laws should not conflict with the Constitution of the United States." The report argued that these stipulations had been violated partly due to the force of changing circumstances: "These stipulations naturally grew out of the situation of the country at the time they were made, and of the character of the Indians with whom they were made. The present growth of the country and its present relations to this territory were not thought of or even dreamed of by either party when they entered into these stipulations." This is why, though the project "seemed successful" for a few years, the conditions that made for this success had "undergone so complete a change" that success soon turned into failure. The report concluded that the failure was "largely the result of outside considerations for which neither is responsible and of the influence of forces which neither can control."

What, then, were these conditions that had undergone so complete a change and that were not susceptible to control? It turns out they

were precisely the "progress" and the "civilization" which the settler population and the United States had always preached to the
native population; the only difference was that, as reality rather than
promise, these changes were evident in their full-blown contradictoriness.
The Commission's report detailed these developments, starting with
railways:

These governments consented to the construction of a number of railways
through the Territory, and thereby consented that they bring into the Territory all that is necessary in the building and operation of such railroads – the
necessary depots, stations, and the inevitable towns which their traffic was sure
to build up, and the large building which white men alone could develop and
which these railroads were sure to stimulate and make profitable.

The report invited whites to come and take *employment* in the Territory
("they have, by their laws, invited men from the border states to become
their employees in the Territory, receiving into their treasuries a monthly
tax for the privilege of such employment"); encouraged the development
of lucrative *commercial crops* such as cotton ("In some sections of the Territory the production of cotton has proved so feasible and profitable that
white men have been permitted to come in by thousands and cultivate it
and build trading marts and populous towns for the successful operation
of this branch of trade alone"), and other resources such as "vast and rich
deposits of *coal*" along with "large and valuable plants for mining coal"
and "vast *pine forests*." Furthermore, "*towns* of considerable importance
have been built by white persons under leases obtained from Indians"; as
a result, "*permanent improvements* of great value have thus been built by
white citizens of the United States, induced and encouraged thereto by
the tribal governments themselves, and have become immovable fixtures
which cannot be taken away" (all cited ibid., italics mine).

The Commission then detailed the downside of progress, from "corruption of the grossest kind" to outright "fraud" making for "large for-
tunes," a trend that none could check for "the courts of justice have
become helpless and paralyzed" in a context where "violence, robbery
and murder are almost of daily occurrence" resulting in nothing less than
"a reign of terror" in Indian Territory. The conclusion notwithstanding,
not only did the details of this charge sheet read like symptoms of "civilization," they seemed no different from what was happening throughout
the western territories in the throes of a gold rush.

In time-honored imperial fashion, the Commission took up the cudgels
on behalf of the poor and oppressed in Indian Territory. The first of these
were "the *full-bloods* who do not speak the English language" (italics
mine):

The governments have fallen into the hands of a few able and energetic Indian citizens, nearly all mixed blood and adopted whites, who have so administered their affairs and have enacted such laws that they are enabled to appropriate to their own exclusive use almost the entire property of the Territory of any kind that can be rendered profitable and available.

In one of these tribes, whose whole territory consists of but 3,040,000 acres of land, within the last few years laws have been enacted under the operation of which 61 citizens have appropriated to themselves and are now holding for pasturage and cultivation 1,237,000 acres. This comprises the arable and greater part of the valuable grazing lands belonging to that tribe. The remainder of that people, largely the full-bloods who do not speak the English language, are excluded from the enjoyment of any portion of this land, and many of them occupy the poor and hilly country where they get a scanty living from such portions as they are able to turn to any account. (ibid.)

The second was the group of those who had before been *slaves* in the tribes and who were to be adopted into the tribes and granted equal rights by provision of the treaties when they were reaffirmed in 1866. Their condition was the worst among the Chickasaws, among whom "they are shut out of the schools of the tribe, and from their courts, and are granted no privileges of occupancy of any part of the land for a home, and are helplessly exposed to the hostilities of the citizen Indian and the personal animosity of the former master." As for the freedmen among the Choctaw and the Cherokee, "although they have been adopted according to the requirements of the treaties," their condition was far from satisfactory: "They are yet very far from the enjoyment of all the rights, privileges and immunities to which they are entitled under the treaties." Finally, there was the group of *poor whites*: "thousands of white children in this territory who are almost wholly without the means of education, and are consequently growing up with no fitting preparation for useful citizenship."

Clearly, the record of the Indian tribes was being measured against rhetorical standards rather than real practice among those said to be custodians of "civilization." When it came to its final recommendation, the Commission pulled no punches:

These tribal governments have wholly perverted their high trusts, and it is the plain duty of the United States to enforce the trust it has so created and recover for its original uses the domain and all the gains derived from the perversions of the trust or discharge the trustees . . . They have demonstrated the incapacity to so govern themselves, and no higher duty can rest upon the Government that granted this authority than to revoke it when it has so lamentably failed.

Having set the terms of the Commission with precisely these objectives in mind, the federal government complied without hesitation. On July 1,

1898, the national governments of the Five Civilized Tribes were stripped
of their powers. The tribes of the Indian Territory were brought under
the full jurisdiction of the territorial courts of Oklahoma. There were
to be no tribal lands and no "Indian Territory" (Harring 1994: 71–3).
Having been promised that the embrace of "civilization" would secure
them autonomy, "civilization" was now advanced as the reason why they
could no longer remain autonomous.[14]

Congress moved in against the Five Tribes with the full force of plenary
powers. In 1906, Congress denied the legislatures of the Five Civilized
Tribes the right to meet more than thirty days per year, and their legislative action was made subject to veto by the President of the United States.
Legislative intervention even extended to federal power over tribal money.
Statutes provided that money due to tribes from tribal assets could be
appropriated at the discretion of Congress (Cohen 1942). Congress even
claimed "the ultimate authority to determine who was a tribal member
for purposes of distributing property, annuities and trust money, and
how that money was spent." Finally, Congress gave to itself the right to
authorize the consolidation of tribes, no matter what their history or eth-
nology (Newton 1983–4: 223–4). In their generality, these powers were
no different from the powers assumed by the colonial governor of the
South African province of Natal over the Zulu tribes towards the end of
the nineteenth century (Mamdani 1996).

But the leaders of the Five Civilized Tribes persisted; their goal was
to preserve their identity within the federal system by promoting separate statehood for Indian Territory. Officials of the Creek, Cherokee and
Choctaw (supported by the Chickasaw as well) met in a joint convention of tribes at Eufaula in the Creek Nation on November 18, 1902, and
adopted a statement against union with Oklahoma Territory. At the same
time, individual tribes also made separate protests.[15] Three years later,
in the summer of 1905, new agitation for a separate state developed, and
strong arguments were presented. Indians pointed to the Atoka Agreement of 1897 which spoke of the preparation of Indian nation lands "for
admission as a state of the Union." In July the heads of four of the five
tribes issued a call for a constitutional convention to meet on August

---

[14] Even against all odds, these native communities survived. Take the example of the
Creek. "The Curtis Act attempted to outlaw their entire tribal existence. 'Final Rolls'
were made for the abolishment of the Creek Nation. And the Muscogee people were to
become citizens without a Native State . . . And yet the Creek nation survived." In 1979,
the Creek Nation ratified a new tribal constitution organized under the provisions of
the Oklahoma Indian Welfare Act (Strickland 1985–6: 746–7).

[15] The Eufaula resolutions are printed in *Congressional Record*, 36: 567. For action by the
various tribes, see *Senate Document* No. 143, 59-1, serial 4912.

21 at Muskogee. All residents of Indian Territory were invited to vote for delegates, and many whites cooperated with the Indians. The convention drew up a constitution for a proposed state of Sequoyah, and in an election of November 7 the document was ratified by a vote of 56,000 to 9,000 (though not more than half the qualified voters went to the polls).[16] Once again, Congress blocked any further development. Although bills for admission of the separate state were introduced in both Houses, no action was taken, and the whole movement simply died. According to a special census of 1907, the population of the new state stood at 1,414,177, slightly less than half of which was in the former Indian Territory. Of this total, there were 101,228 persons in the Five Civilized Tribes, including intermarried whites and the freedmen, and 15,603 other Indians (Prucha 1984: 756–7).

The Dawes and Curtis Acts gave the appropriate authorities in reservations the power to grant to deserving Indians a "trust patent" to his allotment of land, whereby the land title was held in trust by the US for twenty-five years, after which the premises were conveyed to the Indian by fee simple patent. The Act initially delegated to the Bureau of Indian Affairs (BIA) authority to allot 160 acres of tribal land to each head of household and 40 acres to each minor, and was soon amended to provide for allotments of 80 acres of agricultural land, or 160 acres of grazing land, to each tribal member. The May 8, 1906, Burke Act provided that the allotted Indian might become a citizen only when he became an unrestricted landowner at the end of twenty-five years (Macleod 1928: 539). Forced allotment, according to the Act, was a deliberate means of destroying "communistic" tribal culture and forcing Indians to assimilate into the mainstream of US life as farmers and ranchers (Harring 1994: 143). Surplus land was then sold to whites. This is how the land in Indian possession fell by more than half over the next half-century (Kiernan 1978: 103).

The Dawes and Curtis Acts had several consequences, but four are of particular concern for our inquiry. The first was a drastic reduction in land under Indian control. Indian landholdings were reduced from 138 million to 52 million acres. More than 26 million acres of allotted land were transferred out of Indian hands after they passed out of trust, by fair means and foul (Wilkinson 1987: 8–9, 20). Sixty million of the 86 million acres lost to Indians by the allotment regime were due to the surplus lands facet of the 1887 Act (ibid.: 19–20). By 1985, according to records of land in the Old Indian Territory at the Bureau of Indian

---

[16] See *Senate Document* No. 143, 59-1, serial 4912; the memorial on p. I-27, and the Constitution on pp. 47–8.

Affairs, only 65,000 acres remained in tribal hands and less than a million acres in individual Indian hands (Strickland 1985–6: 733).

Second, instead of turning Indians into farmers, the Dawes Act led to leasing of land. By 1898, 112,000 of the 140,000 allotted acres had been leased. This involved two-thirds of the men with allotted land (Prucha 1984: 873). Third, through the sale and lease of land, the Dawes Act opened up reservations to non-Indian settlement. Finally, as the ownership and population of reservations changed, "the BIA moved in as the real government" (Wilkinson 1987: 21). Ironically, the Dawes Act turned Indians from collective to individual wards and the paternalism of the federal government grew instead of diminishing, "until the bureaucracy of the Indian Service dominated every aspect of the Indians' lives" (Prucha 1984: 759).

The fact is that the grant of individual titles did not erode the power of federal agents to incarcerate Indians for infractions of reservation rules and to enforce their "civilization program" with military power: "School masters continued to separate children from their parents. Religious organizations continued to operate with a level of federal support that clearly violated the First Amendment of the US Constitution. Authorities continued to break up unauthorized religious activities and destroy sacred objects. Officials could even 'withhold rations' from tribal members who opposed them" (Castile and Bee 1992: 38).

Not even the allotment law's grant of citizenship to Indians taking up individual landholdings ended federal supervision over native communities. In 1910 the Supreme Court spoke for the entire bureaucracy when it declared that "Congress, in pursuance of the long-established policy of the Government, has the right to determine for itself when the guardianship which has been maintained over the Indian shall cease. It is for that body, and not for the courts, to determine when the true interests of the Indian require his release from such condition" (US Supreme Court 1910, cited in Castile and Bee 1992: 39). The simple fact was that, citizens or not, Indians were wards of Congress and only Congress could terminate that colonial relationship.

V.   Compulsory segregation

Towards the end of the twentieth century, the Native American writer Vine Deloria Jr. reflected on the sharply contrasting historical experiences of Native and African-Americans (Deloria 1988). He explained that the difference arose from two different objects coveted by "civilization": if the Indian was an exotic "wild animal" who had to be tamed by "civilization," the Black person was a "beast of burden" who had to be kept in his place.

The white man adopted two basic approaches...He systematically excluded blacks from all programmes, policies, social events, and economic schemes...With the Indian the process was simply reversed...Indians were...subjected to the most intense pressure to become white...The white man forbade the black to enter his own social and economic system and at the same time force-fed the Indian what he was denying the black. Yet the white man demanded that the black conform to white standards and insisted that the Indian don feathers and beads periodically to perform for him.

The difference, according to Deloria, was this: unlike Black Americans who bore the brunt of compulsory segregation, Native Americans confronted the demand that they assimilate. The two responses were shaped by two different situations and contrasting objects of desire. Whereas Black Americans signified labor, Native Americans signified land. Whereas compulsory segregation went alongside a regime of coerced labor, forced assimilation began with the disbanding of native communities and the fragmentation of communal land into individual agricultural plots and the designation of the commons as surplus land that could be sold cheaply to land-hungry settlers. One of the most enthusiastic champions of assimilation was Thomas Jefferson, who called for a program to civilize Indians by making Christians of them, getting them to take up farming, and teaching them literacy (Hall 2005: 432).

But Deloria was only partly right. The difference between the experience of the African-American and that of the Native American is relative. The fact is that the Native American experience was not single but differentiated: whereas some Native American communities were forcibly dismantled, others were just as forcibly confined to reservations. Both lost land, but with different outcomes. Native Americans experienced *both* forced assimilation *and* forced segregation. The institution that combined forced assimilation and compulsory segregation in one was the reservation.

As the reservation era gathered pace, forced assimilation and compulsory segregation turned out to be like Siamese twins, more complementary halves of a single policy than alternatives. This became clear as the nineteenth century drew to a close, and the Bureau of Indian Affairs took control of reservations. The turning point was when the House of Representatives decreed in a rider to the Appropriations Act of 1871 that henceforth "[n]o Indian nation or tribe within the territory of the United States shall be acknowledged or recognized as an independent nation, tribe, or power with whom the United States may contract by treaty." Henceforth, Indian law became more a matter of domestic law, and Indians were regarded as subjects to be governed, rather than foreign

nationals.[17] The formal end of treaty-making went alongside "the conscious intention thereby to denigrate the power of the chiefs" (Prucha
1976: 329). Not only did treaties with Indians cease to receive constitutionally backed protection, the federal government even abandoned
a rhetorical commitment to obtaining Indian consent. The era of conquest was over and the era of peace was dawning. If conquest had been
associated with a wholesale slaughter of Indians, peace was associated
with forced appropriation and semi-captivity. Semi-captivity, in turn,
was identified with a set of institutions. The first was the reservation; the
second was the BIA.

The Peace Policy was elaborated during the post-Civil War tenure of
President Grant. Congress established the Board of Indian Commissioners on April 10, 1869. When he met the new Board on May 27, 1869,
Grant delineated the main lines of his Indian policy: to abandon the
treaty system, replace it with reservations, and secure Indian titles to
"such lands as they could be induced to cultivate" (ibid.: 36). The Board
began its tenure with an all-round critique of government Indian policy,
issued in its first annual report of November 23, 1869: that the treatment
of Indians had been "unjust and iniquitous beyond the power of words
to express," that the history of the government's relations with the tribes
had been "a shameful record of broken treaties and unfulfilled promises,"
and that the primary blame for Indian wars lay with frontiersmen. "Para-
doxical as it may seem," the commissioners acknowledged, "the white
man has been the chief obstacle in the way of Indian civilization" (Prucha
1973: 38).

That this bit of history was meant for the archives rather than as
guidelines for future policy became clear when the President's Secretary
of the Interior, Columbus Delano, spelt out the fourfold objectives of his
"peace policy" in a statement in 1873. The first was to segregate Indians
on reservations where they could be kept away from frontier settlements.
The second was forcibly to assimilate them, by "all needed severity," so
as "to punish them for their outrages according to their merits, thereby
teaching that it is better to follow the advice of the government, live
upon reservations and become civilized, than to continue their native
habits and practices." The third was to ensure that funds for procuring
Indian supplies were properly spent. And the fourth was to secure the
cooperation of religious organizations to procure "competent, upright,
faithful, moral and religious" agents to run the reservations, as well as

---

[17] VII Newton, 206 Act of March 3, 1871, ch. 120, #1, 16 Stat. 566 (codified at 25 USC
#71 (1976)).

churches and schools meant to bring them "the comforts and benefits of a Christian civilization" (Prucha 1976: 31–2).

Reservations

As an institution designed to hold a subject population captive, the reservation had a long history, starting with seventeenth-century Ireland and the Puritan colonies in North America. The modern reservation, however, came into being only in the second half of the nineteenth century. Its inauguration signaled the final defeat of Native Americans in North America.

To install a reservation system required more or less the complete subjugation of natives. When Queen Elizabeth's nobles received lands and governing powers in Ireland, the condition was that they conquer the natives in the assigned territories. Many concluded that it would be necessary to exterminate the Irish. But this was not possible "since neither the Crown not any feudal lord was wealthy enough to finance the work of extermination" (Macleod 1928: 162–3). The alternative to extermination, Chichester suggested in 1607 (also the year of the settlement of Jamestown, Virginia), was a reservation system for the leaderless natives. King James used this plan in 1600 in his final scheme for the colonization of Ulster. According to the plan, the natives of the region, divided into six British counties, were ordered to leave the country immediately or to gather together on reservations. But they were also left with little choice in the matter, given that they had nowhere else to go, and that the order called for death for any person found outside reservations after a certain date (ibid.: 163–4).

The reservation system was born of a compromise: the king wanted the tribal system of government utterly and completely abolished, but the bishops counseled compromise to avoid bloodshed. Not only were the strategies pursued by Puritans in North America remarkably similar to those executed by English Protestants in Ireland, early Indian treaties were also remarkably like the treaties with Celtic tribes. The tribes were required to submit to the crown's sovereignty, and stop internecine warfare, but they were allowed to retain their tribal organization for administrative purposes. Three different kinds of prohibition were enforced. The first provided for a virtual ban on the sale or transportation of liquor, permitting only home brew, save permission for the chiefs to import a little good whisky or wine for their personal use. The second targeted specific cultural practices identified as barbaric: trial marriage, a native custom, was forbidden; also the tribes, hitherto Catholics – first Celtic, then Roman – were required to submit in religion to the established episcopal church, to build churches and support a clergy. Oliver Cromwell suppressed religious freedom from 1651 to 1660 as rigorously as did his fellow Puritans in America. Anglicans, Jews, and Catholics were forbidden to worship except in Presbyterian or Congregationalist churches. When Cromwell led his army into Ireland, he was determined to wipe out both the tribal system and the native religion, thereby forcing natives to submit both to English rule and to Congregationalist religious belief and organization (ibid.: 170). Finally, there was the strictest prohibition against the cultural and intellectual leadership of the tribes, combined with provisions to create an alternative intellectual leadership. So the bards or *seannachies* were forbidden to sing to remind the tribesmen of their ancient, primitive glory, and the chiefs of their age-long genealogies. The chiefs were even forbidden to support them, and the bards were to be doomed to starvation or manual labor – and silence. At the same time, the eldest children of the chiefs and nobles were to be educated in English schools, under the direction of the crown but at the expense of their parents (ibid.: 167–8). From the outset, compulsory segregation went hand in hand with forced assimilation.

The first reservations in the English colonies were made up of survivors from among the conquered Pequot. These Christianized Indians were called the "Praying Indians." They were allocated a bounded piece of land as their domicile under colonial jurisdiction. The first of these reservations was the "town" of Natick. Over time, these reservations became like magnetic islands attracting freed slaves seeking refuge. The freedmen intermarried, acquired land, and settled down, in the process bringing accumulated skills in European agriculture to the Indian population (ibid.: 389, 392).

The modern American reservation system dates from the middle of the nineteenth century when William Medill, Commissioner of Indian Affairs, renounced the concept of a barrier state in his annual report of 1848 and suggested two reservations (called colonies) for the tribes standing in the way of expansion: "one north, on the dead waters of the Mississippi and the other south, on the western borders of Missouri and Arkansas" (Trennert 1975: 30). *In other words, the reservation system emerged as a successor to Indian Removal and an alternative to a Native American state.* The following year, on March 3, 1849, the Senate approved the creation of the Department of the Interior to which it transferred Indian Affairs. There ensued a division of labor between the army and the Indian Office, the former retaining responsibility for the hostile tribes and the latter for the subdued tribes (ibid.: 41–2). The first of the agents was sent out in 1849, and a single consolidated Indian Department was created by the federal government in 1851 (ibid.: 57–60).

Gold-rush California became a state of the Union in 1850, and soon afterwards became an implementation site for the untested policy of reservations. Federal officials first proposed reserves for the Golden State in a series of eighteen treaties negotiated in 1851 and 1852 with numerous bands and villages of natives. These agreements assigned Indians to specific territories in the state, promised a subsidy of food and livestock, and offered instruction and supervision for at least five years. When the US Senate refused to ratify the treaties on July 8, 1852, the Office of Indian Affairs proceeded to found reservations in a manner that would not require Senate ratification. It appointed Edward F. Beale, a prominent frontier adventurer and office-holder, as superintendent of Indian affairs in the state, and instructed him to establish a "system of colonization" for the purpose of "making useful, our present worthless, and troublesome Indian population." Beale and his successors focused attention away from the coastal strip, where Hispanic settlement had either eliminated or absorbed most natives, to the great interior valley and the northern coast, where contact with Indians had been limited before the 1840s. This is where the first three experimental reserves – El Tejon, Nome Lackee and Fresno farm – were first started (Findlay 1992: 15–17). Six more reservations or farms founded by agents of the Office of Indian Affairs followed in 1852–5, and yet another six in 1856–70; but only three survived up to 1871 (ibid.: 18). In an analysis of the early California reservations, John M. Findlay identifies three factors as shaping their demise: starvation, violence by encroaching white settlers, and incompetence or corruption on the part of Indian agents. "The institution was too weak to provide them with food and clothing, too weak to protect them from white attacks, and too weak to make them stay . . . If Indians tried to drive off or kill the white man's stock, they were threatened, beaten or shot." Without adequate security and subsistence, most Indians who went to California's first three reservations "either died there or departed," whereas the rest avoided the reservations altogether (ibid.: 23).

As officials looked for familiar models with which to identify this new institution, "reserves were variously likened to farms, fortresses, asylums, schools, final refuges, and Spanish missions." Even if the context made for a shift of meanings, one model, that of the asylum, endured more than any other (ibid.: 14). If anything, the reservation was designed as a movable asylum. Since Indians were marched from one site to another, early reservation policy "assumed not only a high degree of impermanence but also a substantial amount of coercion." Indian agents looked to the military both for an example of how to organize life within the reservation and for assistance in forcing the Indians to do as they were told. But the role of the military was inconsistent with the reservation's reform and welfare functions (ibid.: 21–2). To facilitate this role, California denied civil and political rights to Indians as soon as it was admitted to the Union in 1850 – and authorized and financed military campaigns against Indians, as part of a larger removal effort (ibid.: 25).

Findlay says that early reservations suffered the same fate as asylums which had been established to rehabilitate deviants and regenerate stability, but by the late 1850s were "losing their reformist mission and becoming storage bins for society's outcasts." In another decade, by the end of the Civil War, reservations too had become places to segregate Indian "misfits" from the rest of society, even if they had been designed for an opposite purpose – as a means to incorporate Native Americans into the mainstream (ibid.: 19). In 1855, US Army Captain E. D. Keyes praised the superintendent at Nome Lackee because, instead of holding expectations about the Indians' ultimate survival and acculturation, he reportedly understood that his chief purpose "must be to deprive the Red Man of his power to do mischief" during the few years he had remaining on earth. "We ought . . . to act," Keyes wrote, "on the determined certainty that the aborigines of this Country will soon become extinct" (ibid.: 20). In this vision, domestication was not seen as an alternative, but as a transit facility to extermination. The early California reservation, which seemed like an early version of the industrial concentration camp, was discredited and supplanted by a new generation of smaller reserves and rancherias during the late nineteenth and early twentieth centuries (ibid.: 28).

Not all settlers were in favor of a reservation policy. Some, as in Texas, preferred a more immediate final solution: extermination. When the federal government proposed the establishment of a reservation in Texas as a way of separating the races and securing peace, newspapers such as the *Democratic Telegraph* and *Texas Register* were bitterly opposed and called for a war of extermination. Some Texan residents called for the removal of all Indians from Texas. The Texas legislature approved a reservation policy on February 16, 1854, but no sooner were reservations established than "armed parties invaded the reservations and began a systematic slaughter of the tribesmen." Finally the government relented, and in 1859 authorized the complete removal of all Texas tribes north of the Red River (Trennert 1975: 68, 77, 92–3). Reservations were eventually set up elsewhere, in 1854 (Missouri), 1867 (Cheyenne and Arapaho), and 1868 (Sioux). The policy was generalized in the context of the "Indian Wars" on the western frontier between 1860 and 1890, when the US "decided to put a full reservation system into operation by defeating or starving the tribes into compliance" (ibid.: 158, 191, 196).

The federal policy of confining Indian tribes to remote reservations was initiated by Abraham Lincoln during the Civil War, and was intensified by President Grant under what he claimed was a Peace Policy. In his 1869 inaugural address, Grant promised to pursue policies that would "civilize" Native Americans and lead to their "ultimate" citizenship. As preparation for the policy turnaround, he fired all existing Indian agents and hired new ones, chosen by Quakers, and later also by other Christian denominations. Thus began the most extensive federal-level collaboration between the state and churches in the history of the United States – one that made "repudiation of native religion and ways of life, and acceptance of middle-class American Christianity with its attendant customs, official prerequisites for admission to US citizenship" (Smith 1997: 318–19).

Eric Foner has noted that, when completed in 1869, the transcontinental railroad "expanded the national market, facilitated the penetration of capital in the West, and heralded the final doom of the Plains Indians." In this west "lay millions of acres of fertile and mineral-rich land roamed by immense buffalo herds that provided food, clothing, and shelter for a population of perhaps a quarter of a million Indians, many of them members of eastern tribes forced inland two centuries before from the east coast, and moved again earlier in the nineteenth century to open the Old Northwest and Southwest to white farmers and planters." This jackpot was now targeted by Grant's Peace Policy, to be executed by military and civilian officials, "nearly all" of whom "shared a common presumption: that the federal government should persuade or coerce the Plains Indians to exchange their religion, communal form of property, and 'nomadic' way of life for Christian worship and settled agriculture on federally supervised reservations. In a word, they should surrender most of their land and cease to be Indians." Towards this end, generals employed methods they had perfected during the Civil War, destroying the "the infrastructure of the Indian economy," even if that meant destroying the buffalo, and abrogating the treaty system that dealt with Indians as independent nations. This step was "strongly supported by railroad corporations, which found tribal sovereignty an obstacle to construction, and by Radical Republicans, to whom the traditional system seemed a form of local autonomy incompatible with the uniform nationality born of the Civil War." By the time Grant left office, the world of the Plains Indian had been shattered by a combination of the railroad, farms, ranches, Indian Wars, and reservations. The population of Plains Indians, hitherto, estimated at a quarter of a million, had diminished drastically, while the settler population of the Middle Border states (Minnesota, the Dakotas, Nebraska and Kansas) had grown from 300,000 in 1860 to well over two million in twenty years. On the ashes of the Plains Indians thus arose, in the words of Eric Foner, "a new agricultural empire" (Foner 1988: 21, 462–3).

The reservation policy, in the words of Kenneth D. McRae, "condemned the Indian and the *métis* to a non-competitive, sheltered, subsidized, and essentially neglected and uneducated existence on reservations of his own" (McRea 1964: 264). But they were not places "of his own." Rather, constructed for him and her, reservations were sites where the Indian was not only detained ("neglected") but also made the butt of a whole array of coercive measures designed to subdue ("civilize") him and her into full obedience ("citizenship").

The Bureau of Indian Affairs

The reservation was presented to white society both as a way of segregating the races, and as a hothouse for the accelerated "civilization" and assimilation of Indians. The Indian agent was to be the key catalyst in this process. This is how the Indian Office's regulations for the Indian service defined the role of an agent: "The chief duty of an agent is to induce his Indians to labor in civilized pursuits. To attain this end every possible influence should be brought to bear, and in proportion as it is attained, other things being equal, an agent's administration is successful or unsuccessful" (Prucha 1984: 643, 645). Created to administer the assimilation of the Indian tribes into the American nation, the BIA turned out to be the instrument of their forced segregation into semi-captivity. BIA agents ruled the reservations without any legally imposed restraint during the plenary power era, which went from 1877 to the 1930s (Harring 1994: 4, 56). Harring says BIA's claim that the tribes were not ready for the full responsibilities of US citizenship rationalized the near-absolute administrative powers exercised by its agents (ibid.: 175).

The BIA intervened in the daily lives of Indian peoples through two extra-legal institutions: the Indian police created in 1879, and the Courts of Indian Offenses established in 1883. The Indian police wore the uniform of army privates and had their roots in the army's Indian scouts (ibid.: 1982). Under the command of the agent, the Indian police functioned as "quasi-military forces" that were "a substitute for army control of the reservations" (Prucha 1976: 201). The strongest objections against having a standing police force under the control of the agent came from the chairman of the House Committee on Indian Affairs in 1880:

This provision turns him [the Indian] over, bound hand and foot, to the agents. These men had authority before almost without restriction, except as they are restricted by the want of physical force. Now we give them eight hundred men armed and equipped and thus the fullest authority is allowed with fearful power to execute not known laws, but the will of the agent. (ibid.: 207–8)

The Indian police were soon joined by Courts of Indian Offenses, introduced by Secretary of the Interior Henry M. Teller, who in December 1882 called attention to several cultural degradations: "the continuance of old heathenish dances" which he insisted led to a war spirit and demoralized the young, the practice of polygamy, and the influence of the medicine men who kept children from attending school and promoted heathenish customs. Together, said Teller, these constituted "a great hindrance to the civilization of the Indian." Not surprisingly, the jurisdiction of the courts set up by Teller included all three: dances, polygamy, and medicine men (Prucha 1984: 646–8). This is how the "Rules for Indian Courts" defined these offenses:

Dance, etc – any Indian who shall engage in the sun dance, scalp dance, or war dance, or any other similar feast, so-called, shall be deemed guilty of an offense . . .

Practices of Medicine Men – Any Indian who shall engage in the practices of so-called medicine men, or who shall resort to any artifice or device to keep the Indians of the reservations from adopting and following civilized habits and pursuits, or shall adopt any means to prevent the attendance of children at school, or shall use any arts of a conjurer to prevent Indians from abandoning their barbarous rites and customs, shall be deemed guilty of an offense . . .

Misdemeanors – And provided further, that if an Indian refuses or neglects to adopt habits of industry or to engage in civilized pursuits or employments, but habitually spends his time in idleness and loafing, he shall be deemed a vagrant and guilty of a misdemeanor. (cited in Strickland 1985–6: 728)

The judges were given specific jurisdiction over these practices, and other misdemeanors. Composed of the first three officers in rank of the police force, or, if the agent did not approve them, of three other persons selected by the agent, the courts were a further "extension of the agent's authority." By 1900, approximately two-thirds of the agencies had courts. The exceptions were the "civilized" tribes with tribal governments: the Five Civilized Tribes, the Indians of New York, the Osages, the Pueblos and the Eastern Cherokees (Prucha 1976: 208–9). For the tribes considered "uncivilized," First Amendment rights were drastically curtailed. Indian religions were banned upon threat of criminal prosecution in the Courts of Indian Offenses set up by the Bureau of Indian Affairs (Newton 1983–4: 227).

Whereas every reservation had a police force, not every reservation had a court system. Many agents never bothered to create them. But where they were created, the judges were appointed by and served at the pleasure of the agents. Occasionally they were police officers, but often they were influential chiefs. The degree of apparent assimilation was a major criterion in the selection of judges, and agents' reports are replete with descriptions of judges as "Christian," "wearing white man's clothing," or "monogamous." The agents placed this legal process in the hands of progressive Sioux, factionalizing the Sioux legal system. These judges did not set out to implement "Indian law" but rather a set of BIA rules. The rules for Indian courts were revised twice, in 1891 and 1904, but the substance remained that of the original 1883 rules (Harring 1994: 186, 191).

With or without the assistance of courts, agents were determined to demonize Indian culture. Herring concludes from a reading of BIA annual reports that the struggle to outlaw traditional dancing was long and drawn out (ibid.: 274). Illustrative of the BIA's views is an observation in the BIA annual report of 1883: "It was found that the longer continuance of certain old heathen and barbarous customs, such as the sun-dance, scalp-dance, war-dance, polygamy & c., were operating as a serious hindrance to the efforts of the Government for the civilization of the Indians" (ibid.: 186).

In practice, assimilation turned into a culture war against practices that distinguished Indian tribes from white neighbors, such as long hair, painted faces, and Indian dress. Commissioner William A. Jones pointed out "a few customs among the Indians which, it is believed, should be modified or discontinued." The first was the wearing of long hair by men, which the Commissioner believed was "not in keeping with the advancement they are making, or will soon be expected to make, in civilization." "Certainly all the younger men should wear short hair," Jones directed, "and it is believed that by tact, perseverance, firmness, and withdrawal of supplies the superintendent can induce *all* to comply with this order." Commissioner Jones also directed action against painting the face and against dances and Indian feasts, which "were simply subterfuges to cover degrading acts and to disguise immoral purposes." Finally, superintendents and agents were directed to encourage the wearing of citizen's dress instead of Indian costumes and blankets (Prucha 1984: 764). If Indians employed by the Indian service refused to comply, they could be discharged and their supplies stopped. If they became obstreperous, "a short confinement in the guard house at hard labor, with shorn locks, should furnish a cure."

Successive commissioners upped the ante, calling for the renaming of Indians. Commissioner Thomas J. Morgan argued in a circular of March 19, 1890 that there will be "needless confusion" and "considerable ultimate loss to the Indians if no attempt is made to have the different members of a family known by the same family name on the records and by general reputation." He contended that "among other customs of the white people it is becoming important that the Indians adopt that in regard to names." He condemned the translation of Indian names into English, a practice which often resulted in "awkward and uncouth" names. He was also against "the habit of adopting sobriquets given to Indians such as 'Tobacco,' 'Mogul,' 'Tom,' 'Pete,' etc. by which they become generally known." He suggested that "unusually long and difficult" Indian names be shortened arbitrarily, and authorized the substitution of English names for Indian ones too difficult for whites to pronounce and the introduction of Christian given names before the surnames (ibid.: 673–4).

In reservations that lacked functioning Courts of Indian Offenses – which was in most – the agent simply jailed whoever he wanted to on his personal authority or he asked the military to do so. The military believed it had authority over Indians because they remained within the United States after their defeat in the Indian wars as a conquered people subject to military discipline (Harring 1994: 193). Harring says there is no question that many thousands of Indians were so detained for offenses ranging from murder to resisting allotment.

The full brunt of the effort of reeducation was directed toward Indian children who were shipped away from the reservation or brought together at reservation schools. The philosophy was most simply expressed by Richard Pratt, the founder of Carlisle School: "Kill the Indian and save the man" (Strickland 1985–6: 729). Vaunted as a key benefit of "civilization," as it was at the World's Columbian Exposition in 1893, the regime at school led to "heartbreaking experiences that drove Native children to commit suicide and to run away repeatedly" (Huhndorf 2001: 201).

In reality, the agent ran an occupation regime. Besides wielding a police force and influencing courts where they existed, he had powers to control the ebb and flow of resources to the reservation. When tribal councils were dissolved in 1906 as a correlative to forced individualization of property, his grip on power was further tightened (Kiernan 1978: 103). "By 1915, the agent, now called a superintendent, had control of all welfare services, and anyone who found fault with his doings could be set down as a malcontent" (ibid.: 101). More often than not, reservations appeared as "mammoth poorhouses rather than nurseries of civilization" (Prucha 1976: 223).

The Board of Indian Commissioners boasted in 1901 that not only was the object of the Indian Office to "make all Indians self-supporting, self-respecting, and useful citizens of the United States," but also that unlike other divisions of the government, "the Indian Bureau should always aim at its own speedy discontinuance" (Report of the Board of Indian

Commissioners, 1901, pp. 4–5; 1906, pp. 8–9, cited in Prucha 1984, 779). But the trend, as Prucha showed, was to the contrary: the employees in the Indian Office increased from 115 in 1900 to 262 in 1920, and the communications received increased from 62,691 to 261,486 over the same period (ibid.: 781). In practice, the reservation was more the site of social decay and social crisis than progress. Forced segregation was perhaps the most important factor fostering this crisis. Forced isolation robbed the Indians' way of life of both vitality and meaning, reducing it to a set of disconnected rituals without the possibility of innovation. Not only were the buffalo and the wide stretches of free territory gone, it was also the case that social organization, built up through generations to protect fundamental interests, no longer met crucial problems, but was preserved as if in a museum. To be sure, there were substitutes, such as agricultural life and Christianity, but they were both unfamiliar and not always relevant. In this spiritual and social vacuum came the rapid development of movements such as the Ghost Dance religion, "engendered by the wish for the old security and distaste of the white man's civilization, and eagerly sought and accepted by one after another of the distraught plains tribes" (Macleod 1928: 530).

The first major critic of forced assimilation was the applied anthropologist John Collier, one of the founders of the Interamerican Indigenista Institute (whose first executive director was Manuel Gamio) (Hall 2005: 223–4). Collier called for an end to "monopolistic and autocratic control over person and property by a single Bureau of the Federal Government" and for protection of Indian property rights, for respect of "elementary rights guaranteed to other Americans by the Constitution or long-established tradition," and for the use of cultural pride and "native social endowments and institutions" in the education of the Indians (Prucha 1984: 806).

Taking office as Commissioner of Indian Affairs on April 21, 1933, Collier modernized Indian Affairs into a version of British-style indirect rule in tropical Africa. To do so, he brought in a flock of anthropologists to shape policies and programs. Collier tried to reconfigure Indians as a tribal government with a tribal economy, even if the group in question was in practice organized into bands and villages (ibid.: 1010).

The centerpiece of Collier's policy was the Indian Reorganization Act (IRA), an ambitious package of interrelated reforms designed to halt and reverse the destruction of Native American communities. The title of the bill he introduced was self-explanatory:

A bill to grant the Indians living under Federal tutelage the freedom to organize for the purposes of local self-government and economic enterprise; to provide for

the necessary training of Indians in administrative and economic affairs; to con-
serve and develop Indian lands; and to promote the more effective administration
of justice in matters affecting Indian tribes and communities by establishing a
Federal Court of Indian Affairs. (ibid.: 957)

Collier made it clear that while a tribe that rejected the Act would not
be discriminated against, there were sure to be consequences born of
official neglect: "it will merely drift to the rear of the great advance open
to the Indian race. It will stand still and will probably continue to lose its
lands while those who accept the Act, its benefits and responsibilities can
preserve and increase their lands and will move forward" (ibid.: 964). He
set up an Indian Organization Division within the Bureau to reorganize
tribes according to newly adopted constitutions, bylaws, and corporate
charters. Within ten years, ninety-three tribes, bands, and Indian
communities had adopted constitutions and bylaws and seventy-three
were granted charters (ibid.: 967–8). The Act authorized preferential
hiring of Indians in the Indian Service. The number of permanent
Indian employees in the service rose from a few hundred in 1933 to
4,682 in 1940. These included eight superintendents, 251 professionals,
935 clerical workers and approximately 3,475 in other skilled jobs
(ibid.: 992). Of all Bureau employees 78 percent were Indians or Alaska
natives by 1980. Within a decade, Collier had successfully created a
combination of self-government and a comprehensive administrative
paternalism (ibid.: 1086).

To stem the continuing erosion of the Indian land-base, all further
allotments were prohibited; the trust status on existing holdings was
extended indefinitely and $2 million a year was appropriated for the
purchase of additional land. At the same time, to help them regain a
measure of autonomy and self-sufficiency, tribes were encouraged to
organize their own governments and to establish business corporations,
with a revolving loan fund of $10 million set up to provide capital for
plant and equipment. But this vision of tribal autonomy was promptly
undermined by making every important decision subject to approval by
the Secretary of the Interior (Wilson 1998: 347–8; Churchill 2001: 292).

The Act's first major critic was Scudder Mekeel, director of the Applied
Anthropology Unit in the Office of Indian Affairs, 1935–7. In a broad-
ranging critique, Mekeel focused on two salient aspects of the Act. First,
that "it closely resembles the British policy of 'indirect rule' in that the
native political and social organization is strengthened by utilizing it
for administrative purposes." The bureaucracy may be Indianized, but
Mekeel felt the strengthened bureaucracy would only have the effect of
furthering a trend begun under the old Indian Service: "Practically all
tribes, aside from certain groups in the Southwest, have seen their native

form of government disintegrate and disappear under the bureaucracy of the Indian Service." Even if "many 'Tribal Councils' have been organized under Indian Office sponsorship," they "have been almost completely controlled by the reservation superintendent." Second, he pointed out that "the Indian Reorganization Act continues the policy of segregating the Indian population from the white – a policy inherent in the reservation system itself" (Mekeel 1944: 209–17). Here, too, Mekeel was spot on.

After Collier left office in 1945 and Harold Ickes (his strong backer) resigned as Secretary of the Interior in 1946, the policy pendulum swung back to forced assimilation as the executive branch of the government joined Congress in a massive drive to assimilate Indians once and for all (Prucha 1984: 1013). President Truman appointed Dillon S. Myer, who had been in charge of the wartime internment and resettlement of Japanese Americans, as Commissioner of Indian Affairs. Myer's forceful methods included interfering in tribal elections, selling land without the tribe's consent, supporting a bill which would have allowed Indian Service employees to carry guns and arrest Native Americans without warrant, and removing a rare BIA superintendent who had upheld Indian rights (Wilson 1998: 362).

The thrust of the Truman administration's Indian policy was known as the Termination Policy. Adopted in August 1953, it declared Congress's intention to make Native Americans "subject to the same laws and entitled to the same privileges and responsibilities as . . . other citizens of the United States" by "freeing" them from "all Federal supervision and control." A few days later, Congress passed Public Law 280, which extended state control over all Indians – with a few specified exceptions – in five states, and empowered other states to enact similar legislation. From 1954 to 1960 some fourteen recognized tribes with reservations were terminated, often without their consent. Most were small, impoverished communities who had little idea of what was happening to them, but a few – most notably the Menominee of Wisconsin and the Klamath of Oregon – were large, wealthy tribes with considerable natural resources, who fought the government's decision for some years (ibid.: 361–2). The Termination Policy was repudiated by the Nixon administration in 1970.

The longer-run impact of Collier and the 1934 Indian Reorganization Act was to move federal policy on reservations, even if fitfully, "away from seeing them as temporary impounding points for ultimate assimilation and toward a recognition of their status as permanent homelands," thus aiming to enhance their economic development and stabilize their internal organization as communities. It is for this reason that, notwithstanding the brief resurgence of assimilationist and abolitionist sentiment epitomized by the "termination" resolution of 1953, most observers are agreed that Collier's influence on Indian policy survives even half a century after he left office. The ultimate legislative expression of this policy is the Indian Self-Determination Act of 1975, which seeks both to make the Native American peoples entirely self-administering and to eliminate their dependent status as administered communities (Castile and Bee 1992: 5–6). As George Pierre Castile and Robert L. Bee observe in their introduction to *State and Reservation*: "New explanations are needed why the reservation system and federal–Indian relations have seemingly become permanent" (ibid.: 8).

VI.   Citizen wards: citizens without rights

If Marshall could see no future for Native American *communities* beyond a perpetual colonial condition, Supreme Court justices such as Taney explored the possibility of *individual* futures beyond colonial subjugation. Taney wrote in *Dred Scott* (1856) that even though Indian tribes had not historically formed a part of the colonial communities and had never "amalgamated" with them, and though the Indians were "uncivilized," "the course of events" had brought them "under subjection" to the white race, "and it has been found necessary, for their sake as well as our own, to regard them as in a state of pupilage, and to legislate to a certain extent over them and over the territories they occupy." Following a trajectory well laid by the Marshall model's guardian–ward principle, Taney noted that Indians could only become naturalized as citizens under the laws of the United States by abandoning their ties to their savage tribes and taking up "abode among the white population" (Williams 2005: 17–18, 72). The alternative Taney offered would today be termed ethnocide, the erasure of their group identity in favor of assimilation into white society as individual citizens of the United States.

Citizenship was first thought of with reference to the "civilized" tribes, and as an alternative to the promised two-state solution. In its very first annual report of 1869, the Board of Indian Commissioners urged citizenship for Indians considered "civilized" – the Five Civilized Tribes in the Indian Territory – and "wards of the government" as the appropriate legal status for "uncivilized Indians" (Prucha 1976: 40). A law conferring citizenship on the "civilized" tribes was passed in 1901. But when a Select Committee of the Senate was sent to investigate conditions in the Indian Territory in connection with the Act of 1906, it remarked on how this law seemed not to have taken any effect:

Yet notwithstanding this express legislative naturalization, Congress in its subsequent legislation, and the Department of the Interior, acting under such legislation, has apparently ignored entirely this established citizenship, and in nearly every instance has treated the questions arising within the Five Civilized Tribes as though no such act had ever been passed and as though the Indians were still in the broadest sense wards of the Government. (Prucha 1984: 899)

Even as Woodrow Wilson paid homage to the right of self-determination globally, the end of his first term coincided with a formal Supreme Court ruling that confirmed the second-class citizenship of Indians, and the fact that the terms of Indian citizenship were not a matter of fundamental right but would continue to be determined at the pleasure of Congress. In *United* v. *Nice*, Justice Van Devanter wrote that citizenship was "not incompatible with tribal existence or continued guardianship, and so may be conferred without completely emancipating the Indians or placing them beyond the reach of congressional regulations adopted for their protection" (cited in Smith 1997: 463).

The formal grant of citizenship to Native Americans took place over two decades, from 1901 to 1924. The first to be granted citizenship were members of the Five Civilized Tribes, who together counted for more than one third of persons officially termed "Indian" in the US. Roughly another third were naturalized between 1907 and 1921: in 1907, all remaining Indians in Oklahoma; in 1919, all Indians who had served in the US army in the First World War; and in 1921, all remaining members of the Osage tribe. The last third of Indians were naturalized with the Act of Congress of June 2, 1924, which provided "that all non-citizen Indians born within the territorial limits of the United States be, and they are hereby declared to be, citizens of the United States" (Macleod 1928: 540; Amar 2006: 439).

As citizens, Indians form a category of their own. At least three different types of limitations set them apart from other native-born American citizens. The first and central limitation to Indian citizenship is that Indians remain legal wards of the US government. This fact was spelt out by the Eighth Circuit Court in a 1912 case: "The word 'Indian' in the statute describes a person of Indian blood. The word 'citizen' describes a political status" (Newton 1983–4: 228). Based on the ward status of the Indian, there were three types of Indian citizens, signifying three different stages in the process of assimilation. The least assimilated are Indians with a tribal membership. They partake of the collective resources of the tribe as members of the tribe. Without allotment of individual plots of land, they are known as the *"unallotted" Indians*. The "allotted" Indians, those who have received individual plots of land from what was previously tribal property, are further divided into two categories: "restricted" and "unrestricted." The second group of Indian citizens comprise the *"allotted" but "restricted" Indians*: these are Indians who have received their allotment of tribal land, but their land title is held in trust by the US government for a period of twenty-five years. The third group of Indian citizens is that of Indians who are "allotted" and "unrestricted": with an unrestricted allotment, only they are full citizens of the US. These were the *"unrestricted" Indians*. The first two groups of Indians are as wards of the federal government: the first group as tribal wards, and the second group as individual wards. In 1920, for example, there were 240,000 restricted Indians. Of these 125,000 were unallotted, and 115,000 allotted (Prucha 1976: 543–4). The arrangement was formally sanctioned by the Supreme Court which held that "citizenship is not incompatible with tribal existence or continued guardianship, and so may be conferred without completely emancipating the Indians or placing them beyond the reach of Congress and regulations adopted for their protection" (Macleod 1928: 540–1). The ward status means that Indians are subject to limitations as Indians – no matter the degree of their assimilation in white society or their citizen status. To take an example, individual Indians can be subjected to liquor laws, whether or not they have severed tribal relations and whether or not they are on a reservation. In *Hallowell* v. *United States* [221 US 317 (1911)], the defendant "had been active in county and state governments as judge, county attorney, county assessor, and director of a public school district," but "he was still subject to the law because of his status as an Indian."

Second, unlike other persons born in the United States, Indians are not citizens by birth. The Court held in *Elk* v. *Wilkins* [112 US 94 (1884)] that the tribal Indian owed allegiance to the tribe from birth and therefore was not born "subject to the jurisdiction" of the United States (Johnson 1973: 993). Citizenship did not necessarily mean enfranchisement. Indians continued to be prohibited from voting in a number of western states, and not until 1948 did Arizona and New Mexico extend the franchise to them (Prucha 1984: 794). Even then, only "unrestricted" Indians had the right to vote. By the time Macleod wrote in 1928, only some 29,000 or so had qualified as voters (Macleod 1928: 541). The rest comprised Indian Country, the name given to settler America's first colony, comprising 200 reservations, with resident agents in about ninety of them. "Today the official 'Indian Country' comprises the aggregate of reservation lands unallotted and of allotted lands the title to which is still held in trust by the government" (ibid.: 541).

Third, Indians are the only citizens without rights constitutionally guaranteed and enshrined in the Bill of Rights. Just as citizenship for Indians came to have a lax meaning – not considered incompatible with federal powers of guardianship, nor with restriction on the right to alienate property – so did civil rights come to be defined in a loose and informal way when Congress passed the Indian Civil Rights Act of 1968 (ICRA). Instead of the full application of the Bill of Rights as contained in the Constitution, Title 1 of the Act speaks of the protection of a select and specific set of individual rights. Title II selectively incorporates portions of the Constitution as a Bill of Rights for Indians. Interestingly, "the Act *omits* some constitutional guarantees including the prohibition against laws respecting the establishment of religion and the right to indictment by a grand jury." It then *limits* other guarantees: "the right to counsel is only available at one's own expense and the right to jury trial is limited to those accused of crimes punishable by imprisonment." Title III directs the Secretary of the Interior to draft and recommend to the Congress a model code governing Courts of Indian Offenses. The code is to "assure that any individual being tried for an offense by a Court of Indian Offenses shall have the same rights, privileges, and immunities under the United States Constitution as would be guaranteed any citizen of the United States being tried in a Federal Court for any similar offense." But the code is not binding on tribal courts; it is only a recommendation (Johnson 1973: 998–9).

That the Act lacked an enforcement mechanism became clear when the Supreme Court in *Santa Clara Pueblo* v. *Martinez* (1978) bluntly denied that it carried any federal remedies, finding that only tribal forums are available to enforce the ICRA. Just as with citizenship, here too we have the anomaly of a federal civil rights act that provides limited federal remedies to enforce it. Application of the full Bill of Rights, argued Prucha, would upset traditional governing practices in Indian Country, including the quasi-theocracies that ran some of them (Prucha 1984: 1107). Tradition, in this case, referred to a colonial mode of governance, not to the historical mode of governance in pre-Columbian America. At its heart is the fact that all Indians are as wards of Congress. The trust relationship means that they possess no constitutionally guaranteed rights in relation to Congress; put differently, the enforceable rights Indians do possess are against the executive branch, a fact that has driven the narrowly conceived struggle for Indian rights in recent times (Newton 1983–4: 233).

Ironically, the colonial paternalism that is the essence of the guardian–ward relationship between the federal government and Indian communities has been defended in the language of self-determination by both sides. Even the resurgence of militancy in the decade of the 1960s that began with the American Indian Chicago conference in 1961 and concluded with the formation of the American Indian Movement in 1968 in Minneapolis did not change this substantially. Take, for example, the "policy for the future" as summed up by the American Indian Policy Review Commission – established in the aftermath of Indian demonstrations at the Bureau of Indian Affairs in 1972 and at Wounded Knee in 1973 – in its final report of May 17, 1977. The report begins with an elaboration of the dual "Foundations of Federal Indian Law":

1. That Indian tribes are sovereign political bodies, having the power to determine their own membership and power to enact laws and enforce them within the boundaries of their reservations, and
2. that the relationship which exists between the tribes and the United States is premised on a special trust that must govern the conduct of the stronger toward the weaker. (Prucha 1984: 1115, 1117–18)

The report proceeds to define "the Trust Responsibility" at the heart of the relationship between the federal government and the Indian community, presenting a total colonial paternalism as some kind of a warm and comforting wraparound administrative blanket:

1. The trust responsibility to American Indians extends from the protection and enhancement of Indian trust resources and tribal self-government to the provision of economic and social programs necessary to raise the standard of living and social well being of the Indian people to a level comparable to the non-Indian society.
2. The trust responsibility extends through tribe to the Indian member, whether on or off the reservation.
3. The trust responsibility applies to all United States agencies and instrumentalities, not just those charged specifically with administration of Indian affairs.

How difficult it has been to think of alternatives to colonial paternalism is evident from the fact that even Indian activists have been unable to come up with a solution that goes beyond a reformed version of that same colonial relationship.

BIBLIOGRAPHY

Amar, Akhil Reed. 2006. *America's Constitution: A Biography*. New York: Random House.
Castile, George Pierre and Robert L. Bee (eds.). 1992. *State and Reservation: New Perspectives on Federal Indian Policy*. Tucson and London: University of Arizona Press.
Cherokee Nation v. Georgia. 1831. 30 US 1; 8 L. Ed. 25; 1831 US LEXIS 337. Decided, pp. 16.
Churchill, Ward. 2001. *A Little Matter of Genocide: Holocaust and Denial in the Americas, 1492 to the Present*. San Francisco: City Lights Publishers.

Cohen, Felix. 1942. *Handbook of Federal Indian Law*. Washington DC: Department of the Interior.

Congressional Record, XXXVI: 567.

Deloria, Vine, Jr. 1988. "The Red and the Black," in *Custer Died for your Sins: An Indian Manifesto*. Norman: University of Oklahoma Press, 168–96.

Dred Scott v. Sandford. 1856. 60 US 393.

Ex Parte Crow Dog. 1883. 109 US 557.

Findlay, John M. 1992. "An Elusive Institution: The Birth of Indian Reservations in Gold Rush California," in *State and Reservation: New Perspectives on Federal Indian Policy*, ed. George Pierre Castile and Robert L. Bee. Tucson and London: University of Arizona Press, 13–37.

Foner, Eric. 1988. *Reconstruction: America's Unfinished Revolution. 1863–1877*. New York: Harper and Row.

Hall, Anthony. 2005. *The American Empire and the Fourth World: The Bowl With One Spoon*, vol. I. Montreal: McGill-Queens University Press.

Harring, Sidney L. 1994. *Crow Dog's Case: American Indian Sovereignty, Tribal Law, and United States Law in the Nineteenth Century*. Cambridge: Cambridge University Press.

Hoxie, Frederick E. 2001. *A Final Promise: The Campaign to Assimilate the Indians, 1880–1920*. Lincoln: University of Nebraska Press.

Huhndorf, Shari M. 2001. *Going Native: Indians in the American Cultural Imagination*. Ithaca, NY: Cornell University Press.

Johnson, Kenneth W. 1973. "Sovereignty, Citizenship and the Indian." *Arizona Law Review* 15 (4): 974–1003.

Johnson v. M'Intosh (1823) 21 US 543.

Kiernan, V. G. 1978. *America: The New Imperialism, From White Settlement to World Hegemony*. London: Zed Press.

Macleod, William Christie. 1928. *The American Indian Frontier*. London: Kegan Paul.

Macpherson, C. B. 1964. *The Political Theory of Possessive Individualism*. Oxford: Oxford University Press.

McRae, Kenneth D. 1964. "The Structure of Canadian History," in *The Founding of New Societies*, ed. Louis Hartz. New York: Harcourt Brace, 219–62.

Mamdani, Mahmood. 1996. *Citizen and Subject*. Princeton, NJ: Princeton University Press.

Mekeel, Scudder. 1944. "An Appraisal of the Indian Reorganization Act." *American Anthropologist* 46 (2): 209–17.

Newton, Nell Jessup. 1983–4. "Federal Power over Indians: Its Sources, Scope and Limitations." *University of Pennsylvania Law Review* 132 (2): 195–288.

Pagden, Anthony. 1998. *Lords of all the World*. New Haven, CT: Yale University Press.

Prucha, Francis Paul. 1973. *Americanizing the American Indian*. Lincoln: University of Nebraska Press.

1976. *American Indian Policy in Crisis: Christian Reformers and the Indian, 1865–1900*. Norman: University of Oklahoma Press.

1984. *The Great Father, the United States Government and the American Indians*, vol. II. Lincoln: University of Nebraska Press.

Smith, Rogers M. 1997. *Civic Ideals: Conflicting Visions of Citizenship in U.S. History*. New Haven, CT: Yale University Press.

Strickland, Rennard. 1985–6. "Genocide-at-Law: An Historic and Contemporary View of the Native American Experience." *University of Kansas Law Review* 34: 713–55.

Talton v. *Mayes*. 1895. 163 US 376.

Trennert, Jr., Robert A. 1975. *Alternative to Extinction: Federal Indian Policy and the Beginnings of the Reservation System, 1846–51*. Philadelphia, PA: Temple University Press.

US v. *Joseph*. 1876. 94 US 614.

US v. *Rogers*. 1846. 45 US 567.

US v. *Sandoval*. 1913. 231 US 28.

Wilkinson, Charles F. 1987. *American Indians, Time, and the Law: Native Societies in a Modern Constitutional Democracy*. New Haven, CT: Yale University Press.

Williams, Jr., Robert A. 2005. *Like a Loaded Weapon: The Rehnquist Court, Indian Rights, and the Legal History of Racism in America*. Minneapolis: University of Minnesota Press.

Wilson, James. 1998. *The Earth Shall Weep: A History of Native America*. New York: Grove Press.

Worcester v. *Georgia*. 1832. 31 US 515.

Part IV

What role for representative quotas?

8   Perverse consequences? The impact of quotas for women on democratization in Africa

Shireen Hassim

I.   Introduction

The emergence of a global political movement agitating for the adoption of gender quotas – what Drude Dahlerup (2005) has described as a "quota fever" – has reinvigorated feminist theorization of representation.[1] The fundamental questions of representation have been posed again: who do elected officials represent; does increased representation improve marginalized groups' access to decision-making institutions; and under what conditions does increased representation lead to improved policy outcomes for marginal groups? Two sorts of disillusionment have coincided in global political discussions about women and representation. On the one hand, feminists in older democracies despair about the slow progress of women in elected bodies. On the other, in new democracies, feminists are skeptical of the willingness of pro-democracy movements to effectively address the interests of women. A remarkable consensus has been forged between these two groups in favor of new mechanisms to increase women's representation, most notably the use of some form of gender quota.

Debates on quotas have advanced in two distinctive phases thus far. In the first phase, feminists were concerned with justifying the idea that special mechanisms were needed to redress the democratic deficit in representation. Most opponents of quotas do indeed focus on normative liberal objections, whether these relate to the relative privileges of groups over individuals, or the value of equal opportunities, or the relative weight of women's claims over those of other groups. I deal very briefly with this set of normative objections, arguing that many of these have been effectively countered by democratically based feminist arguments. One

---

An early version of the arguments in this chapter was first elaborated in Shireen Hassim, "Women, Parliaments and Gender Equality in Africa: Exploring the Virtuous Circle of Representation," in Bauer and Britton (2006).

[1] See the special issue on representation in *Politics and Gender* 2 (4) (December 2006); also *International Feminist Journal of Politics* 10 (3) (2008).

outcome of the first phase of outlining the problem of representation is that substantial expectations were raised as to what quotas might be able to achieve with regard to deepening liberal democracy at least. For many advocates of gender quotas, there is a causal relation between greater descriptive representation and substantive, or interest, representation, a relationship I have described elsewhere as a "virtuous circle of representation" (Hassim 2006a). This assumption is equally widely held by women's movements, leading to a global campaign for equal representation. Building on this assumption, in the second phase of research, the majority of researchers focused attention on analyzing the *kinds of mechanisms* that could be employed to ensure that women gained fair access to the processes and institutions of representation – or, to use the new parlance, to "fast-track" representation (Krook 2006).

In this chapter, rather than debate the efficacy of different types of quotas, I suggest that the foundational questions with regard to representation are worth attention with the benefit of some years of experience with the implementation of quotas in Africa. First, is the expectation that quotas lead to increased democratization of the institutions of political representation (political parties and legislatures in particular) borne out by empirical evidence in new democracies? Second, do quotas facilitate the representation of women's interests and if so, which interests are more likely to be advanced? What evidence is there that increasing women's representation enhances the extent of democracy in political systems? I argue that the use of the fast-track model of women's representation opens new concerns about whether quotas are indeed more likely to advance feminism's democratic aims. I draw attention to two factors generally neglected in the quota literature: first, political cultures of responsiveness and accountability of elected officials, and second institutional maturity. Drawing on research on women and parliaments in Africa, I argue that expectations that quotas will democratize political systems in ways that slower incremental changes might not is questionable. Quotas, I argue, can have profoundly negative effects on deepening democracy when adopted in contexts where the key institutions of democracy and human rights are weakly developed or absent, and where elected political actors are weakly accountable to electoral constituencies. Quotas may fast-track women's representation but they do not fast-track equality or democracy.

II.   The persistent deficit in representation

Women's underrepresentation in elected office is depressingly similar in political systems around the world. Even in advanced industrial

Table 8.1 *Women in national parliaments by region, 2005*

Region	Percentage women
Nordic countries	40.1
Americas	18.6
Europe (OSCE excl. Nordic)	16.8
Asia	15.0
Sub-Saharan Africa	14.8
Pacific	13.2
Arab states	6.5

Note: From Inter-Parliamentary Union (IPU) (2005). OSCE = Organization for Security and Cooperation in Europe.

countries, the deficit in representation remains large despite decades (in some cases over a century) of women's suffrage. As Table 8.1 shows, if one factors out the Nordic countries, Europe and the Americas have made as few strides in including women in legislatures as Asia, where there are supposedly greater social barriers to women's participation in public life. Although early explanations of women's inclusion in the public sphere emphasized modernization as the crucial determinant – levels of socioeconomic development, women's participation in the paid labor force and the erosion of traditional attitudes to women's public roles (Matland 1998) – by the twenty-first century it is apparent that the link between socioeconomic development and political representation is tenuous. With respect to women's political representation (but not other aspects of gender equality), barriers and biases in institutions (in electoral and party systems especially) and resistant political cultures appear to override the gains made in socioeconomic status. In these contexts, there is a growing view that quotas might create a desirable exogenous "shock" and introduce rupture in institutions (Baldez 2006). The proponents of quotas focus on the mechanism as a remedy for political exclusion in advanced democracies, but they assume the existence of a range of democratic conditions: respect for freedom of speech and association, well-institutionalized party and legislative systems and horizontal and vertical guarantees of accountability of elected representatives.

Feminists studying "new democracies" – those that emerged in the transition from various forms of authoritarianism in Africa, East and Central Europe, Asia and Latin America from the 1980s – express equally strong disillusionment with liberal democracy. Transitions offered unique opportunities, both ideological and practical, to redesign institutions to facilitate inclusion. Transitions also created space to debate the underlying values of the "new" society and to reshape constitutional and political principles in ways that might accommodate oppressed and marginal groups (Waylen 2007). The broader acceptance of gender equality in international human rights discourse facilitated the inclusion of some kind of gesture in this direction by the new political leadership (even if only rhetorical). These processes of institutional design and constitutional-ideological debate propelled a stronger expectation that inclusion of women in decision-making would indeed advance gender equality.

The global consensus on the need to increase women's representation was underpinned in many countries by significant levels of women's participation in pro-democracy movements – indeed, in many Latin American and African countries women's organizations ensured the survival of these movements in contexts of extreme authoritarianism. One noteworthy lesson from women's involvement in such movements was that liberation movements that depended on women in their struggles against authoritarianism were nevertheless quite likely to abandon their support for women's liberation once they came to power. The demand for quotas was, therefore, in many cases a demand for a guarantee that history would not repeat itself.

The demand for quotas (which may be reserved seats, candidate quotas, or intraparty quotas) as a mechanism for breaking through entrenched structural and cultural barriers to women's entry into elected office is thus a consequence of a frustration with liberal democracy itself. Various claims are made in relation to what quotas may achieve. Quota demands are based on the assumption that increasing the representation of women is a democratic good in itself. This seems fairly uncontestable; women's consistent underrepresentation in legislatures undoubtedly constitutes a democratic deficit. The now extensive research on women and parliamentary politics demonstrates that at the very least the rapid inclusion of substantial numbers of women (usually through quotas) does change perceptions of women's role in politics and may even shift gendered modes of deliberation within parliament. In both old and new democracies, similar arguments are made for the democratic importance of increasing women's representation. Women's claims to representation entail the claim to equal *inclusion* in the nation-state. This claim, in its most minimal form, draws attention to the denial of suffrage to women as well as to the gap between women's distribution among voters and their presence as elected members of legislatures. Women's underrepresentation is undoubtedly a function of systematic historical discrimination against and marginalization of women as a group.

Demands for inclusion can signal different understandings of the body politic: for some feminists, equality means women taking their place in the modernist, liberal democratic state as it is currently constituted. For others, inclusion is a necessary but insufficient step in the process of redistributing resources in a more equitable manner. For the latter group, demands for inclusion emphasize the representation of women as a group and the *recognition* of women's historical disadvantages. Where minimalist claims for inclusion see equality of access and level playing fields as sufficient redress of the democratic deficit, maximalist claims demand more active intervention in electoral systems and institutional designs to guarantee women's inclusion. In either case, there is a consensus that representation matters, that the pattern of women's underrepresentation devalues the quality of citizenship, and that interventions are needed to facilitate the election of more women in legislatures. Feminists promoted quotas as mechanisms for democratizing both political parties (by giving women guaranteed access to candidate selection processes) and legislatures (by forcing open space for the inclusion of new legislative and policy agendas).

A significant core of the proponents of quotas make a further, more powerful claim that increasing the number of women in decision-making institutions increases women's influence over decision-making in regard to national budgets, policy priorities, and the ideological direction of government policies, skewing these in ways that redress inequalities. For example, the Women's Environment and Development Organization (WEDO), the NGO spearheading the global campaign for parity in parliaments, argues that increasing women's representation will increase the likelihood that issues such as childcare, violence against women, and unpaid labor will become policy priorities (Beaman *et al.* 2007). In many cases, it can indeed be shown that women parliamentarians introduce new policy issues onto the agenda. Jane Mansbridge argues that "descriptive representation by gender improves substantive outcomes for women in every polity for which we have a measure" (Mansbridge 2005: 622). The idea of a "virtuous circle of representation" also underpins many women's movements' views that achieving higher levels of representation will extend political activism into the state and allow them policy leverage. An influential team of researchers attached to the International Institute for Democracy and Electoral Assistance (IDEA) sweeps away theoretical objections to quotas and argues for the importance of "fast-tracking" women's representation, saying "women's impatience is growing worldwide" and that the "incrementalist" Scandinavian route to the empowerment of women can no longer be (if it ever was) the strategic model (Dahlerup and Friedenvall 2005; Dahlerup 2006). In part their view is justified; if the assumed relationship between modernization and women's representation is patently false, there seems little reason why women should wait for the "correct conditions" to be achieved.

The quota literature lists a number of institutional factors that underpin the success of quotas. These include an electoral system based on proportional representation with a closed list, "placement mandates" for ensuring that women are placed in winnable positions on the list (for example the "zebra" or "zipper" model proposes that every alternate candidate on a list is a woman), multimember districts, and sanctions for the non-enforcement of quotas (Dahlerup 2005). These institutional reforms accompany virtually all campaigns for quotas.

Nevertheless, for those concerned with deep democracy the concern is how to ensure that descriptive representation will have virtuous effects, that is, that it will increase the effective representation of women's interests. Based on experiences in Scandinavian parliaments, the notion emerged that increases in representation exhibit an impact on interest representation when the numbers of women in legislatures reaches a critical mass of 30 percent of the legislature. This is based on an argument by Drude Dahlerup (1988) that representation of a marginal group shifts from token representation to influential representation when this critical mass has been achieved. Many studies of European democracies do indeed show that policy concerns relating to care-work and women's rights are more likely to be introduced when women attain a significant proportion among decision-makers. The idea of a critical mass has become a kind of magic number, seen in demands for 30 percent representation of women in global campaigns, and as a target set in various national and transnational feminist documents. For example, the Beijing Conference set a target of 30 percent of women in parliaments by 2005, and this target was subsequently adopted by the Southern African Development Community (SADC). The targets have strategic value in that they constitute a measurable standard by which government commitments to gender equality can be assessed. They have had some effect, though perhaps not as spectacular as is often claimed: in 1995 women accounted for 11.3 percent of members of parliament worldwide; by 2005 this number had increased to close to 16 percent (see Table 8.2) (Ballington 2005: 25).

Quotas undoubtedly address the claim to inclusion and the importance of descriptive representation in dramatic fashion. They instantaneously impose a significant number of new actors onto institutions,

Table 8.2 *Women's representation in African countries*

Country	Type of quota	Year quota introduced	% women in national legislature, 2003
Burkina Faso	Voluntary party	2002	11.7
Botswana	No quota	–	11.1 (2004)
Cameroon	Voluntary party	1996	8.9
Côte d'Ivoire	Voluntary party	–	8.5
Djibouti	Legislative	2002	10.8
Malawi	No quota	–	13.9 (2004)
Mali	Voluntary party	–	10.2
Mauritius	No quota		17.1 (2005)
Mozambique	Voluntary party	1994	30.0
Namibia	Voluntary party	1997/9	29.2
South Africa	Voluntary party	1994	29.8
Tunisia	Voluntary party	–	11.5
Djibouti	Legislative	2002	10.8
Eritrea	Constitutional	1995	22.0
Kenya	Constitutional	1997	7.1
Morocco	Legislative	2002	10.8
Niger	Legislative	2000	1.2
Rwanda	Constitutional	2003	48.8
Somalia	Constitutional	2001	10.0
Sudan	Legislative	2000	9.7
Tanzania	Constitutional (reserved seats)	2000	22.3
Uganda	Constitutional	1989	24.7

Note: Adapted from Tripp (2006); Dahlerup and Friedenvall (2005); and Dahlerup (2006).

disrupt male monopolies, and may have downstream effects on the gender composition of party elites through the "contagion" effect (Matland and Studlar 1996). There is considerable evidence to show that institutional trust and legitimacy are enhanced by greater descriptive representation (Htun 2005). There are also studies that demonstrate the democratizing effects of women's inclusion on the everyday features of institutions (Bauer and Britton 2006). Proponents of quotas argue that the mere presence of women in parliaments shifts "the patriarchal demeanor of political institutions" (www.gender.ac.za/50/50, accessed September 20, 2006) and forces institutions to recognize women. Indeed women parliamentarians in South Africa are fond of retelling what happened in 1994 when the number of women MPs rose from 14 to 111. There was only one small toilet for women in the vicinity of the general assembly; the air-conditioned temperature of the House was set at a level that, in the words

Table 8.3 *Highest ranking countries in terms of women's representation, 2003*

Rank	Country	Percentage women
1	Rwanda	48.8
2	Sweden	45.0
3	Denmark	38.0
4	Finland	36.5
5	Norway	36.4
6	Costa Rica	35.1
7	Iceland	34.9
8	Netherlands	34.0
9	Germany	32.2
10	Argentina	30.7
11	Mozambique	30.0
12	South Africa	29.9
13	Seychelles	29.4

Note: From Ballington (2004).

of one MP, was "comfortable for overweight men in suits"; and House sitting times were organized on the assumption that children were cared for by stay-at-home wives. Mansbridge makes an even stronger claim for descriptive representation in arguing that descriptive representatives have greater advantages in communicating their constituents' interests with other representatives – "they can speak with authenticity and be believed" (Mansbridge 2005).

While there is political convergence among feminists on the importance of representation, a considerable reserve of skepticism about quotas remains in mainstream political science. In Western liberal democracies, and particularly in the United States, the idea of quotas raises a series of normative objections. The first objection is procedural. Quotas are opposed because they place external restrictions on voters' rights to choose their representatives. This is a weak objection, in my view. Quota supporters may counter this objection by pointing out that political parties are in any case gatekeepers to political office, and that decisions about the composition of candidate slates frequently employ "informal quotas" in relation to regional, occupational, or ethnic criteria.

Stronger objections relate to the argument that quotas promote essentialist and homogenized views of social groups, reinforce stereotypes, and rigidify identities. A closely related objection is that quotas are based on the problematic assumption that descriptive representation is in some sense better than other forms of representation – that is, that women are better represented by women. In responding to these objections, supporters of the minimalist approach to quotas frequently argue that support for more women in legislatures does not necessarily imply that their role, once elected, is to specifically represent women. As Krook (2006) points out, these are *sex* quotas, not *feminist* quotas. Rather, the concern is to include new actors and perspectives so that the link between maleness and political office is irrevocably broken. To the extent that feminists are concerned with the representation of women's interests, it is argued, this will be advanced by using the access created by quotas to build on other forms of political action, including alliances with male democrats, to shift policy agendas. Others, of a maximalist persuasion, argue that historical discrimination does create a minimal set of group interests among women that transcend race, class, ethnic, and other differences (Phillips 1995). These include the elimination of overtly discriminatory practices (that is, ensuring the implementation of commitments to gender equality) as well as attention to the specific needs of women arising out of gendered divisions of labor. These ought be to be understood as "shared experiences" rather than as a set of essentialized identities or interests.

Although not necessarily based on essentialist understandings of women, quota demands do tend to emphasize the creation of collective identity; they rest on the successful articulation of women's group-based interest in entering arenas of power. Quotas are a means of achieving recognition; indeed they are best understood as a form of symbolic politics. Quota advocates are agnostic on the issue of the outcomes of representation (e.g. Dahlerup and Friedenvall 2005; Nanivadekar 2006); they are willing to concede that once representatives begin to claim that they represent women's interests the notion of women as a homogeneous group will be abandoned. This will be the inevitable result of addressing interests, as the resource claims of some women based on their class and/or race disadvantages may come into conflict with the interests of other women, or require privileging the building of alliances with other social actors. Yet of course quotas "make" women a group as much as they presuppose group existence. Seen from the social movement perspective of framing, quotas are "a constitutive act of social definition that can have important consequences" (Brubaker 2005) that are both positive and negative, albeit in the latter case unintended. In this sense quotas are not neutral in relation to the politics of identity and it is equally likely that women representatives elected through a quota-based system will resist addressing those interests of women that stem from their class and/or race positions. In other words, it is conceivable that the manner in which feminist claims are advanced can itself constitute the boundaries of what kinds of interests are addressed by elected officials.

This outline of the key arguments for quotas and their objections still leaves unresolved a wide range of questions about whether quotas will facilitate the democratization of political systems and enhance the substantive representation of women. The growing political consensus among feminist activists that quotas are the "magic key" that will unlock the door to political power has produced, with a few notable exceptions, superficial analyses of the effects of quotas on democratic process and democratic culture. Proponents of quotas are to some extent justified in making arguments that stop short of predicting the policy outcomes of increasing women's representation; the arguments for democratizing access are strong enough. This should not be good enough for those seeking to advance democracy though. The supporters of the fast-track approach to representation imply that there are no inherent benefits to incremental processes of changing representation imbalances. In other words, the process matters less than the numerical outcome. As I will argue, though, in African countries it is apparent that short-circuiting the political process of creating strong constituencies and defining policy agendas has negative consequences for the extent to which democratic culture takes root in new democracies.

For the most part, quotas are seen as at best improving substantive representation and at worst having little or no effect on the political system. Yet looking at quotas in African countries – traditionally seen as the success stories of the quota strategy – opens new sets of considerations for democratic debates and suggests that in certain circumstances quotas can indeed have harmful effects on processes of democratization.

III.   Do quotas democratize political institutions? The impact of electoral systems in Africa

Transitions from various forms of non-democratic rule in African countries opened new opportunities for women's movements to make claims on the political system. The wave of political liberalization that swept through the continent in the 1990s ushered in liberal democracy with its attendant features of multiparty competition, regular elections, and the removal of restrictions on the media, political organization and civil society mobilization. No fewer than forty-eight African countries held multiparty elections in the 1990s, most of these for the first time in decades.

Why would men allow women to take seats in legislatures when they might themselves be displaced? One reason is that in these new democracies, elections conducted under new rules and with new demarcations of voting districts allowed women to enter the political process without directly displacing male incumbents (although competition for a limited number of seats does imply that the use of quotas will reduce the opportunities for aspiring male politicians). Where the political landscape is dominated by a single party, as in South Africa, Rwanda and Uganda, quotas can be a relatively costless strategy that has little impact on election outcomes. By way of contrast, in one of Africa's oldest and most stable democracies, Botswana, quotas are resisted by political parties, partly because they would alter the gender composition in a "winner-takes-all system," i.e. some men would lose their seats. Similarly, stable Mauritius has not adopted quotas – in the absence of violent political conflict, it has retained the first-past-the-post electoral system with no plan to change the electoral system.

Designing the appropriate electoral system is key to the acceptance of quotas. Electoral systems play a key role in determining the nature of the relationship between elected representatives, political parties, and constituencies. Proportional representation (PR) systems are now commonly assumed to be the most favorable for women, and closed list PR is particularly effective in increasing women's representation. But the system carries costs that are less frequently detailed in discussions of quotas. On the one hand, a PR system allows progressive parties to bypass customary and cultural objections to women's election – no small factor in societies where conservative religious forces dominate civil society. On the other hand, it also allows parties to establish mechanisms of control over elected leaders and exacerbate party paternalism. PR systems breed loyalty to party rather than constituency, and this tendency is intensified in political systems where the conditions for full and free contestation between different interest groups are limited. Tripp (2006) argues that in Uganda allegiances to the National Resistance Movement (NRM) at times hamper the ability of women MPs to support legislation favored by the women's movement.[2] Similar concerns have been expressed in the South African case, where women MPs have found it difficult to establish a set of priorities for feminist intervention (Hassim 2006b). A strong dominant party with a centralist political culture results in women MPs being more likely to believe that policy-making is legitimately the responsibility of party elites.

The ability of women representatives to mobilize within their parties and their willingness to challenge party hierarchies is an important determinant of the extent to which women will be effectively represented, yet

[2] See also Tamale (1999).

individual women MPs often find it difficult to develop the confidence and political base from which to push for gender equality platforms. The argument for a critical mass suggests that at the tipping point of 30 percent women MPs can begin to develop significant mechanisms of support. In many countries parliamentary women's caucuses have been mooted as a strategy for setting priorities and building support and confidence among women MPs. However, in Uganda and South Africa these have not been as successful as feminists anticipated, precisely because of the electoral system. Women are, after all, elected to represent the party and not women. The challenge is therefore whether and how women's gender interests can be articulated in a way that is distinct from their party interests and identities. Uganda is an intriguing example in this respect. There, women are elected to seats reserved for women by an electoral college made up of women and men councilors, but rather than unambiguously representing women, they are required to represent the district as a whole. Unlike other special groups (soldiers, youth, workers, and people with disabilities), women are not elected members of their group, arguably because the relative strength of the women's movement might result in women MPs who are hostile to the NRM leadership (Tamale 1999; Tripp 2006). (Independent women's organizations have been key opponents of Museveni's attempts to lift term limits on the President, for example.) This means that women MPs remain beholden to the movement as the primary political force and that the election of women MPs who might challenge movement policies in parliament is as unlikely as in a multiparty PR system. As Tripp (2006) argues, this has led women's movement activists to argue for a change in the electoral process so that the women's seats are elected by universal adult suffrage – unsurprisingly, a move opposed by the President.

In both Uganda and Rwanda, women are constructed as a group that stands outside ethnic categories. This suits certain explanations of political conflict in Africa, which see ethnic groups as either fixed and primordial, or purely as colonial constructs used instrumentally to divide African populations. Both, as Newbury and Newbury (1999) point out, are inadequate depictions of ethnicity and ethnic mobilization. Summarizing an extensive body of scholarship on ethnicity in Africa, they remind us that individual identities need to be separated from corporate concepts of identity; that ethnicity as an identity is not coterminous with ethnic mobilization as a political force; and that ethnic identities are historical products that are neither essentialist nor easily politically fabricated from "outside." In Rwanda and Uganda, ethnic mobilization was closely tied to resource contestations by the political class; yet at the local level regional and clan affiliations were more dominant than corporate ethnic identities. "Ethnicity served as a language through which fears and ambitions were expressed, but it was not ethnicity that 'caused' the violence" (ibid.: 316). During the Rwandan genocide, "connection to the state apparatus seems to have been the common characteristic of local leadership in the massacres" (ibid.: 314). It is outside the scope of this chapter to look at all the underlying causes for and forms of mobilization of violence in Rwanda and Uganda. Of particular interest here, though, is the way in which one form of group identity and representation is treated as illegitimate, and the other as acceptable and even progressive. It could be argued that in both countries women's representation provided a kind of alibi for the progressive, "democratic" nature of new governments that at their core nevertheless remained authoritarian, and are increasingly so. And indeed, as some of the examples discussed above suggest, some women MPs colluded in the politics of silencing opponents of the ruling parties on the grounds that they represented an "illegitimate" base.

A different set of objections relates to the ways that certain types of quotas might reinforce rather than challenge the social biases against women in politics. One effect that has been documented by Indian and Ugandan scholars is the emergence of a hierarchy of legitimacy: "quota candidates" are seen as token appointments – less effective and less accountable representatives than those elected on "open" tickets. In India, for example, women who stood for the reserved seats in the *panchayats* were accused of "fronting" for their husbands, fathers, and brothers. For women politicians, the effect is to intensify their second-class status – in other words, while quotas may facilitate women's election to office, they have the consequence of reinforcing existing patriarchal biases. Special seats for women at local government level in Uganda have had similar responses. Women occupying "special" seats are bypassed by citizens who go to "real" representatives with their problems (Tamale 2003; Tripp 2000; Ahikire 2003). Tamale argues that support for women's agendas in fact can act as a disqualification for broader political support, thus limiting women's attempts to be seen as legitimate representatives of a wider constituency.

Senegal, with its mixed electoral system, also offers an interesting counterpoint to the conventional PR system. Although more women are elected to parliament through PR than through the plurality system, Creevey (2006) points out that an increasing number of women are elected through the plurality system. She shows the role that political leadership and a modernizing party can play in shifting attitudes toward women – showing what possibilities there are for feminist politics even in constituency-based systems. Similarly, Longman (2006) writes that in Rwanda it would be erroneous to attribute the massive gains in gender representation to quotas alone, as the number of women in non-reserved elected seats has also increased dramatically – with women winning nearly half of all the seats in the national assembly in the 2003 elections (against a guaranteed 30 percent of seats). Longman (ibid.) points out that women won offices where quotas did not apply, as in the election of judges. The involvement of women in previous governments, and particularly in the democracy movement, appears to account for the rapid increases in the number of women in elected seats.

Strong support for women's rights and women's political representation from the president of the leading party, sometimes against the views of other male leaders, is a double-edged sword. Both Uganda and Rwanda, and possibly also South Africa, show the potentially ugly side of presidentialism and single-party dominance, with rising authoritarian tendencies in the ruling party unable to be checked by women MPs (Tripp 2000; Longman 2006; Hassim 2006a). Indeed, Longman argues that the increase in women's representation in parliament "serves more as an instrument of legitimizing and preserving RPF [Rwandan Patriotic Front] power" (Longman 2006: 147). In Uganda and Rwanda, the extension of patronage to women by the dominant party has been highly instrumental in building up a core of loyal, "progressive" cadres. In Uganda, women are the central actors in the parliamentary NRM caucus that ensures the NRM leadership's support. In several cases, female NRM loyalists acted to limit the participation and voice of NRM opponents, and "those who contested the outcomes of various [electoral] races watched helplessly as the courts dismissed one petition after another in favour of NRM loyalists" (Tripp 2006: 119, citing Tamale 1999). Tripp quotes a woman opposition leader explaining that many NRM women MPs "will rather go by the position of the government because they look to the government as the only agency that has brought them where they are. So in other words, we are now turning our affirmative action into patronage" (Tripp 2000: 119). President Museveni himself has congratulated women MPs for helping him defeat the "multipartyists." On the flip side, women (like men) who go against the President may see the end of their political careers, even if they are not in parliament. Winnie Byanyima, a leading Ugandan feminist and MP married to opposition presidential contender Kiiza Besigye, was forced to exit local politics and take up a post in the African Union after both she and Besigye were accused of treason, and Besigye was accused of rape.

In Rwanda, the head of a women's organization who "questioned the effectiveness of the country's female legislators in solving women's problems, likening them to flowers which look good but do little else . . . was condemned and threatened. Shortly afterward, she fled the country" (Lacey 2005). The RPF pushed through new legislation to create a Forum of Political Parties that would have the power to determine who was fit to stand as an MP. Critics of the government were deemed "divisionist" and hence unfit to stand (Longman 2006: 147). Women MPs stood by while Kagame rewrote the Constitution to make parliament in effect a one-party institution.

In South Africa, political culture and oppositional movements are strong enough to allow women politicians to criticize and question both the government and the President. There is enormous room for dissent in the system more broadly and no threat of imprisonment or torture. Even so, room for dissent *within* the African National Congress (ANC) is more limited. Leading feminist MP Pregs Govender, who had headed up the parliamentary committee responsible for the removal of discriminatory legislation and the promulgation of pro-choice legislation, left parliament in 2002 after clashing with the President and party leadership over an arms deal and the government's policy on HIV/AIDS. Since her departure, the parliamentary committee on women has been virtually defunct, despite the large number of women MPs and a substantial proportion of ministers who are women (including the Deputy President).

These tendencies suggest that, in order to be successful, democratic women's movements would have to move quickly to buttress the openings allowed in transitional periods to build strong movements outside parliament that will sustain women's rapid representational gains through quotas. Women cannot rely on political parties as their only vehicles for representation. While women's movements do well to build relationships with political parties, their success in representational politics also depends on their degree of autonomy from those parties. This ensures that women are not only mobilized for their votes but as electoral constituencies – that is, constituencies with clearly articulated policy interests. I will return to this point below.

IV.   Quotas and procedural democracy

The argument that quotas will at the minimum impact positively on procedural democracy bears interrogation. African experiences of quotas implicitly reinforce the importance of linking representation to accountability. Formally, this accountability operates both internally (within political parties) as well as externally (accountability to constituencies). In most African democracies, however, political parties are poorly institutionalized and operate in a highly centralized fashion. Opposition parties tend to be weak and political contestation seldom revolves around debating the content of political manifestos. Rather, histories of struggle against colonialism and accusations and counter-accusations of corruption – fiscal or electoral – are the stuff of party contestation. In conditions where the basic principles of free and fair elections are constantly violated by the party in government, quotas can achieve very little unless they are backed up by strong campaigns to change the rules of the game. In some cases, they can even harm struggles for procedural democracy. For example, Ugandan feminists have argued that Museveni's acceptance of reserved seats for women might have helped give women seats in parliament but it was based on an attempt to create a solid and reliable block of women supporters of the NRM in government. At crucial moments, this dependent bloc of women MPs observed silently as Museveni repressed opposition to the NRM.

Of course, women can benefit from multipartyism, even if women's organizations have to affiliate to a party in order to have a political voice. In mass parties that have emerged from nationalist movements, for example South Africa's ANC or Zimbabwe's ZANU-PF, national women's organizations operate as the women's wing of the party. The valid vehicle for political voice is through the nationalist party, based on the assumption that the nation is a singular homogeneous entity with one legitimate representative party. Support for gender quotas in many African countries was won by the women's movement aligned with the dominant party and has reinforced the hegemony of that dominant party. If opposition parties were to develop their own internal women's wings, however, the landscape could change. This would entail an acceptance that political constituencies are not pre-given, or the moral preserve of one particular movement/party, but that there is a socially and politically constructed relationship between citizens and political parties that needs to be constantly nurtured. Quotas work best in multiparty systems where several parties are well institutionalized, have clear relationships of accountability for their political actions and represent a diversity of interests. In these cases, we see evidence of the contagion effect, where constituencies of women can push parties into supporting gender equality because of the threat that they can vote for other parties. In Sweden, for example, feminists successfully advanced the argument that they would switch their allegiances from the Social Democratic Party if women's views on party policies (such as nuclear weapons) were not taken into account. Without the threat of electoral retaliation, strategies that focus exclusively on descriptive representation make limited contributions to democratization.

However, the ability to democratize political parties, enforce accountability and clean up the electoral game is dependent on the strength of women's organizations in civil society and the development of strong relationships between women legislators and their supporters. The relationship between women parliamentarians and the women's movement is as difficult as the relationship between women activists and leaders *within* political parties. In some respects there are organic political ties within these spheres; many women parliamentarians cut their political teeth in women's organizations. As a result, the relationship between party/parliament and civil society can often be fluid, as women activists can move back and forth between state and civil society. This fluidity may enhance policy influence but can also have negative impacts in countries with small political elites. Close personal and political relationships can breed a sense of loyalty to comrades that undermines criticism. Yet even if political elites were a much larger segment of the population, there are inherent tensions in the relationship between feminists in politics and those in civil society. Anne Summers (1986) has characterized this as the tension between missionaries (activists in civil society) and mandarins (politicians) with each expecting relationships of support and accountability that may be hard to fulfill. Accountability relationships depend on quota mechanisms working in tandem with strategies to strengthen women's organizations outside the state.

V.   The impact of quotas on the articulation of interests

In the previous section, I addressed the claim that, at a minimum, quotas have a positive effect on democratizing political procedures. I have shown that this can only be achieved if quota campaigns are tied to other processes of party and system reform. What about the stronger claim made by Mansbridge (2005) that descriptive representation is causally related to substantive representation? Here too the evidence from African countries is mixed. The demands for institutional inclusion can galvanize and reinforce women's movements – although the extent to which this will happen depends on whether strong relationships can be maintained between women in parliament and women's organizations in civil society.

If inclusion in the strong sense is to be advanced (that is, if the citizenship claim is framed in terms of women's access to decision-making as part of a strategy to redress inequalities), then the crucial factor is the existence of strong associations that have the capacity to articulate the particular interests of their constituencies, to mobilize those constituencies in defense of those interests, and to develop independent strategies to achieve their aims. A strong social movement requires a degree of political autonomy in order to retain its relative power within any alliance. Although in general the importance of robust civil societies is widely supported in Africa, there is far less tolerance of independent feminist organizations. While autonomy was highly valued in Western women's movements – and in many was seen to be a *condition* of existence – in postcolonial countries autonomy is less highly valued. Because women's political activism in postcolonial contexts has been enabled by larger struggles against colonial and class oppression, the result is a more highly developed politics of alliance rather than autonomy. In many African countries, women's movements have been weakly developed, and feminism as a mobilizing ideology has been delegitimated. Quota proponents tend to neglect these "thicker" understandings of participation as an activity that encompasses *collective* mobilization, through associational vehicles over which women have control. Indeed, it can be argued that quotas are likely to be supported by women's movements that recognize their organizational weaknesses – that is, they can be seen as a compensatory strategy.

Quotas must be distinguished from effective participation, where the emphasis is on more effective interest articulation and representation – i.e. making the "voice" of particular constituencies of women louder in processes of policy-making (Goetz and Hassim 2003). Supporters of quotas might argue that they have the strategic value of fast-tracking a "critical mass" of women into parliament who will then demonstrate/model the value of women's participation. As I have argued in the previous section, however, mere numerical presence does not translate into voice, nor does amplified voice "automatically strengthen the moral and social claims of the powerless on the powerful and produce better accountability to that group" (ibid.: 34). Not only presidential or party control, but also institutional norms and procedures and the nature of processes of deliberation can undermine the extent and impact of women's voice in the public sphere. The more subtle patterns by which power hierarchies are upheld, even when new groups are included in institutions, are both hard to make visible as well as hard to change. Studies of parliament have shown that women's participation as individuals in institutions of decision-making is generally limited – women are less likely to participate in parliamentary debates than men and are more likely to feel intimidated by the demands of public speaking, even when the women elected are highly skilled professionals (Norris and Lovenduski 1996).

A stronger understanding of representation locates interest articulation and interest representation through parties and civil society organizations as central, and is more clearly tied to a politics of transformation. Interest articulation has a checkered history in African governments, as it has been associated most closely with the idea of national machineries for women, which have treated women's interests as narrow and "special" and in need of patronage. Creating a set of specialized institutions for the consideration of gender shifted the issues of gender inequality out of the realm of politics and into the technical realm of policy-making. As Banaszak, Beckwith, and Rucht (2003: 6) point out, this is increasingly a problem with national machineries around the world: "women's movements have been presented with an increasingly depoliticized and remote set of policy-making agencies at the national level . . . The relocation of responsibility to non-elected state bodies eventually reduces social movement influence." In the administration, gender equality concerns have fallen hostage to a range of institutional hierarchies and systemic blockages that are hard to deal with from outside the bureaucracy. In these contexts, interest articulation becomes not just de-politicized but also *anti-political*, to the extent that women's policy demands are shunted into bureaucratic alleys.

To be sure, state actors are central to the process of articulating interests. But bottom-up politics, in which different constituencies of women identify and define policy demands which can be advanced as part of a horizontal coalition of interests (for example, poor urban women linking up with housing movements), as well as through policy-focused alliances with (or where necessary pressure on) women parliamentarians, is a crucial corollary. The emphasis on building a constituency-based politics recognizes that not all women have the same interests, that women's organizations might conceive of their interests differently from women politicians, and that strong organizations of women at the local level enhance the virtuous circle of representation. In Uganda, women's organizations have been partially successful in pursuing such strategies, although their effectiveness is highly constrained by the authoritarian political culture in which they are operating, where building alliances outside of Museveni's approved network can impact negatively on parliamentary politics. Similarly, it can be argued that in South Africa women who are elected into parliament are increasingly distant from movements of poor people. For example, witness the political (and constitutional) contestation between the Treatment Action Campaign and the Health Minister (and ANC Women's League leader) Manto Tshabalala Msimang over access to retroviral treatment for people who are HIV-positive. As Sylvia Tamale has argued, male African politicians are more willing to allow descriptive representation where women MPs symbolically "stand for" women rather than being representatives who "act for" women (Tamale 2003).

Consequently there is a tendency for quotas to produce an increasingly elite-based body of representatives. This kind of politics may bring certain sections of the women's movement into contestation with elite and party-oriented members, as it is a form of politics that is likely to take a more confrontational approach over party manifestos and state policies. The outcome of such alliances may be a marginalization of these actors from the state and political parties.

I would argue that recognition through quotas is a deceptively easy strategy. A much more transformative demand for representation (that is, that women need access to decision-making in order to advance a project of eliminating gender hierarchies of power) is reduced to a simple mechanism. Although it is generally accepted in feminist literature that a combination of factors is responsible for women's increased access to political office – the nature of the political system and the organization of political competition, the nature of civil society and especially of the feminist lobby within it, and the nature and power of the state – all too often actual political strategies are collapsed into a demand for a quota. This is not surprising; it is without doubt more difficult to reshape the nature of the political system.

This is not to suggest that there have been no gains from the increase in the number of women in African parliaments. Perhaps the most visible gain has been to remove many of the most overt examples of discriminatory legislation from the statute books. In some new democracies, women MPs can point to the introduction of legislation that erodes women's formal inequality. For example, in South Africa, the right to abortion, legal and institutional protection for victims of domestic violence, and the inclusion of quotas for women in economic affirmative action legislation and policies are all claimed by women MPs as the product of their presence in the parliament. I scanned the literature to find examples of women's impact on legislation that went beyond changes in electoral laws and the introduction of quotas at different levels of decision-making – I have found few examples other than in South Africa, where there is a relatively well-developed women's movement. Critics could point, on the other hand, to the failure of women MPs to stand firm on broader issues of democracy and human rights and – in Uganda and South Africa, for example – to the failure of political presence in cases where the interests of women have come into contestation with those of men. Even demands for formal equality can be muted when they come up against intense mobilization of competing groups in society. For example, key women MPs in Uganda did not support the amendments to the 1998 Land Act that would increase women's rights to property ownership (a watered-down right for spousal co-ownership, at that). Despite intense lobbying by women activists outside parliament, Museveni and his women loyalists in parliament opposed extending land ownership rights to women, eventually using the technical rules of parliament to prevent the key clause from being read into the Act. According to Museveni, "when I learnt that the Bill was empowering the newly-married women to share the properties of the husbands, I smelt a disaster" (Tripp 2006: 125). Key women MPs, including Vice-President Speciosa Kazibwe, opposed women's ownership of land on the grounds that access was the issue, not control. Kazibwe held a meeting of women MPs with the specific aim of ensuring that they remained loyal to the President.

In South Africa, the case of the Communal Land Rights Act (championed by a woman minister) dramatically showed up the limits of women's representation, as the Act failed to extend full rights of land ownership and control to women living under the jurisdiction of traditional leaders. In this case, the ANC was subjected to conflicting pressures from a constituency hostile to women's interests and, moreover, it was a constituency that posed a perceived electoral threat. While women MPs might see themselves as organically linked to women's organizations in civil society, they placed considerable emphasis on intraparty debates and were aware of their need to survive within the party. They voted with the party leadership on the Act, despite protests from women's organizations in civil society. Without an electoral constituency to back them up, the reality was that women activists remained hostage to the goodwill and support of the party leadership.

These examples show the difficulty of making claims for the importance of quotas when one goes beyond very thin versions of formal equality. Throughout the continent, women's movements have historically struggled for forms of liberation that included but were not restricted to the achievement of equal rights and opportunities. This is not to deny the importance of formal political and civil rights, especially in contexts where there is tremendous resistance to the idea of women's equality. Yet poor women's movements have consistently held out for an understanding of liberation that would include economic transformation and (to a lesser extent) the social reordering of gender relations. These expectations of women's organizations have specific implications for social policy, as it would require that resources be directed in such a way that they serve not only to address the needs of the poorest women, but also become part of an incremental process of enhancing the recognition of women's personhood and their full participation in political and economic processes. This would entail considerable debate about the relationship between the public and private sphere, the cultural recognition of women's unpaid work, and at the very least a public debate about how to negotiate women's individual rights against those of the communities to which they belong. On these measures, there is little to show as yet for women's increased representation.

If the particular content of gender equality ought to be left to women's organizations themselves to define, in their particular socioeconomic and cultural contexts, the argument for the collective mobilization of women and the building of electoral constituencies as the undergirding of representational politics is strengthened. Disaggregating representation from the debate about desirable policy directions and policy outcomes – however strategically useful such a strategy might be in the short term – carries the danger that political party elites (albeit with a gender-neutral face) will continue to determine the content of policies.

VI.   Conclusion

This chapter argues that while there is a strong democratic case for the inclusion of women in institutions of political representation through the use of affirmative action mechanisms, these mechanisms do not necessarily advance feminist ambitions for deep democracy. Arguments for quotas tend to neglect the context in which quotas are adopted, and assume that the institutional conditions for effective representation are easily built by new entrants to political structures. This neglect stems from assumptions that multiparty, liberal democracies are globally similar. However, as these examples from African countries suggest, the weaknesses of party systems and of mechanisms of accountability of representatives to voters may in certain conditions be exacerbated by the adoption of quotas The political conditions that facilitate the adoption of quotas in many new democracies – party systems that are only thinly institutionalized, centralist political cultures, and elite control of politics – may limit the effectiveness of quotas, and at times have negative consequences for deepening democracy.

I argue that quota mechanisms can result in demands for representation being disembedded from processes of constituency formation. This impacts significantly on feminist ambitions to shift the nature of gender power relations. Rapid inclusion into political institutions through mechanisms such as quotas has many advantages. However, if these are not tied to processes of extra-parliamentary collective mobilization in a free political environment on the one hand, and broad public deliberation on the principles and priorities underpinning legislative and policy proposals on the other, the impact on more transformative feminist ambitions is limited. As far as the impact of increased representation of women in legislatures is concerned, this has to be analyzed in the broader context of the political system. There is little value in promoting women's representation in authoritarian systems: at best, a substantial amount of political energy is expended for little substantial gain; at worst, women simply become collaborators in the process of restricting the political rights of oppositional groups.

BIBLIOGRAPHY

Ahikire, Josephine. 2003. "Gender Equity and Local Democracy in Contemporary Uganda: Addressing the Challenge of Women's Political Effectiveness in Local Government," in *No Shortcuts to Power: African Women in Politics and Policymaking*, ed. Anne Marie Goetz and Shireen Hassim. London: Zed Books, 213–39.

Baldez, Lisa. 2006. "The Pros and Cons of Gender Quota Laws: What Happens when you Kick Men Out and Let Women In?" *Politics and Gender* 2 (1): 102–9.

Ballington, Julie (ed.). 2004. *The Implementation of Quotas: African Experiences*. Stockholm: International IDEA.

2005. "Introduction," in *International IDEA Handbook: Women in Parliament: Beyond Numbers*, ed. Julie Ballington and Azza Karam. Stockholm: International IDEA, 23–30.

Banaszak, Lee Ann, Karen Beckwith, and Dieter Rucht (eds.). 2003. *Women's Movements Facing the Reconfigured State*. New York: Cambridge University Press.

Bauer, Gretchen and Hannah Britton (eds.). 2006. *Women in African Parliaments*. Boulder, CO: Lynne Rienner.

Beaman, Lori, Esther Duflo, Rohini Pande, and Petia Topolova. 2007. *Women Politicians, Gender Bias and Policy-Making in Rural India*. State of the World's Children 2007 Background Paper, UNICEF.

Brubaker, Rogers. 2005. "Ethnicity Without Groups," in *Remaking Modernity: Politics, History, and Sociology*, ed. Julia Adams, Elisabeth S. Clemens, and Ann Shola Orloff. Durham, NC: Duke University Press, 470–92.

Creevey, Lucy. 2006. "Senegal: Contending with Religious Constraints," in *Women in African Parliaments*, ed. Gretchen Bauer and Hannah E. Britton. Boulder, CO: Lynne Rienner, 215–45.

Dahlerup, Drude. 1988. "From a Small to a Large Minority: Women in Scandinavian Politics." *Scandinavian Political Studies* 11 (4): 275–98.

2005. "Increasing Women's Political Representation: New Trends in Gender Quotas," in *International IDEA Handbook: Women in Parliament: Beyond Numbers*, ed. Julie Ballington and Azza Karam. Stockholm: International IDEA, 141–53.

2006. "The Story of the Theory of Critical Mass." *Politics and Gender* 2 (4): 511–22.

Dahlerup, Drude and Lenita Friedenvall. 2005. "Quotas as a Fast-Track to Equal Representation for Women." *International Feminist Journal of Politics* 7 (1): 26–48.

Goetz, Anne Marie and Shireen Hassim (eds.). 2003. *No Shortcuts to Power: African Women in Politics and Policy Making*. New York: Zed Books.

Hassim, Shireen. 2006a. "Women, Parliaments and Gender Equality in Africa: Exploring the Virtuous Circle of Representation," in *Women in African*

Parliaments, ed. Gretchen Bauer and Hannah Britton. Boulder, CO: Lynne Rienner, 246–66.

2006b. *Women's Organizations and Democracy in South Africa: Contesting Authority*. Madison: University of Wisconsin Press.

Htun, Mala. 2005. "Women, Political Parties and Electoral Systems in Latin America," in *International IDEA Handbook: Women in Parliament: Beyond Numbers*, ed. Julie Ballington and Azza Karam. Stockholm: International IDEA, 112–21.

Inter-Parliamentary Union (IPU). 2005. "Women in National Parliaments: Situation as of 31 January 2005." Available at: www.ipu.org (accessed September 3, 2006).

Krook, Mona Lena. 2006. "Gender Quotas, Norms and Politics." *Politics and Gender* 2 (1): 110–18.

Lacey, Marc. 2005. "Women's Voices Rise as Rwanda Reinvents Itself." *New York Times*, February 26, 2005.

Longman, Timothy. 2006. "Rwanda: Achieving Equality or Serving an Authoritarian State?" in *Women in African Parliaments*, ed. Gretchen Bauer and Hannah E. Britton. Boulder, CO: Lynne Rienner, 210–33.

Mansbridge, Jane. 2005. "Quota Problems: Combating the Dangers of Essentialism." *Politics and Gender* 1 (4): 622–37.

Matland, Richard E. 1998. "Women's Representation in National Legislatures: Developed and Developing Countries." *Legislative Studies Quarterly* 23 (1): 109–25.

Matland, Richard E. and Donley T. Studlar. 1996. "The Contagion of Women Candidates in Single-Member District and Proportional Representation Systems: Canada and Norway." *Journal of Politics* 58: 707–33.

Nanivadekar, Medha. 2006. "Are Quotas a Good Idea? The Indian Experience with Reserved Seats for Women." *Politics and Gender* 2 (1): 119–28.

Newbury, Catharine and David Newbury. 1999. "A Catholic Mass in Kigali: Contested Views of the Genocide and Ethnicity in Rwanda." *Canadian Journal of African Studies / Revue Canadienne des Études Africaines* 33 (2/3): 292–328. Special issue on French-Speaking Central Africa: Political Dynamics of Identities and Representations.

Norris, Pippa and Joni Lovenduski (eds.). 1996. *Women in Party Politics*. New York: Cambridge University Press.

Phillips, Anne. 1995. *The Politics of Presence*. London: Polity Press.

Sawer, Marian. 2002. "Representation of Women: Meaning and Make-Believe," in *Women, Politics and Change*, ed. Karen Ross. Oxford: Oxford University Press, 5–17.

Summers, Anne. 1986. "Mandarins or Missionaries: Women in the Federal Bureaucracy," in *Australian Women: New Feminist Perspectives*, ed. Norma Grieve and Alisa Burns. Melbourne: Oxford University Press.

Tamale, Sylvia. 1999. *When Hens Begin to Crow*. Kampala: Fountain Publishers.

2003. "Introducing Quotas in Africa: Discourse and Legal Reform in Uganda." Paper presented at International Institute for Democracy and Electoral Assistance (IDEA) / Electoral Institute of Southern Africa (EISA) / Southern African Development Community (SADC)

Parliamentary Forum Conference, Pretoria, South Africa, November 11–13, 2003.

Tripp, Aili Mari. 2000. *Women and Politics in Uganda.* Kampala: Fountain Publishers.

2006. "Uganda: Agents of Change for Women's Advancement?" in *Women in African Parliaments*, ed. Gretchen Bauer and Hannah E. Britton. Boulder, CO: Lynne Rienner, 158–89.

Waylen, Georgina. 2007. *Engendering Transitions: Mobilization, Institutions and Gender Outcomes.* Oxford: Oxford University Press.

9   On quotas and qualifications for office

Andrew Rehfeld

I.   Introduction

In every existing democracy, qualifications for office restrict who may run for various elected offices. Most frequently, these qualifications require that the candidate be older than a certain minimal age, that she be a citizen of the nation in which she is running, and that she be a member of the party or resident of the district that she stands to represent. Increasingly, qualifications for office are being crafted based on gender, race, and ethnicity. In the last twenty years, dozens of democratic governments around the globe have established secured seats in the legislature or on party lists for women (Baldez 2004; Krook 2006). And the effect of other rules and circumstances – such as the need for large sums of money to mount a campaign in the United States – has created virtual qualifications for office, stacking the deck in favor of some kinds of candidates at the expense of others.

The use of qualifications is hardly new, nor is the desire to use them to achieve desirable results. For example, on December 4, 1820, in a debate on alterations to the Massachusetts State Constitution, Daniel Webster defended the inclusion of a "profession of belief" in Christian principles as a qualification for office (Webster 1903). As a general matter, Webster argued, the use of qualifications for office was consistent with principles of representative government that depended on voters themselves making good principled judgments about the types of people who should represent them. Voters used their own standards to filter out

For comments on earlier versions of this argument I thank Corey Bretschneider, Randy Calvert, David Estlund, Susan Hyde, Jack Knight, Mona Lena Krook, Charles Larmore, Frank Lovett, Andrew Martin, Larry May, Robert Reich, Margo Schlanger, Ian Shapiro, Anna Stilz, Susan Stokes, Daniel Weinstock, Elisabeth Wood, and participants in the Washington University Law School faculty seminar, the Brown University political philosophy workshop, the Yale University conference on Representation and Popular Rule, and the 2008 annual meeting of the Association for Political Theory.

all sorts of undesirable types, and rightly so.[1] More specifically, Webster argued, voters regularly elected those with a strong Christian faith so that requiring a profession of belief would not substantively change any voting outcome (a claim that was most probably true at the time). A constitution, he argued, should not be prevented from institutionalizing the very distinctions that voters use, and would like to use, as a sort of insurance policy for their own considered judgments (ibid.).

Presuming Webster was right that requiring a profession of belief would not alter any intended election results (and leaving aside the discrimination that this particular qualification involved) what good reasons are there to object to externalizing voter judgments in the forms of qualifications for office? Certainly, qualifications make these judgments inflexible; no matter how good a judgment may appear to voters at a particular time, legal qualifications make revision difficult, if not impossible, when the need or desire arises (Manin 1997; Schwartzberg 2007). Yet if we presume that voters have a right, and perhaps even an obligation, to use value-based preferences when voting by choosing "better" candidates over "worse" ones; if we presume that individual voters ought to use internal constraints such as "must have good policy ideas" or "must be competent," or "must have a good character" to guide their own choices; and if we acknowledge that such preferences and constraints tend to be robust over time; what principled reasons are there to object to formalizing these preferences into democratic constitutions?

The goals of this chapter are to explain how qualifications for office operate conceptually; to describe their unique relationship to the underlying principles of representative government; and to explain why their use always violates two presumptive democratic rights: that of citizens to run for office, and that of voters to choose whomever they wish to rule them. The goal here is neither to defend nor assail their use, but rather to precisely specify the conceptual bounds of these institutions, and the necessary normative tradeoffs they entail.

In large part, the present project is meant to clear the ground for the normative and empirical analysis of these institutions, something of particular importance given the explosion of gender quota laws[2] in emerging and established democracies over the last two decades (Baldez 2004; Krook 2006). The empirical literature now emerging by and large addresses the effects of these laws on women's representation,

---

[1] The filtration argument has been a staple of theories of representative government for over 300 years. For early variants of this filtration argument see Harrington (1992), Hume (1987), and Madison (1961). For a more recent account see Manin (1997).

[2] I outline a defense of treating gender quota laws as a qualification in Section II below.

or details the robust and differentiated political discourse that surrounds their adoption or defeat (Kittilson 2006; Krook 2009; Opello 2006). The normative literature has treated this material indirectly, as a means of securing a more completely defended principle of justice. Thus theorists have argued for secured seats (creating a qualification for that seat) as a way of achieving descriptive representation, correcting past harms, or promoting greater justice and deliberative legitimacy going forward (James 2004; Young 2000; Mansbridge 1999; Williams 1998; Phillips 1995; Young 1990).

In both empirical and normative literatures, the institution of a qualification for office itself is poorly described and unclearly articulated. Nowhere are the conceptual problems clearly delineated, nor are the democratic potential and pitfalls that accompany their use specified. In large part this is understandable and typical of how the study of politics often (and justifiably) proceeds: particular political problems are identified and struggled with, and only later are the conceptual and normative underpinnings developed and clarified. If successful, such clarification can then feed back into the study of politics by seeing and developing new ways to solve these practical problems. The fact that such an analysis has not yet been done, despite the attention to the expanding use of qualifications around the world, is thus hardly surprising.

Although I will not make the argument here, my own view is that qualifications may only legitimately be used to solve collective action problems brought about by institutional limitations, and not to limit democratic options by an appeal to substantive justice. I state, without defending, this position because it deviates significantly from the way qualifications are usually justified. In many empirical cases, qualifications have been justified by reference to principles of substantive justice or a commitment to a certain view of democratic deliberation. A commitment to justice, for example, is sometimes said to require that individuals of a certain sort, say African-Americans in the United States, be given representation in a legislature as a form of reparation for past harms. A commitment to democratic deliberation, for example, is sometimes said to require descriptive representation in a legislature in order to ensure that a diversity of opinions, ways of thinking, or mere "presence" of that group is made real (Phillips 1995). And of course there are many other kinds of arguments that might support the use of quotas and qualifications: from increasing sociological legitimacy to maintaining stable political institutions.[3]

---

[3] Related arguments may be found in Phillips (1995), Kymlicka (1996), Williams (1998), Mansbridge (1999) and James (2004). This literature generally fails to distinguish between "group representation," in which a group is given the power to elect its own

But qualifications to limit voter choice in the service of principles of justice – whether to ensure that representatives profess religious belief or to ensure that representatives have a certain set of descriptive characteristics – violate the very principles upon which representative government is endorsable as a form of democratic self-rule. Qualifications entail high democratic costs because they violate two presumptive democratic rights: the right of citizens to run for any office that stands to make and enforce law over them; and the right of citizens to choose whomever they want to fill those offices.[4] Furthermore those committed to democratic principles should view the use of qualifications for office with suspicion based on past experience: historically, they have been motivated by democratic distrust, and used to exclude vast portions of the population from office due to the "questionable" judgment of the *demos*. In the past, qualifications excluded those without property, the non-white, and the female. Today, the excluded groups are different, and the exclusion is motivated by a desire to act justly by including those who were previously excluded. But the arguments are structurally the same: we need quotas and qualifications today, it is said, because the judgment of the *demos* cannot be trusted (they only vote for men after all).

Whether the two presumptive democratic rights are *worth* violating and whether quotas can be secured without democratic distrust is our ultimate concern. For surely many anti-democratic rules that restrict voter choice are defended to promote democratic values (or more precisely in order to promote a certain kind of robust democracy). The answer to these substantive questions can only be addressed by first laying out clearly what tradeoffs are involved.

In this chapter I present a systematic way of thinking about qualifications for office as any rule or circumstance that has the effect of creating different probabilities of success for individual candidates prior to election. In Section II I provide a conceptual road map distinguishing qualifications and quotas from claims to group representation, define the terms, illustrate three variants of these institutions, and delineate between three kinds of justifications for their use. I conclude the conceptual section by distinguishing between qualifications such as "conforming to voter judgment" (i.e. winning an election) that are endorsable by foundational principles of representative government, and qualifications such as "profession of religious belief" that do not reference voter judgment at all. In

---

representative, and "legislative presence," in which legislative seats are secured for members of a particular group. Quotas and qualifications for office secure legislative presence, but not necessarily group representation; similarly giving a group the right to elect its own representative may secure group representation but not necessarily legislative presence. I take this up in Section II.1.1 below.

[4] I will defend these as core democratic rights later in the chapter.

Section III I lay out the necessary democratic costs of any qualification for office, explaining why they always constitute a presumptive violation of two core democratic rights: the rights of citizens to run for office and the rights of voters to choose whomever they want to rule them. I conclude by suggesting (but not defending) that qualifications for office should only be used in conditions that amount to democratic self-limiting rather than imposition of substantive justice that forecloses the exercise of voter judgment at election time.

II.   A conceptual roadmap to qualifications for office

In this section I offer a number of conceptual clarifications to guide the normative discussion that remains. In Section II.1 I propose treating qualifications for office as rules that create differential probabilities of candidates' success prior to voter judgment. In Section II.2 I offer a typology of justifications for qualifications drawn from empirical cases. And in Section II.3 I differentiate between different sorts of justifications.

II.1   *Defining "qualifications for office"*

Traditionally a "qualification for office" has been any rule that limits legal eligibility for an office to a specific set of people. This eligible set may be a subset of all citizens (e.g. "*citizens* over thirty-five years old"); it may include non-citizens (e.g. "*anyone* over the age of thirty-five years old"); it may be identical to all citizens (e.g. "any citizen of this nation"); or limited to a single person ("the first male heir of the king"). The hallmark of a qualification for office is simply that it has the effect of limiting who may run for office and, by extension, limiting the set of candidates for whom a voter may vote. Framed in this way, quotas that set aside a certain number of seats in the legislature or on party lists (without setting up restrictions on who may vote for those seats) are a type of qualification for office. Examples of these include the *parité* laws in France that require party lists to have a certain percentage of women on them, and rules in Rwanda that require 30 percent of all legislative seats to be held by women. These rules create a gender qualification for those seats.

In this section I make three formal distinctions. First, I argue that qualifications (and quotas) should be distinguished from group representation (II.1.1). Second, they should be framed in terms of probability assessments rather than as "legal eligibility" (II.1.2). And they should be framed in reference to the effect of rules and circumstances on candidates, rather than the language of a rule itself (II.1.3). Finally, I will differentiate between qualifications that emerge from voter preferences and those that do not (II.1.4).

II.1.1   Qualifications versus *group representation*   Qualifications for office make more likely what has been called, following Anne Phillips, "legislative presence" for a member of a particular group, whether the group is "citizens over thirty-five years old" or "women" (Philips 1995). Legislative presence for a particular group is secured when there is a member of that group in the legislature *regardless of who elects that member to office.* Thus, we can secure the legislative presence of *women*, that is, ensure that there are women in office, simply by establishing qualifications that require women to be elected without changing anything about the makeup of the electoral constituency that elects that member. By contrast, we can precisely describe "group representation" as a case of substantive representation, where a group's interests are substantively represented by a representative's activity in office, *regardless of the descriptive characteristics of that representative.*

Frequently "group representation" is secured by defining electoral constituencies around members of a particular group. To use the American example again, drawing electoral districts that create African-American majorities secures the substantive representation of blacks to the extent that the elected representative is responsive to the interests of those black voters. But "group representation" (as in the substantive representation of a group) may also be achieved when a group's interests are pursued by a representative "virtually," even in cases where the group does not formally elect a representative: as a group, poor Americans are represented to the extent that US Senator Ted Kennedy defends their interests in Congress. This "virtual" representation may be inadequate to secure a group's interests over time. Nor does it have a democratic basis, since the group being represented has no authority over the representative himself. These considerations point at the limits of *virtual* versus *actual* representation, but do not affect the "groupness" of the representation itself: the poor in this case are represented to the extent their interests as a group are pursued in the legislature.[5]

In much of the literature the term "group representation" blurs the distinction between using group membership as the basis of an electoral constituency (e.g. an African-American electoral district) and having a

---

[5] For a defense of the underlying conception of representation on which this depends, see Rehfeld (2006). For the inadequacy of the traditional distinctions upon which this relies, including those by Hanna Pitkin and Jane Mansbridge see Rehfeld (2009), Pitkin (1967), Mansbridge (2003).

member of the group be a member of the legislature (e.g. having an African-American representative). Because of this, "group representation" is sometimes described as giving a group electoral autonomy over their representative, or at other times described as securing seats in a legislature for members of that group. By precisely delineating the bounds of these two concepts we can thus more precisely describe and explain some confusions that arise when one, but not the other, of these two is secured. So, for example, when white voters elect a conservative African-American (like J. C. Watts, the Republican former member of the US Congress from the state of Oklahoma), the legislative presence of African-Americans is secured (by definition). Conversely, when a white man is elected mayor of a predominantly black American city (like Martin O'Malley, former mayor of Baltimore, MD), we can say that blacks there achieved group representation, but not legislative presence.

Some readers may want to object to the claim that Watts counts as achieving "legislative presence" for blacks *at all*, because Watts does not speak as the majority of blacks would, nor perhaps is he representative of American blacks. (A related example is that of Clarence Thomas on the US Supreme Court.) Such a claim generally confuses group representation with legislative presence itself. We may all agree that Watts does not defend African-American interests but we cannot seriously claim he does not provide *black* presence in the legislature since he is African-American himself. More plausibly, when critics say that Watts does not achieve "legislative presence" for blacks (despite being an African-American himself) it is only because critics do not want legislative presence *of blacks*. Rather they mean legislative presence *of certain kinds of African-Americans* and Watts is not one of those kinds. Thus, making clear the kinds of presence that one wants, and making clear the modes of group representation, we can more precisely explain what is going on here.

The distinction between "group representation" and "legislative presence" is an important one, but in practice these two concepts admittedly blur and overlap. For example, sometimes legislative presence may be best achieved by giving a group the right to elect its own representative, which may well be the best way of making sure a member of that group gets elected. Similarly, group representation may be best achieved by securing legislative presence for a member of that group. This is particularly true when it is difficult or undesirable to define an electoral constituency by reference to a particular group characteristic. The defense of securing seats for women as a way of promoting their interests (i.e. using legislative presence to secure group representation) is often made on the impracticality or impossibility of defining "women-only" electoral constituencies. But the fact that in practice legislative presence may secure group

representation or vice versa should not lead us into blurring the underlying conceptual distinctions between presence, constituency definition,
and group representation.[6]

II.1.2   Framing qualifications as probabilities of success   Traditionally,
qualifications for office have been treated as necessary legal conditions:
either a candidate meets a stated qualification and he can run for office,
or a candidate does not meet this standard and is legally forbidden to
run. But we might express qualifications in more functional, probabilistic terms rather than as a dichotomous legal permission. In this broader
framing, traditional qualifications are rules relative to which some candidates have a zero probability ($p = 0$) of success in an upcoming election,
while others have a non-zero ($p > 0$) probability of success. The traditional framing of qualifications as legal permissions and exclusions can
then be translated into these terms: candidates that meet a qualification
are legally permitted to run, and thus have a non-zero probability of success, relative to that rule, in the election; candidates that fail to meet the
qualification are forbidden from running and thus have a zero probability
of success (again relative to that rule) in the election.

   (What does "relative to that rule" add to the account? First, it acknowledges that there are many rules and circumstances that affect someone's
probability of success. In any particular case we want to isolate a given
rule or circumstance independent of these other factors, to the extent
such isolation is possible. Second, "relative to that rule" acknowledges
that these rules work in so far as the rule is in fact followed. A candidate may be legally forbidden from running for office by some rule, but
still fake his eligibility, legally challenge the rule, or take arms to coerce
authorities to let him run. Thus the probability of success is only relative
to that particular rule, since there is always some probability that the rule
may not be followed or something else would intervene.)

   Once seen in probabilistic terms, qualifications for office can be generalized to rules that assign *non-equal* probabilities of success to individual
candidates. In the traditional case there is a binary assignment of probabilities: the rule assigns some individuals a $p = 0$, and to other it assigns
a $p > 0$, where p takes the same value for all individuals in each of the
two groups. But there are other rules that have the effect of assigning different non-zero probabilities of success across candidates. Indeed, from

---

[6] Mansbridge distinguishes between flexible and inflexible ways of securing group representation, treating quotas as an inflexible way. But I think such a view fails to see
the conceptual limits of "constituency," as well as "qualifications." For an extended
treatment of "constituency," see Rehfeld (2005).

the standpoint of democratic theory, in which we presumably want to be sensitive to inequalities in political power, it is the assignment of *different* probabilities of success to each individual that should be of concern to us rather than one particular case in which some have a probability of "0" of winning, and others have a probability "$p > 0$" of winning. Put differently, the traditional dichotomous treatment of qualifications ($p = 0$, $p > 0$) is simply a special case in which rules give some candidates a greater probability of winning than others. We will thus treat qualifications for office more expansively as any rule whose effect is to create *differential probabilities of success across a set of individual candidates* even in cases where all individuals are legally permitted to run (i.e. even in cases where no individual has a $p = 0$ relative to that rule).

With this treatment we can see why some rules that do not follow the traditional form are properly described as "virtual" qualifications for office. Consider the case of gerrymandered districts in the United States in which 70 percent of all voters are registered members of the Democratic Party, or a district in which 70 percent of all voters are African-American. Candidates running in these districts are far more likely to win if they share the quality upon which the constituency was defined, be it party ID, race, and so on. Treating qualifications as the assignment of different probabilities of success, regardless of what value p actually takes on, explains why in these districts "race" or "political party" forms a very real if implicit qualification for office: the probability of winning in a majority–minority African-American district is greater if one is black than if one is not, even though one *need* not be an African-American to win. To use another case, there is no formal rule with the effect of *requiring* candidates to be wealthy (or be good fundraisers) in order to successfully compete for office or *forbidding* those who are neither of these to run. But given other rules that make it almost impossible to win without access to funds, we may treat access to wealth as a qualification for office, since those without it are much less likely to win than those with it. So long as we limit the term "qualification" to denote legal permissibility or exclusion, we cannot explain why, in these cases, race and wealth indeed are qualifications for office. Instead we say that these are qualifications for office because they distribute probabilities of success differentially across candidates.

II.1.3   Qualifications as the effects of rules and circumstances   Traditionally, qualifications for office have been treated as explicit rules, such as an age or residency requirement, that set legal permissions ($p > 0$) and exclusions ($p = 0$) to run for office. In addition to framing them in terms of differential probabilities of success, I want to broaden the treatment in two other ways: by considering the *effects* of rules, rather than the rules themselves; and by considering *circumstances* as well as rules. I will take each in turn.

First, we should consider the *effect* of a rule, rather than the rule itself, as what constitutes a qualification for office. If the effect of two different laws or rules is the same, and if that effect is to differentially distribute the probabilities of success in an election, then both rules will be treated as a qualification for office no matter what the language of the rule actually is. This is consistent with other features of election law, and in fact governs the US Justice Department's oversight of electoral districts.

As an example, consider these two proposed voting rules:

"Women with young children may not vote."

and

"No strollers are allowed within one mile of a polling booth."

Only the first rule explicitly forbids women with young children from voting. But the second creates a de facto, if not absolute, limit and should rightly be treated as a voting rights infringement. Less fanciful and more heinous examples are readily available throughout American history, particularly in the attempt to disenfranchise African-Americans. The point is, we should look to the effects of rules, rather than their explicit language, to judge whether differential probabilities of success are created and thus whether the rule counts as a qualification for office.

Once we see that it is the *effects* of rules that matter, but not the explicit rules themselves, we can justify the expansion of our treatment from *rules* to *circumstances* as well. Here "circumstances" refer to constraints that affect the probabilities of candidate success. These might include circumstances personal to a candidate – the health of their family – or more broadly social facts like the number of opponents they face in the election (the more candidates there are in an election the less likely any particular one of them is to win, all things considered[7]). Here, as in the case of rules, qualifications for office refer only to those circumstances that assign *unequal* probabilities of success to different candidates. Thus, the fact that all candidates faced the same diminished probability of success the more candidates there are that run does not form a qualification

---

[7] Recall that we consider the effect of the rule by itself and not other subsequent reactions to the rule. So, all things considered, the more candidates run for office the less likely any one of them is to win, even though it may be the case that an individual may benefit from the entry into a race of a polarizing candidate.

for office. By contrast, access to money would be a qualification for office since it creates differential probabilities of success.[8]

Focusing on "circumstances" is a way to acknowledge structural inequalities that create differential probabilities of success for different candidates, even in the absence of formal rules. I leave open the possibility that "circumstances" may well be reducible to a set of very specific rules that form these circumstances – in this case perhaps treating political speech as commercial speech or the rules of the free market. Circumstances thus allow us to consider more fully the set of social facts that have the effect of creating unequal probabilities of success for different candidates.

Finally, I note that although conceptually we need not differentiate between qualifications that emerge from circumstances, and qualifications that emerge from rules, as a normative matter we may well care about their etiology. For various reasons we may want only to regulate formal rules whose effect is to form qualifications for office, but not attempt to intervene in circumstances that are hard to pin down even though they have a particular effect. But the fact that there may be good normative reasons for dealing with some but not all qualifications for office in a certain way does not explain what should count conceptually as a "qualification." Thus we will leave open the possibility that there may be normative reasons to treat the different etiologies of qualifications differently without presuming that conceptual separation in advance.

In sum, then, I define qualifications for office in this way:

> Qualifications for office = Rules or circumstances that have the effect of differentially distributing probabilities of success to candidates for office.

II.1.4   Voter-endogenous and voter-exogenous qualifications for office   Qualifications for office as just stated refer to any rule or circumstance that differentially affects the probability of a candidate's success. Although we normally think of qualifications as external to voters, voters themselves regularly constrain their own choices to a set of individuals possessing features they take to be important. Some voters will *only* vote for members of a particular party; others will choose between a few parties; still

---

[8] I call "access to money" a qualification instead of "money" itself because each candidate's probabilities of success are equally changed by each additional dollar they have. Money itself thus does not create differential probabilities of success; rather "access to money" must form the qualification. I acknowledge that this is not as precise as it could be, but it is precise enough to proceed with the present account.

others make their choice based on the personal characteristics of the candidates. These internal judgments differentially distribute probabilities of success among candidates no more or less than external choice constraints would if written to correspond with the internal judgments of a particular voter.

The fact that individual voters use their judgment to select candidates (rather than choose randomly) means that "corresponding to voter preferences" should itself be counted as a qualification for office, since candidates are not equally likely to so correspond. This should not be particularly controversial since "winning an election" is about the most readily used "qualification for office" around and even conforms to the traditional use of legal permission, in that it assigns those who meet that standard (i.e. who win the election) a $p = 1$, and all others a $p = 0$. But it allows us to make an important distinction between voter-exogenous and voter-endogenous qualifications that will be of significance to normative analysis.

Let *voter-endogenous* qualifications for office denote qualifications emerging from the exercise of voter judgment.

Let *voter-exogenous* qualifications for office refer to all non-voter-endogenous qualifications for office.

Since representative government is often defended on the ability of voters to promote into office "better" representatives than would otherwise be selected were random selection (Manin 1997) or direct democracy (Mill 1991 [1861]; Madison 1961) employed, we should distinguish between voter-endogenous and voter-exogenous qualifications for office and treat them differently. Indeed, while there are normative reasons to be concerned about the kinds of judgments that voters make, we have different reasons to be concerned about rules and circumstances *external to voters* that create differential probabilities of success among candidates. And the reason we should treat voter judgment differently from exogenous factors has to do with the presumptions of democratic representative government. Representative government is built on the presumption that voters will indeed make non-arbitrary judgments built upon non-random preferences, and thus systematically favor some kinds of candidates and disfavor others. This is not only a fact of representative government, it is arguably why representative government is preferable to direct forms. By contrast, we should be extremely suspicious of voter-exogenous qualifications because they restrict democratic options while voter-endogenous qualifications are more difficult to assail on democratic principles. At the very least, we should expect different sorts of arguments concerning voter-exogenous interventions and voter-endogenous interventions.

Of course, different individuals cast votes for numerous reasons. But the point here is that we can differentiate constraints internal to voters (their preferences, judgments about their interests or the interests of the nation) from those externally applied to voter choice prior to the exercise of their judgment. These external constraints are distinctive precisely because they operate external to voters and prior to the exercise of their judgment. The aristocratic nature of elections that Manin was right to emphasize can thus be institutionalized in two different ways, by internal and external constraints.

I will say more about voter-endogenous and voter-exogenous constraints below in Section III.2. But notice that relying on constraints imposed by voters to select "proper" candidates depends on trusting voters to make good choices and to allow for flexibility when necessary. The US founders, for example, thought that candidates for political office *ought to* be property owners of a certain level. But rather than making this requirement rigid as law, they opted to rely on voters' internal judgment that the founders believed would have the same effect of promoting only prominent property owners to elective office. Further, by relying on voter judgment rather than external constraints, the proposed system was less rigid and allowed for flexible response by voters if the circumstances warranted it.[9]

> If the advantage of the propertied classes is assured by a statistically proven regularity of electoral behavior, the system offers a measure of flexibility: circumstances may arise where the effect [i.e. property ownership] does not obtain, because an exceptional concern overrides voters' ordinary inclination toward "conspicuous" candidates. The situation is different if legislative position is reserved by law to the higher social classes, because the law is by definition rigid. (Manin 1997: 126)

Relying only on internal constraints maintains flexibility.

II.2   *A typology of qualifications*

Having mapped out the conceptual space surrounding qualifications for office, I turn to a typology of qualifications that differentiates three distinct types of ends for which formal qualifications (i.e. explicit rules) have been used. Note that formal qualifications (like most rules) use proxies

---

[9] The flexibility of the American system is in sharp contrast to the English and French systems of the times which used qualifications more robustly (Manin 1997: 126–9). For more on the value of revisability in constitutional democracies see Schwartzberg (2007).

for the desired end. For example, age qualifications are brute devices that are meant to secure "political maturity" – for lack of a better term – of legislators. Few people care that a legislator is of a certain age, but many of them care that they have some minimal maturity or life experience. Since age is closely related to maturity of all kinds, age qualifications are used because they increase the likelihood that legislators will have political maturity. Here the age requirement stands as a proxy for "political maturity" or simply "maturity" that corresponds systematically to age. The point is that "being age X" is not itself the desideratum of the rule; rather the rule is a proxy for the desideratum of political maturity.

Consider some other examples in which proxies are used to achieve a substantive end. Property ownership was proposed to secure a variety of aims including independent judgment and having a stake in society. Gender and race requirements today are used to secure diverse perspectives within the legislature, as well as provide a remedy for past discrimination and harm. Term limits are supposed to protect representatives from becoming too entrenched. And ethnic and subnational group membership qualifications are often seen as the only way to guarantee stability and/or give a population a sense of participation within the whole. Without presuming the correctness of the argument (that is, the proxy used may or may not achieve these ends), qualifications are most often used in order to aim at a purported end, rather than being the end in themselves.

Historically, formal qualifications have been used to secure three different kinds of ends: (i) to secure the same minimal competency for each member of a legislature; (ii) to ensure correspondence between an individual representative and her constituents; or (iii) to create legislatures that are composed of different kinds of people. These three aims – *competency, correspondence,* and *composition* – sometimes overlap but they are conceptually distinct. I will take each in turn. (A summary of this discussion appears in Table 9.1.)

First, qualifications have historically been used to increase the probability that each candidate will have *minimal competency.* By "competency" I mean: (i) an acquirable trait; that is (ii) purportedly necessary for the job; and (iii) applies to everyone who is a member of the body (say, a legislature). A minimal age requirement in a legislature, for example, is precisely of this kind: it is an acquirable trait that is purportedly necessary for the job[10] and everyone in the legislature is required to have it. Religious oaths for office might also be considered under this category since they were acquirable, purportedly necessary for the job, and applicable

---

[10] Or in light of what we just said, "political maturity" is required for the job; minimal ages act as proxies for this.

Table 9.1 *Three general aims of qualifications with examples*

Purported general aim of qualification	Description of aim	Specific examples of aim
Competency: To set minimal competence of all representatives	Competencies are: (i) features that any individual can acquire; (ii) purportedly necessary for the job; and (iii) applicable to all who serve.	Age qualifications; religious oaths; term limits
Correspondence: To maintain correspondence between representatives and their electoral constituents	Correspondence qualifications ensure that office-holders share some characteristic feature(s) used to define their electoral constituency.	Residency requirements; party membership requirements; citizenship requirements.
Composition: To craft how the legislature (or other body) looks.	Composition qualifications are: (i) seat specific; and (ii) determined with an eye to the membership of the whole body.	Group membership; gender quota laws; district gerrymandering.

to all who served. Literacy tests and qualifying examinations would be further examples of this kind of qualification.

A second kind of qualification aims to increase the probability that officer-holders *correspond* to a particular group, most often to their particular electoral constituencies. The most familiar of these types of qualifications are residency requirements, in which representatives are required to live in the state (frequently in the electoral district) of the voters that vote for them. Correspondence between representatives and their electoral constituents is also secured in proportional representation systems in which electoral constituencies are defined by the votes that voters cast at each election (Rehfeld 2005). And here, correspondence between, say, the Labor constituency and its representatives is guaranteed by the requirement that those who offer themselves up as Labor candidates in fact support Labor policies. It is this obvious fact (that party candidates support the party platforms for which they stand) that guarantees correspondence even in these systems. The correspondence requirement is perhaps most readily seen in cases of professional representation in which, for example, pediatricians elect pediatricians, psychiatrists elect psychiatrists, etc., for representation on their own professional councils. Importantly, "correspondence" does not specify the competency of a representative, but indicates an identity between a representative and her constituents on some particular dimension.

In addition to securing minimal *competencies* for all office-holders, and to ensuring that all office-holders *correspond* to some feature of their electoral constituents, qualifications for office can also be used to shape the *composition* of the legislature when considered as a whole. In this case, qualifications for office can increase the likelihood that a legislature (or other body) looks a certain way by establishing different rules for each seat in the legislature. For example, gender and racial quotas are often said to be important to secure deliberative or descriptive diversity within the legislature – what we have called "legislative presence." Unlike *competence* and *correspondence*, which could apply to all offices, qualifications that alter the composition of a legislature differ for each seat or group of seats in the same corporate body. So, for example, if we wanted more gender diversity in the legislature we might set aside certain seats for men and certain seats for women by creating different qualifications for each seat. Similarly, we might specify that a certain percentage of seats be set aside for ethnic groups whether to protect their rights or for other reasons.

These three kinds of qualifications are conceptually distinct, and the typology is meant to delineate and describe how these institutions are used, and have been used historically. Importantly, they are not mutually exclusive and whether they are used to ensure *competence, correspondence,* or *composition* may depend on other political factors. One might use a residency qualification that ensures *correspondence* between voters and representatives in order to secure a certain kind of *composition* of the legislature. Or, if electoral constituencies were defined by gender, then a qualification for office to ensure *correspondence* between constituencies and their representatives would also ensure that the legislature was *composed* in a certain way. Whether this result is the primary aim, or a secondary consequence, will depend on how the qualification itself is conceived based on one of these categories. Further, the normative justification for qualifications for office may indeed rest as much on which of these three aims the qualification is meant to secure, as it is on what the consequences are of securing that aim.

II.3   Kinds of justifications

In II.1 I offered a conceptual framework for qualifications including a reconceptualization of what they were; in Section II.2 I offered a typology of the three ends qualifications for office are used to secure. I turn now to a final typology about the kinds of justifications that are used for qualifications for office. These will be critical to assessing the normative legitimacy of their use.

Why take up "justifications" for qualifications at all? At a formal level, justifications for these rules are not about qualifications per se but about the ways we justify any rule to each other. Here I presume, rather than defend, what is the dominant, if not universally agreed upon, account of political legitimacy in which democratic institutions are normatively legitimate in so far as they are justifiable to all reasonable citizens.[11] In plain language this means that a government has a right to make and enforce its laws when they are justifiable to citizens over whom they govern.[12] The ultimate question is whether any qualification can be justifiable to democratic citizens on this basis.

Allowing that a range of specific justifications for qualifications for office have in practice been offered for their use, at a general level of abstraction there have been three substantive justifications for them: *justice* (they aim at purportedly just ends); *democratic distrust* (they limit the harms that voters can cause); *public choice* (they solve irresolvable conflicts of public choice). I will take each in turn. (A summary of this section appears below in Table 9.2.)

First, qualifications may be justified by a principle of *justice*; i.e. the purportedly just ends at which they aim. In the case of contemporary gender qualifications, for example, *ensuring* that the legislature's *composition* includes men and women is purportedly just for a set of reasons (e.g. because a legislature without many women is *ipso facto* unjust; because ensuring gender parity is presumed to secure fairer laws and policies; because of the role modeling effects of seeing all kinds of people in the legislature, etc.). When qualifications are rejected, they are also rejected by reference to substantive principles of justice that they purportedly violate: e.g. the rejection of property or literacy tests or racial requirements to run for political office.

A second kind of justification for these rules is based on *democratic distrust*. Following a robust tradition dating at least back to Plato, the use of formal qualifications in England and America in the seventeenth

---

[11] This is a simplification of a vast and important literature on justification. The contemporary touchstone is of course Rawls (1993). What such justification means in practice is developed in a masterly way in MacGilvray (2004). See also the discussion in Rehfeld (2005) that provides a more complete summary of this.

[12] As stated, this is a presumption; I am not defending this claim here. Famously, the meaning of "reasonable" is contentious, and whether or not individuals actually have to be reasonable for a government to be legitimate raises some problems of consent. It would seem that a government might be legitimate so long as it was endorsed by "reasonable" people who gave their hypothetical consent even if none existed and therefore none consented to the current regime.

Table 9.2 *A typology of justifications*

Kind of justification	Description	Examples
Principles of justice	The end towards which a qualification aims is defended by the substantive justice it brings about.	Gender qualifications that create better policies; secure seats for ethnic groups as a remedy for past harms.
Democratic distrust	Qualifications limit the bad judgment that voters can make.	Property qualifications that kept the poor from running lest they dupe voters; gender and racial qualifications that are imposed because voters are racist and sexist.
Problems of choice	Qualifications can resolve decisional conflicts that emerge from any system of rules.	Racial gerrymanders in cases where voters both want to vote for "someone like me" and want representatives that look like the nation as whole.

and eighteenth centuries made this explicit: motivated by spite and envy rather than love of the whole, the masses could not be trusted to elect leaders who would pursue the public good. Thus, for example, were higher property qualifications for office justified: those with property purportedly had a stake in society and without the use of qualifications they were unlikely to be elected (Lerner 1995). The large electoral district was similarly intended to create a de facto qualification for office because it was designed in large part to increase the likelihood that men of good reputation would be elected (Madison 1961; Harrington 1992; Manin 1997; Rehfeld 2005). Again, the use of these qualifications was purportedly justified to protect the nation from outcomes resulting from the venality or stupidity of voters.

To the extent that prejudice explains why women are not elected, the contemporary use of gender quotas appears to be motivated in large part by the same sense of democratic distrust that animated earlier campaigns. Voters today no longer lack "moral virtue"; today they are merely "racist" or "sexist," or unjustly refuse to acknowledge the claims of the oppressed. Voters are no longer said to be stupid or uneducated; rather they are said not to know what their own interests are or ought to be. These are precisely the same kinds of arguments that were made to justify other sorts of now rejected qualifications for office.

A third justification is based on the limits that emerge from the use of voting rules themselves. As has been well developed, institutional problems, rather than ignorance or malice, can prevent desired outcomes from being achieved. For example, imagine all voters in the United States used the following principle of "racial correspondence" to decide their vote: "I will vote for someone who's the same race as I am."[13] And imagine that the US is racially integrated at the level of the enormous congressional district.[14] In such a case, most electoral constituencies might contain a majority of whites and the legislature would be entirely white *even if all voters would prefer a racially diverse legislature*. Whites might endorse this principle of racial correspondence for the same reasons that non-whites do (because they believe race is a good proxy for whether a candidate shares a citizen's perspectives and interests), yet sincerely lament the fact that there are no blacks elected to Congress. Electoral gerrymanders are premised upon this very principle and supporters of them are often explicit about this in their endorsement.[15]

Some gender quota laws may be designed (and justified) to remedy similar sorts of institutional limits. Even absent venal discrimination at the time of voting (in this and the last case), if individual candidates are selected simply using the decision rule "I will vote for whomever has the most experience" or "I will vote for whomever is likely to be the most effective politician given ongoing sexism (that I lament but which nevertheless exists)," then men will almost always be elected even as we all lament the fact that there are no female representatives.[16] The only way around that is to impose external constraints (and in this case such

---

[13] When whites use "racial correspondence" as a principle of selection they are often accused of racism or merely excluding black voices; when blacks use it they are lauded for trying get their perspective in the legislature. I suspect voters in each group are motivated by a combination of "keeping out" the other and "getting in" their own. In either case, if the principle of racial similarity is a good one, there seems to be no prima facie reason to restrict its use by any individual. The problem is only a problem collectively. Unless, of course, one thinks that using racial correspondence itself is not in fact a good principle on which to select political representatives.

[14] The population of the United States is roughly 300,000,000 people. Although each congressional district does not have precisely the same population owing to differences in state population and in apportionment rules, the size of each district is roughly the same: 690,000 individuals per electoral district. The territorial scope will of course differ given population density. The territorially large state of Montana has but a single member of the US House of Representatives, the same number that can be found in a relatively small area of Manhattan.

[15] In law, gerrymanders are justified based on the inability of blacks to elect whomever they want, and not on whether blacks in fact are in the legislature. And yet in the United States the test of whether a community has been able to elect one of their own has often been based on how successful blacks have been in getting into office. Thus however else racial gerrymanders are justified, they do appeal to the election of blacks themselves, and not merely to giving the black community more autonomy to choose their own representatives.

[16] Indeed when *parité* was passed in France, it was difficult to recruit women to run as candidates because there were relatively few of them with any political experience.

constraints would simultaneously bring about the conditions by which these particular internal constraints would fail to be salient).

To sum up here, qualifications for office need not be based on anxieties about the masses. When justified as a corrective for the presumed incompetence of voters they are explicitly anti-democratic. But when justified for their potential to solve conflicts of democratic values or collective action problems they are no more or less democratic than any other such provision of preemptive restraints in the law. But appreciating qualifications for office in this light, rather than as a reflection of anti-democratic sentiments, demonstrates that they need not be anti-democratic, and that they need not fail the test of public justifiability. And, as I will argue later, it is necessary for qualifications to be justified based on the solution to institutional conflict, rather than as an anti-democratic corrective, for them to be reasonably democratic at all.[17]

III.   The normative implications of qualifications for office

Having delineated the conceptual space surrounding qualifications for office, I turn now to a discussion of the normative implications of their use. As defined, qualifications for office differentially alter the probability that a potential candidate will win an election. Further, in cases where they set a $p = 0$ for some candidates they limit a voter's choice set by excluding these candidates. Both of these constitute the prima facie limits of two core democratic rights: a right to run for office and a right to vote for an unconstrained choice of candidates. The goal of this section is to explain why qualifications so limit these rights. (What follows merely describes the normative terrain and explains the normative stakes involved. While it suggests some ways that qualifications might be justified, owing to the limits of this chapter it does not offer a full defense of these positions.)

The two rights can be illustrated by considering again Daniel Webster's argument about transforming the internal judgments of voters (who wanted candidates to profess Christian beliefs) into an external institutional constraint (that required the profession of belief as a condition of office-holding). Webster's proposal was problematic for three reasons. First, any formalized rule creates a rigid rule in place of flexible voter judgment. Second, qualifications for office also abrogate a right to offer

---

[17] It may be that qualifications are also necessary for justice. And indeed, I think sometimes considerations of justice may limit democratic institutions, as checks on the majority do. This presumes that "democratic" and "just" as categories do not precisely overlap, and that it is possible to have at least an unjust democracy (whether or not a "just nondemocracy"), though I acknowledge this is a disputed point. See for example Shapiro (1996).

oneself as a contender to rule; Webster failed to distinguish the right to *serve* from the right to *run*. Third, to argue that in a democracy people can enact *any* precommitment in law it wants so long as it is consistent with what they would do anyway is an overstatement. Qualifications for office do not merely stand to *reshape* democratic institutions, they stand to *unmake* democracy: imagine that only those with some individual's DNA are legally permitted to run; the result is an elective dictatorship or monarchy, not a recognizable democracy.

To state this more formally, qualifications are problematic because they limit or violate two presumptive democratic rights: (i) citizens have a right to run for offices whose occupants make and enforce the law that governs them; and (ii) voters have a right to choose whomever they wish to rule them. As I said above, I presume that legitimate democracies begin with a strong presumption in favor of these rights forming an institutional default position of any purportedly legitimate democratic government. Justifying qualifications for office will thus mean explaining the conditions under which violations of these rights are acceptable. And that requires first specifying in greater detail what these rights amount to.

In this section I will argue that an equal right to run is institutionalized, first, in the legal permission to run for office, and, second, in the absence of formal rules that alter the external probability of success for one kind of candidate over another kind. A right to run for office is only minimally secured first by the legal permission to run, and further presumes the absence of institutional rules that differentially distribute the probabilities of success among different kinds of candidates. In this way the right to run for office parallels the treatment of "equal voting rights": the equal right to vote has meant not merely a legal permission to cast a ballot, but also the equal probability of a vote to affect the outcome of an election, as well as the absence of other rules that would encourage or suppress voting by certain kinds of voters. Understood in this way, qualifications for office thus always violate this core, presumptive right. I develop this in two sections, first more generally in terms of political equality (III.1) and then in a specification of an equal right to run (III.2).

III.1   Political equality

I presume at a minimum that any reasonably democratic government will secure these three political rights for all citizens:

(1) The right to vote: *citizens have a right to vote of equal value in choosing among candidates for office*;

(2) The right to an unconstrained choice set: *citizens have a right to be ruled by anyone they choose (i.e. to an unrestricted choice set of candidates)*;

(3) The right to run for office: *citizens have a right to compete for the offices that govern them.*

The view that these are core democratic rights is treated here as a presumptive, non-exhaustive, conditional view, rather than a view that is metaphysically justified or ontologically defended. By this I mean three things. First, these rights are presumptive rather than necessary: for a polity to be reasonably democratic it must either secure these rights for its citizens *or* it must justify a deviation from them. Second, these rights are not exhaustive: I presume that there are other political rights that must be guaranteed by any reasonable conception of democracy – rights that govern influence over or access to power, rights of expression, etc. – though I do think that these three are more fundamental or democratically *prior* to those. Finally, these rights are conditional in the sense that *if* one values democracy *then* one presumptively gives these rights a prominent place. By contrast, an unconditional defense of these rights would explain whether they or democracy were primary; whether they were endorsable for *detached* or *dependent* reasons, as Dworkin has described it; and perhaps whether they derived from natural law, social norms and agreement, or God's will.[18] Though these are important questions to any full account of democratic rights, they need not concern us here. Instead, I presume these rights have a primacy but not necessity for anyone who endorses democracy, for whatever reasons they do: these rights derive from a conception of democracy as equal distribution of power, but they nevertheless may be abrogated if there are good reasons to do so.

There are a few things to notice about these core rights. First, while they are rights that purportedly accrue to citizens, they leave unaddressed important questions of membership – of who gets to be a "citizen." This is at least consistent with the historical development of these rights: arguments for universal suffrage, for example, were premised on what citizenship entailed, and not on who ought to be a citizen per se.[19]

Second, the first two rights are interrelated: the right to vote is meaningless without a sufficiently expansive choice set: that is, without the

---

[18] Dworkin (2000: 186–7). Though I presume these are detached, they may also be dependent. In fact, Dworkin uses these terms in slightly different ways: dependent views depend on across-the-board measures of equality; detached views of democracy are premised only on the equal distribution of power. Thus do I say, "among other things." I find Pettit's version of this tradeoff of principle and consequences to be clearer, but I use Dworkin's here because it speaks more directly to issues of political equality (Pettit 1997).

[19] As Keyssar (2000) has documented, there have been and continue to be many arguments for the extension of suffrage to non-citizen residents or workers of a nation who might not be eligible to receive full rights of citizenship. Here I am only considering why these three rights should correspond to citizenship, and I leave unaddressed whether others should also be afforded them.

right to choose. It is unlikely that any system in which only one candidate were legally permitted to run (say, Hussein or Castro) would be a plausible democracy at all (let alone normatively legitimate) *even if* universal suffrage were guaranteed. The right to vote must be paired with a right to an unconstrained choice for office as a starting point for any plausible theory of self-rule. Of course, the fact that a *completely* constrained choice set is not reasonably democratic leaves open the question of how unconstrained a voter's choice set can be. Maybe legitimate democracies need merely to guarantee voters some *sufficient* but not *unlimited* choice for each office. If so, the task would be to specify what this sufficiency requirement would amount to – perhaps it is sufficient to have a limited choice between candidates who hold differing views, or who are members of different groups.[20] But the point here is to establish a default position. Limits on unconstrained choice, rather than unlimited choice need to be justified.

A third and longer clarification is needed concerning the relationship between the right to run for office and the right of voters to have an unconstrained choice set at election time. Although a truly unconstrained choice set necessarily entails a universal right to run for office,[21] the former is conceptually distinct from the latter. In fact, each concerns different citizenship roles. A voter's right to an unconstrained choice set is derived from the citizen as voter: as I said above, the unconstrained set gives meaning to the right to vote. By contrast, the right to run for office concerns the ability of citizens to offer themselves as potential rulers. While both are forms of political participation we should not necessarily presume, nor do we usually presume, that all forms of participation are justified by the same sorts of arguments. Given that there will likely be justifiable limitations on a voter's choice set and that these limits will likely restrict which citizens may run for office,[22] we should work separately to establish these rights on two different bases.

I want to raise three issues concerning the right to run, explaining: (i) why we should presume such a right; (ii) its distinction as a mid-point between conceptions of ancient and modern equality; and (iii) why

---

[20] I remind readers that many other conditions would have to be met for a government to be democratically legitimate, including, I presume, the necessity for robust free debate between candidates.

[21] It is logically impossible for a voter's choice set to include *every human being who wants to run* and to forbid some human beings from running despite wanting to.

[22] This is only a probable limit. We could well imagine that the only constraint on voters is to vote for fellow citizens. In such a case their choice set is radically limited (from "all human beings" to "all citizens of this state"), without limiting at all a citizen's right to run themselves.

the right to run provides a rights-based articulation of the principle of distinction that is a hallmark of representative government.

(i) First, a citizen's right to run for office emerges from a consideration of democratic political equality, of what it means to equally participate in a democratic polity. The intuition here is that politically equal citizens should all have an equal right to offer themselves up for selection, even if we cannot reasonably demand an equal right to be chosen (for reasons to be developed momentarily). The intuition can be generated by imagining that only one small group – say white men – are legally permitted to offer themselves for selection. We would rightly reject such a provision as anti-democratic and presumptively wrong. This right to run for office is broadly endorsed by a range of democratic theorists, even though none of them has specified what it means in practice or in any other systematic way[23] (Dahl 1991: 222; Beitz 1989; Dworkin 2000; Christiano 1996; Rawls 1971).

(ii) Second, it is useful to note that a right to run for office is also not expressible in the distinction between ancient and modern forms made familiar by Constant and expanded more recently by Manin.[24] In this first distinction, ancient political equality meant that each citizen had an equal right *to serve* in office; modern political equality means that each citizen has the equal right *to choose* who serves in office. Modern political equality has thus emphasized the rights of citizens to *choose* their rulers, to participate as voters (deliberate *about* candidates and issues; have equality of influence over who represents them, etc.). Midway between the ancient and modern ends, midway between the equal right *to serve* and the *equal right to choose*, stands a third form of political equality: the equal right *to run* for the offices that govern us.

(iii) Framed in this way, a political right to run for office is an institutional method of tempering the aristocratic tendency of government. With

---

[23] Dahl comes closest to *justifying* a right to run for office with a discussion of why each citizen has a right to fully participate in ruling the polity (Dahl 1991). But this leads only to a right of equal participation in citizen deliberation and voting and never actually establishes a right to run for office as differentiated from these other citizen activities.

[24] Constant (1988), Manin (1997). There are other ways of conceiving of political equality, and most promising are the distinctions introduced by Beitz: equality of the individual vote, equality of (group) electoral success, and equality of legislative outcome. As Beitz rightly observes, these three may not be mutually achievable. As Lublin has shown, for example, ensuring group electoral success may come at the cost of worse legislative outcomes for that group. Similarly, equal voting shares may not produce group electoral success. In a sense my questions arise from the other side of the coin: ensuring these kinds of political equalities (particularly of group electoral success) often means a cost of individual political rights intimately related to core democratic presumptions (Beitz 1989; Lublin 1997).

Manin, in pure democracies the right to rule is reflected in the institution of rotation in office, whereby any citizen who wishes stands an equal chance to serve, their selection being overseen by the use of lot. Indeed, corresponding also to Aristotle's argument in *The Politics*, a polity can claim to rule itself in part so long as its citizens have a reasonable expectation to rule and be ruled in turn. In contrast, citizens of representative government cannot reasonably expect to rule *at any time*. As Manin argues, the distinction is what Madison and Sieyès explicitly argued for, and we might add it is endorsed by Guizot and Mill in the nineteenth century and in admittedly different forms by both Schumpeter and Dahl in the twentieth century. The exclusion found in contemporary representative government means that most citizens are more likely to be hit by lightning than ever to serve in their national legislature (Rehfeld 2005).

At the same time as securing that these presumptive rights move representative governments in a democratic direction, the possibility that they might be abridged in order to enhance democracy allows institutional designers to embrace publicly the aristocratic formulation and help self-consciously to shape, rather than be shaped by, the exclusion of representative government. Here, we can now be sensitive to whether qualifications for office create a de facto governing elite that, as Manin has illustrated, ensures that being a millionaire is a virtual qualification for office. Rather, it is to be far more explicit and public about the kind of aristocracy we are forming, in an attempt to make it more democratic in spirit if not in nature.[25]

The discussion in this section can now be summarized in Table 9.3, which outlines these three principles of political equality (column 1), lists types of regimes that are commensurate with that principle (column 2), and provides examples of regimes that fit (column 3). As the table shows, modern political equality in the Constant/Manin articulation is incomplete because dictatorships, and tyrannies more generally, can guarantee an equal right of voters to choose who rules.[26] What is needed, as I said above, is a provision about the real choice set they face which requires that citizens be permitted to run, and that they stand a chance of winning that is institutionally equal to others who are running, an issue to which we now return.

---

[25] Justifications for qualifications thus explicitly conform to the prescriptions of Republicanism as articulated by Philip Pettit (1997). For one recent example of this, see McCormick (2006).

[26] Similarly, Dworkin notes the inadequacy of equal voting power: "In totalitarian dictatorships private citizens have equal political power: none" (Dworkin 2000: 191).

Table 9.3 *Three forms of political equality*

Principle of political equality	Commensurate with these kinds of regimes	Examples
Equal right to rule (i.e., ancient political equality)	Democracies	Fourth-century Athens
Equal right to select those who rule (i.e., modern political equality)	Dictatorships; representative systems; democracies	Present-day Syria; Iraq 1979–2003; United States; France; India; fourth-century Athens
Equal right to run for office/right to choose whomever one wants.	Democracies; representative systems	US; France; India; fourth-century Athens.

III.2   What an equal *right to run for office entails*

The right to an unconstrained choice set is relatively straightforward: citizens should have the right to choose *whomever* or *whatever* they want to fill the offices that will make and enforce the laws that govern them. This right extends even to choices that are bafflingly stupid: for example, the right to choose a fichus tree for their President, a choice no more or less sensible than the choice of a newborn or merely an adult with decreased or marginal capacity for rational thought. The right to an unconstrained choice set is a right of self-determination, even to the extreme. Some might think that completely undifferentiated choices would not be covered by this right since it is a right to choose *someone with the capacity to rule*, but fichus trees (along with babies and incompetents) have no ruling capacities.[27] While I acknowledge the apparent force of this problem, it is ultimately question-begging: there is no way to create a criterion of "meaningful choice" or "proper objects of choice" without limiting a voter's choice set in the same way that "only women for this seat" or "only Jews for this one" does. Now it may be that the criterion "meaningful" or "proper" is less democratically problematic than some other (say, the securing of descriptive representation). But that is precisely what has to be worked out.[28]

What, then, does "an equal right to run for office" mean? At a minimum, a right to run for office appears to be dichotomous: either one is *permitted* to run or one is *forbidden* to run. By this view, an *equal* right to

---

[27] I thank David Estlund for sharing this objection.
[28] I thank Estlund and members of the Brown political philosophy workshop for their comments on a version of this argument presented there in October 2006.

run for all citizens would be realized when every citizen had the permission to run. But treating this right as dichotomous would separate it from the treatment of other political rights that are considered by reference to their *enjoyment* and not mere *permission*. To use a close analogy, it would not be sufficient to grant every citizen the permission to vote without considering whether other systematic or institutional factors restricted the enjoyment of that right. The equality we care about refers to citizens having an equal ability to actually cast a vote. Equal voting rights, and equal rights to run, constitute two parts – permission and enjoyment. A similar approach should apply to this right.

What then does it mean to equalize the enjoyment of a right to run for office? For one thing, it does *not* mean that all citizens have *an equal probability of success*, for this would make an equal right to run identical to an *equal right to serve*. Further, we must find an articulation of this right that does not impinge on a voter's ability to use their own internal judgments to determine for whom to vote, even though these rules (such as "vote for the most competent") may radically reduce the probability of success for many candidates.

I want to propose that the enjoyment of an equal right to run means equalizing the effect of external constraints on each candidate's probability of success; or, in terms we developed in Section II, a set of institutions in which no voter-exogenous qualifications for office existed. Institutional rules should treat citizens equally who choose to run *or* compensate for external social factors that leave citizens unequally situated relative to these external constraints. In more formal terms, an *equal* right to run for office means that voter-exogenous probabilities of success must be equal *prior to being filtered, unequally, by internal voter judgment*.

To put this more formally, then, an equal right to run for office entails the following:

Equal Right to Run for Office = For every elective office with authority over any individual citizen or with the authority to vote on laws that will govern the citizen:

i) the citizen must be legally permitted to run for office;

and

ii) the citizen's voter-exogenous probability of success in her run for office must be equal to any other citizen's.

As I said above, the first clause expresses a necessary but insufficient condition: an equal right to run for office must at least entail the permission to run. The key provision is the second clause, particularly its specification of a "voter-exogenous probability of success." I will treat this now at some length.

In any given election, many factors will affect a candidate's probability of success. Taller, conventionally attractive, and articulate candidates will stand a better chance than shorter, inarticulate, and conventionally unattractive candidates. Candidates whose views are closer to a majority of voters may be more likely to win than those whose views are farther from a majority of voters. And if you live in a district that has a majority of African-Americans, being black increases your probability of success. Of these kinds of factors, we can distinguish those that result primarily from voter judgment (i.e. internal voter constraints) versus those that result primarily from rules that are external to voter judgment (even if they are written with voter judgments in mind). So, for example, of the factors I have just listed, all except gerrymandering are factors that are endogenous to voters – the *reason* that taller, articulate, and conventionally attractive candidates have a better probability of winning is due almost entirely to voter preference for these things. By contrast, the reason that African-Americans stand a better probability of winning in a black electoral district is a combination of voter-endogenous and voter-exogenous factors: (i) voters prefer to vote for someone of their own race (voter-endogenous); and (ii) electoral laws group similar races together (voter-exogenous). So, "voter-exogenous probability of success" simply means the probability of success given the rules that shape electoral contests.

Focusing on exogenous factors means that the use by voters of internal systematic rules (such as "only vote for Republicans") to choose candidates does not constitute a presumptive violation of a citizen's right to run for office. And this corresponds to our notion of what modern representative government entails vis-à-vis democratic exclusion and distinction, and now makes clear the importance of that initial discussion. As we saw above, representative government is a distinctive form because it allows for such distinctions to be made. And often these distinctions (such as "vote for the most competent") are advisable, should be encouraged, and arguably justify representative government as preferable to direct democracies. But even when voters use *bad* rules to decide for whom to vote – rules that are unjust or ill informed – it seems inappropriate to describe this activity as a violation of another citizen's right to run for office. When a voter is a racist, or sexist, or merely votes with an eye to his own good despite the harm it will cause the whole, it expresses the venality, ignorance, or simply unjustness of voters, but it is not an obvious violation of anyone's right to run. So an equal right to run for office is thus consistent with formal systematic rules that voters may use internally to limit their own choice set in exercising their judgment about for whom to vote. An equal right to run is violated only by systematic rules exogenous to voter judgment that alter the probability of one kind of candidate winning a contest. Put simply, qualifications for office always violate the equal right to run for office at the heart of any plausible account of democratic legitimacy. However, they may at times be used to counterbalance other voter-exogenous qualifications.

The distinction here maps closely onto the conceptual distinction between justice and legitimacy: conceptually, a citizen may rely on bad judgment to choose for whom to vote without that choice being *obviously* illegitimate for the use of that bad judgment. This could happen, for example, if the legitimacy of an outcome was merely a question of consensual procedures and nothing else. Of course, one may, with Dworkin and Shapiro, believe that in practice and substance these two concepts are intertwined. But conceptually I take them to denote very different things. Legitimacy here specifies the conditions under which the state has a moral right to make and enforce its rules. Justice specifies the kinds of rules and political behavior (including voting) that are morally good. And while one may in fact be required for the other, this is a contingent fact not a necessary one.

IV.   Conclusion

Quotas and qualifications for office stand not merely to structure the legislature but to undo the democratic nature of any polity. Qualifications for office may secure some principles of justice at a direct cost to two presumptive political rights at the core of democratic institutions: that voters have a right to elect whomever they want to rule them; and that citizens have a political right to offer themselves to rule. To illustrate the problem in extremis, we might endorse the qualification that limits all offices to those with the DNA of Smith, Jones, and Cooper. Although this might be a just policy (Smith, Jones, and Cooper are really good, smart, and decent people), it is insufficiently democratic to be endorsable. Do current qualifications that restrict in a less dramatic but no less limiting way, whose intention is purportedly different from earlier exclusionary institutions, violate similar principles or not?

The purpose of this chapter was to clear the conceptual and normative ground required to answer such a question: to provide a conceptually precise definition of qualifications for office, explain how they connect to foundational principles of representative government, and articulate the basic problems that qualifications for office pose for democratic theory. As I have argued, qualifications are usefully conceptualized as the assignment of differential probabilities of success among candidates. As a normative matter, we should be concerned with voter-exogenous qualifications because they always violate two presumptive democratic rights: a voter's right to an unrestricted choice set for voting; and a citizen's equal right to run for any office that makes and enforces laws over them. As I have argued, I do not presume that these are inviolable rights: legitimate democracies may well want to violate these rights in pursuit of other normative ends.[29] But framing these institutions by reference to their rights violations is a first step in figuring out precisely when their abrogation is justified.

The starting point of any subsequent analysis should be a presumption against the use of qualifications in favor instead of unlimited constraints for voters, and for citizens to run for office. Because the right to run for office, and the right to vote for whomever one wants, are core democratic rights – political rights that accrue to a citizen on account of their being a citizen of a liberal democracy – then qualifications for office must be justified not merely by reference to their purported pragmatic benefits (to secure voice, political maturity, correspondence with a constituency, etc.), but against the costs to democratic legitimacy that are involved in their use at any time. To put it in the more familiar terms of the right to vote, even if limiting voting rights to an elite class of citizens *would* produce better and more just outcomes, this alone would not justify limiting the vote to that elite group.[30] If qualifications are to be used, we need instead to justify them against their democratic costs.

The next step is to consider the conditions under which such rights violations are justified, and to do so in a manner that is consistent with democratic principles. In the international debate about qualifications these normative costs have been underemphasized. Instead, qualifications and quotas are defended by reference either to derision of voter judgment (voters are said to be sexist, racist, or stupid) or to principles of justice (e.g. correcting for past oppression; combatting current voter discrimination; better law). Such violations may be justified for these reasons. Doing so entails a preference for justice (as we now conceive it) over

---

[29] I have argued elsewhere that equal voting rights are of trivial value when framed consequentially ("one-person-one-vote"; "make votes count"), as many advocates of alternative voting systems do (Rehfeld 2005: 192–7).

[30] But see Estlund (2007) for the oppposite view. Some might argue that universal suffrage is itself pragmatically recommendable. That may be true and may be an additional reason to grant universal suffrage. But it is incidental to the point: the right to vote is guaranteed by reference to a non-instrumental commitment to political equality and not simply because of the policy outcomes it may or may not produce. I acknowledge here that this appears to commit me to a certain non-consequentialist account of rights. I would say this is an appearance only – I think it is consequentially useful to act as if these rights were non-consequentialist, and this is ultimately why I think such an account and framework are useful. I do acknowledge the familiar bag of worms this opens, and cannot adequately address it in the context of this chapter.

democracy. Or qualifications may be defensible to correct for inescapable tradeoffs involved in public choice. Whether these tradeoffs are worth it depends on having a clear picture of how qualifications function and their precise democratic costs.

BIBLIOGRAPHY

Baldez, Lisa. 2004. "Elected Bodies: The Gender Quota Law for Legislative Candidates in Mexico." *Legislative Studies Quarterly* 29 (May): 231–58.

Beitz, Charles R. 1989. *Political Equality: An Essay in Democratic Theory*. Princeton, NJ: Princeton University Press.

Christiano, Thomas. 1996. *Rule of the Many*. Boulder, CO: Westview Press.

Constant, Benjamin. 1988. "The Liberty of the Ancients Compared with that of the Moderns," in *Benjamin Constant: Political Writings*, ed. Biancamaria Fontana. Cambridge: Cambridge University Press, 308–28.

Dahl, Robert. 1991. *Democracy and its Critics*. New Haven, CT: Yale University Press.

Dahlerup, Drude (ed.). 2006. *Women, Quotas and Politics*. New York: Routledge.

Dworkin, Ronald. 2000. *Sovereign Virtue: The Theory and Practice of Equality*. Cambridge, MA: Harvard University Press.

Estlund, David. 2007. *Democratic Authority: A Philosophical Framework*. Princeton, NJ: Princeton University Press.

Goodin, Robert. 1995. *Utilitarianism as a Public Philosophy*. New York: Cambridge University Press.

Guizot, François. 2002. *The History of the Origins of Representative Government in Europe*, trans. Aurelian Craiutu. Indianapolis, IN: Liberty Press.

Gutmann, Amy, and Dennis Thompson. 1996. *Democracy and Disagreement*. Cambridge, MA: Belknap Press.

Harrington, James. 1992 [1656]. *The Commonwealth of Oceana*. New York: Cambridge University Press.

Holmes, Stephen. 1995. *Passions and Constraint*. Chicago: University of Chicago Press.

Hume, David. 1987. "Idea of a Perfect Commonwealth," in *Essays: Moral Political and Literary*, ed. Eugene F. Miller. Indianapolis, IN: Liberty Fund, 512–29.

James, Michael. 2004. *Deliberative Democracy and the Plural Polity*. Lawrence: University of Kansas Press.

Keyssar, Alexander. 2000. *The Right to Vote: The Contested History of Democracy in the United States, with a New Afterword*. New York: Basic Books.

Kittilson, Miki Caul. 2006. *Challenging Parties, Changing Parliaments: Women and Elected Office in Contemporary Western Europe*. Columbus: Ohio State University Press.

Krook, Mona. 2006. "Reforming Representation: The Diffusion of Candidate Gender Quotas Worldwide." *Politics and Gender* 2 (3): 303–27.

  2009. *Quotas for Women in Politics: Gender and Candidate Selection Reform Worldwide*. New York: Oxford University Press.

Kymlicka, Will. 1996. *Multicultural Citizenship*. New York: Oxford University Press.

Lerner, Ralph. 1995. "Giving Voice." Paper presented at the Giornate Atlantiche di Storia Constituzionale, Laboratorio di Storia Constituzionale "Antoine Barnave," Università degli Studi di Macerata.

Lublin, David. 1997. *The Paradox of Representation*. Princeton, NJ: Princeton University Press.

McCormick, John. 2006. "Contain the Wealthy and Patrol the Magistrates: Restoring Elite Accountability to Popular Government." *American Political Science Review* 100 (2): 147–63.

MacGilvray, Eric. 2004. *Reconstructing Public Reason*. New York: Harvard University Press.

Madison, James. 1961 [1787–8]. *The Federalist*, ed. Jacob E. Cooke. Middletown, CT: Wesleyan University Press.

Manin, Bernard. 1997. *The Principles of Representative Government*. New York: Cambridge University Press.

Mansbridge, Jane J. 1999. "Should Blacks Represent Blacks And Women Represent Women? A Contingent 'Yes.'" *Journal of Politics* 61 (3): 628–57.

   2003. "Rethinking Representation." *American Political Science Review* 97 (4): 515–28.

Mill, John Stuart. 1991 [1861]. *Considerations on Representative Government*. Amherst: Prometheus Books.

Opello, K. A. R. 2006. *Gender Quotas, Parity Reform, and Political Parties in France*. Lanham, MD: Lexington Books.

Pettit, Philip. 1997. *Republicanism: A Theory of Freedom and Government*. Oxford: Clarendon Press.

Phillips, Anne. 1995. *The Politics of Presence*. New York: Oxford University Press.

Phillips, Herbert. 1921. *The Development of the Residential Qualification for Representatives in Colonial Legislatures*. Cincinnati, OH: Abingdon Press.

Pitkin, Hanna Fenichel. 1967. *The Concept of Representation*. Berkeley: University of California Press.

Rakove, Jack. 1996. *Original Meanings: Politics and Ideas in the Making of the Constitution*. New York: Alfred A. Knopf.

Rawls, John. 1971. *A Theory of Justice*. Cambridge, MA: Harvard University Press.

   1993. *Political Liberalism*. New York: Columbia University Press.

Rehfeld, Andrew. 2002. "Representation," in *Dictionary of American History*. New York: Charles Scribner's Sons.

   2005. *The Concept of Constituency: Political Representation, Democratic Legitimacy and Institutional Design*. New York: Cambridge University Press.

   2006. "Towards a General Theory of Political Representation." *Journal of Politics* 68 (1): 1–21.

   2008. "Extremism in Moderation: A Response to my Critics." *Polity* 40 (2): 254–71.

   2009. "Representation Rethought: Trustees, Delegates and Gyroscopes in the Study of Political Representation and Democracy." *American Political Science Review* 102 (2): 214–30.

Schwartzberg, Melissa. 2007. *Democracy and Legal Change*. New York: Cambridge University Press.

Shapiro, Ian. 1996. *Democracy's Place*. Ithaca, NY: Cornell University Press.

Smith, Rogers. 1996. *Civic Ideals*. New Haven, CT: Yale University Press.

Waldron, Jeremy. 2002. *God, Locke, and Equality: Christian Foundations in Locke's Political Thought*. Cambridge: Cambridge University Press.

Webster, Daniel. 1903 [1820]. "Testimony Before the Massachusetts Constitutional Convention," in *The Writings and Speeches of Daniel Webster*. Boston: Little, Brown: vol. III, 3–7.

Williams, Melissa S. 1998. *Voice, Trust, and Memory*. Princeton, NJ: Princeton University Press.

Young, Iris Marion. 1990. *Justice and the Politics of Difference*. Princeton, NJ: Princeton University Press.

2000. *Inclusion and Democracy*. Oxford: Oxford University Press.

Part V

Preferences, persuasion, and democratic representation

10 Electoral representation and the aristocratic thesis

John Ferejohn and Frances Rosenbluth

I.   Introduction

A modern democracy is conducted by a small body of elected officials who make the laws and control the state. This fact has been taken by some to mean that modern democracy is really a kind of elite rule. In its strong form, this claim implies that modern democratic governments pursue the interests of an elite or aristocracy; the weak form claims no more than the evident fact that government is run by a relatively narrow class of people and leaves open the question of whose interests may be served by this arrangement. Strong form elite theorists do not necessarily reject the possibility that the people may have some influence in picking and choosing which parts of the elite class control government. But they typically stress how weak and ineffective such controls are, especially when it comes to getting the elite to pursue public interests. If public interests are served, on the strong account, they are served gratuitously, by leaders who happen to be publically motivated, and not because of any strong incentive leaders may have to govern for the people.

Versions of the elitist view were stated by Schumpeter years ago and have been developed in various ways by Przeworski, Manin, and Dunn. The emphases of these theories vary quite a bit but all concur in seeing elections as devices for picking an elite and not an instrument by which the people exercise real control over these leaders. All of them reject the democratic idea that government is, in any intelligible sense, "by" the people. The core idea shared by these thinkers – that a government of elected representatives is necessarily aristocratic in some sense – is quite ancient, dating back at least to Aristotle. And the common conclusion of this view is that electoral democracy is really nothing at all like direct democracy as was practiced, for example, by the Athenians.

Two typical complaints about Athenian-style direct democracy are often run together but they are independent of one another. One, attributable to Thucydides, is that democratic rule is turbulent and unstable. Emblematic of this worry is the example he gives of the Athenian assembly deciding to put an uppity city to the sword and then, a few hours later, reversing the decision, dispatching a fast ship to stop the slaughter. Another example was the rash decision to attack Syracuse. The idea is that there is something about direct rule by a large assembly that makes it vulnerable to demagogic oratory and other kinds of deliberative failures. Madison summarized this worry when he remarked that even if the Athenian assembly was made up of copies of Socrates it would still have been a mob.

The second complaint, due to Aristotle, is that direct democracy is rule by the poor who are more numerous, and it systematically reflects their class interest. Democracy's defect on this account is not that it is willful or arbitrary but that it is biased to prefer one part of the city. These two complaints, while they may be held by the same person (as they were in the case of Madison, for example), would seem to have different kinds of remedies.

For the first complaint – turbulence, unsteadiness, emotionality – the best remedy according to Kant (and Montesquieu and Madison among others) was to ensure that government is indirect or conducted by representatives, rather than by the sovereign people themselves.[1] Many writers hoped that in an indirect or representative government power would be exercised by a better sort of person – by those skilled in leadership, or at least by educated people, or people who specialized in government. But many of them thought that, even if none of that was true, indirect government would minimize or eliminate appeals to the public that might corrode governmental stability and rule of law. Arguably, changes in Athenian government in the fourth century provide an example: while every citizen could attend the assembly or be selected to most executive offices, certain kinds of vital decisions (military and financial) were reserved to elected magistrates. In this respect even democratic Athens came to practice a degree of indirect government.

The second complaint may require a different sort of remedy. Assuming the poor are actually a majority, Aristotle thought that either the electoral franchise ought to be restricted, or else that the other interests in the city be given some voice or check on what policies should be pursued.[2] Essentially, each of these is a strategy of representation: in the first case, by disenfranchising some of the poor, political representation

---

[1] The sovereign we are speaking of here is, of course, the people, but Kant saw that the argument also implied that a monarchy, if it is to avoid despotism, ought to work through representatives rather than through the direct imposition of the will of the monarch.

[2] There is a third option. The majority may be motivated to pursue common rather than class interests but it seems unrealistic to rely on that motivation in designing political institutions of a large heterogeneous polity.

will tend to weigh the interests of the wealthy more heavily. The second strategy gives institutional roles to people with wealth that permit them to project and protect their interests; in this sense the wealthy are over-represented in the corridors of power. This second strategy amounts to a kind of mixed government strategy and is exemplified by the system of institutional checks of the kind that Polybius admired in the Roman constitution.

The strategy of mixed government has been especially attractive in modern democratic conditions where franchise restrictions are generally hard to justify. Aristotle himself proposed both strategies at various points in the *Politics*, sometimes favoring a restriction on citizenship, and some-times favoring a kind of mixed democracy. And many other classical and modern writers have done so as well. Interestingly, one of the institutions that Aristotle thought could help moderate democracy into a good form of government (*politeia*) was election. So for Aristotle it seems that the two evils of democracy – turbulence and class bias – may yield to the same remedy.

While the idea of a government conducted by elected representatives has become commonplace in the modern world, it has two distinct fea-tures that Madison, Rousseau, and many others have noticed. First, if representatives are drawn from an elite class, they may pursue the inter-ests of that elite, at least to some extent. This is, of course, exactly what those who favored mixed government anticipated and endorsed. Second, and more problematically, whether or not representatives come from a distinct social class, they may themselves constitute a class of a certain kind and would be expected to some extent to pursue their own interests at least some of the time. If they do, then there is a natural sense in which we could understand representatives to be a kind of oligarchy, united in pursuing their own interests rather that those of the public. Nowadays we call this a problem of agency, and it seems to us to form an alternative basis for the aristocratic hypothesis.

Political representation is prone to a distinctive class of agency prob-lems for several reasons. In ordinary agency relations the concern is to design a "contract" – or incentive system – for agents who want to pursue private remuneration or leisure. This is ordinarily done by establishing a system of rewards and punishments for the agent which are condi-tioned on some measure of her actions. But the actions of political agents are very hard to observe, and elections, the typical way of disciplining political agents, are a crude and imperfect way to control officials; they happen infrequently and they can usually only punish or reward officials by withholding or awarding office. Second, representatives have a wide range of possible motivations: like ordinary agents they may desire to increase their own wealth and leisure but they may also desire to pursue ideological goals. Finally, there is a reluctance on the part of many people to see elected representatives as employees hired to pursue the interests of the public. Elected officials of course foster this view, claiming not to be mere servants but to be leaders who symbolize the dignity of the public and who ought to be trusted to exercise their own vision and resourcefulness.[3] Such deferential attitudes towards elected officials may further limit the kinds of electoral "contracts" that are available for selecting and incentivizing leaders; and they may limit the willingness of voters to enforce such contracts by punishing poor behavior. For these reasons, elected representatives usually have a great deal of latitude to pursue their own goals. On the surface, then, there appears be a great opportunity for a kind of aristocratic rule – rule by elected officials – under the cloak of nominally democratic procedures.

There are, however, countervailing forces. Because elective office offers so many attractive options, we expect there to be intense competition for it. In equilibrium, we expect the value of office to be dissipated in this competition; indeed, in some models, one would expect aspirants to willingly incur in campaign costs the full expected value of the office, discounted by their chance of winning it. Or they might promise post-election benefits that would reduce their (private) value of winning office. Aspiring office-holders might be expected to provide benefits to electors such as by bribing them with favors prior to the election, as was described in Lewis Namier's (1929) wonderful study of eighteenth-century England. Mark Kishlansky (1981) has documented such activities in the previous century, as has Gordon Wood (1991) during the early years of the American republic. More generally, we expect campaigns to be based on promises of future rewards for voters, sometimes private, sometimes public. Such practices will not always benefit voters, but they will tend to erode any gains from office that might otherwise accrue to the elected officials. Rather, policies are likely be chosen that will please those who have effective control over access to office such as contributors and activists.

---

[3] Perhaps this phenomenon is not confined to political agents. Potential agents have a generic incentive to reduce interagent competition, and to some extent high-status agents (usually labeled "professionals") have succeeded in getting state assistance in doing this by imposing entry restrictions in the form of licensing or training requirements. Such professional requests are always, more or less plausibly, based on concerns to protect the health or safety of the public (i.e. the potential principals), but they invariably result in conceding more freedom of action for agents. Often part of the price for getting the public to go along with such regulations is a more or less credible commitment on the part of the profession to self-regulate by means of a code of conduct or something of that sort.

The point is that competition can limit the capacity of the elected officials to rule in their own interest.

The thrust of our argument is not, on balance, very supportive of any strong form of the aristocratic hypothesis. While political agents have a great deal of scope for autonomy while in office, they are unlikely to gain much from it. The potential agency gains are liable to be competed away by other aspirants to public office.[4] Instead, political agency is likely to favor those in society – voters and contributors – who have a comparative advantage in monitoring the actions of representatives. Insofar as there is a political aristocracy, it is to be found in those privileged principals rather than among the agents.

II.   Democracy

Definitions of democracy are inherently controversial because any definition involves value judgments. One kind of definition focuses on particular institutions and how they function. In the classical period the focus was on the use of lottery to choose officials, and direct rule by popular assemblies. More recently, many have followed Dahl (1971) in requiring well-functioning competitive elections as the defining feature. Another approach emphasizes democracy's connection with equality and requires that everyone have an equal opportunity to rule. (Aristotle's notion was that democracy is a system in which everyone takes turns ruling and being ruled.) As we want to leave open the possibility that a government of elected officials may (or may not) be democratic, our definition of democracy focuses on whose interests guide governmental policy. We claim that a government is democratic if its policies reliably track the interests of a majority, and that this tracking is accomplished through the agency of the citizens.

In a representative government, our definition requires that government policy generally follows the public's opinion about what its interests are, at least at times before elections. Political leaders may to some extent shape or persuade the public, but if they fail at this, leaders may have to give up on a policy altogether – at least eventually. Other background conditions must of course be satisfied as well so that the desires of the majority may reasonably be counted as expressing the views of a large part of the people as a whole. The specifics here seem historically variable but nowadays we would insist that both the franchise and

---

[4] This suggests that those who have good outside opportunities have little reason to choose a career as a representative, so that selection into the political occupation may be drawn from among the others.

eligibility for office be open to (virtually) every adult, that information circulate quite freely, that elections are frequent, and that votes be counted equally.

Admittedly this definition is weaker than the idea that the people rule themselves directly, as the Athenians were supposed to have done when they determined policy in their popular assembly or decided verdicts in their popular courts. But, as we emphasized above, even the Athenians eventually chose to leave the most important matters to elected officials, and they also relied extensively on mechanisms of legal accountability to ensure that, generally speaking, all officials (however they were chosen) had reason to act for the general interest.[5] Our definition is not the mere requirement that policy track the interests of a majority or of the people as a whole. That might as well be accomplished by a wise, poll-taking, and benevolent monarch. We insist that the best account of why policy tracks majority or popular interests must be that voters have some way of motivating their leaders to take their opinions as to their interests into account. This implies that leaders have reason to pay attention to what the voters actually want (their opinions) and not only what is thought to be best for them (their interests). Democracy can be a poor form of government if citizens tend to have defective views about what is in their own interests and if its policies therefore do not reflect their real interests. This is, in fact, what Schumpeter and Aristotle thought.[6]

How leaders will respond to public opinion depends on the structure of the democracy in question. Elected officials may, in some systems, be held personally accountable before voters in single-member districts (or open-list systems), or be collectively responsible to them as members of a party. Either way, as long as voters have a real opportunity to demand such an account at regular intervals, we would say the system is democratic. This opportunity must be real, of course. Elected officials or parties must face a prospect of losing office and this "reality" test implies that elections

---

[5] The use of mechanisms of accountability in Athens was ubiquitous and far more pervasive than anything in the modern world. For one thing, the terms of office were very short – only a year – and there was a requirement that officials be examined before assuming office, and especially upon leaving it. Then too, officials could be impeached before the assembly or before the courts. And anyone carrying out a public function, whether elected as an official or selected by lot, or simply acting on his own initiative to push a proposal before the assembly, was subject to legal liability before the courts. Finally, there was always the possibility that someone (any citizen) could simply be ostracized for no stated reason at all, though as far as we know the reason almost always amounted to getting "too big for one's britches."

[6] This was also Churchill's view when he remarked in 1945 upon being voted out of office, "In my country the people can do as they like, although it often happens that they don't like what they have done" (Gilbert 2007: 864).

must generally be competitive.[7] And what that requires depends on the institutional structure in various ways. But if those conditions are fulfilled, it seems to us that a system could be democratic while being governed by a small class of potential aspirants for office. That small class might well be described as an aristocracy in some circumstances, such as if membership in it were determined by heredity or wealth or education. What is critical is that each leader or party be genuinely vulnerable to the judgments of the electorate.

We think it is a ubiquitous fact about modern democracies that positions of leadership are precarious. While journalists often complain of an insulated and protected political class, the fact is that public officials are always in danger of losing their jobs, and they know it. If you want to be, or remain, in public office you need public approval, and no matter how far you have debased yourself in its pursuit, you can never be sure that you have enough to survive the next test. Fear of losing office is an existential fact of political life. We need only recall a few prominent political careers, such as that of Richard Nixon, to see how realistic that fear is, and to imagine the lengths to which leaders might go to cope with it. American scholars of congressional elections have long observed that nearly every congressman has, at one time or another, suffered defeat or at least a close call that she did not expect. From the perspective of governing officials in a democracy, then, public life is characteristically a treacherous business. Perhaps this is less so today than for the Athenians: Themistocles, the creator of the fleet that destroyed the Persian armies and brought about the possibility of a vast Athenian empire, was ostracized from the city. And even Pericles himself suffered the loss of office. The point is that, in a democracy, political leaders can never forget that they serve at the pleasure of a fickle and unpredictable master.

This "democratic condition" implies that even if politicians as a class share some interests in common, which of course they do, it is exceedingly dangerous for them to try to pursue these interests if that pursuit would risk support among the people. Moreover, even if elected and appointed officials share some interests, the democratic condition forces them to compete with each other for scarce political rewards, and this gives them reason to undercut and double-cross each other. Elected officials may be described as an aristocracy in virtue of possessing or seeming to possess

---

[7] It is too much to ask that every election be genuinely competitive; rather what is required is that control of government be competitive among parties or leaders. Therefore, as is the case in all democracies, the seats of many backbench members of parliament may be quite securely held even if control of government is insecure.

rare and valuable skills, but they are likely to have a very hard time converting these advantages into personal or class gains. That is not to say they cannot succeed, but success in pursuing private interests is not guaranteed, and from a certain perspective looks doubtful.

III.   Representation

As our purpose is to analyze a feature of representative government rather than studying representation in general, we shall not follow Pitkin's (1967) lead in trying to unravel the concept of representation.[8] We shall work instead with a stipulative definition that we think illuminates the "core" aspects of political representation. Specifically, we take what Pitkin calls a formalistic view and focus on the relationships of authorization and accountability to try to understand the constraints on official representatives and ask whether or in what sense representatives can be characterized as an elite. There are two separate ideas here: a person is authorized to act for a group by being given authority prior to taking action. Moreover, a person is accountable for her actions on behalf of a group if she can be rewarded or punished for those actions if they fail to respond to the group's interests (by some entity, not necessarily by the group itself).

The authorization/accountability view significantly narrows our focus, in that it marginalizes certain normative claims that may work within practices of representation, such as the idea that a representative is supposed to mirror the represented. But such views are only marginalized as potential definitions. There may still be reasons for a representative to try to, or claim to, mirror her constituents in some way or other.[9] Doing so may help her to get selected and to hold onto office, or even to make wise decisions. And it may make her constituents more inclined to take her words and acts as authoritative for them.

Election is one way that a representative may be authorized. Representatives could, alternatively, be appointed as Senators are in Canada, or selected by lotteries as in classical Athens, or inherit their office as do members of the House of Lords. Such officials are rightly regarded as representatives as long as it is accepted that those chosen owe duties to

---

[8] We take the analysis in her book to demonstrate the extreme difficulty of such an endeavor. In any case, if it is true that representation is essentially contested, any such effort must fail.

[9] In fact, the agency view can illuminate such appeals by showing when they might be persuasive. If potential agents can differ in the degree to which they resemble principals, perhaps in the sense of sharing their preferences, there is a competitive reason for each of them to be seen as similar to the principal as possible.

advance certain interests of the represented in appropriate contexts.[10] To be a representative is, in this sense, to be selected according to a conventionally accepted scheme and thereby to be embedded in a certain kind of normative relationship with a group.[11] This normative relationship may be to represent the desires or opinions of the group (to act as its ambassador or delegate) or to represent its interests (to act as a trustee).

A representative may be accountable for his failure to fulfill his normative obligation to represent. Duties to represent might be enforced, if they are enforced at all, directly by those to whom the duties are owed – in which case the representative is made accountable before the represented – or they may be enforced by whoever has the authority to select the representative. For example, while a representative may have a duty to pursue the common interests of the people, she may be selected by voters in a particular geographic district. This is another form of political accountability. As before, the representative is or is not reelected according to the will of a majority. Alternatively, as in the case of fiduciary duties, duties might be enforced by a third party or by courts of law, according to some legal or normative standard.[12] We call this an instance

[10] Regarding representation as a normative relation of a certain kind has the additional advantage of making sense of "informal" claims to represent, such as when someone claims to speak for a group or subset of the population. Such claims remain informal because there is no accepted convention for conferring authority, and because informal representatives are not entitled to exercise state authority.

[11] We are employing an interpretive construct here in order to facilitate institutional comparisons. If a people has a set of practices that can best be explained by positing their possession of a unified concept that supports the idea, then they actually have something like that concept even if they have no single word for it. For example, the Athenians had an extraordinary range of practices of holding public figures to account. They required magistrates (whether selected by lottery or election) to give an ex post account of their official behavior before a court (and sometimes in the assembly as well). They exposed anyone proposing decrees or laws to public law prosecutions. And they exposed everyone to ostracism (and this must have been most dangerous for public leaders). Moreover, the content of these interrogations – the questions posed – appeared to relate mostly to whether the official had acted in ways that served the common interests of the city as expressed in its laws. That the magistrates and other public figures owed duties to act in the interest of the city, and that, in addition, these duties were enforced through making them accountable to the people, suggests that the magistrates were expected to act as representatives. This is obviously a kind of functional definition and is situation-specific.

[12] Legal accountability is one mode of enforcement, and traces of it remain in impeachment procedures in modern polities. The Athenian requirement was not only legal but also popular or political since the courts were popular institutions without professional judges or lawyers. Modern systems tend to rely mostly on political rather than legal accountability, a practice the Athenians had largely abandoned by the end of the fourth century. Impeachment and criminal sanction remain supplementary forms of accountability relations as well, even if they are used rarely in practice. We emphasize that duties may not be enforceable at all: duties can sensibly exist that cannot be enforced. Moral duties are an example. Where duties cannot be enforced or enforced very well, it is important that the people select representatives who are likely to have a kind of moral

of "legal" accountability. When an agent is politically accountable to the represented, the representatives are free to decide to retain her or not, according to their will. When an agent is legally accountable before a tribunal, the agent may be removed only for cause: for failing to perform up to some legal or normative standard. Persuasive reasons have to be given to the tribunal to justify the removal.

Traces of legal accountability remain in the impeachment procedures in modern polities, and in the fact that political officials are not completely immune to prosecution for criminal acts. But mostly modern governments rely on political accountability to select and de-select representatives. We can appreciate this by contrasting it with Athenian practices. Democratic Athens required its officials and other public actors to account for their actions in legal as well as political forums and, after 403 BC the balance was heavily toward legal rather than political accountability. Their courts were themselves popular institutions without professional judges or lawyers, so the difference between the two forms is perhaps less sharply etched than in modern polities.[13] But they did retain some distinctly political forms, permitting impeachment before the assembly and ostracism as well.[14]

We emphasize that some duties may not be enforceable at all. Moral duties often are not. Indeed, we think representatives have moral duties to constituents even if, and especially if, their actions cannot be observed by their constituents. Where duties to represent cannot be enforced or enforced very well, the people have reason to select representatives who are likely to have some kind of internal motivation to pursue their interests. Perhaps this is best done by choosing representatives whose private interest and/or ideology are correlated somehow with the public interest they are to serve. But perhaps there is a residual need for public officials to have moral motivations.

The expression "representative" government is usually used to refer to a government made up of representatives selected according to

motivation to pursue their interests. Perhaps this is best done by choosing representatives whose private interest is correlated somehow with the public interest they are to serve.

[13] Still, there was a distinction in that legal judgments are supposed to be based on reasons (of law and fact), whereas political judgments can be more or less arbitrary.

[14] The emblematic case of this is the story of the poor and nearly illiterate farmer struggling to spell a name on a pottery shard (*ostraca*). The philosopher Aristedes (who was generally known as Aristedes the Just) asked if he could help: "Whose name are you trying to write?" The farmer replied "Aristedes." "But why?" asked the philosopher. The farmer snorted in reply, "I am sick and tired of hearing of this 'Aristedes' always being called 'the Just'." Ostracism was often aimed not so much at those who abused power or popular trust, it seems, but simply at the famous who had grown perhaps too big for the city.

conventionally accepted procedures for allocating offices. It is often used descriptively, though there are some who think that calling a government representative is a kind of praise. When "representative" is used as a qualifier of "democracy," as in the expression "representative democracy," the normative terrain is more divided: some people take it to indicate a kind of qualification or even a negation of the real thing (genuine democracy), made necessary by the scale and complexity of the modern nation-state.[15] Others regard representative government as a kind of improvement over direct democracy, either by making democracy more attractive by moderating its democratic aspect, or by making it more rational or deliberative (in Madison's expression: representatives were expected to "refine and enlarge" public opinion).

Everyone agrees that representatives, as political agents, are supposed to act in the interests of the people in settings where they are authorized to act and, as a means of achieving this, to be answerable to them in some way. But citizens have only meager means for disciplining their representatives. Representatives' actions are hard to observe; the occasions for demanding an account are few, and are shared by a heterogeneous group of people. For that reason, elected officials do not seem to be on a very tight leash. Why is this? Perhaps we think of political officials differently than we do other kinds of agents: as leaders rather than servants. Because of this we may want to provide them with a fair amount of autonomy to take the kinds of actions that might best advance our interests. So we may not insist, as we might in other agency relations, on being able to audit their actions closely.

These "distortions" in the agency relation remind us that political agency may be distinctive in permitting political agents a lot of slack or autonomy. Elite theorists, starting with Aristotle, think that giving leaders the chance to take independent action can increase the prospects for beneficial policy choices and stability in government. The distinctive slack in political agency is what makes room for the aristocratic hypothesis. Those with more popular sympathies worry that slack will allow official corruption or the capture of government by private interests. Discussions of political agency are marked therefore by controversy over how much scope should be permitted to an agent and how agency duties are best enforced or at least encouraged.

---

[15] Kant and Madison and legions of modern writers have thought representation constitutes an improvement over direct democracy because it introduces non-democratic elements in a kind of mixed government, which moderates populist impulses and produces reasonable or moderate policy. Others have argued that genuinely democratic rule must be representative for other reasons: for example, representatives are better able to deliberate effectively and to pursue common interests than the people would be.

IV.   Political agency

We argue that, suitably modified, the agency model – a version of what Pitkin has called the authorization/accountability model – captures the central aspects of formal representation.[16] We hire an official by means of an election and expect her to employ her legal authority to pursue our interests in government. We hire a private lawyer for similar reasons: we expect that lawyer to advance the interests we entrust to her within the confines of legality and professional norms. In both cases we retain some degree of control over our representative both ex ante and ex post: before the fact we make it known what we expect, sometimes implicitly by voting for the candidate who makes the most attractive offer; and after the fact we can punish or reward her for her performance. In both cases, our representative is expected to act in our interest, to be accountable to us, to warrant our trust, and to explain and justify her behavior when she appears to fall short.[17] And she runs risks of being fired or not paid (or sued) if she fails to fulfill our expectations.[18]

We do not deny, of course, that the word "representation" is used in other ways to describe other activities: as metaphor or synecdoche, as a theory of meaning or a concept of mind, or as a particular way of drawing or painting. Some thinkers have sought to put some of these other meanings on a par with the idea of representation as authorization, arguing that political representation must make sense of these other usages. Within political life, people sometimes make claims that someone can speak for another only insofar as he is "like" the other in some way. Sometimes this is applied to elected representatives and sometimes to competitors for leadership. Such claims may be persuasive in various contexts – usually they are aimed to persuade – but they are essentially normative arguments aimed at influencing action, or perhaps undercutting claimed authority, rather than conceptual claims. Moreover, such

---

[16] Pitkin's criticism of this view is that it focuses too narrowly on aspects of representation – that the agent has been given authorization to take certain actions – to the exclusion of others: she lists several including "having one's actions attributed to another" and "having the right to command another" (Pitkin 1967: 51). Neither of these is a part of the agency view at all as far as we can see, and neither seems necessarily a part of representation either, unless the principal somehow authorizes them. This may or may not occur.

[17] The best ethnographic account of this relationship, as it appears to the representative, is still Richard Fenno (1978).

[18] This does not imply that agents can easily be removed for non-performance. The typical situation in agency relations is, indeed, that some non-performance occurs in equilibrium. And we do not deny that punishment is harder in political settings, but it is hard in many non-political settings as well. The difference is not a matter of degree, and depends on specific features of the agency relationship, political or non-political.

arguments are not confined to the political realm: you might want to have as a doctor someone of your own age or gender. But those wants count only as normative reasons for choosing between doctors. In the end, the actual picking remains the crucial thing: until you actually do that you do not have a doctor at all. And once you have picked a doctor she will be authorized to make certain choices on your behalf, whether or not she happens to share your gender or age.

We used the expression "suitably modified" to signify that the kind of agency relations found in public life may differ from agency relations in the private sphere. In what we shall call the standard model, the agency "contract" provides ongoing incentives for the agent by attaching rewards or punishments to her actions. Such contracts also serve to screen or filter potential agents by making the role of agent more or less valuable to different kinds of people. There are really two distinct ideas here: agents, having different preferences than the principal, need to be given incentives to take actions that are in the principal's interest. And, some potential agents are better than others for the principal in some way: they may be more competent, more ethical, or have preferences more like those of the principal. These two ideas correspond to the "moral hazard" and "adverse selection" perspectives. In the first, the focus is on controlling an agent's actions while she is in office; in the second it is on selecting the right kind of agent in the first place.

In either case, there will normally be more slack in political agency relations than in other kinds of agency relations. One reason for this is that political principals tend to be collectivities rather than individuals. This requires that there be some way of making collective decisions – elections, for example – for resolving disputes among principals who may disagree about what they want their common agent to do. Virtually every way of making such decisions creates problems of collective action of various kinds and opportunities for agents to exploit.[19] Second, political agency "contracts" are typically crude, in that it is not only costly or impossible for voters to observe most activities done by their representatives,

---

[19] Both of these features of political agency are explored in Ferejohn (1986), in the context of a very simple model. In that paper, the principal's only way of controlling the policymaker was the possibility of firing her. Even so, as long as the policy space is one-dimensional so that there is a median voter, the principal could exert some degree of control on the agent. But in higher dimensions the agent is basically uncontrollable unless the principals could somehow agree to judge the agent using a one-dimensional performance criterion. In effect, only if the principals can solve the collective action problem and act as a kind of "person" can they hope to get the agent to pursue or represent their interests. That model was extreme in limiting the tools available to the principals to control the agent, but the logic of the situation will carry over to much more complex settings.

but it is also impossible to make rewards and punishments sensitively contingent even on observed differences. Voter opportunities for expressing disapproval are limited to infrequent elections and perhaps by some legal institutions that permit impeachment or criminal accusation.[20] So, for various reasons, we are unable to treat officials differently depending on the actions they take or the outcomes that result. Finally, political agency relations may be subject to relatively weak competitive pressures. Normally we would expect that a person would refrain from hiring an agent whose behavior she has little control over. But, as we pointed out earlier, a citizen cannot really refuse to enter the relationship if its terms seem unattractive. Such a refusal requires costly efforts at coordination.

In market settings one expects that competition among agents will lead to the creation of more attractive agency contracts – that is, contracts that can be conditioned on a finer description of events and that are more effective in motivating and screening agents. But this process is often blocked in the political sector (and it is occasionally blocked in markets as well). Why is this? Political agency relationships differ from ordinary agency relations in a way that does not really seem to track any formal feature of agency models. When someone hires an agent, one might think that a kind of hierarchical relationship is established: the agent is an employee, a hireling, whose duty it is to do what the principal wants and whose compensation depends on performance in some way. Think of hiring a person to mow your lawn or fix your car or sell your home. This model breaks down a bit in the case of high-status professions such as surgeons, but for reasons that seems to have nothing to do with the agency relation. No doubt surgeons have skills and information that permit them to do things for us that we cannot do for ourselves; and, in the course of surgery, our ability to monitor the physician's actions is probably compromised. And maybe in certain areas of surgery, the important skills are rare and there is little competition among potential agents. Anyway, someone who needs surgical services probably is in a hurry, which places further limits on competition. But these circumstances are not special to surgeons. Think of having your car break down on an isolated road with only one garage in the vicinity. Remember, a couple of centuries ago people thought of surgeons as on a par with barbers and mechanics.

---

[20] In market settings one expects that competition among agents can improve this situation. But even there, competition may not eliminate problems. The reason we see doctors and lawyers and other professionals adopting ethical codes and organizational modes of enforcing them is precisely because agency relations are imperfectly policed by incentive contracts, and potential agents seek efficiency gains through self-policing or governmental regulation.

Perhaps officials in a democracy enjoy an especially high status because, though they may be our employees, they are expected to "lead" us, to direct or command our actions. Why would that matter? Possibly, it is a matter of psychology: it may be difficult to accept orders from a subordinate, so people may psychologically "elevate" political agents, projecting onto them some undeserved superiority. Another answer is to say that elected officials are not "our" servants as collections of individuals but are servants of our collective interest. We elect them not to subordinate ourselves but because we think they have special political skills that make them better able to discern what is in our collective interest than we, as disparate individuals and groups, would be. These seem plausible enough answers, but dangerous ones, and we doubt that robust democracies could concede so much to their leaders. Another possibility, one that seems more consonant with a democratic culture, is that elected leaders enjoy a kind of democratic deference out of respect for elections: that representatives who have been chosen in orderly and fair elections may be due a special degree of respect that is traceable not to them as individuals but to the people.

The belief that political leaders are somehow above individual citizens may explain why we are reluctant to demand more effective agency contracts concerning them. This may account for why elected officials enjoy relatively long terms, why popular recall is rarely available, and why binding instructions to elected officials are almost never countenanced. To restrict the terms or employment conditions of our elected officials may be to express a kind of contempt and not only for them as officials, but also for the people who elected them. To be sure, these are all variables rather than constants because there is nothing that dictates the appropriate length of a term, for example. Therefore, if we are right, hierarchical beliefs are probably variable as well. The Athenians, for example, permitted officials to serve only a year and required them to undergo ex ante oaths as well as stringent ex post audits, and subjected them to a number of other ongoing checks on their official performance. Of course many of their officials were ordinary citizens chosen by lottery, and people may have thought they had to be kept on a short leash. But their elected officials were constrained in the same way.

It seems significant that most of the restrictions on the agency contract are not in any sense "natural," but are actually imposed on us by our political agents. Political manipulation rather than deference may explain the distance at which politicians hold voters at bay. In competitive settings one would expect agents who offer poor contract terms to disappear, so one expects agency contracts to be attractive. But typically the restrictions on political agency are imposed collectively and not individually.

286 John Ferejohn and Frances Rosenbluth

Sometimes they are placed in the constitution: the Bonn Constitution forbids binding instructions on representatives and the American Constitution has been interpreted to resist term limitations, to take two examples. More often, agents set the rules by statutes or chamber rules that govern how observable their actions are and the extent to which their rewards and punishments can be made to depend on them. These practices limit the extent to which contract terms can be subjected to competitive pressures that might force them to be more favorable to principals. Sometimes competitors do try to offer new and more attractive terms – such an offer was the basis of the "Contract with America," with its pledge of term limits and the like – but such offers are neither credible nor, if they are accepted by gullible voters, actually implemented.

V.   Representative government and aristocratic rule

Madison thought that part of the genius of American government was that it was indirect: the sovereign power, the people, had no actual role in government (*Federalist* 63). Governing is done by delegates who obtain grants of power from voters, through election, and are entitled for a period of time and within certain limits to exercise it on behalf of the people. There is no doubt that Madison thought this feature of the new Constitution – the fact that the people had no direct role in government – was not an unhappy compromise forced upon it by the size or extent of the new republic, but an essential feature of a good form of popular government.[21]

---

[21] He voiced apprehension of a direct appeal to the people in *Federalist* 49 as well, where he explained that such appeals would undermine the development of popular veneration for the new Constitution. That Madison worried about direct popular involvement does not make him anti-democratic in the way that term is used nowadays. His preference was explicitly for a republican government in which all authority was drawn directly or indirectly from the people. He thought, however, that direct popular involvement in government would undermine the possibility of stable republican government by unleashing passionate appeals to transient majority sentiment. In fact Madison went much further than this in seeking to limit the indirect influence of popular majorities in government. He thought the more dependent a government was on the people, the more dangerous it was, and the more need there was to control and check its power. The state legislatures were dangerous to liberty precisely because of their popular proximity, and the federal House of Representatives similarly dangerous, though less so, for the same reason. For that reason the legislative branch, which was necessarily close to the people, posed a powerful threat to republican rule: Madison said that the legislative "vortex" was the chronic source of turbulence, irrationality and danger to stability. His central arguments for establishing a national government (in *Federalist* 10), for federalism (in *Federalist* 45–46), for checks and balances (*Federalist* 51), all aimed at restraining popular influence. Finally, in what seems the direct expression of a desire for a kind of aristocratic rule, albeit of the republican kind associated with Rome, he argued that by adopting large

Madison was not alone in thinking that a government of representatives was to be preferred to a direct democracy. Kant also thought that democratic government – by which he meant a direct democracy – was necessarily will-driven and for that reason despotic.[22] "Every form of government that is not representative is properly speaking without form, because one and same person can no more be at one and same time the legislator and executive of his will (than the universal proposition can serve as the major premise in a syllogism at the same time as be the subsumption of the particular under it in the minor premise)" (Kant 1970 [1795]: 114). A government of representatives was much more likely to be able to act under the control of reason and therefore to be moderate or temperate.

Kant's reasons for preferring representative government have nothing to do with representatives being in some sense "better" or more virtuous than the people. Rather, his argument is based on the defining feature of indirect rule: the person who takes action – the representative – is not the one source of valuation or preference. He is an executive who acts on the interests, passions, preferences, or opinions of others rather than on his own valuations and he is, for that reason, better able to act rationally. This is a kind of separation-of-powers argument in which the passions and emotions of the people are acted on, and disciplined by, their representatives. One sees in it echoes of Plato's division of the soul (Plato 1987), where the rational part controls the appetitive and passionate parts. In that respect, it also echoes Montesquieu's idea that the separation of legislative (evaluative) and executive powers is necessary to avoid tyrannical rule, by which he meant rule by passions rather than reason. But Kant argues here for a vertical (between people and their representatives) rather than a horizontal (between departments of government) separation of powers.

Several Greek writers had already expressed similar misgivings about direct democracy. Thucydides chronicled the passionate and turbulent politics of democratic Athens during the Peloponnesian War which he attributed partly to the effects of democratic rule. Xenophon,

---

constituencies for the House of Representatives one could hope that elections would tend to choose virtuous leaders who would be likely to "refine and enlarge" on public opinion.

22 "[D]emocracy, in the proper sense of the term, is necessarily a despotism" (Kant 1970: 114). By "proper" democracy Kant meant direct democracy, and he went on to specify what was defective about direct rule (whether democratic or not). Kant, like Madison, favored a popular component in government but insisted that the authority of the people be exercised only through representatives. He went on to criticize the ancient republics – surely referring to Rome and possibly to Athens as well – for failing to understand this and therefore degenerating into despotism.

condemning the popular reaction to an attempt to introduce legal process into the famous trial of the generals, quoted an incensed member of the assembly as saying, "It is outrageous to say that the people cannot do whatever they want." Unmediated or direct democracy was seen as impulsive and subject to bouts of irrationality. Indeed, there is reason to think that even ordinary Athenians thought there was reason to temper or moderate direct rule: after the democracy was restored at the end of the fifth century, the Athenians embraced various judicial institutions that could limit and control the actions taken by the assembly.[23]

Aristotle's normative views were complex. He did not reject democracy as such but sought ways to ensure that a democratic government would act moderately. In Book VI of *Politics*, for example, he expressed admiration for an agrarian democracy in which most of the people lived outside the city and were too busy farming to take much interest in politics, and would therefore prefer to use elections to select their leaders (rather than choosing them by lottery as the Athenians did).[24] He had already defined democracy as a kind of government in which the citizens actually rule in some direct sense, whether they take turns ruling as in a good constitution, or rule at the same time as in Athens. He did not expect either kind of direct rule in an agrarian democracy. Elections would be employed to choose magistrates and would select only certain kinds of people into office. Possibly these would be especially able or wealthy which might conduce to a better government. In any case, electing the able or the wealthy would recruit them into public service rather than leaving them outside of government where they could cause trouble. We imagine that he thought it a saving feature of Athenian democratic practice that some of its officials – the most important ones – were chosen by election rather than by lottery.[25] That, at least, permitted the selection of officials with

---

[23] Even in the heyday of direct democracy in the fifth century, Athenian government had important elements of mixture that incorporated the rich and upper middle-class governmental institutions. Election of the generals was an important kind of mixing – the generals tended to come from those who had military or naval equipment and experience as far as we know – as was the extension of elections to choose financial officers.

[24] Aristotle (1962: Book VI, ch. 4).

[25] While we present the argument from "competence" here it is by no means clear that that is the reason the Athenians used elections to pick generals throughout their history, and to pick financial magistrates in the fourth century. It may also be that elections allowed the state to harness potentially dangerous people with private armies. The powerful families that produced Themistocles, Cleisthenes, Pericles, and others would have been a danger to the state if they were not in its service. Indeed, Themistocles ended his life in exile. The oligarchic coups of 411 and 404 were led by such people who may have been eclipsed or threatened by parvenus. And the creation of elected financial offices may have been an attempt to enlist wealth-holders in the service of the state rather than any recognition of competence or superiority.

the ability to make reasoned policy decisions in complex and dangerous policy domains, though it did not guarantee that they would.

Later thinkers, such as Schumpeter, have put a somewhat different spin on their preference for a government of representatives. Schumpeter (1942) thought that ordinary people, being unfamiliar with political life and issues of public policy, would be incompetent to make reasonable political choices. Public officials may or may not be talented in this respect but their day-to-day experience would at least lead them to acquire some skills relevant to governing. So he argued that the people ought to confine their involvement in politics to choosing a government and perhaps removing it later if they did not like the results. While he did not argue this directly, he probably thought that the comparative advantage of elected elites partly explains why it is that modern democracy takes the representative form that it does.

We imagine a representative government can become a system of elite rule in two different ways. Michels (1915) claimed in his "iron law of oligarchy" that any organization will devolve ruling authority on a small set of people. Michels thought elite rule could be an emergent feature of any organization irrespective of the beliefs or values of the organization's members or of the mechanisms for choosing leaders. Schumpeter appears to have shared a similar view, since his arguments do not seem to turn directly on the use of election itself, though we admit it is less than clear from his writings. On this view we would expect to see elite rule within the lottery-selected Athenian boule as well as in an elected assembly.

Against this view, we may contrast theories that claim that an organization is elite-dominated if it employs a method of leadership selection that tends to choose leaders who have special qualities. That is to say, certain selection processes may "recognize" certain people with special qualities relevant for leadership. Madison and Aristotle entertained theories of this kind and so does, with qualifications, Bernard Manin (1997). Aristotle and Manin thought that the electoral mechanism was a device for elite selection. Madison thought that elections in large districts would perform in this way.

Manin appears to accept the idea that elected representatives will govern differently than ordinary citizens would if they were rotated into office. It is not that he thinks that representatives are likely to be a better sort of person. Nor does he claim, like Schumpeter, that elected representatives are likely to be more competent in matters of policy and government. Manin argues that it is simply the use of elections as the device for selecting leaders that produces aristocratic tendencies, locating its critical feature in the tendency of voters to make choices based on certain kinds of considerations. He sought "to deduce the inegalitarian and aristocratic effects [directly] from an abstract analysis of election" (ibid.: 135). By doing this he hoped to drive home the conclusion that these effects are intrinsic to the electoral mechanism itself.[26] However, he acknowledged that his deductive argument depended on certain empirical (contingent) assumptions – essentially that voters will tend to elect those they think are superior in some relevant way: "The dynamics of choice and cognitive constraints usually leads to the election of representatives perceived as superior to those who elect them" (ibid.: 145).[27] So he could not reach all the way to the analytic conclusion he sought.[28] Still he thought these contingencies were likely to be satisfied in most circumstances of modern democracy.

We agree. The most that can be said is that voters tend to choose those whom they believe to possess some valuable characteristic for political leadership, and they may well be wrong both in the value of the characteristic and who are likely to possess it. Second, whether this constitutes an aristocratic tendency seems to depend on the idea that the characteristics in question are somehow valuable or attractive in some wider sense. Third, we have to think that these characteristics are fixed prior to election and not conferred by the fact of being elected. After all, if elite characteristics were automatically attributed to those who happen to be elected, election would simply *constitute* an aristocracy. It may be true that marks of superiority are not too mutable, at least not deliberately so, in a variety of circumstances, but we doubt that that it is anything like universally true. Moreover, to say that contingent factors matter is to

---

[26] Manin presents his argument as a kind of completion of a project begun by Aristotle, showing that elections are an aristocratic device and are, for this reason, incompatible with democracy. In the case of Aristotle we are not yet persuaded. Aristotle could be read as speaking merely of tendencies or statistical regularities – that lottery tends to be employed in democracies and election in oligarchies – or else as making something like a constitutive claim – that something is not a democracy if it uses elections for important offices. But Aristotle plainly thought that Athens was democratic and it employed election for significant offices. Moreover, the constitutive claim seems even harder to defend in light of *Politics*, VI, 4 where he discusses (agrarian) democracies that employ elections. In any case, both the constitutive claim (that democracies necessarily employ lottery) and the statistical claim are distinct from the claim that we think Manin wants to make: that democracies have good reason to employ lottery and that they will therefore tend to make that choice. This seems a causal claim and Manin's "deduction" is an attempt to elucidate the causal elements of that story. And, of course, it is no defect of a causal argument that contingencies play an essential part.

[27] And even here he qualifies the sense of "superiority" as being only in respect to relevant qualities for government. There is little sense that the elected are more virtuous in any moral sense or even more competent except with respect to political skills – or, rather, reputed political skills.

[28] The four assumptions are these: the unequal treatment of candidates by voters which says that voters *may* choose candidates in an arbitrary fashion; distinction of candidates due to the circumstance of choice, which says that voters choose candidates thought to have some mark of superiority; that certain persons are more salient or visible than others; and that it is costly to secure public recognition. We agree, of course, that these factors make it unlikely that as a matter of fact election will treat everyone equally.

leave open which factors actually matter and how likely they are to arise in practice. Perhaps other contingent factors operate to defeat the effects of the contingent factors that Manin cites.

In any case, the qualities of the candidates may not be as important for the aristocratic hypothesis as what the governmental officials actually do and what policies they produce. Thucydides' criticism of Athens was based at least partly on his judgment that disastrous or unstable policies were chosen and other writers seem largely to agree. No doubt Thucydides thought that there was some connection between the quality of the officials and their policies, but after all it was Pericles who led Athens into the war with Sparta (whose qualities Thucydides would not have doubted), and Alcibiades (another highly capable leader, even if he was a flawed character) who convinced the Athenians to undertake the disastrous Sicilian expedition. One has to be open to the possibility that that connection between capable leaders and good policy is uncertain. Why not, instead, ask the policy question directly? Doing this may indeed support an alternative version of the aristocratic hypothesis: the idea is that, even if elections do not produce better officials, the policies produced tend to support the public interest or perhaps the interest of some elite.

VI.   Policies in representative v. direct democracy

Athenian democracy had three characteristic institutional features. The first was what is now called direct democracy: any citizen who wanted to could attend the assembly and vote or speak on any issue. Second, every citizen was eligible to be chosen by lottery to serve in the magistracies that governed the city. Third, every citizen was eligible to be selected a juror, again by lottery, in the very powerful court system. In these respects everyone could take (equal) turns in ruling the city. In this section we want to compare direct democracy – where the people choose policies by some kind of popular referendum – with representative democracy.

Since the appearance of Downs's (1957) work half a century ago, many positive political theorists have shared the intuition that majority rule tends to perform similarly in different institutional settings, independently of whether people are choosing between policies or candidates.[29]

---

[29] This intuition is supported by the median voter theorem which is thought of as a general tendency of majority rule in a one-dimensional setting. However, to be accurate, the statement needs to be qualified by saying it represents a kind of intuition. After all, it is easy to create game theoretic specifications in which majority rules are extremely sensitive to institutional details in the sense of departing from the preferred outcome of the median voter.

If additional institutional structure matters, it is only because these additional details introduce some kind of bias that constrains the majoritarian property. In a one-dimensional world this intuition is supported in median voter models, in which the preferences of the median voter determine the outcome, assuming that distorting institutional frictions, such as monopoly agenda control, are absent.

For example, in two-candidate competition over a one-dimensional policy space, under very weak assumptions, both candidates "converge" on the position of the median voter. And, in an open-agenda legislature (where anyone is free to make proposals), the legislative outcome will be at the same point. The median voter theorem may not hold in some settings, such as when someone has agenda control or if candidates are insufficiently motivated to seek office or are not somehow free to pick winning platforms. Except for imperfections or frictions of this sort, the intuition is that the majoritarian aspect of the institution will dominate.

At least in some special cases results of this kind extend to higher dimensions, though many complications arise that define such extensions, since in many models equilibria frequently do not exist. But when an equilibrium does exist in a "legislative game" in which people are free to propose alternative policies under an open agenda, then a two-candidate equilibrium exists as well in which both candidates propose the legislative outcome. So there is at least some support for the majoritarian intuition even in this unpromising setting.

In the same spirit, we can sensibly ask the comparative institutional question posed in the introduction: when will an elective/representative democracy produce similar policies to a direct democracy? Let us assume, to begin, a one-dimensional policy space and direct democratic rule with an open agenda, as in the Athenian *ekklesia*, where everyone is free to propose whatever they want. Such an institution would tend to select policy at the preferred position of the median voter. Assume, now, the simplest possible representative government: one person is elected who then is to set policy, and this person is elected in a two-person election (we leave details aside for now). As argued above, the two candidates will have reason to promise to implement the preferred policy of the median voter. In this simple case, therefore, the Downsian intuition is satisfied. One can imagine extending this argument to a multidistrict setting if, for example, the districts are ideologically identical to the voting population so that each representative will advocate policies at the median position of her constituency. In that case the representatives will all have preferred policies at the population median. It is easy to see that this result could be further extended (a bit) by permitting constituencies to vary as long as the median legislator is located at the population median.

And, again in somewhat special cases, one could devise extensions to higher dimensions.

Ideas of this kind have been pursued further in two-stage models, which take account of how representatives would campaign for legislative office. When standing for election, a legislative candidate cannot plausibly claim that she alone would set policy if elected. Rather, she could only argue that she will play a more or less predictable part in producing legislation. Such models contemplate that the voters form beliefs as to the consequences of electing one representative rather than another – in effect, voters are assumed to have a model of the legislative process that allows them to assess the policy consequences of electing one or another candidate – and then vote based on a full assessment of the policy effects of their vote. One such model was developed by Austen-Smith and Banks (1988) in which they establish a connection between the preferred policy of the median voter in the population – which we could assume would be chosen in a direct democracy – and equilibrium in the representative democracy game. Their results depend on a number of other quite restrictive assumptions about the structure of elections and about the kind of electoral competition that takes place. But their basic finding is that equilibrium policy is related to the position of the median voter.

These arguments sidestep problems of political agency which we have discussed earlier by assuming that representatives will do as they promise after the election. If that assumption is relaxed it is not clear how con-strained representatives are by having to compete for election. It is easy to imagine models in which it is a powerful constraint: a world where a single elected official wants to stay in office, faces frequent elections, and can choose among policies contained in a one-dimensional space, for exam-ple. In that world, if information about the official's actions is sufficiently available to voters, and sufficiently easy to interpret, it might be hard for the official to stray far from the preferred policy of the median voter. But these informational assumptions are stringent, as is the notion that the space of policy has such a simple structure. And, as we depart from dras-tically simplifying assumptions of this model, by permitting numerous politicians to make decisions, allowing the policy space to be complex and to map uncertainly into a multidimensional space of outcomes, the reelection constraint facing the representatives probably diminishes in its force. Once account is taken of these considerations, the theoretical perspective adopted here, therefore, seems unlikely to support the idea that representative and direct democracy will generally produce the same or similar policy outcomes. So we turn, for now, to examine empirical evidence that may bear on this issue.

To examine the question of policy convergence, some authors have asked about the effects of introducing direct democratic mechanisms – the referendum or the initiative – into representative democracies. While the resulting literature is somewhat diverse, the basic finding so far is that the introduction of such devices tends to push policies in the direction of the median voter (Frey 1994; Gerber 1999; Matsusaka 2004; Funk and Gathmann 2005). This effect sometimes is direct: a popular initiative is enacted that moves policy in the direction of the median on that issue. And sometimes it is indirect in that the legislature in initiative states may tend to produce policies nearer the median, presumably out of worry that failure to do so would provoke popular policymaking. Indeed, sometimes one can actually observe such thinking at work where the legislature enacts a law after seeing initiative petitions being gathered; or where the legislature puts a referendum on the same ballot as the initiative in an effort to undercut support for the initiative (Gerber, Lupia, McCubbins, and Kiewiet 2001).

These phenomena suggest that states without the initiative tend to produce systematically different policies than states with such an option. In effect they lend support to the idea that representative democracy chooses different policies than direct democracy would. Of course, the comparison is very imperfect as we are forced to make an extrapolation from those polities permitting popular initiatives to a polity that makes all its policies in this way. That is a very long extrapolation indeed, and so evidence of this kind can only be suggestive.

In any case, from a normative viewpoint it is not very reassuring to learn that our government will tend to do whatever the median voter happens to want. After all, the median voter is, like the rest of us, a private person occupied with making a living or raising a family and probably not very familiar with the world of policy. As Schumpeter worried, her policy preferences are likely to be influenced by superficial beliefs and emotional responses rather than being well thought out or consistent.

There is reason to think, both theoretically and empirically, that direct and indirect democracies tend to choose different policies, except in the special circumstances we have outlined. This difference seems to be systematic rather than random: direct democracy, as far as we can see, tends to pick out median voter outcomes and representative governments depart from that in some direction or another. And the difference seems regularly related to how purely representative the government is: partial systems, which include some institutions of direct democracy, exhibit policies closer to the position of the median voter. Finally, we do not have any idea whether these differences are properly traceable to the use of elections as such or to the specifics of how elections are implemented (e.g. the absence of rotation, term limits, instructions, and the presence of many incumbent-favoring features).

The evidence seems weaker when it comes to the question of whether the policies of representative government favor the interests of an elite rather than the general interest. Madison, for example, would have expected systematic differences of the kind we discuss but thought that, in the right constitutional setting, these policies may simply have been better at advancing the common good than the median voter's preferred policy. But there is some evidence on this issue and it will be discussed in the conclusion.

VII.   Election or lottery

Bernard Manin reminds us that until the eighteenth century, educated people thought that lottery was the selection mechanism most compatible with democracy. The assumption was that officials chosen by lottery would be more likely to pursue policies that most citizens (who were poor) would want, whereas elected officials would tend to choose systematically different policies. We saw in the previous section that recent empirical evidence suggests that elected leaders probably do choose differently than the people themselves when asked to choose policies directly. But would elected officials choose differently than officials selected by lottery? We do not know a way to examine this issue empirically, so we shall resort to theory.

Let us start with Aristotle's political ontology which divides the city into wealth classes – sometimes he speaks only of the rich and the poor, but sometimes he refers to a middle class (*mesoi*) – and assumes that each class will necessarily seek to pursue its own interest. And, in his two-class model, assuming that the poor are much more numerous than the rich, a democratic government will tend to be a government of the poor. Aristotle had two ideas for moderating this tendency: one was to impose a property requirement for citizenship that was sufficiently high that the new democracy would tend to choose moderate policies for the whole city (including those who were not permitted to be citizens). Such a strategy could work, of course, only if there were a middle class: otherwise franchise restrictions would have no effect or else would shift authority directly from the poor to the rich. The Athenians, who we assume had a large middle class, attempted to achieve something like this following the oligarchic coup of 411, when there was an effort to reduce the number of citizens to 5,000, but this effort collapsed quickly and the democracy was restored.

Aristotle's second idea was more robust to social circumstances and could work, in principle, even if the city was strictly divided between the rich and the poor. It was to devise institutions that would permit the rich to take part in ruling the city along with the poor. It is in this context that he saw election as a device by which the rich could participate in government, while lottery would tend to select the poor. If some offices were chosen according to each principle, that would implement a kind of balance in government. Overall policy would then be a kind of moderate compromise that was likely, he thought, to approximate, to the common interest, an interest that neither class would pursue if it monopolized the government. He recognized, of course, that neither class would be satisfied and thought that, in his own day, the establishment of democracy (rule by the poor) was more or less inevitable, partly because there were so many poor people in every city. But he thought it was partly inevitable too because of the kind of deep egalitarianism of Greek popular culture at the time.

Aristotle framed the aristocratic hypothesis by comparing elections and lottery as a device for picking officials. We can make this comparison by using citizen candidate models, in which any citizen is free to stand for election, and so election, like lottery, is simply a device for selecting leaders. The question posed is this: who (or which kinds of people) will be selected as a representative out of the population, and which will tend to be chosen by lottery? Citizen candidate models allow us to examine the aristocratic hypothesis in a particularly precise manner since every other feature of the city is held constant in the comparison. Of course this precision is won within the context of very simple and stylized models.

To begin, it seems plausible to think that lottery will pick a person whose characteristic is an unbiased estimate of the mean of the population distribution. And these models also allow us to ask whether, or when, election by itself will produce officials who might plausibly be regarded as an elite in some way. We do not offer a definition of "elite" at this point, leaving the idea to emerge from the specific model (hopefully) intuitively.

In many of the early models, voters had complete information about each other's characteristics and each had to decide whether to stand for election. This can be seen as a very simple kind of agency model in which voters have no ex post control over the behavior of an official and can achieve their ends only by selecting agents with the right kind of (internal) motivation. In the simplest two-period model, plurality rule is used to elect a single official (Osborne and Slivinski 1996; Besley and Coate 1997) who, after being elected in the first period, sets policy in the second. Citizens differ only in their policy preferences in a one-dimensional policy space and these are commonly known. Any voter is free to declare her candidacy in period 1 and declared candidates (voters) pay an entry cost. Once entry decisions are made, the election takes place under a plurality rule with ties broken by a fair random device. In the second (policymaking) period the official will necessarily choose her most preferred policy. Any first-period promise to do otherwise would not be credible. The fact that promises are not credible is what permits voters to form preferences between the declared candidates and to decide how to vote.

In this setting, depending on entry costs and the benefits of winning office, only a small number of citizens will declare candidacy (how many depends on the cost of entry), and each will receive the same number of votes. If entry costs are high enough, there will be two-candidate equilibria, and we confine our discussion to those. In a two-candidate equilibrium, policy positions of the leading vote-getters will be moderate (not "too far" from the median) and will be symmetrically situated around the position of the median voter (in the sense that the median voter must not prefer one candidate over the other). The intuition is that their positions are close enough to the median that no one near the median would find it worthwhile to enter the election, but sufficiently separated that no one at either extreme would want to enter either. Many pairs of candidates can actually satisfy this condition so there are many such equilibria, and in each one the leading vote-getters must receive the same number of votes. And the policies of the leaders will be moderate (not too far from the median) but separated from each other.[30]

It is a little hard to see how this kind of result could support the aristocratic hypothesis, for two reasons. First, the set of electable candidates is different from the kind of voter likely to be picked in a lottery. A lottery pick in this model has an expected value at the mean of the distribution of the population over the issue space. If we think of the electoral elite as the set of all voters who could be office-holders in some equilibrium, this elite will be symmetrically arranged around the position of the median voter. So if the mean and the median are identical – as they would be in a symmetric voter distribution – there is a sense in which election and lottery picks would both be centered on the mean of the population distribution. Roemer (2001) has shown that the set of electable candidates is of the same dimensionality as the original issue space, so it is, in this respect, a large subset of the population, and this set is centered at the

---

[30] The trick in these models is accomplished by the assumption that candidates cannot commit to a policy different from their ideal point. So candidates can merely decide whether or not to enter and not which position to offer. This may be sensible in a single election but is less so when elections take place over time. And it is less sensible where there is incomplete information.

mean of the population. While it is true that the set of people who could be picked by lottery is even larger (it includes everyone), the most likely lottery choices are close to the mean/median in the symmetric setting and resemble in policy terms those who are electable. In this setting it is hard to see how the electables can be seen as an elite in any interesting sense.

There is a natural interpretation of this model that is still more damaging to the aristocracy hypothesis. Assume that voters have identical preferences over consumption of a single commodity, but differ only in their initial wealth levels. The collective decision to be made is to set a uniform wealth tax, with the proceeds to be distributed on an equal per capita basis, perhaps with some attenuation. In this model policy preferences are wholly determined by initial wealth, with the richer voters preferring lower tax rates and the poorer ones higher taxes. In a two-candidate equilibrium, the candidates will be located near the median, with one a bit richer than the median voter and the other a bit poorer. In each equilibrium, the expected policy outcome is at the median. Moreover, if we assume that the wealth distribution is skewed in the way that wealth distributions generally are – so that the median income is less than the mean – in each equilibrium the candidates will be two relatively poor citizens (relative to the mean of the distribution). But, in this model, the lottery pick is centered at the mean and so will tend to be richer than the citizen elected. Again, it is hard to see policy as manifesting any kind of elite bias; what bias there is seems to be in another direction. Moreover, Roemer's argument shows that the set of people who could be the elite will be large, as well as relatively poor.

Something like an aristocratic tendency may be observed in a slightly more complex model of the political economy.[31] Suppose a two-period model in which capital investment is productive and that people have identical utility functions but different wealth endowments. In the first period each person has to decide how much to invest, which will yield a second-period return, and to consume what remains. Assume the government has an option to set the second-period tax rate and to redistribute the proceeds on an equal per capita basis. In the second period, the investment decisions have been made and the government could tax productive returns in a non-distortionary manner. But if it is expected to set second-period tax rates too high it will discourage investment, leading to low levels of redistribution. So the government (i.e. the median

---

[31]   The model in this section is a simplification of one in Chapter 7 of Persson and Tabellini (2002). In their more complex settings they reach similar general conclusions.

voter) would want to commit to optimally low second-period taxes. Let us assume for illustrative purposes that the median voter has no wealth endowment so that all of her income comes from redistribution. Then she needs to assure high-income voters, credibly, that second-period taxes will not be set too high. One way to do this might be to give the power to set second-period tax rates to a voter with sufficient wealth to want to set the rate at the optimal level.[32] One might be tempted to say that in this model an "aristocrat" is given the power to make policy in her own interest. Of course that is true, but the policy she chooses is the best policy from the standpoint of the median voter, who is poor. While there is a kind of aristocracy in this model, the aristocrats are forced by a kind of invisible hand to do the bidding of the median voter.

In view of these results, it is not clear that anything like an aristocratic tendency can be generated in simple settings of the kind that have been studied in these models, but we do not want to belabor results of this kind that are set in very sparse environments. Citizen-candidate models are of potential interest because they allow us to focus on how elections select candidates. Citizen-candidate models suggest that elections generate something like a weak median voter outcome even if voters lack the power to monitor and punish their behavior in office. But these models abstract away the strategic complexity introduced by multiple principals and multiple agents, which we take to be the core problem of political agency.

In a somewhat more complex model where information is not complete about some relevant characteristic which we may call "competence," voters would like to choose highly competent candidates but it is hard to identify them. Given the difficulty of measuring competence, one would expect that if office is valuable, people with low levels of competence will try to imitate more highly competent types. And, assuming that the electoral mechanism can create only very imperfect incentives for screening candidates (as we have argued), some of these imitators will be expected to succeed in equilibrium. Moreover, which people find it worthwhile to become candidates for office depends importantly on their other opportunities. If good political leaders are those that have skills with a high market value and poor ones do not, then one expects talented leaders to avoid running for office and the resulting pool of potential

---

[32] Doing this entails another credibility problem: how can the median voter commit to not taking back the power to set policy in the second period? One could imagine various "solutions" but none is really fully satisfying. Perhaps the policymaker could be given the control of the military. This is a kind of neo-Hobbesian solution but it is still vulnerable to ex post revolution.

candidates to be mediocre. If that assumption is right, then the election mechanism, taken as a whole, will be likely to select inferior candidates – candidates who voters would agree are inferior if they could directly observe their attributes. Elections will, in short, select the mediocre and not the aristocratic, if that term is used to refer to high-quality potential officials.

Of course we are not claiming that such a sweeping and dismal conclusion is actually warranted. Possibly the talented will sometimes choose to run out of a desire to serve. Or perhaps political skills are not marketable and competent political leaders have poor outside prospects. In any case it seems possible that the important qualities can be learned after election and that, even if elections have a tendency to choose those with meager inherited gifts, those who take office will tend to form a professional elite and get better with practice. Thus it seems possible that under some circumstances elections may select different and better candidates. But the circumstances in which this may happen seem fairly special.

VIII.   Conclusions

The Romans thought that elections could not be trusted to produce or reproduce the kind of elite that they thought was central to the stable and conservative rule of the Republic. They fretted mightily, as far as can be inferred from their practices, over the details of the voting procedures that were employed in their lawmaking assemblies (*comitia*). They were careful to assemble voting classes so that the rich and well-armed had greater voting weight, to manage tribal membership, and to ensure that the poor of Rome were "packed and stacked" into a small subset of tribes. And they tried to ensure that the order and procedure of voting were such that the elite would get the results they wanted (Staveley 1972). As far as we know, usually this worked as expected. But there were several notorious exceptions where laws were enacted over the objections of the elites.

In modern times, things are arranged less bluntly. But probably they may still be arranged in ways that permit the reliable reproduction of an elected elite of some kind. Almost everywhere the representatives get to choose the details of the electoral system by which they get and hold their jobs, and to change it if they think it is working unacceptably. They have nearly universally avoided term limitations and instructions from their constitutions and usually too the institutions of direct democracy. Almost everywhere they have succeeded in gaining or keeping working conditions that make them hard to monitor and control even by the most attentive voters and interest groups.[33] These are "aristocratic" achievements of a sort. But are they traceable to elections as such or to many additional restrictions on the way that election is employed? More importantly, is there any reason to think that the benefits of their achievements are kept by political incumbents?

Political office is valuable precisely because of these (slack producing) achievements, and so one would expect this value to be the object of intense competition. Competition for office makes political aspirants dependent on the favor of those who can help them to get it and keep it. Sometimes this forces dependence on parties or on others who can help mobilize voters. More recently, however, the dependence seems to run in the direction of those with disposable wealth. Martin Gilens (2001) and Larry Bartels (2002) have presented evidence that seems, on the face of things, to support this view. They argue that representatives tend to respond disproportionately to those from upper income groups who have greater access to the tools of political influence, and that policy exhibits a kind of class bias as a result. To the extent that representatives are forced to compete away the privileges that they would want to reserve to themselves, rendering them beholden to those who control the means to put them in office and keep them there, the elected are a strange and dependent kind of aristocracy.

BIBLIOGRAPHY

Aristotle. 1962. *The Politics of Aristotle*, ed. and trans. Ernest Barker. New York: Galaxy Books.

Austen-Smith, David, and Jeffrey Banks. 1988. "Elections, Coalitions, and Legislative Outcomes." *American Political Science Review* 82 (2): 405–22.

Bartels, Larry. 2002. "Economic Inequality and Partisan Politics." Paper presented at the Annual Meeting of the American Political Science Association, September, Boston.

Besley, Timothy. 2006. *Principled Agents? The Political Economy of Good Government.* New York: Oxford University Press.

Besley, Timothy, and Stephen Coate. 1997. "An Economic Model of Representative Democracy." *Quarterly Journal of Economics* 112 (1): 85–114.

Dahl, Robert. 1971. *Polyarchy: Participation and Opposition.* New Haven, CT: Yale University Press.

---

[33] For a qualification to this argument see John Ferejohn (1999). That paper argues that under certain conditions elected officials may voluntarily increase the degree to which they may be monitored in order to induce people to support a larger public sector. In effect, this argument, like others in this chapter, cuts against any strong form of the aristocratic hypothesis.

Disch, Lisa. 2006. "Rethinking Re-presentation." Paper prepared for delivery at the Annual Meeting of the American Political Science Association, September, Philadelphia, PA.

Downs, Anthony. 1957. *An Economic Theory of Democracy.* New York: Harper and Row.

Dunn, John. 2005. *Setting the People Free: The Story of Democracy.* London: Atlantic Books.

Fenno, Richard. 1978. *Home Style.* Boston: Little, Brown.

Ferejohn, John. 1986. "Incumbent Performance and Electoral Control." *Public Choice* 50: 5–25.

——— 1999. "Accountability and Authority: Toward a Political Theory of Electoral Accountability," in *Democracy, Accountability, and Representation,* ed. Adam Przeworski, Susan Stokes, and Bernard Manin. New York: Cambridge University Press, 131–53.

Frey, Bruno. 1994. "Direct Democracy: Politico-Economic Lessons from Swiss Experience. *American Economic Review* 84 (2): 338–42.

Funk, Patricia, and Christina Gathmann. 2005. "Estimating the Effect of Direct Democracy on Policy Outcomes: Preferences Matter." Working paper, Stanford University Department of Economics.

Gerber, Elisabeth. 1999. *The Populist Paradox: Interest Group Influence and the Promise of Direct Legislation.* Princeton, NJ: Princeton University Press.

Gerber, Elisabeth, Arthur Lupia, Mathew McCubbins, and Roderick Kiewiet. 2001. *Stealing the Initiative: How State Government Responds to Direct Democracy.* Upper Saddle River, NJ: Prentice Hall.

Gilbert, Martin. 2007. *Churchill: A Life.* New York: Henry Holt.

Gilens, Martin. 2001. "Political Ignorance and Collective Policy Preferences." *American Political Science Review* 95 (2): 379–96.

Hamilton, Alexander, John Jay, and James Madison. 1961. *The Federalist,* ed. Jacob E. Cooke. Middletown, CT: Wesleyan University Press.

Kant, Immanuel. 1970 [1795]. "Perpetual Peace," in *Kant's Political Writings,* ed. Han Reiss. New York: Cambridge University Press.

Kishlansky, Mark. 1981. *Parliamentary Selection.* New York: Cambridge University Press.

Manin, Bernard. 1997. *The Principles of Representative Government.* New York: Cambridge University Press.

Matsusaka, John. 2004. *For the Many or the Few: The Initiative, Public Policy, and American Democracy.* Chicago: University of Chicago Press.

Michels, Robert. 1915 [1911]. *Political Parties: A Sociological Study of the Oligarchical Tendencies of Modern Democracy,* English trans. Eden Paul and Cedar Paul. New York: The Free Press.

Montesquieu, Charles de Secondat. 2002. *The Spirit of the Laws.* Amherst, NY: Prometheus Books.

Namier, Lewis. 1929. *The Structure of Politics at the Ascension of George III.* London: Macmillan.

Osborne, M. J. and A. Slivinski. 1996. "A Model of Political Competition with Citizen Candidates." *Quarterly Journal of Economics* 111 (1): 65–96.

Persson, Torsten, and Guido Tabellini. 2002. *Macroeconomic Policy, Credibility and Politics*. London: Routledge.

Pitkin, Hanna. 1967. *The Concept of Representation*. Berkeley: University of California Press.

Plato. 1987. *The Republic*. London: Penguin Classics.

Rousseau, Jean-Jacques. 1968. *The Social Contract*. London: Penguin Books.

Schumpeter, Joseph. 1942. *Capitalism, Socialism, and Democracy*. New York: Harper Colophon Books.

Staveley, E. S. 1972. *Greek and Roman Voting and Elections*. Ithaca, NY: Cornell University Press.

Wood, Gordon. 1991. *The Radicalism of the American Revolution*. New York: A. A. Knopf.

11   Why does the Republican Party win half the votes?

John E. Roemer

I.   Introduction

How can a political party whose economic policies are in the interests of only a small fraction of the richest citizens maintain a sizable vote share in a democracy with full enfranchisement? The prime example of this puzzle today occurs in the United States. My aim in this chapter is to outline the possible answers to the question and then to present in some detail a study of one of the possibilities. I cannot claim, however, to know the answer.

One might, first of all, challenge my presumption that the economic policies advanced by the US Republican Party are indeed only in the interests of a small fraction of citizens at the top of the wealth distribution. Indeed, by the standards of one hundred years ago, the US has a progressive economic policy. About 31 percent of the national product is collected in taxes (at the federal, state, and local levels), and these taxes are used predominantly for transfer payments and expenditure on public goods. There is universal public education through age seventeen, and many states provide publicly financed tertiary education with modest private co-payments. Although the United States remains unique in the degree of private financing of its health services, nevertheless approximately 50 percent of health expenditures are public. There is a universal publicly financed pension system which is redistributive.

Yet the Republican Party seems intent on rolling back many of these practices or institutions, and it has maintained roughly one-half the vote share in national elections, despite its open attack on them. The Bush administration passed the most regressive tax rollback in many years, and has refused to mollify its anti-tax posture despite a large growth in the fiscal deficit, entailed in part by military expenditures in Iraq and Afghanistan, but also by virtue of its not matching tax cuts with cuts in public expenditure. It has tried, unsuccessfully, to privatize social security, a move which would have increased debt financing even more (because of the pay-as-you-go nature of social security finance), and also would have reduced dramatically the redistributive nature of social security. It has vociferously supported repeal of the estate tax, a repeal which would again increase the deficit, and would be only in the clear economic interests of fewer than 1 percent of American dynasties. These policies are only the most obvious ones. Somewhat less obviously sectarian is the Republican Party's position on global warming and energy policy. Given current scientific consensus of the effect of industrial production on global warming, it is almost certainly objectively the case that strong measures to reduce energy consumption (such as a stiff gasoline tax) are in the interest of the vast majority of citizens – I say, however, this policy is less obviously sectarian because it would entail short-run costs for citizens.

I will without further argument assume that Republican Party economic policy is only in the interest of a small fraction of the wealthiest citizens, and proceed to a discussion of how the party is able to maintain its large vote share. I believe there are six categories of possible explanation:

- policy bundling;
- imperfect political representation;
- voters' conceptions of distributive justice;
- voter misunderstanding of "how the economy works," that is, of the mapping from *policies* to *outcomes*;
- voters' incorrect beliefs about the probability of becoming rich;
- manipulative policy framing.

Let me give examples of these phenomena. By policy bundling, I mean that the Republican Party maintains its large vote share by bundling its unpopular economic policy with other policies that do attract voters. In the period after the Civil Rights Movement until the 1990s these were policies on race issues, and in the last decade they have been policies of patriotism and "family values": prayer in schools, and opposition to gay marriage and abortion.

By imperfect representation I mean the fact, if it is one, that legislators do not represent constituent interests in proportion to their numbers, but are unduly influenced by their wealthy constituents, or other wealthy institutions, particularly corporations. Among the six categories of explanation, this is the one that is most easily conceived to be a failure of democracy.

The third explanation is, of course, related to the view that voters behave sociotropically – they vote not primarily according to self-interest, but according to what they think will be good for society – a behavior which is not identical to, but similar to, voting according to justice.

Perhaps the most prominent example of the fourth category is the relationship between taxation and "effort," by which I mean the effort of economic agents to become educated, to work hard, to innovate, or to invest. Republicans argue that effort elasticities with respect to taxation are high, while Democrats tend to argue that they are low. Thus, "supply side economics" is the view that lowering taxes will not only increase the size of GNP, but will also increase government revenue. The most prominent expositors of this view were Ronald Reagan and his economist Arthur Laffer. (Lee and Roemer [2006] recently calculated that the maximum of the Laffer curve for the US economy in the Reagan period was over 50 percent – meaning that income tax revenues would have *risen* at least to the point of 50 percent marginal tax rates, contrary to Laffer's claim.)

The fifth category of explanation really requires two suppositions: that voters believe that the probability of their or their children becoming rich is much greater than it actually is, *and* that voters are sufficiently risk loving that they are willing to take the gamble – keeping redistribution at a low level to their present (relatively poor) selves, against the possible gain of being lightly taxed as their possibly rich future selves (or dynasties). Clearly, America as the "land of opportunity" is an important motivating folk tale for this explanation.

By the sixth explanation I mean that regressive economic policies are framed as being consonant with desirable personal characteristics – individualism, self-reliance, and so on.

My own current view is that the power of these explanations is roughly ordered in the way I have listed them: I believe the first three explanations are the most important. I cannot say, however, that I have proof. I have done some work on policy bundling, and some on imperfect representation (Roemer 2006); I will describe the former below. Otherwise, I am relying on a view about political fundamentals that I summarize in the next section.

There is a cognitive problem for the social scientist. One chooses to work on one of these explanations – say, policy bundling – because one has a prior belief that it is important. If one gets positive results, that view is reinforced: one updates the prior belief in a positive direction. One can, however, find researchers who advocate the primacy of each of these explanations. I do not feel that political science currently has a full grasp of the problem.

II.   What are the fundamentals?

My own view is that we should be guided by looking at the fundamentals. Just as economists seek to explain the values of economic variables over the long term by the fundamentals of preferences, technology, and distribution of endowments, so political scientists should be guided by political fundamentals – preferences of voters on policy issues and the nature of democratic institutions that mediate between voter preferences and political outcomes. My assumption is that the phenomenon of Republican Party strength in the United States is not a flash in the pan; it is a long-term phenomenon, and hence we should search for its fundamental determinants. I am therefore not attracted to the sixth explanation, offered above, that the Republicans have succeeded in manipulative policy framing. Over the long period, they should be no better at this than Democrats, and so even if such manipulation is politically important, it cannot be the kind of fundamental explanation that interests me. I must underscore the point, however, that this is a methodological presumption on my part: perhaps I have too short a view of what constitutes the long run, and one hundred years from now Republican power will, in retrospect, be seen to have been a flash in the pan. (See Smith [2007] for a serious piece of analysis that places more importance than I do on manipulative policy framing.)

On the other hand, I do not have much sympathy for the view that the *only* true fundamentals are the economic interests of voters. Marxists of yore would say that a voter who is swayed by, for example, religion or the church in his political choices, is a victim of false consciousness – the implication being that only political behavior which advances one's economic interests is true consciousness. I will take the *preferences* of voters as fundamentals – not their true economic interests. I am not willing to take economic interests as more fundamental than other kinds of values and preferences that people possess. Whether they are more fundamental in determining political outcomes is an empirical question; it should not be postulated. Indeed there may well be a presumption *against* the necessary primacy of self-centered economic interests, especially as economic development makes survival a less pressing concern. Non-economic preferences may be like a luxury good, becoming more salient as income rises.

I place less importance on voters' misunderstanding of the mapping from policies to outcomes than I used to (see Roemer 1994), and for the same reason that I place relatively little importance on framing. It is certainly in the interests of the wealthy, and of the Republican Party, if it is the primary representative of that stratum, to convince voters that effort elasticities are high – but if the Democratic Party represents the poorer half of society, it should be just as convincing in arguing that effort elasticities are low. In addition, we might expect that in the long run the *more* convincing arguments on this question can be given by the side that is right, and Lindert's important book (2004) gives convincing historical evidence that the low-elasticity side *is* right. Lindert argues that the high-tax welfare states have paid essentially *no* price in terms of lower productivity for their policies. (These countries have lower GDPs per capita than the US because of the labor–leisure choice their citizenries have made, not because of lower productivity. Surely choosing more leisure is a possible response to high taxation. But we do not hear conservatives arguing to the American polity that they should vote for low taxes because otherwise they will want to spend more time on vacation with their families.)

One of the most persuasive studies that focuses upon the mapping from policies to outcomes is Hirschman (1991), who writes that reactionaries have exploited three main rhetorical strategies: to argue that progressive reforms are either perverse (they will have consequences which are the opposite of what is intended), futile, or will put into jeopardy other more valuable social characteristics. But again one must ask: if the claims of perversity, futility, and jeopardy are false, which Hirschman himself believes, then why should progressives not have the edge in the argument? How does one explain the fact that in the United States today each side has the support of about half of the polity?

Another proposal of recent vintage is due to Piketty (1995). In his model, voters are uncertain about the importance of effort versus luck in producing income, where income is a random variable. They update their beliefs about the true importance of effort based upon their own experiences. Eventually, a society will converge to having a distribution of beliefs on this question. Thus people come to have either a "right-wing" view that effort is important for producing income and luck is relatively unimportant, or a "left-wing" view that luck is more important than effort. Based upon these views, voters advocate little or much redistribution. Importantly, two societies with the same distribution of initial beliefs can end up with very different political equilibria.

I have suggested, conditionally, and surely controversially, that the Democratic Party *represents* the poorer half of society. Now in a representative democracy, it would: that is, in a representative two-party system the natural outcome is that the polity partitions into two elements, each of which is represented by one party, and so if the Republicans represent the wealthy, then the Democrats should represent the rest.[1] One of the main ways in which imperfect representation could be an explanation of the question of my title is that the Democrats fail to do this. I believe that

---

[1] I take it as an axiom of (good) representation that every citizen is represented by at least one political party, and that citizens of different types are represented by parties in proportion to their numbers (whatever that turns out to mean).

this is a substantial possibility, although I will not address it seriously in this chapter.

I did not list as one of the possible explanations that Republicans have offered candidates who are or seem to be more competent or personally attractive than Democrats. There is a line of research in contemporary formal political science which focuses upon voter perceptions of candidate competence or attractiveness, or "valence." I am unmoved by this work: I grant such questions may be important in particular elections, but they are not fundamental, and hence not of concern to someone who is interested in long-term political trends. Over the long run, no party's candidates should have a monopoly on these randomly distributed characteristics.

Against my view, you could take a "quantum-mechanical" stance, or perhaps I should say a "catastrophe-theoretic" or "chaos-theoretic" stance. To wit, you might say: the outcomes of some particular elections, like that of the US President, may be determined by non-fundamentals (like the butterfly ballot in some Florida precincts, or George W. Bush's homey veneer), and these may set the political dynamic on a path quite different from what it otherwise would have been, thus engendering a very different future than otherwise would have occurred. I cannot say that I understand the laws of motion of political economy sufficiently well to argue that this is wrong – only that I take a methodologically conservative stance, which is, if you will, "Newtonian." The catastrophe theory view, indeed, challenges the whole idea of fundamentals. If we come to believe it is true, we will have to give up much of what we think of as political science and become more like anthropologists.

What about false beliefs? Can we attribute the quite significant support for repeal of the estate tax to voters' false beliefs in the probability of becoming rich, and their high degrees of risk tolerance? (Perhaps the loss of revenue from repealing the estate tax is sufficiently small that voting for its repeal is like going to a gambling casino – people understand that the odds are against them, but the expected losses are sufficiently small that people behave in a risk-loving manner.) Behavioral economics certainly teaches us to treat cognitive errors (in this case, misunderstanding the probabilities of becoming rich) seriously. But in this case I am more persuaded by the view that the stakes are small (from the viewpoint of government revenue) and that, because of this, a particularly dedicated group of "death tax" opponents has succeeded in framing repeal in an attractive way. (See Graetz and Shapiro [2005] for a detailed study.)

Before moving on, I must mention one non-fundamental explanation for Republican ideological power that I find quite persuasive, but that I did not list: that American conservatives have been prescient in establishing conservative think-tanks that have succeeded, by patient and careful work, in disseminating conservative and reactionary ideas among the public. A persuasive advocate of this view is Mark A. Smith, who has studied the possibility in two books (Smith 2000, 2007). Conservative American foundations, particularly the Olin Foundation, have funded think-tanks (the Manhattan Institute, Hudson Institute, Heritage Foundation, Cato Institute, American Enterprise Institute, Hoover Institute) which hired intellectuals to produce and disseminate broadly conservative and libertarian ideas. While social science in the academy has been predominantly liberal, professors have made little effort to reach the public as the think-tanks have. The atrophy of American unions, which were formerly to some extent schools for solidaristic ideology, has left a vacuum which conservative intellectuals have filled via the think-tank conduit. Ironically, perhaps, the right understood the importance of ideas and theory, while the left did not. I say this explanation is of a non-fundamental sort because there seems to be no reason why the right should have a long-term advantage in employing this strategy. But it may be an important explanation of the present American political landscape.

III.   Policy bundling

The research I describe in this section has been published in Lee and Roemer (2006), and is described in even more detail in Roemer, Lee, and Van der Straeten (2007), so I limit myself here to a non-technical summary.

   We study the extent to which voters' views on the *race issue* in the United States influence the politically determined equilibrium values on the *tax issue*. We analyze presidential elections over the period 1976–92; we postulate a spatial model to describe these elections, in which the policy space is two-dimensional – one dimension concerns taxation and redistribution, the second concerns the race issue. By the race issue, we mean policies specifically concerning the race question: school integration, busing, affirmative action, racial justice issues, and the like. Denote the space of policies by T, which consists of ordered pairs (t, r) where t is a party's position on the tax issue, and r is the party's position on the race issue. Voters are assumed to have preferences over these two issues, which are represented by utility functions with a parametric form to be given below. Each voter is of a *type* specified by two numbers – his ideal policy on the race issue (ρ) and his annual wage rate (w). Thus the *space of voter types* is a space H of ordered pairs (w, ρ) endowed with a probability measure F.

The utility function of a voter of type (w, ρ) over policies (t, r) is postulated to be of the form:

$$v(t, r; w, \rho) = \varphi(t, w) - \alpha(r - \rho)^2 + (\delta_0 - \delta_2\rho)\frac{\log y(t, 0.20)}{\log y(t, 0.80)}. \quad (1)$$

The first term, $\varphi(t, w)$, is the voter–worker's self-interested economic utility, gotten from maximizing a traditional Cobb–Douglas utility function over labor and income, given by $\log((1 - t)wL + b(t)) + \beta \log(\lambda - L)$, where $(1 - t)wL + b(t)$ will be the worker's after-tax income under an affine tax system with marginal rate t and lump-sum payment $b(t)$, should the worker choose to work L fraction of year, and $(\lambda - L)$ is the worker's leisure time. The second term, $-\alpha(r - \rho)^2$, is the voter's utility from the race policy r, which is assumed to be a Euclidean loss increasing as the policy departs from his ideal policy, ρ. The number $y(t, \pi)$ is the after-tax income of the worker whose wage is at the πth quantile of the wage distribution, if the tax policy is t. Thus the last term is a measure of the degree of equality in the distribution of after-tax income, for as t increases, redistribution increases, and this term increases. Thus it is assumed that all voters care about equality to the extent that δ_0 is positive, but that more racist voters (who have a larger value of ρ) care less about equality than less racist voters – to the extent that the parameter δ_2 is positive. The parameters of the utility function that are assumed to be the same across all voters are thus $(\beta, \lambda, \alpha, \delta_0, \delta_2)$ These parameters will be estimated from the data.

Two comments are in order. In actual fact, we modeled households with two adults (man and woman), and we made the utility of each member a function of family income and the leisure of each member; we estimated male and female parameters separately. We also allowed the two household members to have different preferences on the race issue. I am eclipsing these complications here for the sake of expositional simplicity. Second, we originally postulated that the coefficient in the last term was of the form $(\delta_0 - \delta_1 w - \delta_2\rho)$, allowing for the possibility that higher-wage workers would care less about equality than lower-wage ones: but we found this was not the case, and so we set the parameter $\delta_1 = 0$.

Thus political parties in presidential elections are assumed to take positions on the tax question and the race question, and voters are assumed to choose between parties based upon their preferences on these issues. Before describing the concept of political equilibrium, I describe our conceptualization of the ways in which preferences on the race issue will influence parties' positions on the tax issue. There are two of these effects, which we denote the *anti-solidarity* and *policy bundle* effects.

The anti-solidarity effect is a direct one: voters who believe that minorities – and blacks in particular – exploit the welfare state may vote for lower tax rates (than otherwise) because they wish to reduce the degree of redistribution to the undeserving. Many writers have noticed this effect: we mention Luttmer (2001), and Alesina, Glaeser, and Sacerdote (2001). Indeed, Alesina *et al.* perform cross-country regressions in which they show that the smaller the size of the welfare state, the larger the size of the poor minority in the country. This is taken to verify, or to be consistent with, what we call the anti-solidarity effect.

The policy bundle effect is indirect and more subtle. Suppose there is a sizable fraction of relatively poor, white voters, who are racist. On grounds of economic self-interest, they should vote for high tax rates and redistribution. But if the race issue is of sufficient importance to them, they would vote for a party that proposes a low tax rate, if that party is sufficiently conservative on the race issue (i.e. proposes a large r). This would be the case if α and ρ were sufficiently large. Thus, if the mass of voter types so described (small w, large ρ) is large, a party, say the Republicans, could maintain a large vote share by proposing a racist, low-tax platform.

Of course, whether the group of voters just described is larger than the group of high-wage, racially liberal voters is an empirical question. The policy bundle effect can also make it possible for Democrats to attract such voters, while maintaining a high-tax policy, which such voters might dislike.

The so-called Southern strategy of the Republican Party since the Goldwater years is, indeed, consistent with the view that the Republicans have exploited the policy bundle effect. That strategy has been to appeal to racism and law-and-order preferences – and to the extent that such appeals attract votes, the Republican Party can be less compromising on the issue of redistribution.

Our equilibrium model will enable us to estimate the anti-solidarity and policy bundle effects on tax policy over the period in question in the US.

I next describe our concept of political equilibrium. The Downsian model, and its famous median-voter theorem, is of no use in this situation, because that model only possesses equilibria (essentially) when the policy space is unidimensional. Our policy space is two-dimensional: indeed, that is the essence of our problem – the policy bundle effect could not exist if taxation were the only issue (although the anti-solidarity effect still could). We use a concept of equilibrium that I have called *party unanimity Nash equilibrium* (PUNE); these equilibria exist even when policy spaces are multidimensional.

The critical way in which PUNE differs from other strategies to deal with multidimensional political competition is that, rather than complexifying the *Nash* concept of competition, it complexifies the concept of what a *player* is. Formally, a player in a game is a payoff function defined on the cross-product of the players' strategy spaces. We propose, in contrast, that a political party is not a single payoff function, but rather a *set* of three payoff functions, held by different factions among the party's entrepreneurs. To wit, the entrepreneurs in a party have different goals – some are Downsian, in desiring to propose a policy that will maximize the party's probability of victory, or in another formulation, its vote share; some are Militant, in desiring not to compromise, but to propose a policy as close as possible to the ideal policy of the party's constituency; and some are Reformist, in desiring to maximize the expected utility, on average, of the party's constituency, with the expectation taken over the two states in which the party, or its opponent, wins. We propose that these three factions within a party bargain with each other, while facing the proposal of the opponent party. A PUNE is a pair of policies each of which is a bargaining outcome in one party, given the policy of the other party. Thus, the Nash notion of best response equilibrium is preserved, but a player's best response is not the maximizer of its (single) payoff function, given the other player's strategy, but rather the consequence of *bargaining* among *three payoff functions*, given the other player's strategy. This equilibrium concept was first used in Roemer (1998, 1999).

Indeed, we need not be terribly sophisticated about the nature of bargaining: we employ only the assumption that bargainers reach a Pareto-efficient solution at the bargaining table – that is, that in their response to the opposition party, there should be no policy that increases (weakly) the payoffs of all three factions over the policy that they propose.

The fortunate fact is that, even with multidimensional policy spaces, equilibria of this kind typically exist. Indeed, it turns out that, from the mathematical viewpoint, the Reformists are gratuitous! Thus the *set* of equilibria is not changed if we conceptualize parties as consisting only of Opportunists and Militants. *Which* equilibrium in this set will in fact be observed depends upon the relative strength of the factions in each party at the bargaining table. We do not attempt to estimate these relative strengths: we will simply take a party's position to be its average platform over the entire set of PUNEs. We justify this approach in the cited publications.

In summary, I make four points. First, we view the bargaining described as taking place among professional party entrepreneurs – those who set policies – not among voters. Parties are viewed as organizations run by politicians, which in an imperfect way represent constituencies.

Do not think of these entrepreneurs as being voters of a particular type. They are professionals who are adopting different protocols to further their careers – one protocol is to maximize the probability of winning, another is to appeal to constituents. Among these entrepreneurs, the Reformists might be viewed as the most selfless ones, who are looking out for the good of the constituency. But that, too, could just be a good protocol for living a long political life.

The second point is that the description of party factions as bargaining with each other is a formalization of something which may be much more amorphous, namely, that among a party's entrepreneurs, there are competing tendencies – maximizing victory probability and representing constituents. I do not assume there are literal negotiations taking place. The idea that is captured by the bargaining metaphor is that the aims of representing constituencies, and of winning elections, are often very different, and it is more appealing to represent these aims as a competition between payoff functions rather than as the maximization of a *single* payoff function.

The third point is that the memberships or constituencies (these two words are synonyms in the model) of the parties are endogenous. A PUNE is *a partition of the polity into two elements* each of which is represented by a party in the sense described, and *a pair of platforms*, one for each party, such that the entrepreneurs of the parties (at least the Militants and Reformists) represent their constituencies in the manner described, *and* each member of each constituency prefers its party's policy to the opposition's. Thus, in equilibrium, every voter is satisfied (at least to the first order) with her party's policy, in the sense that she will vote for it against the opposition party.[2]

Fourth, in modeling the average utility function of a party's constituency, we do not take a simple average of the voter types assigned to the party, weighted by the probability distribution F. Rather, we attempt to capture the apparent fact that politicians represent more faithfully the preferences of the richer voters in their constituencies. Bartels (2002) has estimated this phenomenon, and we have devised a system for weighting voters' representation in the payoff function of the Militants using his data. Indeed, we found we got better estimates of observed policies by doing this than by taking a simple unbiased average of voter types associated with the parties.

---

[2] Where does "probability of victory" come in? We assume that there is some macropolitical uncertainty in the elections, either because of party uncertainty over voter preferences, or voter misperception of policies, or shocks that may occur between the statement of party policies and elections.

I next describe the estimation of the data of the model. We used two data sets, the Panel Study on Income Dynamics (PSID) and the American National Election Studies (ANES). The PSID is used to estimate the economic parameters β and λ. The ANES is used to estimate, in each election year, the joint distribution of types, F: that is, of wages and racial views. We also used the ANES to estimate the positions of presidential candidates on the issues in each election year, based on what voters' perceptions of these positions were. We then chose the remaining parameters α, δ_0, and δ_2 to give a good fit of the model to the data – that is, so that the calculated PUNEs are close to the observed party positions in those elections.

I will not summarize the details of this estimation, except to describe how we estimated voters' positions on the race issue, the parameter ρ. We used, as a first-order approximation, the voter's answer to the survey question: "Do you think the government gives [too little, about right, too much] aid to blacks?" The respondent gives an answer on a seven-point scale from 1 (far too little help) to 7 (far too much help). To a first approximation, we identify these answers as going from anti-racist (1) to racist (7). However, this identification is problematical, for a voter might answer "7" not because she is racist but because she is libertarian, and believes the government gives too much help to everyone. So we needed to sterilize the answer to the "aid to blacks" question of its libertarian factor.

To do so we ran a factor analysis on a set of ten questions from the ANES: we located four orthogonal factors of political ideology, which we named racism, libertarianism, compassion for the poor, and feminism. (The names come from the nature of the questions upon which these four factors load highly.) We were then able to extract the libertarian component from the "aid to blacks" question: it turned out that that component was rather small. Indeed, "racism" is about three times as important a determinant of the answer to "aid to blacks" as libertarianism, a fact of independent interest. Thus we constructed a measure of racism as the "racism-induced response to the aid to blacks" question. This gave us the value of ρ for the individual.

Next, we calculated the equilibria of the model for various choices of the parameters that are not directly estimated, the vector $(\alpha, \delta_0, \delta_2)$. For each election year, we chose values for this vector that give us a good estimate of the observed platforms for that year. Figure 11.1 shows the equilibria for two of the election years. The plane of the figure is (t, r). Each PUNE consists of a pair of policies, one small black point (Republican policy) and one small gray point (Democratic policy). The large dots are the observed policies for that year (actually, as you observe, we

1976–80	1984–88

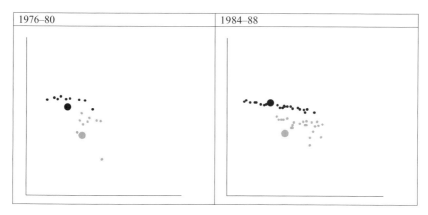

Figure 11.1 PUNEs and observed policies in two pooled election years (dark points are Democratic, light points are Republican).

pooled data for pairs of consecutive election years). The model appears to do quite well in capturing the observed policies. Denote the average PUNE policies in this election for the Democratic and Republican Parties (t^D, r^D) and (t^R, r^R).

Before proceeding to the next step, examine the utility function in eqn. (1), and note that the critical parameter for the anti-solidarity effect is δ_2: it is this parameter, along with the individual's value of ρ, that determines the extent to which racism reduces the desire for redistribution. In like manner, it is the value of the parameter α, along with ρ, that determines the policy bundle effect.

We now move to the heart of our project, the estimation of the anti-solidarity and policy bundle effects. We run a counterfactual election in which we set the race policies of both parties to be identical – it does not matter what policy value we choose. This will be an election on just one dimension: tax policy. In this election, voters will have no reason to vote for the Republican Party because they prefer its race policy: so there will be *no* policy bundle effect in this election. Equivalently, we could set α equal to zero, because the race policies of the parties will have no effect in this election on voter choice. However, the anti-solidarity effect will still be active: a voter who thinks blacks exploit the welfare state will still have reason to vote for lower tax rates. Denote the average tax policies[3] in the equilibria of this election t_I^D and t_I^R. We consequently estimate the

---

[3] In point of fact, we used a method of averaging which weighted equilibria according to their expected frequencies; the reader is referred to the cited paper for clarification.

policy bundle effects on the D and R party policies as the differences $t_I^D - t^D$ and $t_I^R - t^R$.

We next ran a second counterfactual election: this time, we not only set the racial policies of both parties to be the same, but we set $\delta_2 = 0$, thus annihilating the anti-solidarity effect. Denote the average equilibrium (tax) policies in these elections by t_{II}^D and t_{II}^R. These policies are purged of both the policy bundle and anti-solidarity effects. We thus estimate the total effect of racism on tax policy for the two parties, as $t_{II}^D - t^D$ and $t_{II}^R - t^R$. In addition, the equilibria come with vote shares for the two parties, so we estimate the *expected effects* as the vote-weighted averages of the effects for the two parties. This is an ad hoc way of modeling the thought that implemented policy will be some average of the platforms of the parties, an average reflecting the vote shares of the parties due to legislative implementation.

Table 11.1 summarizes the results of these computations: as I mentioned, we pooled data for adjacent election years, so we performed four experiments. We estimated that the expected income tax rate would have been between 11 percentage points (in the 1980–4 experiment) and 18 percentage points (in the 1976–80 experiment) higher, had racism not been a political factor. The decomposition of this effect between anti-solidarity (ASE) and policy bundle (PBE) varies between the two parties and across the years: we may say that the PBE is significant, so the Southern strategy appears to have been a good one for a Republican Party whose central focus was maintaining low tax rates. Indeed, if our estimates are to be credited, then racism would appear to explain the difference between the size of the public sector in the US and the advanced European democracies.

I conclude this section with a discussion of Figure 11.2. The three panels in this figure present the estimated density function of voter types: thus the plane of the domain in these figures is the type space (w, ρ). The two "mountains" of the density function represent white and black voters: all black voters are coded as non-racist (a value $\rho = 1$). In the "full model" panel, the "hyperplane" illustrated separates the space of types into voters who form the constituencies of the R (above the hyperplane) and D (below the hyperplane) parties. Now examine panel (b): here, the hyperplane again partitions the type space into R and D voters, but in the first counterfactual election. Panel (c) presents the partition into party members in the second counterfactual election. Of course, in the second counterfactual election, the racial issue has entirely disappeared, so the only relevant dimension of a person's type is his wage: therefore, we have in panel (c) purely "class politics": that is, a party partition which is completely characterized by a pivotal wage rate. Now the interesting

Table 11.1 *PUNEs and the decomposition of racism's effect* ($\delta_0 = 1$)

1976–80	Full	First counterfactual	Second counterfactual	Total effect	PBE	ASE	PBE (%)	ASE (%)
tD	0.3473	0.3791	0.4824	0.1351	0.0318	0.1033	23.54%	76.46%
tR	0.2212	0.3432	0.4450	0.2238	0.1220	0.1018	54.51%	45.49%
rD	2.7663							
rR	4.1144							
Exp tax rate	**0.2927**	**0.3696**	**0.4742**	**0.1815**	0.0769	0.1046	42.36%	57.64%
D vote share	0.5166	0.7351	0.7814	0.2648	0.2185	0.0463	82.52%	17.48%
# of PUNEs	9	45	26					
1980–4	**Full**	**First counterfactual**	**Second counterfactual**	**Total effect**	**PBE**	**ASE**	**PBE (%)**	**ASE (%)**
tD	0.4025	0.4137	0.4666	0.0641	0.0112	0.0529	17.47%	82.53%
tR	0.2129	0.3638	0.4391	0.2262	0.1509	0.0753	66.71%	33.29%
rD	3.4307							
rR	3.7914							
Exp tax rate	**0.3465**	**0.4011**	**0.4567**	**0.1102**	0.0546	0.0557	49.48%	50.52%
D vote share	0.5609	0.7466	0.6417	0.0808	0.1857	−0.1049	229.83%	−129.83%
# of PUNEs	11	42	19					

1984–8	Full	First counterfactual	Second counterfactual	Total effect	PBE	ASE	PBE (%)	ASE (%)
tD	0.3709	0.3859	0.4993	0.1284	0.0150	0.1134	11.68%	88.32%
tR	0.2392	0.3234	0.4042	0.1650	0.0842	0.0808	51.03%	48.97%
rD	2.7771							
rR	3.6483							
Exp tax rate	0.3109	0.3659	0.4699	0.1590	0.0550	0.1040	34.61%	65.39%
D vote share	0.4049	0.6804	0.7906	0.3857	0.2755	0.1102	71.43%	28.57%
# of PUNEs	23	52	15					
1988–92	**Full**	**First counterfactual**	**Second counterfactual**	**Total effect**	**PBE**	**ASE**	**PBE (%)**	**ASE (%)**
tD	0.3154	0.3320	0.4409	0.1255	0.0166	0.1089	13.23%	86.77%
tR	0.1504	0.3004	0.4030	0.2526	0.1500	0.1026	59.38%	40.62%
rD	2.8738							
rR	4.1953							
Exp tax rate	0.2870	0.3241	0.4270	0.1400	0.0371	0.1028	26.53%	73.47%
D vote share	0.5797	0.7508	0.6320	0.0523	0.1711	−0.1188	327.15%	−227.15%
# of PUNEs	15	36	11					

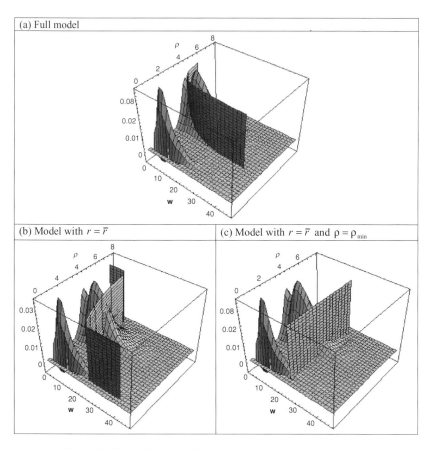

Figure 11.2 (a) Full model
(b) Model with $r = \bar{r}$
(c) Model with $r = \bar{r}$ and $\rho = \rho_{\min}$
Party-separation "hyperplanes" for the full model and the two counterfactual elections. The space of the domain is (w, ρ).

observation is that in passing from the full model to the first counterfactual, we move from a situation in which the racial issue is very important, to one in which politics is *very largely* class politics: that is, in panel (b), the separating hyperplane appears to be almost perpendicular to the w axis. It is important to underscore the fact that *preferences of voters have not changed* in the move from panel (a) to panel (b): all that has changed is that we have excluded *the race issue* as something on which parties may take different positions. The ASE is still active in the political competition of panel (b). Thus, these figures suggest that the existence of the race issue in American politics during this period altered what would have otherwise been predominantly class politics to politics in which race issues are very important.

We note that this inference is quite different from the one made by Poole and Rosenthal (1997), who argue, on the basis of congressional vote analysis, that the race issue was relatively unimportant in this period compared to the economic issue. One crucial difference between their analysis and ours is that ours uses an equilibrium model, in which party constituencies, inter alia, are endogenous. Thus we are able to simulate *how party composition would have changed*, were race to have not been an issue in American politics. This is the drama described in Figure 11.2.

I do not wish to urge overdue credence in the *magnitudes* of our results. If racism has indeed lowered the tax take of the state by between 11 and 18 percentage points, I would be surprised. There are many criticisms one can lodge against our model – and I will mention several in a moment. But I do believe that we have made a serious effort at estimating the effect in question; the ways that I can think of to improve our model would be quite computationally difficult and time-consuming. Therefore, I believe that we have shown that the race issue significantly reduces redistribution in the US from what it otherwise would be.

Let me explain the limitations of the model just referred to. Typical equilibrium analysis in political economy can be characterized as "one by one" (i.e. 1×1); it assumes a policy space of one dimension and a type space of one dimension. The policy is a tax rate, the type dimension is "income." We have employed a 2×2 model: both the policy space and the type space are two-dimensional. This necessitated not only a new concept of political equilibrium (moving from Hotelling–Downs to PUNE), but computationally expensive procedures of calculation. (The equilibrium computations described in this paper took about 500 computer hours.) Now it would be very nice to be able to increase the dimension of both the policy space and the type space. For instance, we might like to allow for non-linear taxation, or for foreign policy, or for preferences over "values" issues – each of these moves would require expanding the dimensions of both type and policy spaces. We might also like to allow voters to possess different values of α – that is, of racial issue salience – in the utility function. This, too, would require expanding the type space to three dimensions. But adding even one extra dimension to the type space would make our calculations of equilibrium an order of magnitude (I am guessing) more time-consuming. My conjecture is that, were we able to do this (or, more optimistically, *when* we will be able to), our estimates of the ASE and PBE will change, and the estimated effect of racism on equilibrium values of tax policies will probably decrease.

IV.   Concluding remarks

I have argued that during the period 1976–92 the Republican Party was able to maintain a significant vote share, without compromising very much its position on redistribution and size of the public sector, by exploiting the race issue. There is reason to believe that the main Republican strategy has shifted in the last decade to relying on issues such as abortion, patriotism, and anti-gay preferences. For some evidence, see Lee and Roemer (2008). Whether this move will be as effective as the race issue has been is, of course, an open question.

I do not wish to claim that Hirschman's observations about the reliance of reactionaries on the arguments of perversity, futility, and jeopardy are out of date: I believe these strategies continue to be important ones, whereby parties that represent the very wealthy can continue to remain viable in a fully enfranchised democracy. Indeed, the American author who has best exploited these strategies in recent years, and to great effect, is Charles Murray (1994). As I said, these arguments fall under the explanation of "the mapping from policies to outcomes," and perhaps I am wrong to place that explanation at a relatively low position (fourth) on my list of explanations.

I have not discussed, very much, the issue of misrepresentation. As I said, we used Bartels's estimates to model the idea that politicians are more responsive to rich voters than to poor ones. But there are many other facets of misrepresentation that may be important, having to do with the role of money in politics (both campaign contributions and lobbying) and with the rules of representation under different democratic systems. I believe I would disagree with those who would argue that the policy bundling phenomenon I have focused upon here, and its apparent effect of keeping extremely conservative economic policy politically viable in a democracy, is an aspect of misrepresentation. Why? Because policy bundling may be an unavoidable characteristic of any viable democracy. The only obvious way of avoiding it is to run referenda on every single issue facing the electorate: but if that is infeasible, or undesirable for other reasons (as I think it is), then we cannot say that electoral systems that bundle policies entail misrepresentation. After all, ought implies can. What we may be able to conclude, however, is that democracy is not the panacea that many appear to think it is.

BIBLIOGRAPHY

Alesina, A., E. Glaeser, and B. Sacerdote, 2001. "Why Doesn't the US Have a European-Style Welfare State?" *Brookings Papers on Economic Activity* (Fall): 187–278.

Bartels, L. 2002. "Economic Inequality and Political Representation." Princeton University.

Graetz, M. and I. Shapiro. 2005. *Death by a Thousand Cuts*. Princeton, NJ: Princeton University Press.

Hirschman, A. O. 1991. *The Rhetoric of Reaction*. Cambridge: Cambridge University Press.

Lee, W. and J. Roemer. 2006. "Racism and Redistribution: A Solution to the Problem of American Exceptionalism." *Journal of Public Economics* 90: 1027–52.

2008. "Moral Values and Distributive Politics: An Analysis of the US 2004 Election," in I. Shapiro, P. Swenson, and D. Donno (eds.) *Divide and Deal: The Politics of Distribution in Democracies*. New York: New York University Press.

Lindert, P. 2004. *Growing Public*. Cambridge: Cambridge University Press.

Luttmer, E. 2001. "Group Loyalty and the Taste for Redistribution." *Journal of Political Economy* 109: 500–28.

Murray, C. 1994. *Losing Ground*. New York: Basic Books.

Piketty, T. 1995. "Social Mobility and Redistributive Politics." *Quarterly Journal of Economics* 110 (3): 551–84.

Poole, K. and H. Rosenthal, 1997. *Congress: A Political-Economic History of Roll Call Voting*. Oxford: Oxford University Press.

Roemer, J. E. 1994. "The Strategic Role of Party Ideology when Voters Are Uncertain about how the Economy Works." *American Political Science Review* 88: 327–35.

1998. "Why the Poor Do Not Expropriate the Rich: An Old Argument in New Garb." *Journal of Public Economics* 70 (3): 399–424.

1999. "The Democratic Political Economy of Progressive Taxation." *Econometrica* 67: 1–19.

2006. "Party Competition under Private and Public Financing: A Comparison of Institutions." *Advances in Theoretical Economics* 6 (1), article 2. Available at: www.bepress.com/bejte/advances/vol6/iss1/art2.

Roemer, J. E., W. Lee, and K. Van der Straeten. 2007. *Racism, Xenophobia, and Distribution: Multi-issue Politics in Advanced Democracies*. Cambridge, MA: Harvard University Press.

Smith, M. A. 2000. *American Business and Political Power*. Chicago: University of Chicago Press.

2007. *The Right Talk: How Conservatives Transformed the Great Society into the Economic Society*. Princeton, NJ: Princeton University Press.

12 The impact of electoral debate on public opinions: an experimental investigation of the 2005 New York City mayoral election

Sendhil Mullainathan, Ebonya Washington, and Julia R. Azari

I.   Introduction

Political debates have long been a part of the American polity. The early practice was aimed primarily at promoting parliamentary and elite deliberation, as well as informing the broader public about issues and candidates (Jamieson and Birdsell 1988: 37).[1] Televised debates have altered this dynamic, structuring debate as a practice to educate the electorate. Yet the impact of televised debates on the quality of democracy has been somewhat controversial, with proponents casting debates as opportunities "to provide sustained analysis of issues and close comparison of candidates" (ibid.: 5), and others expressing the concern that the televised debates would increase the emphasis on image rather than substance (Druckman 2003).

Whether debates influence opinions by showcasing candidate viewpoints or by simply presenting shallow cues of candidate image, conventional wisdom assumes that televised debates will somehow influence viewers' opinions regarding the candidates. Information in the electoral process is presumed to help voters make decisions more in line with their preferences (Lupia and McCubbins 1998). In light of the emphasis on the informative potential of debates, it is natural to pose the question of whether debates truly provide citizens with information that influences their opinions or choices.

To this end, there is a large literature examining the impact of debates on citizens' political opinions and voting behavior. This research has concluded that debates are able to alter viewers' opinions of candidates,

We are grateful to Tiffany Davenport and Meredith Levine for research assistance, Gregory Huber for his discussion, and ISPS for funding.
[1] The Lincoln–Douglas debates of 1858 were notable in this regard. They were well attended and addressed a number of issues related to the national question of slavery (Jamieson and Birdsell 1988: 49).

but only in a small way. This literature states that debates have more influence the earlier in the electoral season they occur. Further, the literature concludes that debates have greater influence over the uninformed than over those who know quite a bit about the election.[2]

Debate studies typically follow a panel design, interviewing voting-aged individuals both before and after the debate of interest. The pre-post-debate opinion change of those who watched is compared with the opinion change of those who did not watch in a "difference-in-difference" style methodology. The limitation of such an analysis is the potential endogeneity of debate watching. Perhaps only those who are most inclined toward opinion change actually watch the debate. In such a case the coefficient on "watch" would be an overestimate of the impact of the debate on the average citizen. Or perhaps only political junkies, who have the longest-held, most intransigent, political opinions, are in the viewing audience. In such a case the coefficient on "watch" would be an underestimate of the impact of the debate on the average citizen.

We overcome this limitation by employing an experimental panel design. During the 2005 election season, in the days leading up to the final debate between mayoral incumbent Republican Michael Bloomberg and Democratic challenger Fernando Ferrer, we interviewed a random sample of 1,000 New York City voters. We randomly assigned these 1,000 individuals to one of two groups: we asked the treatment group to watch the November 1 debate, and we asked the control group to watch a "placebo" program, PBS's *The NewsHour with Jim Lehrer*, which aired opposite WNBC's debate broadcast. Our intervention was effective. Statistically indistinguishable from controls in the pre-debate interviews, in post-debate interviews treatment group members reported watching the debate at a rate that was more than twice as high as controls. (We verified viewership by asking factual questions about the debate.) Thus we can take opinion differences between treatment and controls as a measure of the causal impact of the debate on political viewpoint.

Using this methodology we find that those in the watch group were 6 percentage points more likely to report that their opinions of one or both candidates had changed from the first to the second interview. However, when asked to rate the candidates on two of the most salient campaign issues, terrorism and housing, the post-debate responses of the treatment group were statistically indistinguishable from those of the control group. Clearly in a short survey we could not address every possible issue on which opinions may have changed. However, the fact that there was also no statistical difference between treatment and control group members'

---

[2] See Hellweg, Pfau, and Brydon (1992), Holbrook (1996), or Kraus (2000), for a review of this literature.

ratings of candidates generally, nor on their likelihood of voting for each candidate, strongly suggests that although the debate led respondents to *believe that their opinions had changed*, the debate actually effected *no meaningful political opinion change*. The study highlights the incongruence between respondents' stated opinion change and respondents' actual opinion change, a discrepancy pointed out by Gerber and Green (1999).

Why do we see no real opinion change in this study? Several possibilities exist: the first is that debates actually change no one's political opinions. Second, it is possible that debates shift everyone's political opinions. Because the highlights of debates are reported through the media and over the water cooler, perhaps one does not need to watch the debate to be affected by it.[3] Third, perhaps debates on average do affect opinion change, and this debate was an exception. In other words, perhaps the external validity of the present work is limited. This could be due to its timing – just days before the general election – or perhaps because of the fact that this particular contest was never close. Or perhaps our sample – older, more educated and more likely to vote than the average New Yorker – is not a population whose views are swayed by debates.

In the next section we detail the history of the 2005 New York City mayoral election. In Section III we describe the data and methodology, before presenting results in Section IV. Section V discusses some potential implications of the findings in the context of the broader question of political knowledge and democracy. The final section concludes.

II.   2005 New York City mayoral election[4]

Former Bronx borough president, Democrat Fernando Ferrer, was never a serious contender in the 2005 New York City general mayoral election. The top vote-getter in the Democratic primary, he garnered only 39.949 percent of the vote. By law, 40 percent must be won by a single candidate to avoid a runoff. Fortunately for Ferrer, the second place finisher decided, for the sake of the party, to refrain from participating in the runoff. And thus Ferrer began his eight-week campaign against Michael Bloomberg, a Republican mayor, who enjoyed a 60 percent approval rating in an overwhelmingly Democratic city. (Seventy-four percent of the city's votes were cast for Democrat John Kerry in the 2004 presidential election [Andersen 2004].)

---

[3] We turn to post-debate interviews conducted the night of the debate to control for this diffusion effect. Unfortunately, the sample interviewed that night was too small for this analysis to be informative.

[4] The sources for this section are various articles from the 2005 *New York Times*: Healy (2005a–d); Anon. (2005); Purnick (2005); Healy and Lueck (2005); Healy and Connelly (2005); Haberman (2005); and Rutenberg (2005).

Even more than approval, Bloomberg had money. In what the *New York Times* regarded as "drowning-by-spending," the billionaire incumbent spent more than $70 million on his campaign. Ferrer's only possible opportunity to present himself on an equal footing with the mayor came through the three debates endorsed by the city's campaign finance program. But as Bloomberg was financing his own campaign, he was under no obligation to participate in these events. He decided to meet Ferrer in two of the three. Bloomberg avoided the first debate because he did not like its format: the October 9 event included Conservative Party candidate Thomas Ognibene who attacked Bloomberg for failing to be a true Republican. Ferrer and Ognibene spent most of the debate throwing criticisms at the empty lectern where the mayor would have stood.

The remaining debates occurred on October 30 and November 1, much later in the electoral season. At this point Bloomberg enjoyed a 27 percentage point lead in the polls. Bloomberg even led Ferrer amongst the more often Democratic subgroups of liberals, blacks and women. Nonetheless, at 9 a.m. on Sunday, October 30, Ferrer "tore into Mayor Michael Bloomberg." Ferrer had what the *New York Times* dubbed "the best day so far in his race for mayor." Two days later, however, Bloomberg evened the debate score. He was "far more assertive" than in the first debate in which he participated. The media and our survey respondents agreed. Bloomberg won this final debate, which is the focus of the inquiry in this chapter. The mayor then went on to win the November 9 election by more than 20 points, a record win for a Republican mayoral candidate in New York City.

III.   Data and methodology

We investigate the question of how this final debate between Bloomberg and Ferrer affected public opinion of these candidates by employing an experimental panel design. Respondents, randomly selected from the New York City voter registration list,[5] were first surveyed by telephone between October 28 and October 31. Using this initial survey we established respondents' pre-debate attitudes about how life was going in New York City and about the two mayoral candidates. Respondents were randomly divided into one of two groups: we asked the treatment group to watch the final mayoral debate on November 1, and we asked the control group to watch a placebo program, PBS's *The NewsHour with Jim Lehrer*, which aired opposite WNBC's debate broadcast. We then interviewed

---

[5] Our selection procedure gave greater weight to likely voters. The survey company phoned the home of likely voters but then asked for the adult registered in New York City whose birthday would come the soonest.

respondents for a second time between November 1 and November 3 to establish post-debate attitudes toward the candidates. Our final sample contains pre- and post-debate interviews with 1,000 New York City residents: 505 in the control group and 495 in the treatment condition.

Our methodology is simple. We measured the debate's impact on political views by examining the difference between treatment and control group members' post-debate views. Given our panel design, an alternative strategy would have been to compare the change (from pre- to post-debate) in political views of treatment and control group members. We did not follow such a strategy because we did not want to ask precisely the same questions in the pre- and post-debate interviews. Given that the pre- and post-debate interviews occurred within days of one another, we wanted to avoid respondents' post-debate answers being influenced (or anchored) by their pre-debate answers. Instead of this explicit differencing, we performed an implicit differencing strategy by assuming that members of the treatment group held, on average, the same political views as controls. Therefore, a comparison of post-debate opinion differences between the groups is equivalent to a comparison of pre-post-debate changes in opinion differences between the groups.

Thus the first assumption that underlies our identification strategy is that treatment and control group members do not differ significantly in political views before viewing the debate. We test this assumption in Table 12.1 by comparing the two groups on pre-debate opinions.

The first column of the table gives the sample mean on the opinion (demographic). For example the 0.77 in the first column indicates that 77 percent of the sample agreed with the statement, "New York City is headed in the right direction." The second and third columns of the table give the means for the Watch (treatment) and Don't Watch (control) groups. These columns indicate that 78 and 75 percent of the Watch and Don't Watch groups respectively agreed that the city was headed in the right direction. In the final column of the table we provide the results of a test of the null hypothesis that the two groups are drawn from populations with the same mean. The fact that the final cell in the first row of the table is blank therefore says that the difference between the Watch and Don't Watch groups in opinion of whether the city is headed in the correct direction is statistically insignificant.

The same is true for the remaining pre-debate opinions. Control and treatment group members are statistically indistinguishable on party preference. The sample mean is 15 percent Republican and 75 percent Democrat. (By treatment status, those figures are 16 percent Republican and 73 percent Democrat for treatments and 13 percent Republican and 76 percent Democrat for controls.) The groups are also equally likely to choose Bloomberg (Ferrer) as their preferred candidate. (The figures are

Table 12.1 *Summary statistics*

	Full sample	Watch group	Don't Watch group	Test of equality of Watch and Don't Watch groups
Pre-debate opinions				
NYC is headed in the right direction	0.77	0.78	0.75	
Republican	0.15	0.16	0.13	
Democrat	0.75	0.73	0.76	
Will vote for Bloomberg (asked of only half the sample)	0.65	0.64	0.66	
Will vote for Ferrer (asked of only half the sample)	0.31	0.34	0.28	
Voting history				
Voted in 2001	0.96	0.96	0.97	
Voted in 1997	0.80	0.78	0.81	
Demographics				
Age	64	63	64	
White	0.71	0.68	0.74	**
Black	0.19	0.21	0.17	
Female	0.61	0.61	0.61	
College graduate	0.52	0.52	0.52	
Post-debate checks				
Watched debate	0.27	0.37	0.16	***
Correctly identified moderator's race (of 268 who claimed to have watched)	0.56	0.6	0.46	**
Correctly identified moderator's gender (of 268 who claimed to have watched)	0.64	0.69	0.54	**
N	1,000	505	495	

Note: *** denotes significance at the 1 percent level, ** at the 5 percent level, and * at the 10 percent level. Sample size varies due to item non-response.

64 percent for Bloomberg and 34 percent for Ferrer among treatments and 66 percent for Bloomberg and 28 percent for Ferrer among controls.) In summary, the evidence in the first section of Table 12.1 supports the assumption that pre-debate opinions are the same for the two groups.

We further test this assumption by looking at voting history. By matching our sample to New York City voting records we examine whether respondents voted in the mayoral elections of 2001 and 1997. The 96 percent voting rate in 2001 reflects the fact that we predominantly sampled those who, based on their voting history, were likely to vote in the upcoming election. In neither year is the difference in voting rate between treatment and controls statistically meaningful. Thus voting history data provide further support for the assumption that pre-debate treatment and controls are the same politically.

Finally, we test the assumption by turning to demographic characteristics. On age, gender, and education there is no meaningful difference between the two groups. Only on one demographic, percentage of whites, do we see a statistically significant difference. The Watch group is 68 percent white; the Don't Watch group is 74 percent white. Clearly one statistically significant difference in 12 is no indictment of our randomization procedure. Nonetheless, we will present our results with and without controls for demographics to adjust for any pre-debate differences between the two groups.

Our assumption of equivalence of opinions among treatments and controls thus seems defensible. A second assumption on which our analysis rests is that our intervention – asking respondents to watch the debate[6] – was in fact effective. In the final section of Table 12.1 entitled "Post-debate checks" we test this assumption. The row marked "Watched debate" indicates that 37 percent of the treatment group but only 16 percent of the control group report having watched the debate. This difference is statistically significant at the 1 percent level. But our assumption is not that those in the treatment group report watching the debate at a greater rate than controls, which could arise out of a desire, on the part of respondents, to please the interviewer.[7] Our assumption is that those in the treatment group actually watched the debate at a greater rate than controls. To test the veracity of respondents' viewing reports, we asked those who claimed to have watched the debate to identify both the race and the gender of the moderator. The moderator of the November 1 debate was a white man, while the panelists (questioners) included a white man, a white woman, a black man and a Latino man.[8] Fifty-six percent of those who claimed to have watched the debate identified the race of the moderator correctly. Sixty-four percent of those who claimed

---

[6] Fifty-four percent of respondents asked in the pre-debate survey indicated that they would watch the debate for us. Thirty-one percent said they would not. The remaining respondents were not sure.

[7] See, for example, Gales and Kendall (1957); Gray (1956); or Hanson and Marks (1958) on interviewer effects.

[8] The moderator's race and gender were the same for both debates in which Bloomberg participated. So unfortunately respondents may be given credit for correctly identifying the moderator when they are in fact correctly identifying the moderator for the wrong debate. Over 80 percent of the sample had their pre-debate interview before October 31 – the date of the first Bloomberg/Ferrer debate. Thus it is possible that some treatment members mistakenly watched the wrong debate. If half of those watching saw the debate that Bloomberg won and half saw the debate in which Ferrer prevailed, then it is possible that the reason we find no debate effects on average is because the debate in fact pulled the two groups in opposite directions. However, such a split in debate watching cannot explain the fact that on average debate watchers claimed to feel relatively more favorable to Ferrer rather than unchanged. In the debate in which the mayor did not participate the moderator was a black man.

Table 12.2 *Impacts of commitment to vote on voting (dependent variable is an indicator for having voted in the 2005 election)*

	(1)	(2)	(3)
Commit group indicator	0.042*	0.043*	0.040*
	(0.023)	(0.024)	(0.024)
Demographic controls		Yes	Yes
Voting history controls			Yes
N	795	721	721

Notes: Demographic controls include age, race, gender, and education. Voting history controls include indicators for voting in the 1997 and 2001 New York City mayoral elections.

to have watched the debate identified the gender of the moderator correctly. Thus it seems that respondents, on average, are truthfully reporting their viewership.[9] Amongst those who claim to have watched the debate, treatment group members are significantly more likely to correctly identify the moderator's race and gender. To the extent that incorrect answers on moderator gender and race proxy for not actually having watched the debate, our results show that those in the treatment group were more likely to have watched.

The idea that simply phoning an individual and asking her to undertake some activity (in this case watching a debate) at a future date for no remuneration would result in compliance is hard to believe. Therefore we tested our methodology with an activity that we could actually verify – voting. In the post-debate survey, respondents, regardless of treatment/control debate status, were randomly assigned to a commit condition or a control condition. Those in the commit condition were asked an additional two questions at the end of the survey. The first was whether they would vote in the upcoming mayoral election (96 percent said they would) and the second was whom they would vote for (58 percent said Bloomberg). Those in the control group were not asked about future expectations for voting nor for vote choice. We then matched our sample to voting records. As the results in Table 12.2 indicate, those in the treatment group voted in the 2005 election at a rate that is a significant 4 percentage points higher than those in the control.

[9] There is, however, the possibility that respondents learned of the moderator's demographics by seeing excerpts of the debate on the news. Fortunately the news outlets were more interested in giving sound bites of candidates responding than of the moderator's questioning.

Table 12.3 *Summary statistics for commitment to vote treatment*

	Commit group	Non-committed group	Test of equality of committed and non-committed groups
Demographics			
Age	65	62	*
White	0.71	0.72	
Black	0.21	0.18	
Female	0.63	0.59	
College graduate	0.50	0.54	
Voting History			
Voted in 2001	0.96	0.97	
Voted in 1997	0.82	0.77	
Pre-debate opinions			
NYC is headed in the right direction	0.77	0.76	
Republican	0.15	0.15	
Democrat	0.75	0.74	
Sample size	500	500	

Note: *** denotes significance at the 1 percent level, ** at the 5 percent level, and * at the 10 percent level. Sample size varies due to item non-response.

This is a sizable increase on a mean of 88 percent voting.[10] As the final columns of the table show, this 4 percentage point difference is robust to the inclusion of controls for demographics and for voting history. The means for these demographics, by voting treatment status, are presented in Table 12.3. Thus this simple voting manipulation experiment provides evidence of the plausibility of the effectiveness of our debate manipulation.

IV.   Results

The basic results of our survey are derived from the post-debate interview. As the results in Table 12.4 indicate, those in the Watch group were more likely than those in the Don't Watch group to believe that their opinion of one or both candidates had changed since the time of their initial interview.

[10] Four percentage points is about half the expected size of the most effective GOTV ("get out the vote") interventions, such as personal canvassing (Gerber and Green 2000).

Table 12.4 *Post-debate summary statistics*

	Full sample	Watch group	Don't Watch group	Test of equality of Watch and Don't Watch groups
Have experienced change in opinion toward one or both candidates	0.48	0.51	0.45	*
Opinion of Bloomberg changed	0.30	0.33	0.27	**
More favorable to Bloomberg	0.10	0.09	0.10	
Opinion of Ferrer changed	0.35	0.37	0.32	
More favorable to Ferrer	0.00	0.04	−0.03	
Bloomberg seems more knowledgeable	0.83	0.82	0.85	
Bloomberg thermometer	69	70	69	
Ferrer thermometer	48	49	47	
Bloomberg–Ferrer thermometer	21	21	21	
Bloomberg better on terrorism	0.89	0.89	0.90	
Bloomberg better on housing	0.53	0.50	0.55	
Will vote for Bloomberg (asked of only half the sample)	0.69	0.70	0.67	
Will vote for Ferrer (asked of only half the sample)	0.28	0.27	0.29	
N	1,000	505	495	

Note: *** denotes significance at the 1 percent level, ** at the 5 percent level, and * at the 10 percent level. Sample size varies due to item non-response.

The first row of Table 12.4 shows the mean answers to precisely that question. Forty-eight percent of the full sample said that their opinion had changed. By treatment status, 51 percent of those in the Watch group and 45 percent of those in the control group agreed with that statement. This 6 percentage point difference, statistically significant at the 10 percent level, is the intention-to-treat effect. However, we know that not everyone in the treatment group actually watched the debate. The difference in viewership between treatments and controls was not 100 percentage points, but merely 21 percentage points. Thus we scale our 0.06 effect size by 0.21 and conclude that the effect of the debate on those who actually watched was a 29 percentage point increase in the belief that their opinion had changed over the past few days. Or if we only consider those who correctly identified the moderator's demographics as having seen the debate, our treatment effect rises to a 43 percentage point increase in the belief that their opinion had changed.[11]

[11] Fifty-seven percent of the 37 percent of treatments who said they watched the debate correctly identified the moderator's race and gender. Or in other words 21 percent (0.37 × 0.57) of treatments correctly identified the moderator's race and gender.

We next asked participants about opinion change regarding each of the candidates individually. Thirty-three percent of the Watch group felt their opinion of Bloomberg had changed; while only 27 percent of controls agreed with that statement, a difference that is statistically significant at the 5 percent level. This 6 percentage point intention to treat effect corresponds with a 29 percentage point treatment effect (or 43 percentage points if we consider only the verified viewership).

While those in the Watch group were more likely to say their opinion of Bloomberg had changed, they were no more likely than those in the Don't Watch group to say that their opinion of Bloomberg had changed in a positive (or negative) direction. The third row of the table examines responses to the question of how opinions toward Bloomberg had changed over the last few days. Respondents were offered the answer choices of "more favorable" coded 1, "unchanged" coded 0 or "less favorable" coded −1. On average survey respondents felt more favorable towards Bloomberg, but there were no significant differences between the two groups. Watch group members saw a mean of 0.09 for this variable and Don't Watch members had a mean of 0.10.[12]

Watch group members were also more likely than controls to say that their opinion of Ferrer had changed. Watch group members expressed this view 37 percent of the time compared to only 32 percent of the time amongst controls. This 5 percentage point difference, however, is not statistically significant. Treatment group members on average saw their opinion of Ferrer rise, while controls saw their opinion fall. This 0.07 point difference (0.04 v. −0.03) is just shy of significance at conventional levels.[13] Thus when asked directly whether their opinions had changed, those who were exogenously induced to watch the debate were more likely than controls to indicate that their opinions had changed in the last few days.

Yet when their opinions were measured directly, those in the treatment group held post-debate opinions that were statistically indistinguishable from those of treatment group members. The remainder of Table 12.4 shows these results. The first direct opinion question (shown in row 6

Viewership of only 7 percent of controls (16 percent claimed to have viewed × 43 percent of those named the moderator race and gender) was verified. Thus the difference between treatment and control verified viewership is 14 percentage points. We divide 0.06 by 0.14 to arrive at a treatment effect of 43 percentage points.

[12] This lack of significance between the two groups is caused not merely by an equal number of positive and negative Bloomberg switchers in the treatment group. The two groups saw comparable positive and negative change: 12 (20) percent of treatments had a less (more) favorable opinion of the mayor and 8 (19) percent of controls had a less (more) favorable opinion of the mayor.

[13] The p value on the t test is 0.1067.

of the table) asked respondents whether they felt Bloomberg or Ferrer was more knowledgeable. Eighty-two percent of the Watch group and 85 percent of the Don't Watch group chose Bloomberg. The three-point difference is statistically indistinguishable. Next, we asked respondents to rate their feelings about each of the two candidates on a scale from 0 to 100.[14] Once again, there were no significant differences between treatment and control group members. The groups rated Bloomberg 70 and 68 respectively and Ferrer 49 and 47. The average difference in rating between the two candidates, 21 points for both groups, was also statistically insignificant. We turned to two hot button issues of the electoral campaign next. We asked which candidate would perform better on (1) terrorism and (2) housing. Eighty-nine percent of Watch group members and 90 percent of Don't Watch group members thought Bloomberg would outperform Ferrer on the terrorism issue. On the housing issue, Bloomberg was favored by 50 percent of treatments and 55 percent of controls. Neither difference was statistically significant. Finally, we asked respondents for whom they planned to vote. Bloomberg was chosen by 70 percent of Watch group members and 67 percent of Don't Watch group members. Ferrer was chosen by 28 and 29 percent of the two groups respectively. Once again, neither difference was statistically significant. Thus the evidence of the second half of Table 12.4 indicates that the debates had no impact on political opinions.

The basic finding of an impact of debate watching on belief of opinion change but of no impact of watching on actual opinion change is robust to the inclusion of demographic and voting history controls, as shown in Table 12.5.

The first column of the table reproduces the results of Table 12.4 in regression form. Thus whereas in Table 12.4 we run t-tests, in Table 12.5 we test the equality of effect between the two groups by running regressions of the following form:

$$(1) \text{ Outcome } = a + B \text{ (Watch group indicator) } + e.$$

We run a separate equation for each outcome of interest. As the tests are equivalent the results are of course identical: we see a significant impact of debate watching on the belief that someone's opinion has changed in general and that their opinion of Bloomberg has changed in particular. In column 2 of the table we add demographic controls (summarized in Table 12.1) to the model. Our qualitative findings remain unchanged. We continue to see significant impacts on changes of opinion of Bloomberg. Additionally, the finding that the Watch group has raised

---

[14] The ordering of the candidates in the questioning varied randomly.

Table 12.5 *Impact of debate on opinions of candidates (each cell presents the coefficient on a different regression).*

	(1)	(2)	(3)
Outcome			
Have experienced change in opinion toward	0.058*	0.057*	0.049
one or both candidates	(0.033)	(0.034)	(0.039)
Opinion of Bloomberg changed	0.06**	0.053*	0.055
	(0.029)	(0.031)	(0.035)
More favorable to Bloomberg	−0.011	−0.023	−0.014
	(0.035)	(0.037)	(0.041)
Opinion of Ferrer changed	0.051	0.053	0.044
	(0.031)	(0.033)	(0.037)
More favorable to Ferrer	0.062	0.082**	0.075*
	(0.039)	(0.041)	(0.046)
Bloomberg seems more knowledgeable	−0.032	−0.033	−0.033
	(0.027)	(0.028)	(0.031)
Bloomberg thermometer	1.234	0.870	−0.774
	(1.731)	(1.798)	(1.925)
Ferrer thermometer	2.117	20.081	0.987
	(1.721)	(1.790)	(1.974)
Bloomberg–Ferrer thermometer	−0.758	−1.344	−2.341
	(2.412)	(2.488)	(2.728)
Bloomberg better on terrorism	−0.001	0.007	0.016
	(0.022)	(0.024)	(0.025)
Bloomberg better on housing	−0.045	−0.033	0.000
	(0.035)	(0.036)	(0.040)
Will vote for Bloomberg (asked of only half	0.028	0.025	0.028
the sample)	(0.045)	(0.046)	(0.050)
Will vote for Ferrer (asked of only half the	−0.013	−0.002	−0.009
sample)	(0.044)	(0.045)	(0.049)
Controls			
Demographic controls		Yes	Yes
Voting history controls			Yes

Note: Sample size varies among specifications due to non-response. Total samples size is 1,000. *** denotes significance at the 1 percent level, ** at the 5 percent level, and * at the 10 percent level.

its opinion of Ferrer more than the control group has is now statistically significant at the 5 percent level. All of the direct measures of opinion change continue to show insignificant coefficients on the treatment status dummy. In column 3 we add voting history controls (also summarized in Table 12.1) to the model of column 2. Coefficients are little changed for all outcomes as we move from column 2 to column 3. However, as we utilize increasing degrees of freedom, the general opinion change and the Bloomberg opinion change specifications no longer show significant treatment/control differences. The only significant difference between the groups remains in their opinions of Ferrer. The treatments believe, more than controls, that their opinion of Ferrer has improved over the last few days.

Thus our basic finding is robust to the inclusion of demographic and voting history controls: we show that debate watching increased participants' beliefs that their opinions of the candidates had changed in the past few days. However, when measuring directly, we find no evidence of actual opinion change.

V. Implications

Since the experimental design used in this study overcomes the endogeneity issues endemic to observational studies of debate effects, we cannot attribute the lack of change in participants' opinions to their preexisting strong opinions (Zaller 1992), or to some other shared characteristic of debate watchers. Therefore, the findings suggest that, independent of the effects of existing views or political awareness, the experience of viewing political debates did not change opinions about the candidates. In this section we discuss the implications of both this finding and the finding that respondents thought their opinions had changed when in fact they had not.

Democratic ideals depend on an informed electorate capable of making reasoned political choices (Delli Carpini and Keeter 1996: 1). Responsible party government enforced through electoral accountability requires mechanisms by which citizens can learn about the policy positions of the candidates vying to be their leaders. More candidate-centered approaches to political competition depend on such processes as well in order for citizens to make judgments about the character or personal qualities of candidates. As stated in the introduction, debates in the contemporary era have been seen as a means of helping candidates communicate their message to citizens and, in turn, for citizens to use the information gained by watching debates to form opinions of candidates (Jamieson and Birdsell 1988). In light of the intended relationship between debates and popular rule, the results of this experiment are particularly striking: we find that debates do not perceptibly change citizens' opinions, and – even more notable – despite the evidence that actual views had not changed, participants in this study were under the impression that their views had changed after watching the debates.

American political thought and history have long grappled with the tension between the ideal of popular rule and the possibility of a poorly informed electorate. While revolutionary ideals may have rested in part on an image of "the people" who are "wiser than their governors" (Morone 1998: 5), a streak of skepticism about this characterization of "the people" runs through early American political thought as well. Madison repeatedly warns in the *Federalist* against the potential for the people to rule using "passion" rather than "reason."[15] While the 1776 Revolution against British rule was based on a radical democratic ideology, the dominant sentiment among ruling elites in the new American republic soon took a more conservative turn, motivated in part by a heavy skepticism about the ability of the mass electorate to make informed political decisions (Wood 1998).

The question of whether popular rule is advisable or even possible under conditions of limited citizen information is very much alive in contemporary normative and empirical studies. Contemporary inquiries into the role of information in the functioning of American democracy call into question the level of information possessed by the American electorate (Delli Carpini and Keeter 1996), the effect of political awareness and reception of political messages on public opinion (Zaller 1992), and the importance of information for making reasoned political decisions (Lupia and McCubbins 1998).

How does the literature on political knowledge bear upon the implications of a study whose findings concern the *opinions*, rather than the political knowledge, of the participants? Implicit in the literature on political knowledge is a link between information and political judgment and behavior. Lupia and McCubbins, who investigate this link systematically, insist that perfect information is not needed for citizens to make reasoned political choices; what is required for reasoned choices is what the authors call "knowledge" (ibid.: 6), defined as "the ability to predict the consequences of actions." Their point speaks directly to the implications of this study: the purpose of practices intended to enhance political knowledge is to give citizens the tools to change their opinions about candidates in order to more closely match their true preferences. Our discussion of the implications of the results of the study in this broader context must be cautious; we do not know anything for sure about the voting behavior of the study participants. Obviously we cannot say anything about the ultimate impact of the perceived shift in opinions following the debates.

---

[15] Madison *et al.* (1982: 310–14). The arguments advanced in these documents center on the concern about creating institutional arrangements that will be conducive to the "people's rule" using reason rather than passion, distinct from more contemporary ideas about creating an informed populace.

We can, however, cautiously consider the implications of the findings for the complex constellation of relationships at stake in the study of mass opinion and knowledge, media events such as televised debates, and broader notions of democratic rule. The fundamental purpose of debates – namely, to inform citizens about candidates' characteristics and issue positions – has been explicitly linked with the objective of changing opinions; contemporary models of political information do not regard such information as an intrinsic good, but as means to an end. That end is the ability of citizens to make political choices that better reflect their underlying values and preferences. Here we return to Lupia and McCubbins's thesis that reasoned political decisions are possible with limited political information as long as meaningful cues are available, and that political information is costly and "provides no instrumental benefit" if it does not change citizens' decisions (ibid.). As stated before, we do not know whether watching the debate had an impact on citizens' vote choice.

However, the results suggest that if opinions of the candidates are the bases of such decisions, we might expect that the debates did not have this kind of impact. Further research is needed to determine whether the stability in opinions after watching the debates is associated with stability in electoral behavior. The absence of substantial opinion shift following the debates may suggest that debates are costly and provide little actual value to citizens who rate political information only insofar as it helps them make political decisions that reflect their preferences and views. The fact that participants thought their opinions had changed when in fact they had not suggests that the process of incorporating new information may be more complex than previously theorized. For instance, we do not know whether the perceived changes in opinion of Bloomberg among the treatment group led to changes in voting behavior. However, the results of this study suggest that there may be a distinction between voting based on an actual opinion, and based on a perceived opinion. Our findings suggest that the relationship between political information, political opinions, and candidate evaluation may be even more complex than current scholarship indicates. Debates and other means of informing citizens about candidates may not function in as straightforward a manner as conventional wisdom would predict.

VI.   Conclusion

Previous research on the impact of candidate debates on public opinion has suffered from potential bias due to the endogeneity of debate viewing. We overcome this limitation by employing an experimental panel design. We randomly assign study participants to watch either the final

2005 New York City mayoral debate or a placebo program. We find that debate watching increased participants' beliefs that their opinions of the candidates had changed in the past few days. However, when measured directly, we find no evidence of actual opinion change. Thus this study highlights the incongruence between respondents' stated opinion change and respondents' actual opinion change, a discrepancy pointed out by Gerber and Green (1999).

We do not conclude, however, that debates never induce opinion change. There are several possible explanations for our lack of opinion change findings in this context. The first is, of course, that debates actually change no one's political opinions. The second is that debates move everyone's political opinions. Because the highlights of debates are reported through the media and over the water cooler, perhaps one does not have to watch the debate to be affected by it. Third, perhaps our findings are not generalizable to the voting population at large. Our research setting – New York City – is one of the most politically homogeneous locales in the nation. Our focal debate occurred just days before the general election. Our sample was older, more educated and more likely to vote than the average New York City resident.

Thus we conclude with a suggestion and a word of caution. We suggest that future work on the persuasive effects of debates be conducted using an experimental research design. Such a design overcomes the bias from the endogeneity of debate viewership. We also caution against the use of stated opinion change as a proxy for actual opinion change. Our results highlight that these two variables do not measure the same underlying construct.

BIBLIOGRAPHY

Andersen, Kurt. 2004. "People Like Us." *New York* 37 (November 22): 24–6.
Anon. 2005. "The Shunned Debate." *New York Times*, October 9, p. CY11.
Delli Carpini, Michael X. and Scott Keeter. 1996. *What Americans Know About Politics and Why it Matters.* New Haven, CT: Yale University Press.
Druckman, James N. 2003. "The Power of Television Images: The First Kennedy–Nixon Debate Revisited." *Journal of Politics* 65 (May): 559–71.
Gales, Kathleen and M. G. Kendall. 1957. "An Inquiry Concerning Interviewer Variability." *Journal of the Royal Statistical Society*, ser. A. (General) 120 (2): 121–47.
Gerber, Alan, and Donald Green. 1999. "Misperceptions about Perceptual Bias." *Annual Review of Political Science* 2 (June): 189–210.
2000. "The Effects of Canvassing, Telephone Calls, and Direct Mail on Voter Turnout: A Field Experiment." *American Political Science Review* 94 (September): 653–63.

Gray, Percy G. 1956. "Examples of Interviewer Variability Taken from Two Sample Surveys." *Applied Statistics* 5 (June): 73–85.

Haberman, Clyde. 2005. "Watch Debate? Sleep In? Boxers? Briefs?" *New York Times*, October 28, p. B1.

Hamilton, Alexander, James Madison, and John Jay. 1982. *The Federalist Papers*. New York: Bantam Books.

Hanson, Robert H. and Eli S. Marks. 1958. "Influence of the Interviewer on the Accuracy of Survey Results." *Journal of the American Statistical Association* 53 (September): 635–55.

Healy, Patrick. 2005a. "Weiner Concedes Race for Mayor to Avert Runoff; Says Ferrer is Nominee." *New York Times*, September 15, p. A1.

2005b. "Ferrer Makes His Candidacy Look Stronger Than the Polls Suggest." *New York Times*, October 31, p. B4.

2005c. "Attacks Escalate in Final Debate of Mayor's Race; Rivals Go on Offensive." *New York Times*, November 2, p. A1.

2005d. "Bloomberg Cruises to Re-Election Victory; Corzine is Winner in Costly New Jersey Race." *New York Times*, November 9, p. A1.

Healy, Patrick, and Marjorie Connelly. 2005. "Even Among Democratic Voters, Poll Finds Ferrer is Well Behind." *New York Times*, October 28, p. A1.

Healy, Patrick, and Thomas Lueck. 2005. "Ferrer Levels Attack on Bloomberg Over Iraq War and the Need for Low-Cost Housing." *New York Times*, October 27, p. B3.

Hellweg, Susan A., Michael Pfau, and Steven R. Brydon. 1992. *Televised Presidential Debates: Advocacy in Contemporary America*. New York: Praeger.

Holbrook, Thomas M. 1996. *Do Campaigns Matter?* Thousand Oaks, CA: Sage Publications.

Jamieson, Kathleen Hall, and David S. Birdsell. 1988. *Presidential Debates: The Challenge of Creating an Informed Electorate*. New York: Oxford University Press.

Kraus, Sidney. 2000. *Televised Presidential Debates and Public Policy*. Mahwah, NJ: Lawrence Erlbaum Associates.

Lupia, Arthur and Mathew D. McCubbins. 1998. *The Democratic Dilemma: Can Citizens Learn What They Really Need to Know?* New York: Cambridge University Press.

Madison, James, Alexander Hamilton, and John Jay. 1982. *The Federalist Papers*. New York: Bantam, 1982.

Morone, James A. 1998. *The Democratic Wish: Popular Participation and the Limits of American Government*. New Haven, CT: Yale University Press.

Purnick, Joyce. 2005. "So Far, a Race Without Chutzpah." *New York Times*, October 20, p. B1.

Rutenberg, Jim. 2005. "In Equal Footing of a Debate, Ferrer Gets Feisty." *New York Times*, October 31, p. A1.

Wood, Gordon S. 1998. *The Creation of the American Republic, 1776–1787*. Chapel Hill: University of North Carolina Press.

Zaller, John R. 1992. *The Nature and Origins of Mass Opinion*. New York: Cambridge University Press.

13 Swing voters, core voters, and distributive politics

Gary W. Cox

How do political parties allocate targetable goods – such as private goods targeted to individuals, local public goods targeted to geographic areas, or tax breaks targeted to specific industries or firms – in order to optimize their electoral prospects? A continuing debate on this question pits those who lean toward Cox and McCubbins's (1986) "core voter model" against those who lean toward Lindbeck and Weibull's (1987) "swing voter model." Both models envision two parties competing to win an election by promising to distribute targetable goods to various groups, should they be elected. Cox and McCubbins argue that vote-maximizing parties will allocate distributive benefits primarily to their core voters. A typical response embodying the swing voter logic is Stokes's (2005: 317): "voters who are predisposed in favor of [a party] on partisan or programmatic grounds [– that is, its core voters –] cannot credibly threaten to punish their favored party if it withholds [distributive] rewards. Therefore the party should not waste rewards on them."

In this chapter, I first review the literature and then note that extant models focus solely on *persuasion* (defined as an attempt to change voters' preferences between given alternatives). Once one brings *coordination* (defined as an attempt to affect the number and character of alternatives from which voters choose) and *mobilization* (defined as an attempt to affect whether or not citizens participate in the election) into analytic view, the argument that vote-maximizing parties should focus their distributive benefits on core voters is substantially strengthened. Lowering the number of ideologically similar competitors on the ballot and mobilizing its base are often more important to maximizing a party's vote than is persuasion; in such situations, parties allocate distributive benefits primarily to individuals and groups providing key coordination and mobilization services, rather than to vote-brokers expert at identifying swing voters.

Another point I make is that parties are interested in votes not just in the electoral arena but also in the legislative arena. Thus parties may engage in "electoral targeting" (distributing benefits to optimize

342

electoral outcomes), "legislative targeting" (distributing benefits to optimize legislative outcomes), or a mixture of the two. Indeed, many studies of the allocation of distributive benefits ignore the core voter versus swing voter debate and focus entirely on legislative variables. Even in this part of the literature, however, an analogous debate appears between those who argue that legislative benefits flow primarily to senior figures in the governing coalition (the analogs of core voters) and those who argue that legislative benefits flow primarily to pivotal legislators (the analogs of swing voters).

The core versus swing debate is important to understanding how and whom parties represent. If parties focus exclusively on persuasion, and hence target swing voters in the electorate and pivotal legislators in the assembly, it is hard to see how they could be reliable agents of their core voters. Core voters could not credibly threaten to punish their party, because the party's vote-maximization strategy focuses solely on persuasion and the core voters are by definition already persuaded. In contrast, if parties focus primarily on coordination and mobilization, and hence target core voters in the electorate and party members in the assembly, there is much less tension between the goals of maximizing votes and serving the interests of core voters.

I.   The previous literature on electoral targeting

A typology of transfers

A preliminary question regarding the electoral payoff of distributing targetable goods regards the nature of the exchange. There are three pure types of transfer that appear to have been used in elections: (1) benefits are delivered upon verification of an individual's vote; (2) benefits are given to a voter before s/he votes (and there is no subsequent effort to verify how s/he voted); (3) benefits are promised upon victory of the relevant candidate or party (again, no effort to verify individual votes).

The first type of transfer is what many think of when the word "bribe" is used. It appears to have become less widespread after the introduction of the secret ballot, simply because parties have a harder time verifying their purchases when ballots are cast secretly. Nonetheless, practices such as the Tasmanian dodge,[1] squeaky voting machines, and so on can make

---

[1] The Tasmanian dodge, invented soon after the introduction of a secret ballot in Australia (first in Victoria, 1856), entailed party workers first securing a blank official ballot, filling it in, and giving it to a voter. The voter then concealed the ballot, went to the polling place and got a ballot, cast the pre-marked ballot, and returned the unmarked ballot to

such bribes feasible even with putatively secret ballots. Moreover, bribes are certainly possible when the parties themselves print and distribute ballots, as in Argentina (cf. Stokes 2005).

The second type of transfer has typically been used to boost turnout among known supporters. Upstate Republicans in New York used to convey their supporters to the polls in carriages well stocked with rum under the seat, for example. This sort of bribe is worth the money only if turnout among likely supporters can be significantly boosted by it. Turnout-enhancing bribery became less attractive after the introduction of the secret ballot worsened parties' ability to identify their supporters (cf. Cox and Kousser 1981).

The third category consists of outcome-contingent transfers. Promising to deliver benefits if and only if one wins avoids the cost of verifying either current or past voting behavior on an individual-by-individual basis. Most of the electoral targeting models in the literature focus on this type of transfer.

The Dixit–Londregan model

Dixit and Londregan (1995, 1996) provide a general model of how outcome-contingent transfers are targeted, from which both the Cox–McCubbins and the Lindbeck–Weibull models emerge as special cases. I follow their exposition here.

Dixit and Londregan envision a left-wing party, L, and a right-wing party, R, competing for votes (implicitly in a single-member district). Each party k announces a vector of transfers, $T_k = (T_{lk}, \ldots, T_{nk})$, where T_{jk} is the per capita transfer that party k promises to group j (voters are partitioned into n groups). Promises are credible ex ante, and if the relevant party wins honored ex post. Party k's transfer policy must satisfy a budget constraint, $\sum_j N_j T_{jk} = B$, where N_j is the number of voters in group j. Party k chooses T_k in order to maximize its vote total, $\sum_j N_j P_{jk}(T_{jL}, T_{jR})$, where P_{jk} (T_{jL}, T_{jR}) is the proportion of group j's members who will vote for party k, given the transfer promises T_{jL} and T_{jR}. Although the model accommodates other possibilities, for expositional ease I shall consider the special case in which $T_{jk} \geq 0$ for all j, k.

To formalize Cox and McCubbins's notion of "core support groups," Dixit and Londregan assume that the consumption benefit that members of group j will actually receive, when party k promises an amount

---

the party worker, whereupon he was paid. The process was then repeated. The same practice in the Philippines goes under the more evocative label of the "chain of love."

T_{jk}, is $t_{jk} = (1 - \theta_{jk})T_{jk}$. Here, $\theta_{jk} \in [0, 1]$ denotes the proportion of the subsidies that k intends to deliver to group j that will not actually reach it. Group j is a core support group for party k when θ_{jk} is relatively small. As Dixit and Londregan (1996: 1134) point out, "A party's core constituencies need not prefer its issue position. It is the party's advantage over its competition at swaying voters in a group with offers of particularistic benefits that makes the group core." In practice, core groups tend also to provide solid support to their party, but it is important to recognize that there are two distinct notions of what makes a group core. For most of this chapter, I shall refer to voters with a strong preference for a particular party as its "core" voters; in the next few pages, however, a party's core voters will be those it knows well and to whom it can more effectively and credibly target benefits.

To provide some micro-foundations for the group response functions, $P_{jk}(T_{jL}, T_{jR})$, Dixit and Londregan proceed as follows. All voters in a given group are assumed to have the same income, denoted y_j for group j (so the groups can be thought of as income or occupational strata). Voter h is assumed to have an innate preference for party R, represented by a real number X_h. If voter h is in group j, then h votes for L if $U_j[y_j + (1 - \theta_{jL})T_{jL}] > U_j[y_j + (1 - \theta_{jR})T_{jR}] + X_h$, and votes for R otherwise. Here, $U_j[y_j + (1 - \theta_{jk})T_{jk}]$ represents the utility that a member of group j derives from his or her total income, $y_j + (1 - \theta_{jk})T_{jk}$. Letting Φ_j be the cumulative distribution function of X_h in group j, $P_{jk}(T_{jL}, T_{jR}) = \Phi_j[U_j[y_j + (1 - \theta_{jL})T_{jL}] - U_j[y_j + (1 - \theta_{jR})T_{jR}]]$.

Dixit and Londregan show that, when the parties have no special relationships with any groups (e.g., $\theta_{jL} = \theta_{jR} = 0$ for all j), the parties' allocations are driven by the density of swing voters in each group – as in the Lindbeck–Weibull model. As larger and larger asymmetries in the parties' abilities to deliver benefits arise, however, the parties' allocations are driven more and more by the core voter logic of promising benefits to those groups to which the party can most effectively deliver benefits.[2]

Multiperiod models

Stokes (2005) and Diaz-Cayeros, Estévez, and Magaloni (2006) consider multiperiod models of distributive politics in which promises by parties

---

[2] Of less relevance for present purposes, the Dixit–Londregan model also predicts that parties should target poor voters – because their votes should be cheaper to buy. Note that poor voters' labor – in mobilizing or coordinating others – should also be cheaper to purchase.

to deliver benefits or by voters to deliver votes are not necessarily credible. Stokes views the voter–party exchange as a repeated prisoner's dilemma. In each stage (election), the voter would like to receive a bribe and then vote for her most preferred party, while the party would like to withhold any bribe and yet have the voter vote for it. In a single stage, the equilibrium outcome (between a party and a voter who does not rank the party first) would be mutual defection: no bribe for the voter and no vote for the party. In repeated play, exchange can arise – but the voters involved in the exchange will only be those who would not otherwise support the party and are cheap to buy (swing voters). Diaz-Cayeros, Estévez, and Magaloni also consider a multiperiod model but allow voters' predispositions for one party or another to shift, depending on their past receipt of transfers. In their model, parties have a reason to target core voters, since if they give them no transfers they will become swing voters in the next election.

Multidistrict models

Distinct from the models reviewed thus far are the mostly empirical studies that look at the allocation of distributive goods across multiple electoral districts. The logic of targeting swing *districts* is particularly compelling, because doing a bit better in a swing district can, by definition, make the difference between losing and winning a seat. The same cannot be said about swing *groups* in the models reviewed above. Doing a bit better in a swing group just means that the party earns a few more votes. As the parties in the standard single-district models are vote-maximizers, they do not even consider how close the election is. In contrast, the (implicit or explicit) maximand in cross-district models is seat maximization, and so swing status is highly relevant.[3]

Note that whether swing *districts* are targeted is not particularly relevant to the debate over whether swing *groups* are targeted. The Cox–McCubbins, Lindbeck–Weibull, and Dixit–Londregan models address the allocation of benefits within a single district. In a multidistrict context, the core voter thesis would be that parties concentrate benefits on their core voters *within* whatever districts they target, swing or otherwise. For example, the Republicans certainly targeted resources toward the

---

[3] McGillivray (2004) notes some structural conditions that affect the extent to which swing districts are targeted, including district magnitude (with larger magnitudes, districts vary less in their marginality) and party strength (weak parties cannot convince members to run personal electoral risks for the sake of a more efficient overall campaign).

swing state of Ohio in the presidential campaign of 2004. However, by all accounts, they pushed those resources more into mobilizing their base than into persuading swing voters. Thus the targeting of Ohio in no way provides support for the swing voter thesis; it provides support for the quite different swing district thesis.

Empirical evidence

The empirical studies conducted to date yield mixed results on how much swing as opposed to core voters are targeted. Empirical studies cited as supporting the thesis that material benefits are disproportionately directed toward swing voters include Wright (1974), Stein and Bickers (1994), Bickers and Stein (1996), Denemark (2000), Herron and Theodos (2004), Stokes (2005), Dahlberg and Johansson (2002), and Case (2001). However, all but the last three studies consider the allocation of benefits across electoral districts rather than the allocation of benefits within districts. These cross-district studies provide evidence that parties target swing districts, but do not shed light on who gets benefits within each district. Dahlberg and Johansson (2002) and Case (2001) study the allocation of benefits across municipalities lying in several different electoral districts, while Stokes (2005) examines the allocation of benefits to individual voters. These studies thus come closer to testing the vote-maximizing models considered thus far.[4]

Empirical studies supporting the thesis that material benefits are disproportionately directed toward core voters include Ansolabehere and Snyder (2003), Levitt and Snyder (1995), Balla, Lawrence, Maltzman, and Sigelman (2002), Diaz-Cayeros, Magaloni, and Weingast (2000), Calvo and Murillo (2004), Bickers and Stein (2000), and Chen (2008). Most of these studies, too, examine the allocation of benefits across electoral districts. Thus they too fail to provide much evidence pertinent to

---

[4] Although the study has many strengths, there is reason to doubt that Dahlberg and Johansson (2002) provide an appropriate test of the swing voter and core voter models. The main problem is that the program they study had a strong programmatic content which appealed to core interests within the Social Democratic Party, whereas the models all assume completely policy-neutral transfers of funds. As Dahlberg and Johansson (ibid.: 27) note, the grants they investigate were "intended to support . . . local investment programs aimed at an ecological sustainable development and at increasing municipal employment." It is possible that the primary beneficiaries of these grants were Greens and public-sector union locals in each municipality, regardless of what the overall Socialist percentage was in the municipality. Violation of the assumption that funds are "policy-neutral" is a general problem with using data on spending that has programmatic content.

the Cox–McCubbins, Lindbeck–Weibull, and Dixit–Londregan models. When such studies find that distributive benefits flow to the strongholds of the governing party or parties, rather than to swing districts, they may be discovering that governments are sometimes probability-of-majority maximizers rather than vote-maximizers: if a government allocates benefits to maximize its probability of retaining a majority, then it may sometimes decide that retaining a vice-like grip on a small majority is the optimal strategy. Alternatively, the targeting of benefits to government strongholds may reflect a purely legislative, rather than electoral, logic (on which more below).

II.   Extending the electoral targeting model(s)

Two key aspects of the Cox–McCubbins, Lindbeck–Weibull, Dixit–Londregan, Stokes, and Diaz-Cayeros–Estévez–Magaloni models are: (a) all voters vote; and (b) the number of parties is exogenously fixed at two. The first assumption puts aside all issues of mobilization and turnout. The second assumption puts aside all issues of coordination. Thus, in all current electoral targeting models, parties can increase their vote shares *only by persuasion*, and the means by which they can persuade voters is limited to offering transfers (there is no endogenous spatial competition, for example).

Let us consider the terms coordination, mobilization and persuasion more carefully, following Cox (2005). We shall consider what actions L, the left-wing party, can take to increase its total vote. The probability that voter h votes for party L depends on whether h participates in the election; whether L is the only left-wing party on the ballot; and whether h prefers L to R. Efforts to ensure that voter h actually participates in the election – a necessary but not sufficient condition for h to support L – fall under the heading of mobilization. Efforts to ensure that there is just one left-wing party on the ballot fall under the heading of coordination. Finally, efforts to ensure that voter h prefers L to R fall under the heading of persuasion. In general, parties can persuade by repositioning themselves along the left–right spectrum, by convincing voters that they are more competent at providing valence goods, by slinging mud at their opponents, and so forth. In the models under consideration here, the method of persuasion is offering transfers.

To generalize the Dixit–Londregan model, we could rewrite the proportion of group j's members voting for party L as $P_{jL}(t_L, t_R) = Q_j(t_L, t_R)S_{jL}(t_L, t_R)/M_j(t_L, t_R)$, where $Q_j(t_L, t_R)$ is the turnout rate in group j, $S_{jL}(t_L, t_R)$ is the proportion of group j's participating members who prefer L to R, and $M_j(t_L, t_R)$ is the number of left-wing parties that campaign for votes among group j's voters. If $M_j(t_L, t_R) = 1$, then L gets votes from all citizens who participate and prefer it to the right-wing alternative, R. If $M_j(t_L, t_R) = 2$, then L gets half the votes of citizens who participate and prefer it to R; implicitly, the new entrant on the left is equally attractive to left-wing voters, and vote coordination fails utterly on the left. This particular functional form embodies the largest possible losses due to miscoordination. A more flexible formulation would be that L receives a fraction of the left-wing vote, with that fraction declining as the number of left-wing parties increases.[5]

What happens if one extends the model(s) in the literature so that the transfers party L offers to group j affect not just how many voters in that group prefer L to R but also how many left-wing competitors L faces within group j and how many citizens in group j participate in the election?

Let us consider adding mobilization and turnout first. The transfers offered in the current models affect only the vote choices made by voters, rather than their participation decisions. If turnout is invariant with respect to transfers, then transfers should indeed go to groups where the marginal persuasive effect will be greatest. Lindbeck and Weibull (1987) and Cox and McCubbins (1986) disagree about which groups will yield the biggest persuasion bang for the transfer buck, but they agree on focusing just on persuasion.

What if voters' preferences are immutable but their turnout decision can be affected by transfers? Suppose, for example, the electorate is highly polarized (almost no swing voters in any group) but not everyone has a high probability of participating. In this case, each party should clearly target transfers to its core support groups. The most valuable voter for a party to offer a transfer to is one with a high probability of voting for that party, conditional on participating; and a probability of participation that is highly responsive to transfers. Thus, the party should target core support groups (in the sense of groups with large proportions of members who strongly prefer L to R) with malleable turnout rates.

Now let us consider adding coordination. The transfers offered in the current models do not affect the decisions of political entrepreneurs or young Turks to start a rival party which caters to the same core groups as one of the existing duopolists. If there is some chance that one of the duopolists might face competition on its home turf, then transfers to the core groups have another value, as they presumably help to depress the probability of internecine competition.

---

[5] Another approach, in which both persuasion and mobilization – but not coordination – are brought into analytic view, is that of Bartels (1998).

Do the claims just made about the importance of coordination and mobilization founder on the canonical swing voter objection, quoted at the outset of the chapter, that core voters "cannot credibly threaten to punish their favored party if it withholds [distributive] benefits" (Stokes 2005: 317)? First, the explicit or implicit threat of sitting the election out is credible, because the individuals issuing the threat must bear private costs to participate in the election. It is true that their abstention raises the probability that the other (and dispreferred) party will win the election; but the change in the probability is negligible. Thus, on an individual calculus, it is rational to abstain and a threat to abstain is by no means empty. Second, the explicit or implicit threat of running a rival candidate in the election can also be credible if the group threatening to split has some chance of forcing a re-coordination of the party system and emerging as the dominant party in its ideological niche. Thus, although only occasionally manifest, threats by core groups to sit the election out or to launch new parties are always possible. Indeed, the better way to view it is that coordination is a full-time job and so is mobilization, so that the party needs full-time "employees" or "consultants" working on these problems, and that these agents then receive a regular and large flow of distributive benefits as compensation for their services.

In a combined model, in which transfers can increase a party's vote share, either due to persuasion or to mobilization or to coordination, one should find: (1) the less persuasion a party thinks possible, and the more mobilization it thinks possible, the more it concentrates its transfers on its core supporters; (2) the less persuasion a party thinks possible, and the more its leaders are worried about splintering, the more it concentrates its transfers on its core supporters; (3) the less able a party is to deliver credible promises to swing groups, the more it concentrates on its core groups.

III.   Maximizing votes in the electoral and legislative arenas

In this section, I argue that the debate over whether parties target swing voters or core voters is similar to the debate in legislative studies between those who view pivotal legislators as the primary determinants of legislative outcomes (Krehbiel 1998) and those who view senior majority-party legislators as the primary determinants (Cox and McCubbins 1993, 2005; Aldrich and Rohde 2001; Kim 2006).

First, note that swing voters and pivotal legislators share a crucial similarity. It is true that the Lindbeck–Weibull model is distributive, while Krehbiel's model is spatial. Nonetheless, both swing voters and pivotal legislators end up being indifferent in equilibrium and thus cheap to buy. Swing voters are by definition indifferent on ideological grounds. Pivotal legislators are those whose support may be crucial in overcoming super-majority requirements in the legislative process, such as invoking cloture in the US Senate. Sometimes securing sixty votes in the Senate to invoke cloture is not a problem – when the status quo is far enough away from the legislative median. In this case, the pivotal legislators are not indifferent. When cloture (or other super-majority) requirements do bind, however, then the pivotal legislators are in equilibrium indifferent between passage and rejection of a bill – and are thus cheap to buy with side payments. As with swing voter models, Krehbiel's pivotal legislator model assumes away both any need for mobilization (all legislators vote) and any need for coordination (there are no fights over which bills and amendments will be considered), leaving parties with only persuasion as a strategy.

Second, note that core voters and majority-party legislators share some similarities. The party knows the preferences of core voters and its own legislators better than it knows the preferences of swing voters or independent legislators. Moreover, the party may look to core voters and its own legislators to help coordinate electoral candidacies or the legislative agenda; and to help mobilize voters or whip legislators.

Cox and McCubbins (2005) argue that legislative parties are not primarily mechanisms to purchase votes on the floor. Rather, they are primarily coordinating and mobilizing devices: they distribute benefits to members primarily to buy their agenda-setting (coordinating) and whipping (mobilizing) services, and only secondarily to buy their votes (persuading). I would argue that electoral parties are similar. Their main purpose is not to buy votes on the spot market on the day of the election, or otherwise persuade during the election. Rather they are primarily coordinating (Cox 1997) and mobilizing (Cox 1999) devices.

As evidence for this view, consider the allocation of offices – e.g. committee chairs in the legislative arena or postal sub-masterships in the electoral arena. Offices are the largest *private* benefits that parties distribute. In the legislature, they go almost exclusively to members of the party (i.e. to its "core voters"); and the recipients are being "paid" mostly for their coordinating and mobilizing services. In the electorate, the consistent finding is that political machines allocate patronage jobs almost exclusively to core supporters, who are then expected not simply to vote for the party but also – and more importantly – to coordinate (prevent rivals from emerging) and mobilize (get out the vote).[6]

---

[6] See e.g. Rakove (1975), Cox and McCubbins (1986), Calvo and Murillo (2004).

IV.   Models of legislative targeting

When investigating the allocation of distributive benefits to multiple districts, one might argue that benefits are not targeted solely in order to optimize electoral outcomes but also – or even instead – in order to optimize legislative outcomes. Indeed, many studies seeking to explain the distribution of targetable government expenditures across districts focus on *legislative* considerations. They examine whether districts represented by powerful senior figures, especially those in the government, get more pork (e.g. Levitt and Poterba 1999; Denemark 2000; Golden and Picci 2006), whether districts represented by members of the relevant committee(s) get more pork (e.g. Hird 1991; Alvarez and Saving 1997), and so on. Occasionally, such legislatively focused studies will include a variable measuring how marginal a particular legislator is, on the theory that more marginal incumbents should work harder to bring home benefits to their districts. But the model is one in which individual legislators pursue benefits in order to maximize their own electoral chances, not one in which a party allocates benefits in order to maximize votes.

Other scholars have suggested that parties play a more consequential role in the allocation of legislative side payments. Cox and McCubbins (1993, appendix 1), Evans (2004), and Kim (2006) argue that distributive benefits are used as side payments to clinch broader legislative deals. Kim stresses that these are payments not so much to buy pivotal votes on the floor – the legislative analog of swing voters – but rather to pay committee chairs for their agenda-setting services – the legislative analog of electoral coordination. For example, Claude Pepper, then chair of a key committee, received numerous distributive benefits for his district in the "transition rules" attached to the Tax Reform Act of 1986. Ideologically, Pepper was nowhere near being pivotal on the floor (indeed, the bill passed by a large margin) and thus he did not need to be paid to vote for the bill. Rather, he was collecting his customary "toll" for allowing the bill to pass through his committee and consume scarce (and valuable) committee time (Kim 2006). In other words, he could slow down the bill or speed it up and the proponents were willing to pay for the latter rather than the former.

Another model of legislative targeting, which corresponds better to the swing voter model in the electoral arena, focuses on the side payments used by Speakers in the US House when they arrange "vest pocket" votes. As explained most clearly by King and Zeckhauser (2003), Speakers regularly negotiate "vote option contracts" with certain members before a close vote. The contract gives the Speaker the option of calling on the member to change his or her vote in exchange for a consideration the two have agreed upon. The important things to note about the side payments conveyed via vest pocket arrangements is that (a) they go to swing legislators; but (b) they are small potatoes compared to the flow of pork controlled by committee actors.

My interpretation of results that show powerful individual legislators getting more benefits than would seem justified on a vote-maximizing calculation is that parties need both electoral and legislative votes; and they pay those skilled at coordinating and mobilizing votes in both arenas. Thus, powerful legislators receive additional benefits to pay them for their legislative services. I am not arguing that all parties in all contexts perfectly control the allocation of distributive benefits and trade off electoral vote-maximizing against legislative vote-maximizing at the optimal rate. I am just pointing out that, if a party is a long-lived entity with both electoral and legislative goals, then one cannot take the electorally irrational bonuses that senior figures get – e.g. the notorious "bridges to nowhere" in Alaska or Japan – as convincing evidence that the party as a whole is weak or poorly organized.

V.   The role of coordination and mobilization in spatial models

As explained above, in electoral targeting models sans mobilization and coordination, parties are more likely to target swing voters; but when mobilization and coordination are brought into the analysis, parties cater more to their core groups. A similar pattern emerges in spatial models.

The pure Downsian model – which ignores coordination (the number of parties is exogenously fixed at two) and mobilization (all voters vote) – predicts that both parties will adopt a platform that coincides with the ideological position of the median voter. They both "target" the median voter. When voters can abstain (e.g. Smithies 1941), the parties may not converge, because when they contemplate a move toward the center, they anticipate more vote losses due to abstention on their extreme wing than vote gains from centrists. When the number of parties is not fixed, one can add another reason for non-convergence: each party's worry that it might be outflanked by a splinter or new party if it moves toward the center (Palfrey 1984).

Spatial and distributive models both focus on persuasion. They differ in their conception of the tools that parties use to persuade voters. In spatial models, parties announce a platform of policies that they will enact if elected. In distributive models, parties announce a package of transfers that they will implement if elected. Regardless of the technology of persuasion, the necessity of coordinating and mobilizing induces parties to cater more to their core groups – either in the sense of advocating policies that appeal to the core groups or in the sense of advocating transfers that appeal to the core groups.

VI.   Conclusion

In this chapter, I have considered how vote-maximizing parties might allocate benefits within a district – the purview of the Dixit–Londregan and other models. The first main point I have urged is simply that the extant models of electoral targeting focus too narrowly on a single vote-getting strategy – offering transfers to voters who have already decided to participate in an election with an exogenously fixed number of competitors in order to persuade them to vote for a particular party (persuasion). It is conceptually easy to extend these models to include other vote-getting strategies – in particular, offering transfers to voters or groups, in order to pay them for either (1) their efforts in mobilizing support for the party; or (2) their efforts in coordinating the menu of choices that appears on the ballot. I argue that empirically the bulk of distributive benefits should flow to those who are crucial in lowering the number of ideologically similar competitors a party faces on the ballot and to those who are crucial in getting out the vote. Experts at buying votes on the spot market on the day of the election can sometimes be important, too, but need not be. Since the key agents in coordination and mobilization are typically the leaders of core groups within the party, I expect that distributive benefits should flow to core groups and their members.

The second point I have urged is that the parallel literature on legislative targeting – in which allocations of benefits across electoral districts are explained in terms of the "clout" that individual legislators wield by virtue of their committee positions, leadership positions, or majority status – also should (and implicitly does) pay attention to coordination and mobilization, in addition to persuasion. The legislative analog of Lindbeck and Weibull's swing voter hypothesis would be Krehbiel's pivotal politics thesis, according to which all the action in side payments should center on legislators whose votes are (or will be) pivotal to the outcome on the floor. The argument that benefits should be targeted to "core groups" within the legislature – that is, the majority party's senior figures – relies on points similar to those made above about maximizing votes in the electoral arena: senior party figures are crucial in setting the agenda (coordination) and whipping (mobilization), and a vote-maximizing party should certainly wish to pay for these important services, in addition to buying pivotal votes on the floor when needed.

Finally, I have noted that the necessity of coordination and mobilization drives parties' spatial positions away from the center to more robust left and right positions; and drives their distributive strategies away from swing voters to core voters. These are abstractly similar responses, in that in both cases more benefits flow to the party's base, as a recognition of its crucial role in maximizing votes.

BIBLIOGRAPHY

Aldrich, John, and David Rohde. 2001. "The Logic of Conditional Party Government," in *Congress Reconsidered*, ed. Lawrence Dodd and Bruce Oppenheimer, 7th edn. Washington DC: Congressional Quarterly Press, 26–92.

Alvarez, R. Michael, and Jason L. Saving. 1997. "Congressional Committees and the Political Economy of Federal Outlays." *Public Choice* 92: 55–73.

Ansolabehere, S. and J. M. Snyder. 2003. "Party Control of State Government and the Distribution of Public Expenditures." Unpublished paper, Departments of Political Science and Economics, Massachusetts Institute of Technology.

Balla, S. J., E. D. Lawrence, F. Maltzman, and L. Sigelman. 2002. "Partisanship, Blame Avoidance, and the Distribution of Legislative Pork." *American Journal of Political Science* 46: 515–25.

Bartels, Larry. 1998. "Where the Ducks Are: Voting Power in a Party System," in *Politicians and Party Politics*, ed. John G. Geer. Baltimore, MD: Johns Hopkins University Press, 43–79.

Bickers, K. N. and R. M. Stein. 1996. "The Electoral Dynamics of the Federal Pork Barrel." *American Journal of Political Science* 40: 1300–25.

2000. "The Congressional Pork Barrel in a Republican Era." *Journal of Politics* 62: 1070–86.

Calvo, E. and M. V. Murillo. 2004. "Who Delivers? Partisan Clients in the Argentine Electoral Market." *American Journal of Political Science* 48: 742–57.

Case, A. 2001. "Election Goals and Income Redistribution: Recent Evidence from Albania." *European Economic Review* 45: 405–23.

Chen, Jowei. 2008. "Republican Vote Buying in the 2004 US Presidential Election." Unpublished typescript, Stanford University.

Cox, Gary W. 1997. *Making Votes Count*. Cambridge: Cambridge University Press.

1999. "Electoral Rules and the Calculus of Mobilization." *Legislative Studies Quarterly* 24: 387–420.

2005. "Electoral Institutions and Political Competition: Coordination, Persuasion and Mobilization," in *Handbook of New Institutional Economics*, ed. Claude Menard and Mary M. Shirley. Dordrecht: Springer, 141–61.

Cox, Gary W. and J. Morgan Kousser. 1981. "Turnout and Rural Corruption: New York as a Test Case." *American Journal of Political Science* 25: 646–63.

Cox, Gary W. and Mathew D. McCubbins. 1986. "Electoral Politics as a Redistributive Game." *Journal of Politics* 48: 370–89.

1993. *Legislative Leviathan: Party Government in the House*. Berkeley: University of California Press.

2005. *Setting the Agenda: Responsible Party Government in the U.S. House of Representatives*. Cambridge: Cambridge University Press.

Cox, Gary W., and Michael Munger. 1989. "Closeness, Expenditure, Turnout: The 1982 U.S. House Elections." *American Political Science Review* 83: 217–32.

Dahlberg, M. and E. Johansson. 2002. "On the Vote-Purchasing Behavior of Incumbent Governments." *American Political Science Review* 96: 27–40.

Denmark, David. 2000. "Partisan Pork Barrel in Parliamentary Systems: Australian Constituency-Level Grants." *Journal of Politics* 62: 896–915.

Diaz-Cayeros, Alberto, Federico Estévez, and Beatriz Magaloni. 2006. "Poverty and Vote Buying: The Politics of Social Transfers in Mexico, 1989–2006." Unpublished book manuscript. Stanford University.

Diaz-Cayeros, Alberto, B. Magaloni, and B. Weingast. 2000. "Federalism and democratization in Mexico." Unpublished paper, Stanford University.

Dixit, A. and J. Londregan. 1995. "Redistributive Politics and Economic Efficiency." *American Political Science Review* 89: 856–66.

1996. "The Determinants of Success of Special Interests in Redistributive Politics." *Journal of Politics* 58: 1132–55.

Drazen, A. 2000. *Political Economy in Macroeconomics*. Princeton, NJ: Princeton University Press.

Evans, Diana. 2004. *Greasing the Wheels: Using Pork Barrel Projects to Build Majority Coalitions in Congress*. Cambridge: Cambridge University Press.

Golden, Miriam, and Lucio Picci. 2006. "Pork Barrel Politics in Postwar Italy, 1953–1994." *American Journal of Political Science* 52: 268–89.

Hall, Richard. 1996. *Participation in Congress*. New Haven, CT: Yale University Press.

Herron, M. C. and B. A. Theodos. 2004. "Government Redistribution in the Shadow of Legislative Elections: A Study of the Illinois Member Initiative Grants Program." *Legislative Studies Quarterly* 29: 287–311.

Hird, John A. 1991. "The Political Economy of Pork: Project Selection at the U.S. Army Corps of Engineers." *American Political Science Review* 85: 429–56.

Kim, Henry. 2006. "Agenda Setting, Clout, and Logrolls in the U.S. House." Unpublished typescript, University of California, San Diego.

King, David, and Richard Zeckhauser. 2003. "Congressional Vote Options." *Legislative Studies Quarterly* 28: 387–411.

Krehbiel, Keith. 1998. *Pivotal Politics*. Chicago: University of Chicago Press.

Levitt, S. D. and M. Poterba. 1999. "Congressional Distributive Politics and State Economic Performance." *Public Choice* 99: 185–216.

Levitt, S. D. and James M. Snyder. 1995. "Political Parties and the Distribution of Federal Outlays." *American Journal of Political Science* 39: 958–80.

Lindbeck, A. and J. Weibull. 1987. "Balanced Budget Redistribution and the Outcome of Political Competition." *Public Choice* 52: 273–97.

McGillivray, F. 2004. *Privileging Industry: The Comparative Politics of Trade and Industrial Policy*. Princeton, NJ: Princeton University Press.

Palfrey, Thomas. 1984. "Spatial Equilibrium with Entry." *Review of Economic Studies* 51: 139–56.

Rakove, Milton. 1975. *Don't Make No Waves, Don't Back No Losers*. Bloomington: Indiana University Press.

Smithies, Arthur. 1941. "Optimum Location in Spatial Competition." *Journal of Political Economy* 49: 423–39.

Stein, R. M. and K. N. Bickers. 1994. "Congressional Elections and the Pork Barrel." *Journal of Politics* 56: 377–99.

Stokes, S. C. 2005. "Perverse Accountability: A Formal Model of Machine Politics with Evidence from Argentina." *American Political Science Review* 99: 315–25.

Wright, G. 1974. "The Political Economy of New Deal Spending: As Econometric Analysis." *Review of Economics and Statistics* 56: 30–8.

Index

accountability, 212, 232, 278, 279, 337
  legal, 279, 280
  political, 280
  and representation, 44, 225
addresses, 3, 35
  quantity of, 45
  royalist addresses, 52–3
  statistics about, 41
  use of, 40
advocacy, 114–16
Africa, 211–18
  electoral systems in, 220–5
  ethnicity in, 222
  formal inequalities in, 230
  impact of quotas for women, 211–18, 230
  political parties, 225, 232
  women's movements, 228, 231
  women's representation in, 217
African-Americans, 119, 122, 130, 188
agency, 9, 76, 125, 145, 296
  autonomy of agents, 275, 281, 283
  incentives for agents, 273, 283
  and interests, 281
  political, 282–6
  problem of, 273, 293
  restriction on the agency contract, 285
Alaska, 169
Albericus de Rosciate, 76
Alcibiades, 291
Alesina, A., 312
American Indian Movement, 205
American Indian Policy Review
    Commission, 206
American National Election Studies, 315
American War of Independence, 67
anti-slavery petitions, 41
anti-solidarity effect, 10, 312, 316, 317
Aristedes, 280
aristocracy, 9
aristocratic rule, and representative
    government, 286–91

aristocratic thesis, 9, 92, 96, 271–301
Aristotle, 260, 271, 273
  concept of democracy, 16, 288
  elections, 290, 295–6
  elections and lottery, 296
  leadership, 289
  rule by the poor, 272
Athenian government, 272, 280, 285, 288
  accountability, 276, 279
  citizenship, 295
  direct democracy, 276
  institutional features of democracy, 291
  lottery system, 67
Atoka Agreement, 185
Austen-Smith, David, 293
authority, 25
  and formal institutions, 52
  Hobbes's conception of, 15
authorization, 15, 22, 74, 278
  by election, 278
  Hobbes's theory of, 17, 18–26
  and representation, 17, 25, 28
Azari, Julia, 11, 324–40

Babcock, Frederick, 122
Baldus de Ubaldis, 76
Banaszak, Lee Ann, 229
Banks, Jeffrey, 293
bargaining, 313
Bartels, Larry M., 90, 301, 314, 322
Bartolus of Sassoforrato, 76
Beale, Edward F., 192
Beckwith, Karen, 229
Bee, Robert L., 202
Besigye, Kiiza, 224
Bilgrami, Akeel, 144
Black, Justice Hugo, 169
Bloomberg, Michael, 325, 326–7
Board of Indian Commissioners, 202
Botswana, 221
Bradley, James, 44
bribes, 343

Britain
    accountability of parliament, 44
    debate about popular representation,
        48–50
    electoral system, 36
    group-level representation of the people,
        85
    instructions to members of parliament,
        50, 51
    petitions and addresses in, 35
    representative authority in, 52, 53
    representative system, 44, 96
    sedition bills, 42
    Westminster model of representation, 4,
        63–4, 84–5
British Columbia's citizens' assembly, 65,
        68, 69, 73, 77
Bureau of Indian Affairs, 188, 195–202
    Courts of Indian Offences, 195–7
    Indian Organization Division, 200
    Indian police, 195–7
Burke, Edmund, 1, 12, 51, 84, 92
Byanyima, Winnie, 224
Byrd, Colonel, 179

Carens, Joseph, 151
Case, A., 347
Castile, George Pierre, 202
charters, royal, 36
checks and balances, 98, 100, 103, 107,
        273
Cherokee nation, 176, 184, 185, 196
    legal status of, 165
Cherokee Nation v. Georgia, 163–5
Chickasaw nation, 184, 185
Choctaw nation, 180, 184, 185
Christiano, Thomas, 73
citizens
    as a collective force, 38
    and governments, 32
    judgment of governments, 28
    membership rights, 26
citizens' assembly, British Columbia, 65,
        68, 69, 73, 77
citizens' juries, 68
citizenship, 139, 152, 257, 258
    culture of, 37
    multicultural, 140, 141, 150
    property requirement for, 295
civil rights disputes, United States, 79,
        81
civil society, 18, 227, 228
civilization, 165, 187
classification of humans, 147
Cohen, Felix, 172

collective action problems, 117, 118, 238,
        255, 283
collective identity, 29, 31, 33, 219
    of the state, 21, 26, 28, 33
Collier, John, 199–202
commonwealth, 19, 22, 23
competition, 274, 277, 284, 301, 313, 337
Constant, Benjamin, 5, 91, 92, 98–107,
        259
    and Rousseau, 99
    usurpation, 100
constitutional assemblies, 30, 103
constitutions, 30, 98, 102, 286
constructivism, 143, 144, 146
contestation, 6, 80, 124–7
    value of, 104, 105, 120, 125, 127, 128
Contract with America, 286
cooperation, 62, 63–4, 81
coordination, 12, 342, 353–4
corporations, urban, 36
Cox, Gary W., 11–12, 342–55
Cox–McCubbins model of electoral
        targeting, 348
Creek nation, 180, 185
Creevey, Lucy, 223
Crow Dog, 170–1, 172
cultural commitments
    privatization of, 141, 142
    protection of, 141
cultural groups, 147, 150, 152
    exemption from democratic politics,
        143
    membership in the state, 144, 145
    rights of, 147

Dahl, Robert, 91, 126, 275
Dahlberg, M., 347
Dahlerup, Drude, 211, 216
Dawes Act, 181–7
Dawes Commission, 182, 183–4, 185
debates during election campaigns, 104,
        339
    data and methodology of investigation
        of, 327–32
    impact on public opinion, 324–32
    informative potential of, 324
    and opinion change, 326, 332–9
    purpose of, 339
Defoe, Daniel, 50
Delano, Columbus, 189
Delaware nation, 176
deliberation, 116, 238
deliberative opinion polls, 68
Deloria, Vine Jr., 187–8
demagogues, 5, 102

democracy, 216, 232
  aggregative, 6, 118, 121
    and interests, 118–20, 121, 126
  ancient Greek view of, 2
  contestation, 128–31
  and debate, 79
  definition of, 275–8
  deliberative, 6, 104, 118, 121, 125
    and interests, 118–20, 121, 126
  and difference, 142
  direct, 9, 271, 291–5, 300
  hostility toward, 37
  impact of televised debates on quality of,
    324
  indirect, 9
  liberal, 98–107
  measuring the performance of, 90
  and multiculturalism, 147, 153
  political culture of, 81
  procedural, 142, 225–7
  and representation, 1, 15–18, 26–31,
    77–82
  representative, 26–31, 291–5
  role of information in, 338
  and self-representation, 78–82
  and statutory officers and bodies, 77
  theory of, 124–7
  transition to, 214, 220
  and women's inclusion, 214, 217
Democratic Party, constituency of, 308
democratization, 139, 211–18
despotism, 103, 128
Diaz-Cayeros, Alberto, 348
discursive dilemma, 75–6, 78
Dixit–Londregan model of electoral
    targeting, 344–5, 346, 348, 354
"doctrine of discovery," 162, 165
dominion, 23, 24
Downs, Anthony, 10, 291–2, 353
Drake, Jemes, 50
Dred Scott case, 202
Dworkin, Ronald, 257

educational resources, racial disparity in
    access to, 120, 123
elections, 98, 226, 300
  determinants of results, 309
  and lotteries, 295–300
  quality of candidates, 291, 309
  spatial model of, 310–21
electoral colleges, 101
electoral constituencies, definition of, 241
electoral parties, 351
electoral qualifications, 8–9, 236–61
electoral systems, 221
electoral targeting, 342

coordination, 348, 349, 350, 353–4
  Cox–McCubbins model, 346, 348
  Dixit–Londregan model, 344–5, 346,
    348, 354
    generalization of, 348
  empirical evidence on, 347–8
  extended models, 348–50
  Lindbeck–Weibull model, 346, 348,
    350, 354
  literature on, 343–8
  mobilization, 348, 349, 350, 353–4
  models of, 345–7, 353–4
  turnout, 348, 349
  typology of transfers, 343–4
The Electors' Right Asserted, 50
Elk v. *Wilkins*, 204
England's Enemies Exposed, 48, 52
equality, 9, 80, 81, 151, 152, 256–60, 275
equilibrium, political, 312–13, 321
  party unanimity Nash equilibrium, 312,
    318
Erikson, Robert S., 90
Estévez, Federico, 348
ethnic groups, 139, 146, 156
  in Africa, 222
  creation of, 6
  and identity, 222
  legitimacy and scope of claims of, 145,
    147, 148, 149
Evans, Diana, 352
executive, 102

Federal Housing Administration, 123
feminism, 213, 226
Ferejohn, John, 9–10, 271–301
Ferrer, Fernando, 325, 326
Findlay, John M., 192–3
First Nations, 148; *see also* Native
    Americans
Five Civilized Tribes, 177, 178, 179, 185,
    196
  citizenship, 203
  constitutional convention, 185
  exemption from federal laws, 181
  legal status of, 202
  legislatures of, 185
  national governments of, 185
  and the Oklahoma Territory, 185
Foner, Eric, 194, 195
Fontaine, Peter, 179
Ford, Richard Thompson, 130
France, *parité* laws, 240
franchise, 40
freedom, 94, 125, 129
  and culture, 142
  of indigenous people, 148

French Revolution, 42, 67, 92, 98

Garsten, Bryan, 5, 90, 109
gender equality, 214, 232
Gerber, Alan, 324, 326, 340
Gilens, Martin, 301
Glaeser, E., 312
Govender, Pregs, 225
government, 32
  legitimate, 126
  limited, 99
  mixed, 273
  multivocal forms of, 5
Grand Petition, 41
Grant, President Ulysses S., 189, 194
Green, Donald, 324, 326, 340
group identity, 154, 223, 242
groups
  constructed character of, 152
  cooperative, 62
  cultural differences of, 139
  identity of, 30
  personality of, 29
  and political interests, 116
  structural origins of, 139

Hallowell v. *United States*, 204
Hamilton, Alexander, 5, 102–3, 161
Harring, Sidney L., 195, 197, 198
Hassim, Shireen, 8, 211–33
Hayward, Clarissa Rile, 5–6, 111–32
Helms, Jesse, 117
hierarchical societies, 115, 117, 128, 132, 223
Hirschman, A. O., 308, 322
The History of the Last Parliament, 50
Hobbes, Thomas, 2, 16, 18–26
  dominion, 23, 24
  influence of, 17
  Leviathan, 15, 16, 17, 18, 20, 22, 105
  membership, 23–4
  personation, 22–3, 24, 26, 74, 79
  theory of representation, 15, 20, 35, 61, 76, 78, 106
Home Owners Loan Corporation, 123
Hopewell Treaty, 168, 176
human rights law, 153, 214

Ickes, Harold, 201
identities, formation of, 6–7
identity, 140
  collective, 31, 33, 219
    of the state, 21, 26, 28, 33
  constructivist theories of, 146, 150
  and culture, 143

ethnic identity, 143, 144
  and ethnicity, 222
  formation of, 146, 150
  group identity, 154, 223, 242
  politics of, 154
identity politics, 151, 154, 156
impeachment, 279, 280, 284
incorporation, 63–4
India, 223
Indian Territory, 177, 178, 181
  commercial crops in, 183
  employment in, 183
  natural resources of, 183
  poor white residents of, 184
  railways in, 183, 194
Indians: *see* Native Americans
indigenous people, 149
initiatives, 10, 294
injustice
  historical, 146, 149
  inherited, 6–8
  structural, 7
institutional design, 100, 214
institutions, 5, 6, 7–8, 112, 220–5
Interamerican Indigenista Institute, 199
interests, 275
  articulation of, 227–32
  constructivist conception of, 124–31
  economic, 307
  formation of, 5, 6–7
  and group membership, 116
  institutional mechanisms and, 116
  and policy, 276
  political construction of, 118–24
  and quotas, 227–32
  role of, 111–29
  and structural inequalities, 112
International IDEA, 215
Ireland, 190–1
Italian city republics, 67, 70

Jefferson, Thomas, 103, 188
Johansson, E., 347
Johnson, Kenneth W., 161
Johnson v. *M'Intosh*, 162–3
Jones, Commissioner William A., 197
Jung, Courtney, 6–7, 139–57
Jura Populi Anglicani, 48
Jura Populi . . . Answer'd, 49
jury system, 67
justice, 255, 265, 305
  compensatory, 150
  distributive, 146
  and legitimacy, 264
  political conception of, 81
  substantive, 238

Kagame, P., 225
Kant, Immanuel, 272, 281, 287
Kazibwe, Speciosa, 231
Kennedy, Senator Ted, 241
Kent petition, 44, 48, 50, 52
Keyes, Captain E. D., 193
Kim, Henry, 352
King, David, 352
Kirshner, Alexander, 1–12
Kislansky, Mark, 274
Klamath nation, 201
Knights, Mark, 3, 35
Krehbiel, Keith, 350, 351, 354
Krook, Mona Lena, 219
Kymlicka, Will, 140–1, 148

Laffer, Arthur, 306
Lawson (of the Carolinas), 179
leadership, 277, 289
   and agency, 285
   and policy, 291
Lee, W., 310
Legion Memorial petition, 44, 48, 50,
      52
legislative parties, 351
legislative presence, 241, 242, 251
legislative targeting, 352–3, 354
legitimacy, 111–29, 223, 252
   and descriptive representation, 112–18
   and justice, 264
   and qualifications for office, 256
   sources of, 37
Leslie, Charles, 50
Levelers, 40
liberalism, 92, 98–107, 139–53
Lincoln, Abraham, 194
Lindbeck, A., 342
Lindbeck–Weibull model of electoral
      targeting, 345, 346, 348, 350, 354
Lindert, P., 307–8
Locke, John, 78
Lone Wolf, 171
Longman, Timothy, 223, 224
lotteries, and elections, 295–300
Lupia, Arthur, 338, 339
Luttmer, E., 312

Macedo, Stephen, 142
Mackuen, Michael B., 90
Macleod, William Christie, 179, 204
Madison, James, 5, 338
   constitutional assemblies, 103
   direct democracy, 286
   "doctrine of discovery," 162, 165
   leadership, 289

policy outcomes, 116, 295
public opinion, 104
representation, 91, 102, 272, 273, 281,
      286
Magaloni, Beatriz, 348
majority principle, 53, 95, 142
Mamdani, Mahmood, 7–8, 159–89
Manin, Bernard, 54, 111, 260
   electoral representation, 35, 248
   leadership, 289–90
   lottery system, 295
   qualifications for office, 260
   right to run for office, 259
Mansbridge, Jane, 117, 215, 218, 227,
      243
Markell, Patchen, 125
Marshall, Chief Justice John, 161–7, 174–5
   Cherokee Nation v. Georgia, 163–5
   "doctrine of discovery," 162, 166
   Johnson v. M'Intosh, 162–3
   political power, 175
   relationship between ward and guardian,
      163
   title by conquest, 174
   Worcester v. Georgia, 165–7
Mathews, Justice, 171, 172
Mauritius, 221
Mayhew, David, 108
McCubbins, Mathew D., 338, 339, 342,
      346
McRae, Kenneth D., 195
media, 105
median voter theorem, 291, 292, 294, 297,
      299, 353
Medill, William, 191
Mekeel, Scudder, 200
membership, 23–4, 139
   cultural group, 140, 148
   rights, 7, 26, 151–6
memory, political significance of, 149, 150
Menominee nation, 173, 201
Menominee Tribe of Indians v. United States,
      173
Michels, Robert, 289
Mill, James, 114, 115
Mill, John Stuart, 73
Miller, Warren E., 90
misrepresentation, 42–51, 52, 322
mobilization, 12, 342, 353–4
monarchy, constitutional, 100
monitoring problem, 1–12
Montesquieu, C. de, 287
Morgan, Commissioner Thomas J., 197–8
Mosely-Braun, Carol, 117
motivation, 73

Msimang, Manto Tshabalala, 229
Mullainathan, Sendhil, 11, 324–32
multiculturalism, 146, 147
  and democracy, 147, 153
Murray, Charles, 322
Museveni, Y., 224, 226, 230
Myer, Dillon S., 201

Namier, Lewis, 274
Napoleon Bonaparte, 100, 102
nation-state, 106
nationhood, conceptions of, 151
Native Americans, 7–8, 159–89
  in Alaska, 169
  assimilation, 142, 188, 194, 199, 201,
    202
    forced, 178–87
  and the churches, 194
  citizenship, 159, 161, 187, 202–6
    and civil rights, 164, 204–5
    and enfranchisement, 204
    limitations on, 203–5
    types of, 203–4
  civilization program for, 187
  colonization of, 159–67, 174
  criminal jurisdiction over, 170
  cultural practices, 196, 197, 199
  "domestic dependent nations", 162,
    163, 165
  education of children, 198
  federal power over, 166, 171–5, 185
  "free persons of color," 164
  group identity, 170
  Indian Country, 167
  Indian courts, 170
  Indian states, 176–8
  land rights, 160, 167–8, 180, 182, 186,
    200
    appropriation of land, 181
    reduction in holdings, 186
    right of use, 168
  loss of political independence, 167
  relationship to the United States
    community, 159
  reservations, 188, 190–5
    in California, 191–3
    in Texas, 193
  rights of, 166
  segregation of, 187–202
  self-administration, 169
  self-determination, 202, 203,
    205
  separate representation, 175–6
  social organization, 199
  sovereignty claims over, 159
    tension between civilization and
      tradition, 179, 182
    Termination Policy, 201
    and trade, 160
    treaties with, 160, 168, 176, 177, 189
      Choctaw Treaty, 180
      Creek treaties, 180
      guarantees given, 180
      Hopewell Treaty, 168, 176
      Treaties of Removal, 180
    Tribal Councils, 201
    tribal sovereignty, 159, 166, 167–75, 200
      historical origin of, 172, 174
      scope of, 172
    voluntary integration, 179
    wards of the state, 161, 168, 171–5,
      202–6
Navajo nation, 169
New York City mayoral debate, 11, 324–32
  candidates in, 326–7
  data and methodology of investigation
    of, 327–32
  experimental panel design to investigate,
    325
  implications of the investigation, 337–9
  results of investigation of, 332–7
  summary statistics on the investigation,
    329, 333
Newbury, Catherine, 222
Newbury, David, 222
Nixon, Richard, 277
North America, settlers and natives in,
  159–89

obligation, 139, 140–5
Oklahoma, 181, 185
Oldmixon, John, 52
Olin Foundation, 310
Oliphant, 173
Osage people, 196

Page, Benjamin I., 90
Paine, Thomas, 38
Panel Study on Income Dynamics, 315
Parker, Ely S., 178
Parsinnen, T. M., 38
participation, 42, 154, 228, 258
  and electoral representation, 37
  informal, 35
  and representation, 61
  before representative democracy, 35
party policies and voter preferences, model
  of, 10
party unanimity Nash equilibrium, 312,
  318

paternalism, 176, 187, 205
the people, 2, 3, 28, 64, 104
Pepper, Claude, 352
Pequot nation, 191
Pericles, 277, 291
personation, 22–3, 24, 26, 74
persuasion, 9–12, 342, 348, 350, 353
petitions, 3, 35
    anti-slavery, 41
    and counter-petitions, 39, 52
    electronic, 54
    and the French Revolution, 42
    Grand Petition, 41
    Kent petition, 44, 48, 50, 52
    Legion Memorial petition, 44, 48, 50,
        52
    and misrepresentation, 42–51, 52
    and the press, 40, 52, 53
    quantity of, 41, 45
    right to petition, 49
    statistics about, 41, 42
Pettit, Philip, 3–5, 61, 104
Pettit, Rory, 82–7
Phillips, Anne, 73, 241
Phillips, John, 44
Piketty, T., 308
Pitkin, Hanna, 2, 15, 54, 74, 105, 282
    criticism of Hobbes, 18, 19, 24
    descriptive representation, 114
Plains Indians, 194
Plato, 287
Plotke, David, 111
policy
    and interests, 276
    and leadership, 291
    mapping from policy to outcomes, 307,
        308, 322
    and types of democracy, 291–5
policy bundle, 10, 305, 310–21, 322
policy outcomes, and voter preferences, 10
political autonomy, 8
political debates, 11
political economy, model of, 298
political elites, 115
political equality, 256–60, 261
    ancient, 259
    modern, 259, 260
political parties, 49, 98, 351
    activities of, 11
    allocation of side payments, 352
    bribes, 343
    constituency of, 314, 343
    coordination, 354
    coordination activities, 12
    democratization of, 226

    electoral targeting, 342, 350–1, 353,
        354
    factions in, 313, 314
    focus of distributive benefits, 342
    leadership, 354
    legislative parties, 12
    legislative targeting, 343, 350–1, 353,
        354
    mobilization, 354
    mobilization activities, 12
    multipartyism, 226
    transfers to boost turnout of supporters,
        344
    types of transfers of benefits, 343–4
political society, 80–1
politics
    constituency-based, 229
    distributive, 342–51
    fundamentals of, 306–10
    identity politics, 151, 154, 156
    mass national, 38
    oppositional, 154, 155
politics of presence, 114
Poole, K., 321
popular sovereignty, 5, 33, 50, 54
    hostility toward, 37
    and an informed electorate, 337, 338
    institutional locus of, 102
    negative function of, 97, 106, 108
    as a normative ideal, 109
    and representative government, 90
    Rousseau on, 93–8
power, 144, 145, 146, 165, 166
    executive, 94
    legislative, 94
    negotiated, 37
    relations of, 115, 127, 128
    and representative institutions, 129
Pratt, Richard, 198
press, free, 40, 52, 53, 54, 105
Prucha, Francis Paul, 199
public opinion, 91, 104, 108
    impact of electoral debates on, 324–32
    and representers, 86–7, 276
public reasons, 79, 80, 81, 104
public sphere, 141
Pueblo Indians, 196

qualifications for office, 8–9, 236–61
    access to wealth, 244
    conceptual roadmap of, 240–55
    definition of, 240–8
        as the effects of rules and
            circumstances, 244–6
        as probabilities of success, 243–4, 263

qualifications versus group
representation, 241–3
voter-endogenous and
voter-exogenous qualifications,
246–8, 262, 264
democratic costs of, 239, 264,
265
and democratic rights, 256
justification for, 251, 265
democratic distrust, 252–3
and justice, 252
limits of voting rules, 253–4
types of, 251–5
normative implications of, 255–64
purpose of, 250
competency of candidates, 249–50
composition of the legislature, 251
correspondence of candidates, 250–1
typology of, 248–51, 253
quotas
debates about, 211
demand for, 214, 219
and democratization, 220–5
and elite representatives, 229
gender-based, 9, 254–5
institutional factors and the success of
quotas, 216
and interests, 227–32
negative effects of, 212
objections to, 218, 223
and participation, 228
and procedural democracy, 225–7
and qualifications for office, 236–61
and representation, 232
role of, 8–9

Rawls, John, 64, 79, 81
Reagan, Ronald, 306
referendums, 10, 96
Rehfeld, Andrew, 8–9, 112, 236–61
Rehnquist, Chief Justice, 173
representation, 278–81
and accountability, 225
and authorization, 17, 25, 28
cultural rights, 154
and democracy, 1, 15–18, 26–31,
77–82
democratic, 9–12, 62, 77–8
democratic value of, 111, 124, 127
descriptive, 65, 112, 132, 212, 227
advantages of, 120
and advocacy, 114–16
and deliberation, 116–18
and legitimacy, 112–18
limits to, 119, 120

and outcomes for women, 215, 216,
218
purpose of, 119, 238
determinative, 104
differences between the Washington and
the Westminster models, 82–7
electoral representation, 35, 37, 54, 62
enactive, 4
factors in, 62
fast-tracking of representation for
women, 212, 215, 220, 228
formal and informal, 42, 44, 51
and group identity, 223
group representation, 241–3
Hobbes's theory of, 15, 20
imperfect, 305
indicative, 66–71, 77, 82
extended conception of, 69–71
standard conception of, 66–9
informal, 38, 52, 53, 54
and inherited injustice, 6–8
interpretive, 4, 66, 78, 82, 104
Lockean conception of, 30
of marginal groups, 216, 222
and the monitoring problem, 1–12
parliamentary, 36, 37
and participation, 43, 61
popular, 30, 77
professional, 250
proportional, 68, 69, 73, 221
and quotas, 232
before representative democracy, 2–3,
35, 53
representers and representees, 4, 35,
62–6, 68, 105
responsive, 71–7, 78, 82, 90, 212
constructive, 76
directed responsiveness, 71–4
interpretive, 66, 74–7
and socioeconomic development, 213
substantive, 212, 241
theory of, 15
varieties of, 61
representative government, 247
and aristocratic rule, 286–91
definition of, 275
and democratic rights, 260
and popular sovereignty, 90
principles of, 264
purpose of, 90, 91, 108
questions about, 107–9
responsiveness of, 108
representative institutions, 38
and contestatory democracy, 128–31
and interests, 121, 132

representative institutions (*cont.*)
  non-electoral, 53
  and power relations, 129
  purpose of, 5
  and structural injustice, 7–8
  types of, 38–9
representatives, 32, 62–4, 81
  autonomy of, 117
  delegates, 72, 73, 78, 82
  deputies, 65, 72, 77
  expressive pressures on, 86
  independence of, 32
  indicative, 65
  indirect election of, 101
  motivation, 73, 114, 131
  pressures on, 86
  professional, 69–71
  proxies, 65, 69, 77
  and public opinion, 86–7
  responsive, 65, 73, 91, 108
  selection of, 290
  as spokespersons, 74, 75
  trustees, 78, 82, 84
representees, 64, 81
  control over representatives, 69, 72, 75,
    78
Republican Party, 10
  economic policies, 304, 305–6
  electoral success, 304–18
  energy policy, 305
  exploitation of the race issue, 322
  ideological power, 310
  manipulative policy framing, 307
  position on global warming, 305
  quality of candidates, 308
  Southern strategy, 312, 317
responsibility, collective, 29
rights, 99, 100, 151
  civil and political rights, 153, 154, 231
  collective rights, 50, 152, 155
  cultural rights, 153, 154
  democratic, 9
    right of citizens to choose, 239
    right of citizens to run for office, 239,
      256, 257, 258–60, 261–2, 264
    right to an unconstrained choice, 256,
      258, 261
    right to vote, 256, 258
  equality of, 231
  group rights, 6, 141, 147
  indigenous rights, 139, 148, 149, 155
  individual rights, 7, 152, 153, 155
  membership rights, 7, 26, 151–6
  political rights, 264
  and politics, 155

right to petition, 49
  social, economic, and cultural rights,
    153, 154
  voting rights, 256
Robespierre, M., 2, 102, 106
Roemer, John, 10–11, 297–8, 304–18
Rosenbluth, Frances, 9–10, 271–301
Rosenthal, H., 321
Rousseau, Jean-Jacques, 16, 92, 105
  direct democracy, 93–4, 95
  general will, 93
  legislation and execution, 94, 97, 99
  opposition to representation, 96, 97,
    273
  popular sovereignty, 5, 78, 93–8, 99,
    108
  referendums, 96
  usurpation, 94, 95, 96, 100
Rucht, Dieter, 229
Runciman, David, 2–3, 15
Rwanda, 8, 221
  ethnic mobilization, 222
  Forum of Political Parties, 225
  women in, 222
  women representatives, 223, 224,
    240

Sacerdote, B., 312
Santa Clara Pueblo v. *Martinez*, 205
Schmitt, Carl, 17
Schumpeter, Joseph, 271, 289, 294
self-determination, 139, 142, 147
self-representation, 114
Seminole nation, 177
Senegal, 223
separation of powers, 103, 287
Sequoyah, 186
Shapiro, Ian, 1–12
Shapiro, Robert Y., 90
Sieyès, Abbé, 17, 101, 105, 106
Sioux nation, 197
Skinner, Quentin, 66
Smith, Mark A., 310
Smith, Melanchton, 67
social groups, construction of, 143
socioeconomic development, and political
  representation, 213
Somers, John, 49
South Africa, 8, 221
  African National Congress, 225, 226,
    231
  Communal Land Rights Act, 231
  electoral system, 221
  formal inequalities in, 230
  impact of quotas for women, 230

parliamentary women's caucuses, 222
space for dissent, 225
Treatment Action Campaign, 229
women representatives, 225
women's organizations, 229
Southern African Development
    Community, 216
sovereignty, 16, 19, 21, 22, 24, 25; *see also*
    popular sovereignty
absolute, 98
conceptions of, 7
constitutional limitations on, 30
democratic, 95
Hobbes's theory of, 19
parliamentary sovereignty, 51
of the people as a whole, 25
source of, 104
unlimited nature of, 18, 19, 24
Spinner-Halev, Jeff, 146
the state, 2, 15, 19, 105, 106
and the multitude, 23
obligations of, 139, 150
personality of, 29, 31
representation of, 32
responsibility of, 145, 148
State v. Forman, 159
Stimson, James A., 90
Stokes, Donald E., 90
Stokes, S. C., 1–12, 342, 347
structural inequalities, 5, 112–13, 131,
    246
and collective decisions, 121, 123
and descriptive representation, 120
and interests, 121, 127
and political interests, 112, 124
structural injustice, 7, 145–56
Summers, Anne, 227
Sweden, 226
Swift, Jonathan, 49, 50

Talton v. Mayes, 171
Tamale, Sylvia, 229
Taney, Justice, 170, 202
taxation, 28, 304, 305–6, 310
Taylor, Charles, 152
Teller, Henry M., 195
Themistocles, 277
Thomas, Justice, 173
Thucydides, 271, 287, 291
Tilly, Charles, 38
trade unions, 310
Tripp, Aili Mari, 221, 222, 224
Truman, President Harry S., 201
Tuck, Richard, 16
Tully, James, 126

Uganda, 8, 221
impact of quotas for women, 230
National Resistance Movement, 224
parliamentary women's caucuses, 222
reserved seats for women, 226
single-party dominance, 224
women in, 222
women's organizations, 229
unions, political, 39
United States
African slaves, 161
Articles of Confederation, 160
Atoka Agreement, 185
autonomy of suburbs, 130
Board of Indian Commissioners, 189,
    198, 202
Bureau of Indian Affairs, 188, 195–202
Burke Act, 186
Civil Rights Act of 1866, 161
civil rights in, 79, 81, 116
Commissioner of Indian Affairs, 169,
    177, 191
conceptions of sovereignty in, 7
Congress, 63
Congress-cum-administration, 82, 83,
    84
Constitution, 83, 103, 107, 160
    Bill of Rights, 205
    and Indian policy, 161, 205
    state and federal sovereignty, 174
constitutional conventions, 177
Contract with America, 286
Curtis Act, 181, 182, 186–7
Dawes Act, 181–7
Dawes Commission, 178, 182, 185
Democratic Party, constituency of, 308
Department of the Interior, 191
elections
    anti-solidarity effect, 312, 316, 317
    policy bundle effect, 312, 316, 317
executive branch of government, 108
Federal Housing Administration, 123
formation of an Indian state, 177
General Allotment Act, 181–7
Harlan Bill, 177
Home Owners Loan Corporation, 123
Indian affairs, 160, 166, 170
Indian Civil Rights Act, 205
Indian Country, 167
Indian Reorganization Act, 199–202
Indian Self-Determination Act, 202
Indian Territory, 178, 181
Intercourse Act of 1834, 169
jurisdiction over Indian reservations,
    159

United States (*cont.*)
  Major Crimes Act, 171
  National Resistance Movement, 221
  paternalism, 176, 187
  Peace Policy, 189, 194
  plenary powers over Native Americans,
    171–5, 185
  political jurisdictions in, 6, 84, 90, 129,
    130, 131
  Public Law 280, 159
  qualifications for office, 236
  race in, 119, 122, 129, 321,
    322
  railways in, 183, 194
  representation of Indians in Congress,
    175, 176
  representation of individuals, 27
  representative institutions, 7
  Republican Party, 10, 304–18
  responsiveness of members of Congress,
    107
  role of information in democracy in, 338
  state sovereignty, 159
  Supreme Court's judicial review, 102–3,
    108
  system of representation, 82–4, 107
  think-tanks, 310
  trade unions, 310
  Treaties of Removal, 180
  two-state policy, 176, 177
United States v. *Joseph*, 169
United States v. *Kagama*, 171
United States v. *Lara*, 173
United States v. *Nice*, 203
United States v. *Rogers*, 170
United States v. *Sandoval*, 169
United States v. *Wheeler*, 172
usurpation, 94, 95, 96, 100, 103

Van der Straeten, K., 310
Van Devanter, Justice, 203
voter preferences, 9–12, 248, 307
  anti-solidarity effect, 10
  policy bundle effect, 10
  and policy outcomes, 10
voters, 305, 307, 331
  belief in opportunities for wealth, 306,
    309
  core voters, 12, 342–51
  information available to, 296, 299, 324,
    337, 338, 339
  swing voters, 12, 342–51, 354
voting systems, 76, 300

Waldron, Jeremy, 149
Washington, Ebonya, 11
Washington model of representation, 4, 63,
    82–4
Webster, Daniel, profession of belief,
    236–7, 255
WEDO, 215
Weibull, J., 342
Westminster model of representation, 4,
    63–4, 84–5
whistle-blowers, 71
Wilkinson, Charles, 162, 172
Williams, Melissa, 116, 150
Williams, Robert Jr., 162, 173
Williams v. *Lee*, 169
Wilson, Woodrow, 203
Wolin, Sheldon, 128
women
  ability of representatives to mobilize, 221
  claim to inclusion, 214, 227, 232
  deficit in representation of, 212–20
  discrimination against, 214
  fast-tracking of representation for, 212,
    215, 220, 228
  influence over decision-making, 215,
    230
  participation in institutions of
    decision-making, 228
  political autonomy, 8, 227
  quotas for, 8, 211–18, 236
  representation in parliaments, 213,
    218
  representation of women's interests,
    212, 219
  rights to property, 230
  support from political leaders, 224
  women parliamentarians and the
    women's movement, 227
  women's movements, 212, 225
  women's organizations, 226
Wood, Elisabeth, 1–12
Wood, Gordon, 274
Worcester v. *Georgia*, 165–7, 171
Wyvill, Christopher, 41

Xenophon, 287

Yorkshire Association, 41
Young, Iris, 113

Zaret, David, 40
Zeckhauser, Richard, 352
Zimbabwe, 226